Fox Populism

Fox Populism offers fresh insights into why the Fox News Channel has been both commercially successful and politically effective. The book traces the historical development of Fox's counter-elite news brand and reveals how its iconoclastic news style was crafted by fusing two class-based traditions of American public culture: one native to the politics in populism and one native to the news field in tabloid journalism. After investigating the origins of Fox News' populist journalistic style, the book goes on to illustrate how it is deployed as a political tool for framing news events, using the network's coverage of the economic crisis of the late 2000s as the book's principal case study. Through close analysis of Fox News's top-rated programs, this study shows how Fox hails its audience as "the real Americans" and effectively re-presents narrow, conservative political demands as popular and universal.

REECE PECK is Assistant Professor of Media Culture at College of Staten Island, City University of New York (CUNY). He provides commentary on media and politics to news organizations, including *New York* magazine and the AFP.

Communication, Society and Politics

Editors

W. Lance Bennett, *University of Washington*
Robert M. Entman, *George Washington University*

Politics and relations among individuals in societies across the world are being transformed by new technologies for targeting individuals and sophisticated methods for shaping personalized messages. The new technologies challenge boundaries of many kinds – between news, information, entertainment, and advertising; between media, with the arrival of the World Wide Web; and even between nations. Communication, Society and Politics probes the political and social impacts of these new communication systems in national, comparative, and global perspective.

Other Books in the Series

Erik Albæk, Arjen van Dalen, Nael Jebril, and Claes de Vreese, *Political Journalism in Comparative Perspective*

Eva Anduiza, Michael James Jensen, and Laia Jorba, eds., *Digital Media and Political Engagement Worldwide: A Comparative Study*

C. Edwin Baker, *Media Concentration and Democracy: Why Ownership Matters*

C. Edwin Baker, *Media, Markets, and Democracy*

W. Lance Bennett and Robert M. Entman, eds., *Mediated Politics: Communication in the Future of Democracy*

Rodney Benson, *Shaping Immigration News: A French-American Comparison*

Bruce Bimber, *Information and American Democracy: Technology in the Evolution of Political Power*

Bruce Bimber, Andrew Flanagin, and Cynthia Stohl, *Collective Action in Organizations: Interaction and Engagement in an Era of Technological Change*

Lynn S. Clark and Regina Marchi, *Young People and the Future of News*

Murray Edelman, *The Politics of Misinformation*

Frank Esser and Barbara Pfetsch, eds., *Comparing Political Communication: Theories, Cases, and Challenges*

Myra Marx Ferree, William Anthony Gamson, Jürgen Gerhards, and Dieter Rucht, *Shaping Abortion Discourse: Democracy and the Public Sphere in Germany and the United States*

Hernan Galperin, *New Television, Old Politics: The Transition to Digital TV in the United States and Britain*

Tim Groeling, *When Politicians Attack: Party Cohesion in the Media*

(continued after the Index)

Fox Populism

Branding Conservatism as Working Class

REECE PECK

College of Staten Island, CUNY

CAMBRIDGE
UNIVERSITY PRESS

CAMBRIDGE
UNIVERSITY PRESS

University Printing House, Cambridge CB2 8BS, United Kingdom

One Liberty Plaza, 20th Floor, New York, NY 10006, USA

477 Williamstown Road, Port Melbourne, VIC 3207, Australia

314–321, 3rd Floor, Plot 3, Splendor Forum, Jasola District Centre, New Delhi – 110025, India

79 Anson Road, #06–04/06, Singapore 079906

Cambridge University Press is part of the University of Cambridge.

It furthers the University's mission by disseminating knowledge in the pursuit of education, learning, and research at the highest international levels of excellence.

www.cambridge.org
Information on this title: www.cambridge.org/9781108496766
DOI: 10.1017/9781108634410

© Reece Peck 2019

First published 2019

Printed and bound in Great Britain by Clays Ltd, Elcograf S.p.A.

A catalogue record for this publication is available from the British Library.

Library of Congress Cataloging-in-Publication Data
NAMES: Peck, Reece, 1979– author.
TITLE: Fox populism : branding conservatism as working class / Reece Peck, College of Staten Island, CUNY.
DESCRIPTION: Cambridge ; New York, NY : Cambridge University Press, 2018. |
SERIES: Communication, society and politics | Includes bibliographical references.
IDENTIFIERS: LCCN 2018026123 | ISBN 9781108496766 (hardback) |
ISBN 9781108721783 (pbk.)
SUBJECTS: LCSH: Fox News. | Television broadcasting of news–United States. | Mass media–Political aspects–United States. | Populism–United States. | Conservatism–United States. | Working class–United States. | Political culture–United States.
CLASSIFICATION: LCC PN4888.T4 P44 2018 | DDC 070.4/30973–dc23
LC record available at https://lccn.loc.gov/2018026123

ISBN 978-1-108-49676-6 Hardback
ISBN 978-1-108-72178-3 Paperback

Contents

Preface   *page* ix

Acknowledgments   xv

Introduction: Fox Populism in the Great Recession   1
    Rethinking Media Partisanship   11
    Beyond "Fair and Balanced": How Conservative Media
        Criticism Heralded a New Journalistic Epistemology   20
    Divergent Conceptions of TV Populism: Organizational
        versus Aesthetic   27
    Chapter-by-Chapter Compendium   37

1 Channeling America's "Tabloid Soul": How Rupert
    Murdoch, Roger Ailes, and Bill O'Reilly Remade
    Television News   40
    The Rise of Partisan Narrowcasting: "Affective Economics"
        Meets "Affective Polarization"   44
    Tabloid!: The Debate Over "Bad" Journalism and Its
        Class-Based Roots   55
    The "Aspirational" News Style: Anti-Tabloid Journalism in
        the Twentieth Century   62
    The Unmaking of Middlebrow News in America   68
    Tabloids for Television: *A Current Affair, Inside Edition,*
        and Bill O'Reilly before Bill O'Reilly   71
    "Partisanship Needs to Be Produced"   81

2 Populism on Cable News: A Theoretical Framework   85
    Fox News versus MSNBC: "Logic of Equivalence" versus
        "Logic of Difference"   88
    A Fox News Hermeneutics: Narrative and Performance   92

Fox News versus *The Daily Show*: Performing Sincerity
versus Irony   99
The Cold Shoulder: No Place for Populists in Liberal
Cable News   104
Populism's Race and Gender Problem   111
The Feminine Populism of Conservative Women   116

3   "I'm a Blue-Collar Guy": How Fox News Hosts Imagine
Themselves and Their Audience as Working Class   121
The Social Logic of Anti-Elitism   125
The "Silent Majority" versus the "New Class": How the
Conservative Movement Redefined Class in America   127
Is Fox News' Audience Working Class?   133
"I Eat at Red Lobster": Performing Working-Class Taste   140
"I'm Not an Expert, but I Am a Thinker": Performing
Working-Class Intellectuality   146
Populist Journalism: An Enemy of Facts or of Cultural
Elitism?   151

4   "The Makers and the Takers": How Fox News Forges
a Working-Class/Business-Class Political Alliance   155
From Traditional Producerism to Entrepreneurial
Producerism   158
"The Job Creators": Fox News' Reinterpretation of the
Labor Theory of Value   165
Racializing the Stimulus Act: The Producerist Narrative
of Theft   173
"Who Have We Turned Into?": The Stimulus Act as a Sign
of Generational Transformation and Moral Decline   178
Why Moral Discourses of Class Matter   182

5   The Populist-Intellectual Tactic: How Fox News Incorporates
Expert Knowledge within Its Populist Framework   185
Creating the "Counter-Intelligentsia": Understanding the
Right's Close but Complicated Relationship with
Intellectual Culture   189
Amity Shlaes and the "Openness" of the Activist-Expert   193
Translating Intellectual Knowledge into the Language of
Cable News   198
Policing the Intellectual Content of a Populist Show   208
The "Invested" Populist and the "Disinvested" Expert   211
Switching Roles: The Communicative Versatility of the
Fox News Pundit   215
Expertise Must Be Performed   218

Conclusion: Trumpian Populism: Fox News' Respectable
Future Clashes with Its Tabloid Past   222
    A Defense of Populism   227
    Learning from Fox News   232
Postscript: Fox News and the "Alt-Right": Populism
and Nationalism   239

Bibliography   245
Index   282

Preface

Being raised in Utah, one of the most conservative states in the country, I felt like I knew everything I needed to know about Fox News. It pervaded my landscape just like Mormonism and "Jazz" basketball. Most of my family watched Fox News simply because they were Republican. "What else is there to know?" I thought. In retrospect, my sense of "knowing" Fox News was largely unfounded. I had never actually watched its programs in full or with any regularity. What I had seen of Fox was mostly in passing or based on brief, edited clips presented on YouTube or by other news sources.

The economic crisis of the late 2000s changed my passing interest in Fox News into a long-term active one. The 2008 financial collapse and the Great Recession that followed had caused profound devastation, inflicting financial pain across both the US population and globally. Some even felt that this Great Recession could pose the gravest threat to capitalism since the Great Depression of the 1930s. Ever since the early 1990s, Democrats had been shouting, "It's the economy, stupid!" However, in the political climate of the Great Recession, they didn't have to shout anymore. The "Culture War" issues that had so frustrated the left (e.g., God, guns, and gays) during the George W. Bush era would no longer be the central topics of national debate. All eyes were now glued to the economy, finally giving Democrats the homefield advantage they had always longed for. With the social and political conditions of the Great Recession presenting such an intriguing case study, I wanted to know how the number one news source for conservative Americans would respond to such a clear crisis of legitimacy for the free-market economic tenets it so passionately endorsed (e.g., deregulation, privatization, and tax cuts for the wealthy). The crisis indeed proved to be a true test of strength for Fox News' rhetorical skills.

In early 2009, I committed myself to watching Fox News closely and systematically. I analyzed over 800 broadcast transcripts and used UCLA's cable television archive to watch hours upon hours of Fox News programming, particularly the network's three top-rated shows at the time: *The O'Reilly Factor, Hannity*, and *Glenn Beck*. I did this for roughly two years. The programming range I analyzed and coded ranged from September 2008 – or the beginning of the financial collapse – to the midterm elections at the end of 2010. It was during this period that Fox News would experience one of the highest ratings surges in its twenty-two-year history and would galvanize a street protest movement in the Tea Party.

The benefit of my becoming so engrossed in the textual world of Fox News is that it allowed me to become intimately familiar with the network's special vocabularies and catchphrases. From such sustained viewing, I began to see how layered the political language of conservative media could be; how its recurrent code words such as "job creators," "the liberal elite," and "the forgotten man" could also carry "residual" (Williams, 1991) meanings from the political past that predated and ran deeper than the partisan alignments and divisions they currently expressed. Indeed, I discovered that this historical embeddedness is the secret to their power.

In 2000, Bill O'Reilly famously said his program was the only television show that presents news "from a working-class point of view."[1] Fox's ability to advance conservative political narratives during the late-2000s economic crisis –a moment when the issue of class inequality stood at the fore of the nation's collective consciousness – convinced me that this claim needed to be taken seriously. Yet all too often the populist rhetoric of Fox's top pundits has been dismissed as a naked form of charlatanism and a simpleminded gimmick. *Fox Populism* seeks to show how the contrary is true. Not only does Fox's populist journalistic style make for clever marketing and dramatic entertainment, it also stands as one of the most sophisticated and culturally astute forms of political communication in recent American history.

While this study relies on literary-critical textual methods, in the course of my research I sought to confirm my interpretations of Fox

---

[1] Farhi, P. (2000, December 13). The Life of O'Reilly. *Washington Post*.

News programming by investigating other important sites for the production of conservative political discourse. From 2009 through 2011, I conducted interviews with political activists and media industry figures and conducted participant observations at various Tea Party–affiliated events in Southern California and Nevada. The media training workshops I attended at various RightOnline conferences in Las Vegas, Nevada in 2010 and in San Diego, California, in 2011 were particularly elucidating. RightOnline is the conservative counterpoint to the liberal Netroots Nation conference. Like Netroots, the conference is dedicated to teaching activists how to use the Internet and digital platforms as political tools. It is hosted by the conservative political advocacy organization Americans for Prosperity, which gains most of its funding from Charles and David Koch of Koch Industries, better known as "the Koch Brothers."

Attending these conferences was useful because many of the discussion panels were small, intimate settings directed by prominent talk radio hosts, Internet publishers, TV personalities and politicians. These included figures such as Judge Napolitano (a Fox News pundit), Herman Cain (conservative talk radio host and former Republican presidential candidate), Representative Michelle Bachman, current Vice-President Mike Pence, and Andrew Breitbart – the late founder of Breitbart News. Observing these figures in person informed and textured my evaluations of their media performances on Fox and elsewhere.

Panels such as "Basic Investigative Reporting Skills" (July 23, 2010) and "Old Media, New Media and The Role of Citizen Journalism" (July 23, 2010) taught activists how to use journalistic practices to investigate political corruption and wasteful spending. They also trained attendees in how to cultivate a compelling mode of address for podcasting, online publishing, and public speaking in general. In a panel entitled, "Speaking Right: Communicating the Message Effectively," I listened to conservative media pioneer Richard Viguerie stress the need to maintain the conservative movement's central themes, which he analogized to a "four legged stool." The first two legs are the Old Right's emphasis on strong national defense and anticommunism and other two legs are founded on the Religious Right's social issues and the Tea Party's anti-government, free-market message.

At the San Diego RightOnline conference, panels such as "Effective Online Radio and Podcasting" and "Using Humor for Effective Content" outlined key presentational priorities of conservative talk media that informed my interpretive framework for studying Fox News. These included "being authentic" and "being likable," establishing a clear media persona and story about oneself, having liberal guests on to create confrontation for entertainment value, and more. In these workshops, I found strong parallels between the verbal rhetoric of conference attendees and Fox News programming discourse. In one panel at the Las Vegas, Nevada conference entitled "Prosperity 101: Citizen Economic Education," panelists Herman Cain, AFP executive director Linda Hansen, and *The Wall Street Journal*'s John Fund gave presentations and passed out DVDs and literature on how to teach friends, employees, and coworkers about the moral virtues of capitalism. Their political literature and verbal discourse were patently identical to the "producerist" rhetorical framing that Fox News utilized in its framing of the Great Recession (see Chapter 4).

"Cultural populist" (see Chapter 3) discourses were pervasive as well in these conferences, especially in the workshops devoted to citizen journalism and amateur news production practices. Audience members were repeatedly told by the panelists running the workshops that most mainstream journalists "look down on ordinary Americans" and question their ability to produce intelligent commentary. In essence, the speakers running these workshops framed the audience of grassroots activists as monadic versions of Fox News. As individuals wielding the tools of social media, the narrative they were told about their political and cultural role mirrored one of Fox News' central institutional narratives about challenging the cultural elitism of the mainstream media.

The last sites of conservative discourse that I turned to in order to test and orient my interpretations of Fox News programming were Tea Party political events that I attended between 2009 and 2011. On April 15, 2009, the day the first nationally coordinated anti-tax Tea Party protest occurred, some colleagues and I went down to the San Diego County Regional US Post Office, where the largest Tea Party protest was being held in San Diego County. There we took notes on the protest signs and conducted numerous audio-recorded interviews with activists. The following year, on April 15, 2010, we attended the second nationally coordinated protest in the same location and again conducted audio-recorded interviews with participants and took notes. Notably, the discourses I observed at these protests in the signs, speeches, and in the interviews predominantly dealt with the issue of wealth distribution. Moreover, they closely resembled the "producerist" rhetoric that is centrally featured in this book. For example, at the April 15, 2009 protest, I noted a middle-aged man wearing work boots and jeans holding a sign

that read "spread my work ethic, not my wealth." Another sign a pro-
testor was carrying read, "socialism: trickle-up poverty," again and again
playing on the themes of unjust wealth distribution.

Throughout 2010 and 2011, I attended other Tea Party events in
smaller towns in the broader San Diego area, such as El Cajon and
Oceanside. As with the RightOnline conferences, these Tea Party events
were promising locations for meeting Fox News viewers, especially ones
that through their investment in activism were likely to be opinion leaders
in their own interpersonal networks. Thanks to an older couple who sold
"patriot t-shirts," I was introduced to a wide range of rank-and-file
participants and had long informal discussions with them about the state
of the US news media and particularly about why they preferred Fox
News over other news sources. At these events, I met congressional Tea
Party candidates and local talk radio hosts who agreed to do extended
recorded interviews at later dates.

I do not mention this fieldwork to suggest that it stands as proof of my
interpretations of Fox News programming. Rather, I stress how this
secondary research functioned as a guiding device and safeguard against
allowing my analysis to veer toward idiosyncratic, overly impressionistic
interpretations that have no or little recursive connection with other
sources and forms of conservative political communication. Because the
discourses and representational practices used at these events and mentioned interviews closely and consistently reflected what I observed on
Fox News, this secondary research, at every step of the way, renewed my
confidence in the core textual arguments of the study.

In addition to this fieldwork, this project relied on audience data
from nonprofit research organizations like the Pew Research Center
and National Annenberg Election Survey (NAES). Beyond publishing
quarterly ratings indices that show who is winning and losing in the
cable news ratings game, commercial ratings companies like Nielsen
tend to guard the more fine-grained data they have on the cable news
audience. In most cases, researchers must pay for access to Nielsen
audience data. Future studies on Fox News would benefit immensely
from having greater access to Nielsen's audience data and also from
more ethnographic research on the Fox News audience, something that
is relatively scarce.

By capturing how Fox News programming operates as a complex
"cultural system" (Norton, 2011) and by historically contextualizing
the key political narratives and performance techniques Fox News
hosts utilize to frame and dramatize news events, I believe this study

offers new insights into why Fox News has been both commercially successful and politically effective. Moreover, this book will provide future quantitative studies on Fox News with descriptive tools and analytical categories that more adequately account for the stylistic nuances and particularities of the conservative media sector and political television more broadly.

Acknowledgments

This book bears my name but it is the collective product of various communities both within and without the academy. I credit the peculiar city of Salt Lake and the two (very large) extended families that raised me there for giving me an early education in ideology critique. My family was divided along the lines of the religious and nonreligious, like Salt Lake City itself. My cheerier Latter-day Saints (LDS) side attuned me to the power of moral philosophy, while my grittier secular side gave me a healthy dose of skepticism. Both sides taught me how to see the humanity in people, regardless of their politics or religion.

I credit the various academic communities that enriched my thinking and expanded my political preoccupations. A doctoral student could not have asked for a more intellectually stimulating environment than the one I enjoyed at the Department of Communication at the University of California, San Diego (UCSD). The insights I gleaned from the versatile faculty at the "La Jolla School" are echoed throughout this book, but the fingerprints of my graduate advisor Chandra Mukerji mark its pages most evidently. Chandra always challenged me to listen to the text and fight against the tendency to impose my own categories and prejudices onto the media I studied. This discipline taught me respect for detail and for evidence. I hope to pass this on to the students I advise now that I am a professor.

From the dissertation to the book proposal to the final monograph, Daniel Hallin has guided this research project every step of the way. Thank you, Dan, for all the care and time you've devoted to this book. I count you as one of my strongest advocates. Robert Horwitz was another key mentor that steered me through graduate school. Robert invited me to join UCSD's Conservative Movement Workshop. This academic collective exposed me to a wide range of disciplinary approaches for studying the political right. I thank all its members, particularly Amy Binder, John Evans, and Isaac Martin. In addition to being an exceptional source of expertise on television, John McMurria affirmed the value of my research and gave me confidence to advance my ideas about class and elitism. Michael Schudson's feedback during my defense proved invaluable, and this book emulates the "culturological" approach to journalism studies that he innovated. Other UCSD mentors that deserve thanks include David Serlin, Shelly Streeby and Natalia Roudakova.

I want to thank the eccentric graduate community at UCSD that challenged me intellectually and supported me emotionally. Many of the doctoral students that contributed the most to this book's development were the people that comprised the parenting support system that enabled me to complete my dissertation. Thank you, Matt Dewey, Harry Simón, and Tara-Lynne Pixley. I am especially grateful to Andy Rice, who generously edited several drafts of this book, and to Muni Citrin, who was my main fieldwork collaborator and intellectual confidant. I owe equal thanks to their partners – Aurora Dewey, Adriana Jasso, Collin Chappelle, Carla Rice, and Naya Colkett – who unselfishly shared in the labor of raising our children. I wish to acknowledge Andrew Whitworth-Smith, Michaela Walsh, Antonieta Mercado, Erin Malone, Regina Marchi, Matt Stahl, Kate Levitt, Carl McKinney, Stephanie Martin, James Perez, and Lauren Berliner. I appreciated all the cover letters, syllabi and bibliographies we traded over the years, but it was your music and dirty jokes that I prized the most. Marisa Brandt, Kim De Wolff, and Jericho Burg were key friends and editors as well.

The empirical heart of this book lies in the programming content that I was able to review at the University of California, Los Angeles, (UCLA) Communication Studies Archive, UCLA Television & Film Archive and The Paley Center for Media. I am grateful to the faculty and staff who helped me navigate these archives over the years, namely Tim Groeling, David Deliema and Darin Hoyer. I also want to thank my trusty research assistant Dominic Provenzano and editor Kathleen Ryan. This project could not have happened without these resources and their assistance.

The transition from graduate student to assistant professor is jarring, especially when it involves moving your family three thousand miles across a continent. I was blessed with a supportive group of faculty mentors at the CUNY College of Staten Island to walk me through the dual challenges of being a tenure-track professor and to life in New York City. This includes Ying Zhu, Edward Miller, Cindy Wong, Michael Mandiberg, Tara Mateik, Valerie Tevere, Jason Simon, Bang-Geul Han and Sherry Millner. A special thanks goes to Jillian Baez and Racquel Gates – the junior faculty members that preceded me at the Department of Media Culture. Our weekly office conversations have been an invaluable source of both camaraderie and knowledge. I thank David Gerstner, Bilge Yesil and Cynthia Chris for your close mentorship, editing help and for lending an open ear. I am grateful for Christopher Anderson who, in addition to offering incisive feedback on my writing, has actively promoted my research and broadened its visibility in the journalism studies field. The labor of writing a book can be very isolating, so I want to thank the small businesses and workers of Bay Ridge, Brooklyn who embraced me as a member of the community and allowed me to turn their restaurants into my office (LY and Rocco's get special love).

I want to thank the Columbia School of Journalism and the Department of Television and Radio at Brooklyn College for inviting me to present earlier iterations of this book project. The comments from the faculty of these programs revealed blind spots in my analysis and helped me formalize the narrative arc of the book. I thank Fred Turner for reviewing my book proposal and for suggesting that the project focus more on Fox News' prehistory. Geoffrey Baym's book *From Cronkite to Colbert* (2009) and Victoria Johnson's *Heartland TV* (2008) were go-to examples that I modeled this book after, and I thank both of them for their critical feedback and support. I owe a special debt to George Lipsitz, who served on my dissertation committee and who continued to advise me through the writing process. So many ideas in this book came from George's scholarship and from the references to which he pointed.

The editors and staff at Cambridge University Press have been wonderful collaborators. I particularly want to thank Sara Doskow for believing in this project when it was only a proposal. The enthusiasm she continued to express throughout the revision process put wind in my sails. I am very appreciative of Lance Bennett and the anonymous readers. Their penetrating reviews and constructive criticism were absolutely pivotal to transforming this project from a dissertation into a book.

Other Cambridge assistants and editors I want to thank include Danielle Menz and Karen Weller.

Portions of this book, primarily Chapter 4, derive from two published articles: (1) Reece Peck, "'You Say Rich, I Say Job Creator': How Fox News Framed the Great Recession through the Moral Discourse of

Producerism," *Media, Culture & Society* 36, no. 4 (May 2014): 526–35, and (2), Reece Peck, "Usurping the Usable Past: How Fox News Remembered the Great Depression during the Great Recession," *Journalism* 18, no. 6 (July 2017): 680–699. I articulated a version of Chapter 1's general argument and historical outline in a short two-page essay entitled, "Is Fox News the Smartest Journalism Ever?: Tabloid Television Is Great at Manipulating America's Long History of Elitism and Class Conflict" (2014, November 4) at *Zócalo Public Square*.

I received generous funding for this project from the University of California President's Dissertation Year Fellowship. I was also awarded various Research Grants from my union – Professional Staff Congress of the City University of New York. This financial support was vital to funding archive trips to UCLA and editing services. Funding from the Provost Office and the Faculty Center for Professional Development at the College of Staten Island allowed me to attend key conferences that shaped the ideas of this book. I owe a big thanks to Distinguished Professor Sarah Schulman, who went through this manuscript with a fine toothcomb and gave me excellent advice on how to improve its organizational structure. I give a heartfelt thank you to my undergraduate mentors Mary Jo Hinsdale, Elree Harris and Jeff McCarthy.

Lastly, I want to thank members of my immediate family, starting with my mother, Linda Green. She has anchored me my entire life. Her fearlessness and optimism in the face of adversity continues to leave me in awe. My father, Don Peck, is easily the most hilarious, authentic person I have ever met. His phone calls from construction sites making fun of my "thinking job" added perspective and levity to the serious (but always air-conditioned) work of academic research. I thank my sister, Krista Bergeron, for being my first academic hero and for encouraging me to go to college. I thank my big brother, Donny Peck, a talented country singer, for inspiring me to explore the politics of country music (I still copy everything he likes). Most importantly, I thank my wife and co-parent, Mercedes Panah, who has been in my life through every facet of this long, arduous journey and who sacrificed the most so I could finish this project. Her practical, in-the-now mind-set has always grounded my thinking, but nothing inspires me more than witnessing the fierce, unabashed way she loves our two sons, Razi and Reece. These two wild, adorable boys deserve my gratitude as well. The adventures we had together on my days off fed my soul and sustained my spirits.

Introduction

Fox Populism in the Great Recession

Shortly after Barack Obama's 2008 presidential victory celebration, *Time* magazine put on its cover a parody of the iconic cigarette-smoking Franklin Roosevelt photo, this time with a photo featuring not FDR but a smiling Obama and a caption reading: "The New New Deal."[1] Indeed, given the Democrats' control of the presidency and both branches of congress, analysts speculated that the party would soon be able to pass a policy program as bold as FDR's New Deal. Yet in a relatively short period of time the national debate over the financial crisis would dramatically shift from one targeting Wall Street greed and corporate malfeasance to one centered around fiscal policy and the national debt, taxpayer victimization, and the "sweetheart" benefits of public-sector workers.

This rhetorical turnaround had grave and lasting political consequences for Democrats. The "Republican tsunami" that swept the nation in 2010 caused Democrats to lose more congressional seats than in any midterm election since 1938.[2] In addition to giving Republicans the House of Representatives and 6 seats in the Senate, Democrats lost 6 governorships and more than 700 seats in state legislatures, handing Republicans the power to redraw voting districts in their favor. The conservative political resurgence during the Great Recession was punctuated by Obama's signing into legislation an extension of the Bush-era tax cuts – a scene that would have been unthinkable two years prior. Somehow the transformative economic agenda that progressives had hoped for was dead in its tracks. What explains this political turnaround?

[1] TIME Magazine Cover (November 24, 2008). [2] Tomasky (November 3, 2010).

I

Conventional wisdom tells us that severe economic downturns like the recession of the late 2000s tend to push the nation's politics leftward, as was the case during the Great Depression of the 1930s. But as cultural theorist Stuart Hall has pointed out in his writings on the rise of the British Right during the 1970s, market failures and the dire material conditions they create do not automatically unfurl leftist political responses. How crises are resolved, Hall stresses, is contingent on the representational work done in what he terms "the 'theatre' of political and ideological struggle" (1988a: 4).

In the twentieth and twenty-first centuries, the US political "theatre" has been largely founded on and expressed through the mass media. Since the 1960s, the medium of television has been the single most dominant form of political communication. Even with the rising influence of the Internet, this remains so today.[3] Within the televisual terrain, cable news is a particularly important battlefront in the contest for ideological hegemony. True, cable news is far from being the number one media source Americans rely on for *general* information; the audiences for local and network news programs are nearly three times as large. It *is*, however, the primary source Americans turn to for *political* information.[4] The 24-hour format allows cable news programs to relentlessly push policy positions and devote sustained coverage to a narrow set of politically contentious issues in a way that local and network news formats simply cannot match.[5] Hence, politicians pay special attention to cable news[6] (President Donald Trump is particularly known for his "obsession" with cable TV[7]).

In political television, one network towers above all others: the Fox News Channel. Since surpassing CNN as ratings leader in 2002, Fox has utterly dominated the cable news arena. In the course of this seventeen-year winning spree, the conservative network has not only beaten its more liberal competitors, CNN and MSNBC, but has consistently garnered

---

[3] Mitchell et al. (July 7, 2016).

[4] Gottfried et al. (February 4, 2016); Huffington Post (February 7, 2012); Blumenthal (May 21, 2010); Pew Research Center (October 30, 2009).

[5] Fitzgerald (November 5, 2013).

[6] As *New York Times* columnist Matt Bai writes in his article "Cable Guise," "a sizable portion of ... [the] paltry cable viewership comprises nearly every congressional aide, White House official and assignment editor in Washington, where it is rare to find a political or news office that doesn't have multiple televisions tuned to the punditry parade" (2009: 13). For academic research on Fox News' special influence on the congress and the political class, see Clinton & Enamorado, 2014; Bartlett, 2015; Arceneaux et al., 2016.

[7] Parker & Costa (April 23, 2017).

higher ratings than both these networks *combined*. Today, the company earns a jaw-dropping 2.3 billion dollars annually, making it the most profitable asset in Rupert Murdoch's global media empire.[8] And these commercial milestones say nothing of the network's political and cultural impact.

Some media critics and scholars have downplayed Fox's significance by pointing out that the cable news audience makes up only a small slice of the national television audience and an even smaller slice of the voting population.[9] However, attempts to correlate Fox's audience size to its political effects miss one critical thing. They assume Fox's influence ends at the borders of its loyal audience's living room. According to Terry McDermott of the *Columbia Journalism Review*, cable news outlets can capture an "outsized portion" of the national "mindshare" because journalists, as a group, are avid news consumers who are highly "self-reflective" (2010: 8). In other words, journalists heavily influence other journalists, and what they say in particularly dominant national news outlets sways the editorial decisions of smaller, local news organizations – a process scholars have called "inter-media agenda setting."[10]

Several content studies on Fox News support this idea showing how, on different occasions, the network, on its own, could drive the editorial agenda of the national press.[11] By the late 1990s, Fox News would begin to demonstrate both its inclination and, more importantly, its ability to help conservatives gain conceptual control over key national issues, such as the Lewinsky-Clinton scandal and Clinton's ensuing impeachment, the

---

[8] Pew Research Center (June 16, 2016).

[9] In *Changing Minds or Changing Channels* (2013), Kevin Arceneaux and Martin Johnson argue that the perception of cable news' influence is overblown. They show how small the cable news audience is in relation to the network news programs and in relation to the US voting population. As they cite, in January of 2012 *Hardball with Chris Mathews* on MSNBC garnered 0.8 million viewers while cable news' number one show of that year, *The O'Reilly Factor*, garnered 3.4 million. By comparison, the network evening news programs dwarf these ratings numbers. In same period, NBC and CBS posted 7.4 million viewers and 10.2 million respectively (4–5).

[10] According to David McKnight, Fox's role as a "inter-media agenda-setter" is the true source of Fox News' influence, not its persuasion over its audience (2013: 13, 27–29, 70). For literature on the concept of "inter-media agenda setting," see Castells, *Communication Power* (2009), p. 91, 164. Also see McCombs, 2005.

[11] Notable examples include: the Iraq War, see Schechter, 2003; Rutenberg, 2003c; Calabrese, 2005. The Swift Boat campaign, see Shaw, 2006; Cappella & Jamieson, 2008: 143, 211–212. The ACORN controversy, see Dreier & Martin, 2010. The Tea Party movement, see Skocpol & Williamson, 2012: chapter 4. The 2009 controversy over President Obama's "green jobs czar" Van Jones, see Levendusky, 2013.

2000 presidential election, and the Iraq invasion. However, Fox's role in shaping the national debate on the late 2000's economic crisis may be its most impressive rhetorical feat to date.

The Great Recession posed a far greater political communication challenge for Republicans than attempts to secure public support for the Bush administration's "War on Terror." The 9/11 attacks of 2001 had already primed the American public for war, significantly assisting Fox's patriotic programming strategy and its hawkish, Republican foreign policy stance. But the 2008 financial collapse and the historic recession that followed presented an entirely different set of political conditions. This was now becoming an environment rife with anti-corporate sentiment as poll after poll showed the public's trust in business dipping to all-time lows.[12] Economy-related news stories now came to utterly dominate the national media,[13] and income inequality – a topic Democrats had "owned" for decades (Petrocik et al., 2003) – was about to become the central political issue of the moment, pushing the national security and "culture war" politics (e.g. God, guns and gays) of the Bush era far to the wayside.

In such a political climate, one might assume a conservative network like Fox News would downplay issues of income inequality. Instead, Fox's top programs placed the topics of wealth distribution and class hierarchy at the top of their editorial agenda but approached these issues in such a way that ingeniously reconfigured the meaning of socioeconomic divisions so as to negate the market's role in producing them. In the place of economic antagonisms, Fox News pundits advanced a *cultural-normative* understanding of class conflict that has been a staple of conservative populism since the McCarthy era.

One of the long-standing political narratives of the conservative movement has focused on how "over-educated elites" use government power to both expropriate the wealth of "producing" Americans and impose non-traditional cultural values on them. Fox News' top hosts have seized

---

[12] A Marist College Public Opinion poll showed, "More than three-quarters of Americans said the moral compass of corporate America is pointing in the wrong direction, compared to 58 percent of business executives." See Carroll (2010). According to the Yankelovich marketing consulting firm, in the year 1968, 70 percent of Americans answered "Yes" to the question "Does business act responsibly?" In 2011, by contrast, a Harris Poll showed that only 13 percent of respondents expressed confidence in "large companies." See Argenti (2013). The public's confidence in Wall Street reached all-time lows as well. See Owens (October 7, 2011).

[13] Pew Research Center (October 5, 2009).

these conservative narratives and skillfully interconnected and rationalized them with the "lowbrow-taste" politics of tabloid media. This potent mix of tabloid taste and populist moral reasoning is the crux of how Fox News has interpellated its audience as the "authentic," working-class majority, thus allowing it to effectively re-present narrow conservative political demands as popular and universal. And indeed, in the most pivotal years of the Great Recession, this rhetorical strategy seemed to be working. In 2009 and 2010, Fox News would post some of the highest ratings in its twenty-two-year history[14] and would help redirect public anger away from corporate America toward government.

Of course, Fox did not accomplish this all by itself. Its free-market interpretation of the Great Recession was reinforced by the other major pillars of the "conservative media establishment," such as the *Rush Limbaugh* talk radio show, the news website the Drudge Report and the op-ed pages of the *Wall Street Journal* (Jamieson & Cappella, 2008). Going beyond media, Fox News' ability to drive the national discussion on the economic crisis was significantly assisted by an actual, on-the-ground protest movement named after the "Boston Tea Party" of the American Revolution. The Tea Party mobilizations of early 2009 provided a real-world referent for Fox's narrative depiction of its audience as being the central protagonist of the economic crisis, the political community most entitled to moral outrage and populist anger. In a reciprocal fashion, Fox News gifted this anti-tax, anti-government movement with a steady stream of life sustaining publicity. Fox News' early and repetitious coverage of Tea Party protest events in February and March of 2009 ultimately pressured CNN and other major news organizations to devote more coverage to the Tea Party than they would have otherwise (Skocpol & Williamson, 2012: chapter 4).

In anticipation of the first nationally coordinated Tea Party protest on Tax Day, April 15, 2009, Fox News shifted into full "advocacy" mode, going from merely reporting Tea Party events to promoting them. The network even sent several of its popular hosts such as Sean Hannity, Glenn Beck and Neil Cavuto to broadcast their programs live at various protest locations across the country (see Figure I.1). "This is the moment," Theda Skocpol and Vanessa Williamson wrote in one of the most definitive books on the Tea Party, "that many people we interviewed got involved [in the movement] for the first time" (2012: 8).

[14] See Holcomb et al. (2012).

FIGURE I.I　Fox News' promotion of Tea Party events

On Tax Day 2009, Fox News fans morphed into activists, and the activists became marketing vehicles for Fox News. This was the fullest expression of a decades-long trend toward an increasingly partisan news industry, the perfect marriage between a media corporation's branding strategy and a political movement's media strategy.[15]

In the summer of 2009, Tea Party protesters besieged town hall events designed to promote Obama's signature healthcare reform bill, the Affordable Care Act, or what became known as "Obamacare." Fox News' top programs gleefully broadcasted camera phone footage showing rank-and-file conservatives overwhelming Democratic Representatives with critical questions that, in many instances, devolved into shouting matches. "Throw the bums out," a crowd of Tea Partiers chanted at one event in Long Island, New York. The protest march, known as The Taxpayer March on Washington, on September 12,

---

[15] Williamson and Skocpol cite a poll taken in April 2010 showing that "63% of Tea Party supporters watched Fox News, compared to 11% of all respondents" (2012: 135). For an in-depth analysis of the intersection between conservative media branding and the political activism of the Tea Party see Khadijah Costley White's recent book (2018) *The Branding of Right-Wing Activism: The News Media and the Tea Party.*

2009, was another flashpoint. An estimated 75,000 conservative activists filled the United States Capitol standing as one of the largest political demonstrations against Obama in his entire eight-year presidency. As indicated by its date, this event was intimately tied to Glenn Beck, a rising star at Fox News at the time who created the Tea Party affiliated organization called the "9/12 Project."

Recognizing Fox's special role in rallying Tea Party protestors against him, President Obama vented his frustration in a June 16, 2009, interview with CNBC telling correspondent John Harwood, "I've got one television station [Fox News] that is entirely devoted to attacking my administration...You'd be hard pressed if you watched the entire day to find a positive story about me."[16] That fall, Anita Dunn, the Communications Director of the Obama White House, explicitly named Fox as the culprit. On CNN's *Reliable Sources*, Dunn said bluntly, "the reality is that Fox almost operates as either the research arm or the communication arm of the Republican Party." Fox, she charged, takes Republican "talking points" and "put[s] them on the air."[17] In the recession years, it seemed liberals and conservatives had switched their traditional rhetorical roles. Now liberals were the ones most readily lamenting the "media bias" against them. This reversal was a testament to how much the conservative media sector had grown and matured since the half-baked film and broadcasting ventures of ultraconservative groups from the 1950s and 1960s, such as the John Birch Society (Hendershot, 2011).

In the wake of an unpopular Bush presidency and amid one of worst economic crises in eighty years, Obama and the Democrats assumed they would enjoy bipartisan support for the Stimulus Act and other Keynesian policy measures they were proposing to address the nation's economic woes. In hindsight, however, they clearly underestimated the ability of Fox News to activate the Republican base and push Republicans in congress further to the right, injecting the party with a zeal for fiscal austerity that surpassed anything seen during the Bush era.

By the time President Obama took office in January of 2009, Fox News' founding CEO Roger Ailes, himself a former Republican media strategist, had raised Fox's political stature to such heights that even some conservatives (mostly moderates) were beginning to complain about the network's disproportionate sway over the Republican Party. In 2010, former Bush speech writer David Frum went so far as to suggest that

---

[16] *New York Times* (June 16, 2009).   [17] CNN (October 11, 2009).

Fox had usurped the party itself telling ABC's *Nightline*, "Republicans originally thought that Fox [News] worked for us and now we are discovering we work for Fox" (Schoestz, 2010, para. 1). That same year *Politico* used the term "Fox primary" to describe the network's role in directing the candidate selection process for Republican primaries. One basic way this was done, the article noted, was by giving or denying an aspiring candidate a paid position at Fox News as a pundit or "contributor" (Hagey & Martin, 2010). Because of Fox's reputation as conservative kingmaker, Republican politicians have been careful not to cross the network's corporate leadership and top stars, that is, until Donald Trump entered the political scene.

During the 2015–2016 Republican presidential primary, Trump openly feuded with Ailes and Megyn Kelly, one of Fox's most popular hosts at the time. Trump even boycotted a Fox News debate in Des Moines, Iowa on January 28, 2016, a move every other Republican candidate viewed as political suicide. But just as Trump warned, Fox would be the one to pay the price for his absence. This Trump-less panel of primary candidates yielded one of the lowest ratings of the twelve debates held. In addition to using the drawing power of his established celebrity status to bend Fox to his will, Trump benefited from an emergent "alt-right" media sector led by online news sites such as InfoWars and Breitbart News. During the primary season, these sites painted Fox News as part of the anti-Trump "Media Establishment." A 2017 study published in the *Columbia Journalism Review* demonstrates how the majority conservative shares and retweets on Facebook and Twitter originated from Breitbart, not Fox News.[18] According to Harvard Law School Professor Yochai Benkler, one of the study's authors, Breitbart's online proliferation pushed the entire conservative media ecosystem in a pro-Trump direction, which isolated #NeverTrump conservatives and compelled Fox News "to join the bandwagon."[19] The outcome of the Republican primary revealed that Fox's hold over conservative voters was not as unassailable as previously thought.

Other events in the Trump era, unrelated to the presidential election, would test Fox News like never before. In 2016 and 2017, we witnessed the ousting of not one but *two* of the network's most important figures, as both CEO Roger Ailes (now deceased) and longtime number one host Bill O'Reilly were forced to leave in the wake of multiple sexual harassment

---

[18] Benkler et al. (March 3, 2017).   [19] Milano (August 31, 2017).

charges against them. Many analysts wondered if Fox News could continue its dominance over cable news without Ailes' leadership and O'Reilly's talent. Despite the drastic changes to its management structure and primetime lineup, Fox News was still able to close out 2017 on top. In fact, during the tumultuous years of 2016 and 2017, Fox broke its own ratings records surpassing the stratospheric numbers it had set in the Great Recession era (Otterson, 2017).

However, the news organization's future is far less secure than it was a decade ago. Trump has incensed liberal audiences, which has boosted the ratings of CNN and MSNBC to unprecedented heights. To make matters worse, for the first time Fox is beginning to feel competitive heat from its right flank, as a crop of new conservative television ventures have recently emerged (e.g., One America News Network, Newsmax TV, Sinclair Broadcasting Group). The growing trend toward "cord-cutting" poses possibly the greatest threat to Fox News' long-term existence (and all of cable television for that matter) as media consumers, especially younger Americans, are rapidly dropping pay-TV services for Internet-based news.

Where Fox News is headed at this precarious juncture of its history is uncertain and one can only speculate about when and if Fox will lose its title as conservative America's main news source.[20] What is certain, however, is the central role that the network has played in spearheading the conservative media revolution of the last two decades and, at a deeper level, in changing how news is presented and marketed in the United States. The example of Fox's breakout commercial success demonstrated its domino effect, since it encouraged other news outlets, namely MSNBC, to also take up a partisan branding approach and, with that kind of linkage, a programming model that favors a politically charged, opinion-based news format over the dispassionate, "straight" newscast of the past.[21] This study asks *how* Fox News pioneered a new style of television journalism and *why* this style has created such a compelling political identity for conservative audiences. To answer these questions, *Fox Populism* examines Fox's institutional history and conducts a close textual analysis of the network's top three programs –*The O'Reilly Factor*, *Hannity*, and *Glenn Beck* – during the pinnacle years of

---

[20] Gottfried et al. (February 4, 2016).
[21] Kurtz, 1997; Delli Carpini & Williams, 2001; Schudson, 2003; Rutenberg, 2003: 112; Collins, 2004; Wormald, 2005; Pew, 2007; Baum & Groeling, 2008; Jaramillo, 2009: 36–38; Peters, 2010; Norton, 2011; Sherman, 2014.

2009 and 2010, a moment when Fox's engagement in American politics was dramatic and undeniable.

The historical sections of this book engage the biographies of Rupert Murdoch, the owner of Fox's parent company News Corp. (now Twenty-First Century Fox, Inc.), founding CEO Roger Ailes and star host Bill O'Reilly, and spotlight how the earlier media enterprises these figures took part in foreshadowed the unique broadcasting formula Fox News would develop. However, this study adopts a "cultural genealogical method"[22] that gives less weight to the individual geniuses of the "great men" of Fox's history and instead focuses on understanding the rhetorical traditions and media styles that these figures wielded as marketing tools and political weapons. This method reveals how Fox built its counter-elite news brand by combining two class-based traditions of public culture – one native to the political field in *populism* and one native to the commercial media field in *tabloid journalism*. Donald Trump, a reality TV star-cum-populist politician, embodies this stylistic synthesis through and through. Yet, he is less the trigger and more the capstone of a populist discursive trend that Fox News set in motion decades before Trump and Breitbart were making headlines.

The historical scholarship on the postwar conservative movement has blossomed in recent years, shedding light on the forces behind the rightward political shift of the last four decades.[23] However, few scholars have mapped the points of convergence between this political history and the history of American media (Hendershot, 2011:13). As a result, the media dimension of the political right's ascendancy remains insufficiently explained. By marrying political theory with cultural theory and by bridging literatures on populism and the postwar conservative movement with journalism and television studies scholarship, *Fox Populism* seeks to account for the complexity of Fox News' populist rhetorical address and the overdetermined nature of its unlikely rise to cable news dominance.

As discussed in the following section, one of the primary objectives of this book is to offer a new conceptual approach to media partisanship and to question the extent to which its popular conceptualization is really about political ideology. To rely only on a left–right ideological schema to define Fox News is to miss how it constructs partisanship as an identity *style*.

---

[22] Nietzsche, 1956; Foucault, 1965, 1970, 1977; Mukerji, 2007.
[23] Davis, 1986; Carter, 1995; Kazin, 1998; McGirr, 2001; Frank, 2004; Phillips-Fein, 2009; Cowie, 2010; Perlstein, 2001, 2008, 2014.

RETHINKING MEDIA PARTISANSHIP

The history of style embraces, not the reasons men voted Democratic or Republican, but only why it was *natural* for them to vote and to vote only for the candidates of a single party.

—Michael McGerr, 1986

A 2009 promo for Fox News' long-reigning number one show *The O'Reilly Factor* begins with a black backdrop. Smoke is swirling in the air as if an explosion just happened. The viewer hears a thumping drum beat: *bump, ba-bump, bump*. Capital letters appear that read: "THE ULTIMATE IN CONFRONTATION TV. A REAL VOICE FOR THE LITTLE GUY. LOVE HIM. HATE HIM. HE'S CLEARLY NUMBER ONE." Then a montage of video clips shows host Bill O'Reilly debating, body leaned in, hands flying. His face abounds with expression, accentuated by extreme close-ups of his eyes. The viewer hears a gruff, movie-trailer-like voice-over: "*Bill O'Reilly, number one in cable news 100 months and counting.*" This is followed by a series of sound bites from O'Reilly: "You're either a moron or a liar," "The American people have a right to be angry," "Look, stop the B.S!"[24]

Compare this to a contemporaneous ad for *The Rachel Maddow Show*, the flagship program of Fox's cable news rival and political opposite MSNBC. The viewer sees host Maddow wearing a hoody and thick-framed glasses kneeling on the carpet. She holds a Sharpie in her mouth as she frenetically marks up various documents. Brooding violin-based background music accompanies this imagery. In the voice-over Maddow says: "News is about stories. It's about finding all the disparate facts and then finding their coherence. Doing this right takes rigor and a devotion to facts that borders on obsessive." The scene then switches to Maddow's standing in front of her research team writing ideas and connections on a white board as if she is leading a seminar. Next, Maddow is shown at a disheveled desk, feverishly typing. It is late, but she, the ad implies, is a driven, investigative reporter.

Contemporary media critics often draw equivalences between the conservative Fox News and the liberal MSNBC due to their common adoption of a partisan branding strategy. However, this superficial commonality tells us little about the stark differences we see in how the two networks have historically represented themselves and their audiences.

---

[24] DirectorJess8 (April 2, 2009).

The O'Reilly Factor promo uses populist language and scenes of confrontation to depict O'Reilly as a fighter, the champion of "the little guy." Dominant ratings numbers are touted to legitimate *The Factor* as the voice of the majority. Maddow, on the other hand, is presented as a researcher, a writer, an intellectual. Her cultural authority rests on her "devotion" to "rigorous" empiricism and sound research. It's an appeal designed for an audience who especially "pride[s] themselves on being members of the 'fact-based community,'" as *Vanity Fair* correspondent Gabriel Sherman has aptly put it (2010).[25]

The aesthetic features of *The Factor* promo – from the music to the sound bites to the visuals to even the font type – are designed to create a sense of physicality and emotional intensity, whereas the presentational style of Maddow's ad elicits a pensive, cerebral mood. In these ads, we see two competing consumer appeals: the first culturally "populist" and the second culturally "aspirational." But these stylistic orientations are by no means exclusive to the field of cable. They shape and direct the market addresses of print, radio, and online news outlets as well.[26]

A television commercial for the venerable *New York Times* in the same era provides an even more illustrative example of the "aspirational" news appeal displayed in the *Maddow* promo. In an ad entitled "The Weekender," the viewer is introduced to different people that represent typical *Times* subscribers. First, we see a professional group dressed in formal business attire standing in a circle, talking. "A subscription puts you at the center of a conversation," the voice-over says. Then the camera shifts to a young woman in a modish maroon skirt. She asks, "Which sections are you fluent in?" A lean, beatnik-looking man wearing a black turtleneck sweater responds with a smile, "I'm fluent in three sections actually: business, travel, and the book review."[27] The ad also emphasizes the *Times'* unmatched prestige as a news organization. However, equally important to discourses of professional distinction is how the ad

---

[25] NBC News (October 10, 2010).

[26] The presence of intellectual or "highbrow" content on Fox News shows complicates attempts to label the network "populist" in the same way the *New York Times'* adoption of certain tabloid presentational elements complicates attempts to define it as elite or aspirational. Every outlet, from the *People Magazine* to the *Economist*, encompasses a composite mix of "tabloid" and "quality" elements. For this reason, it is better to evaluate the aesthetic politics of news organizations less in terms of bright line distinctions and more in terms of a stylistic spectrum.

[27] nytimers (February 25, 2009).

associates the *Times* with a *professional class* social world and cosmopolitan "taste culture" (Bourdieu, 1984). (See Figures I.2–I.4.)

To maintain its special status as the national "paper of record," the *Times'* marketing stresses the professionalism and enduring commitment

FIGURE I.2 The O'Reilly Factor

FIGURE I.3 The Rachel Maddow Show

FIGURE I.4 *New York Times*

to the "objective" journalism tradition it has had such a historic role in creating. And yet, like National Public Radio, itself an outlet that bends over backwards to prove its professionalism, the *Times* is still predominantly viewed as liberal and by conservatives as "far left."[28] This points to the problem of assuming that the partisan mapping of the American news environment is based solely on oppositional political opinions and editorial biases. This conceptualization of media partisanship tends to overlook the *indirect* ways in which the marketing strategies of news outlets actually *create* political associations through social identifiers and taste-based appeals.

The bulk of voluminous writing and commentary on Fox News has been devoted to the "media bias" narrative conveyed in Fox's founding slogan "Fair & Balanced." This corporate motto invokes, through insinuation, a story about how Fox heroically "restored objectivity" to US journalism by providing a counterpoint to the "liberal" mainstream media. Corresponding with its marketing, the "liberal bias" frame has

[28] Pew Research Center (September 27, 2012).

been a pervasive trope in Fox's programming discourse. In fact, Eleanor Townsley and Ronald Jacobs (2011) credit Fox, along with talk radio, for creating a greater emphasis on media *criticism* in the national news culture at large. They call this "media metacommentary" – or news about news. Townsley and Jacobs explain how contemporary news stories increasingly focus on how other news outlets cover a given event, rather than just reporting on the event itself.

Invariably intermeshed with Fox's media bias themes, however, is another equally foundational media metanarrative about how Fox has earned the allegiance of "ordinary Americans" by challenging the *cultural elitism* of the news industry. These twin narratives – the liberal bias story and the populist story – have been so utterly synthesized in Fox's programming discourse that the terms "the liberal media" and "the elite" are treated as interchangeable. Conversely, phrases such as "the folks," "the heartland," and "blue-collar Americans" have come to signify the conservative segment of the national news audience automatically and exclusively.

Placing the focus on Fox's media bias narrative in order to understand Fox's partisan mode of address makes sense if one believes partisanship is fundamentally about representing ideological differences. However, if social background and cultural affinities shape and direct partisan identifications as much, if not more, than pure philosophical beliefs and policy preferences, how the network represents its audience as a sociocultural group requires at least the same amount of scrutiny.

Political science scholarship has shown that social identity has a greater influence on political affiliation than ideology. As John Bartle and Poalo Bellucci point out, "[I]t is far easier to adjust political preferences to match" those of one's family, class, ethnicity and neighborhood "than [it is to] select group memberships on the basis of political preferences" (2009: 8). In other words, people tend to identify less with a particular party and its platform than with their fellow party members – i.e., the social groups tied to the partisan label.[29]

Historians have observed this phenomenon when looking at the relationship party members have had with the partisan newspapers that predominated in nineteenth-century America. The popularity of the partisan papers was not based on the information they imparted or the political ideology they promoted. Their popularity was instead due to

[29] Campbell et al., 1960; Schuessle, 2000; Green et al., 2002; Green & Shickler, 2009; Iyengar et al., 2012; Taub, 2017.

what historian Michael McGerr calls the papers' "political style," or in how the papers would rhetorically engage their readers by (re)presenting the political world in a familiar, identifiable way (1986). Reading partisan journals served an *expressive* function for the public, McGerr stresses. Much like the pole-raising contests and street parades, journal reading provided nineteenth-century Americans with a ritual occasion and public context for displaying group identities and communal values.

At the dawn of the twenty-first century, we see the dramatic return of partisan journalistic styles and media markets but, in this electronic age of partisanship, TV screens have taken the place of political flags. When you see Fox News on the television in a gym, a bar or in someone's living room, you may be prompted to think more about the people who selected the channel than you are about the news content itself. The network's mode of address immediately conjures up a distinct social group in your mind, and its confrontational tone compels you, the viewer, to decide whether you are a supportive member of this group or a hostile outsider. What often goes unquestioned is the idea that political ideology is the essential bond that defines the Fox News tribe. Or at least this was more or less *my* assumption before I approached Fox News as a research topic. The insights I gained in my many years studying Fox's institutional history and programming content has led to me to conclude that the network's real ideological force derives not from its talking points but rather from the *cultural-stylistic referents* Fox producers and pundits use to make such talking points socially meaningful.

It is easy to recognize how style organizes film genres and musical subcultures. However, political analysts have been slower to recognize how politics, and by extension, political news, can be shaped and struc- tured along stylistic lines as well (Hariman, 1995: 10). Like their nineteenth-century ancestors, partisan news outlets in the twenty-first century exhibit different kinds of expressive politics complete with their own signature story themes, aesthetic inclinations, and performative qualities. And as Aristotle's treatise *Rhetoric* arguably suggests, this has been a fact of political communication since antiquity. But such inten- tional shaping is undeniably the case in the contemporary era where the separation between media entertainment and politics has nearly col- lapsed. "[T]he contemporary political landscape is intensely mediated and 'stylised,'" political communication scholars Benjamin Moffitt and Simon Tormey write, and "as such the so-called 'aesthetic' or 'performa- tive' features are particularly (and increasingly) more important" (2014: 388). The presidential victory of Donald Trump punctuates the necessity of style as an analytical category more than ever. Trump ran one of the most unorthodox Republican campaigns in recent memory. Yet as a longtime tabloid figure, he was able to leverage his knowledge of media publicity to defeat more ideologically pure opponents in the Republican primary like Senator Ted Cruz.

In regard to Fox News, I am far from being the first person to stress how vital the network's style and entertainment qualities have been to its success. In fact, style is a central concept in one of the few academic books about Fox News. In the first pages of *Dark Genius: The Influential Career of Legendary Political Operative and Fox News Founder Roger Ailes* (2008), Kerwin Swint states outright, "What the world needs to understand about Roger Ailes is that he is not so much a newsman as he is a showman" (3). Swint's analysis describes the stylistic innovations Ailes devised earlier in his career as a daytime television producer and shows how he deployed these media techniques across a wide range of other communications fields, from political campaigning to corporate PR to television news. The interdisciplinary, multi-field approach that Swint develops in *Dark Genius* provides an excellent model for studying Fox News. It is a model this book seeks to emulate.

But despite all its merits, *Dark Genius* does have some analytical limitations, many of which are representative of larger analytical trends in the Fox News literature. Its main shortcoming is the "style over substance" (3, 10) argument that Swint adopts. From this perspective, the duty of the analyst is to see through Fox's flashy presentation –i.e., the sugar coating – in order to reveal its political-ideological core – i.e., the pill. While Swint astutely recognizes the tabloid influences in Fox's presentation and rightfully stresses the premium Roger Ailes placed on "performance" and interpersonal conversation, ultimately his analysis treats these presentational traits as little more than entertainment-based palliatives ("made-for-TV-imagery") for Ailes and Rupert Murdoch's rightwing political views. Prioritizing political analysis above all else, *Dark Genius* leaves the *cultural politics* of Fox's broadcasting style underexamined.

The notion that stylized political communication plays to emotions and not to the mind and the attendant belief that "images" or "visuals" are inherently "anti-rational," especially in comparison to the written word, is many centuries old (Caldwell, 1995: 336–358). During the network era of television journalism (1940s–1980s), this Cartesian understanding of style was codified in broadcasting policy. As Deborah Jaramillo cites, CBS' 1976 Standards Handbook barred "the use of music, reenactments and any tactics of a 'showbiz' nature in the news" (2009: 30). Yet what the proponents of this anti-style broadcasting philosophy had consistently failed to recognize was that the austere broadcasting aesthetic they considered the telltale sign of "serious" journalism was *itself* a type of style, one that specifically had been designed to express an aspirational class appeal.

This book strives to make the reader more aware of the value judgments media analysts and critics implicitly convey when they lament the entertainment aspects of contemporary political media. In addition, it does not approach style as a garnish or subsidiary element of political ideology but rather as a fundamental precondition for its communication. Political ideas and values, rhetorical scholar Robert Hariman stresses, "can only be taken seriously once performed successfully" (1995: 10). The style being exuded by a given news outlet, whether it be from the left or the right, is as substantive and important to the formation of its political identity as its ideology alone. Hence, to a significant degree, Fox's style *is* its politics.

With this said, it would be equally problematic to provide only a stylistic analysis of Fox News' political communication strategies and not address the political interest that such strategies serve. It would be akin to taking a machine apart to see how it operates without considering what the machine itself is used for. Offering an "inside look" into the Fox News organization, investigative journalists like Gabriel Sherman have revealed the political goals and intentions underlying Fox's programming choices and news framing (2014).[30] In the past decade, numerous content analyses of Fox's programming have *empirically* demonstrated Fox's conservative ideological slant.[31] Even the longtime face of Fox News, Bill O'Reilly, publicly admitted in 2004 that Fox "tilts" rightward.[32]

To have a comprehensive understanding of Fox News, then, we need a framework that can explain the relationship between the network's style and its political ideology. The theory of hegemony is useful in this regard

---

[30] Through obtaining leaked internal memos and emails, liberal activist groups such as Media Matters and Brave New Films have exposed how Fox's executive editors have, on occasion, directly prompted Fox journalists to cover events in ways that have helped Republicans and hurt Democrats (Greenwald, 2004; Brock & Rabin-Havt, 2012: 86–90).

[31] Kull et al., 2003; Aday, 2005; Groseclose & Milyo, 2005; Conway et al., 2007; Pew Research Center (October 29, 2008); Groeling, 2008; McDermott, 2010; Brock & Rabin-Havt, 2012; Feldman et al., 2012; Huertas & Kriegsman, 2014.

[32] Media Matters for America (July 2004).

as it combines a political analytical lens with a cultural one. Hegemony theory, as Raymond Williams explained, moves beyond strictly cultural and aesthetic concerns in that it involves questioning how discourses are guided by political interest and shows how such discourses reinforce "specific distributions of power and influence" (1978: 108). Yet, hegemony cannot be reduced to "ideology" alone because it also accounts for the way dominant values and meanings circulating in the culture at large bear down on and delimit the machinations of any given political group or media organization. In other words, political and media elites cannot just fabricate popular culture at will to suit their agenda. "[C]ulture," to use sociologist Michael Schudson's words, "constrains how we tell the tale" (1992: 53).

Cultural theorist Stuart Hall's book *Hard Road to Renewal: Thatcherism and the Crisis of the Left* (1988a) showed how to use hegemony theory to explain conservative populism. The book engages the rise of the British right in the late 1970s to consider how the Thatcher coalition's anti-government, free-market politics came to supersede the Labour Party's welfare appeals. A political mode of analysis, Hall maintains, could only reveal the "aggressive themes" of Thatcherite populism – that is, its free-market ideas and agenda. A cultural analysis is required to reveal what Hall terms the "organic themes" of Thatcher's political project, or the deep-seated cultural values Thatcher and pro-Thatcher media outlets (namely Rupert Murdoch's British tabloids) had to tap to make the historically specific ideology of conservative Toryism appear to be intuitively aligned with timeless British beliefs about what is right and what is good.

To build its corporate brand and programming style, Fox News' creative leadership drew ideas from one of the greatest repositories for "organic themes" about class, wealth and social status in the US national culture: the "populist rhetorical tradition" (Kazin, 1998). Learning from colossal defeats (e.g., Barry Goldwater's landslide defeat in 1964) and colossal victories (e.g., the "Reagan Revolution" of 1980s), the postwar conservative movement gradually forged a version of populism compatible with both free-market ideology and *white* working-class identity (Chapters 2 and 4 underscore the gendered and race-based dimensions of this political formation). Conservative think tanks of the 1970s and 1980s developed a knowledge infrastructure for transmitting the populist repertoire the movement cultivated.[33] This infrastructure and set of

---

[33] Himmelstein, 1990: 145–151; Nash, 1998; Rich, 2001, 2004; O'Connor, 2007; Phillips-Fein, 2009; Medvetz, 2012.

discourses provided subsequent generations of conservative activists, including media creators, with a "collective intelligence" (Mukerji, 2009) about how to work within existing American political styles to augment their power. While no single puppet master figure or funding source creates or controls the ideas associated with conservative populism, their gestalt produces a unifying thrust all the same.

In line with the conservative movement strategy described above, Fox News' programming discourse emphasizes aspects of the populist tradition that dovetail with free-market ideology and occludes those that do not. This book investigates the process of "selective tradition" (Williams, 1991) that Fox News' top programs performed during the Great Recession. It identifies the deep moral logics Fox programs deploy to legitimate conservative economic policies, while also revealing how Fox pundits managed the limitations, contradictions and risks inherent in using populist rhetoric to defend the business class and the wealthy. Such contradictions are all the more palpable in the context of a spiraling economy.

BEYOND "FAIR AND BALANCED": HOW CONSERVATIVE MEDIA CRITICISM HERALDED A NEW JOURNALISTIC EPISTEMOLOGY

In 1993, *USA Today* ran a story entitled "Conservative TV" about the "first ideologically designed network."[34] That same year the *New York Times* ran a similar story: "TV Channel Plans Conservative Talk, All Day, All Night."[35] This channel, the article explained, "is supposed to do for conservative political views what Court TV has done for the legal system: make them a fixture of popular culture." *Newsweek* also ran a story about a new, "unabashedly ideological ... 24-hour-a-day cable network," a network that was, the article noted, "the first of its kind in America."[36] All this commentary, however, was *not* about Fox News, which launched in October of 1996. Instead, it was about four short-lived conservative news channels that history has all but forgotten.

These upstart networks launched between 1993 and 1996 and included National Empowerment Television (NET), the most successful

---

[34] Lee (1993).   [35] Kolbert (November 27, 1993).

[36] Meacham (January 30, 1995). Smaller regional papers followed suit with titles such as "Conservatives Broadcasting Own Message" (*The Oklahoman*, 1993) and "GOP to Invade TV" (*Greensboro News & Record*, 1994).

of the failed conservative TV projects, airing for seven years running from 1993 to 2000.[37] Next came the Republican Exchange Satellite Network (RESN). This network lasted from 1993 to 1995. The third was GOP-TV, a network that was produced by the Republican National Committee and broadcasted from 1994 to 1997. Lastly, the Conservative Television Network, a venture that struggled to raise capital and never got beyond the promotion and planning stage.

Fox's founding CEO Roger Ailes, a man many credit as the mastermind behind Fox, told a reporter in 1998, "If you come out and try to do right-wing news, you're going to die. You can't get away with it." A few years later in a *New York Times* interview, Ailes – without giving specific names – hinted at these forgotten conservative networks, saying there had been "four failures" that attempted to do this. But Fox News, Ailes insisted, had a "different mission entirely."[38] Seeing Fox News as a pure "propaganda machine," liberal critics like David Brock and Tim Dickinson would jeer at the distinction Ailes was attempting to draw here. From their view, "right-wing news" describes Fox News to a tee. However, in certain respects, Ailes was right. Fox News did have a different mission, or, at the very least, its approach for delivering ideological news was quite unique.

The conservative TV projects that launched just before Fox News falsely assumed their enterprises would prosper simply by stamping their networks Republican and by dishing out the good gospel of Reagan conservatism. However, as it turns out, the idea of launching a conservative television network is one thing; the successful *execution* of one is quite another. As these "four failures" attest, Fox News was not the first to rail against "media elites" and "liberal bias." It was, however, the first to achieve national distribution and to effectively make the populist tropes and political styles of the conservative movement intelligible within *popular* formats of news and entertainment (Jones, 2012). But before delving further into the question of what made Fox News different from the previous attempts at creating "Conservative TV," let us recognize the central genealogical trait that Fox News shared with its prototypes, this being the long tradition of conservative media criticism.

The press releases of the conservative TV ventures of the 1990s reveal company narratives and selling points that are strikingly similar to those

---

[37] For one of the few contemporaneous academic articles on NET, see Dooley & Grosswiler (1997).

[38] These quotes were found in Sherman, *Loudest Voice in the Room*, p. 241.

subsequently used by Fox News. In one interview, for example, the vice-chairman of National Empowerment Television (NET), Burton Pines, said there are "tens of millions of Americans who feel they are out of the mainstream."[39] NET, Pines maintained, would provide an "alternative" news source, "at a time when the press is being criticized for being too liberal."[40] Like NET, the Conservative Television Network (CTN) framed its whole raison d'être as serving conservative news consumers who, by their estimation, were being ignored by the national press. In a 1994 interview, network president Anthony Fabrizio explained CTN's basic market strategy: "More than 60 million Americans, or 31% of the country identify themselves as conservatives." There is, he continued, "a disenfranchised core of individuals who feel they do not get the news the way they want to get it. These are the same people who listen to Rush Limbaugh daily."[41]

Fabrizio's mention of Rush Limbaugh is important to the story of conservative television. The commercial success of Limbaugh's talk radio show – though a different medium – emboldened conservative entrepreneurs interested in television. Included among them was Roger Ailes and the man who would become Fox News' top star, Bill O'Reilly.[42] *The Rush Limbaugh Show* was nationally syndicated in 1988 and by the early 1990s its audience had swelled to 20 million, making "El Rushbo" the number one radio host in the country (Bolce et al., 1996). Many conservative politicians believed that it was Limbaugh's media influence that "turned the tide" in the 1994 midterm election. In this midterm, Republicans took both the House of Representatives and the Senate as well the majority of state legislatures and governorships across the country. As a token of their appreciation, Republicans named Limbaugh an honorary member of the 104th freshman congressional class (Seelye, 1994). Limbaugh's meteoric rise in the

---

[39] Lee (1993).   [40] Kolbert (November 27. 1993).

[41] *The Indianapolis Star* (November 20, 1994).

[42] In years just before launching Fox News, Roger Ailes produced a television adaptation of *The Rush Limbaugh* radio show. This show ran as a syndicated program from 1992 to 1996. Limbaugh's success also inspired the man who would become the face of Fox News, Bill O'Reilly. In the early 1990s, O'Reilly told a friend, "I'm not sure where the [news] business is going but my gut says it is going in the direction of Rush and, man, I'm going to be there." Working as an anchor on the tabloid show *Inside Edition* at the time, O'Reilly pitched a newsmagazine version of Limbaugh's conservative-populist show to his corporate superiors at King World Production, but they did not pursue the idea. See Collins, *Crazy Like a Fox*, p. 143.

1990s proved, for the first time, that right-wing broadcasting could be *both* profitable and politically influential.

Like CTN, Fox News planned to tap into the massive conservative listener base Limbaugh had already solidified and then bring them over to cable news (Swint, 2008: 138). In Fox's first critical years on-air, Limbaugh – a friend and associate of Roger Ailes – promoted Fox News to his audience, the self-described "ditto heads." The on-air pitch Limbaugh verbalized was quite similar to NET and CTN's. "Check any recent polls," Limbaugh bellowed in his typical self-assured voice, "it's clear Americans think the media are biased. But there's now an alternative. Fox News is fair news" (Meroney, 1997: 41).

In contrast to the "four failures," however, Fox News did not overtly claim a partisan, political orientation. While Fox's spokespeople consistently hinted at the "underserved market in news" they sought to reach, they were far more careful not to explicitly label this market as conservative. In raising the issue of media bias, however, Fox's marketing discourse *implicitly* signaled its kinship with conservatives, yet it was always worded in such a way as to give Fox "a plausible deniability to the charge that it was a conservative organ," as Ailes biographer Zev Chafets nicely put it (2013: 125). A masterful example of this wording can be found in an interview with the *New York Daily News*, when Ailes told the paper, "We're not programming to conservatives. We're just not eliminating their point of view" (Battaglio, 2003).[43]

Ultimately, however, it was not hard for the public to guess the ideological direction to which Fox swayed. In the years leading up to Fox's launch, Rupert Murdoch, the owner of Fox's parent company News Corp., publicly accused the cable news leader at the time, CNN, of being "too liberal." In a 1996 interview with *American Journalism Review*, Murdoch blamed his archrival and CNN's founder Ted Turner for pushing the network "further and further to the left." Fox News, he boasted, would reintroduce "objective news coverage" to the cable field (Gomery, 1996).

Turner retorted – wrongly, it turned out – that he would "squish" Murdoch's Fox News Channel "like a bug" (Collins, 2004: 68). Instead,

---

[43] An episode of *The O'Reilly Factor* illustrates how slippery the distinction that Ailes is making here can be, even for an experienced host like Bill O'Reilly. In a brief moment of candidness, O'Reilly tells fellow Fox host Chris Wallace that, "this [Fox News] is a conservative," then catching himself, "NOT a conservative network but," returning to his point, "we give voice to conservatives, which ... others don't at all" (January 22, 2010).

to the shock of Turner and everyone else in the television industry, in 2002 Fox News surpassed CNN as the ratings leader – a position of dominance that Fox has held to the present day. Evidence suggests that the leaders and historians of mainstream TV news never really got their heads around the underpinnings of Fox's rise. In 2003, CNN's lead anchor Aaron Brown attributed Fox's success in taking the top spot to clever "marketing slogans," a backhanded compliment of sorts, as it denies the quality of Fox's programming as a possible reason (Auletta, 2003). Brown was not the only one advancing this thesis. Both critical and celebratory histories of Fox News give the network's original "Fair & Balanced" marketing campaign a great deal of credit.[44] I do not deny its importance to the development of Fox's brand. However, taking account of the failed conservative broadcasting ventures prior to Fox News, I argue that the "Fair & Balanced" campaign was the least original element of Fox's broader corporate strategy. In fact, a short-lived conservative television network that launched in the early 1970s, Television News Incorporated (TVN), anticipated Fox's famous company slogan by more than two decades (Swint, 2008: 67–69; Sherman, 2014: 106–107).[45] What truly distinguished Fox News from everything that came before was the enormous amount of corporate capital it had at its disposable and the populist *style* of journalism it put forth.

Conservative media organizations claimed to champion the cause of "balance" and raised the specter of "liberal bias" in broadcast media at least as far back as the 1940s and 1950s (Hendershot, 2011: Hemmer,

---

[44] Viguerie & Franke, 2004; Kitty & Greenwald, 2005; Brock & Rabin-Havt, 2012; Chafets, 2013; Sherman, 2014.

[45] Television News Incorporated (TVN) was launched in 1973 and received the bulk of its seed money from the conservative beer magnate Joseph Coors. TVN adopted the same narrative of liberal media bias that Fox News and the other conservative TV projects would deploy in 1990s (Gould, 1975; *Rocky Mountain News*, 1974). However, the more obvious reason TVN has been historically linked to Fox News is because it stands as Roger Ailes' first foray into the news business, as he served as TVN's news director from 1974 until October of 1975, when the network officially closed down. The network's demise was largely due to distributional obstacles. TVN's method of transmitting pre-recorded news packages to local stations over phone lines was a costly delivery option. The high transmission rates AT&T charged local stations to use TVN's video wire service inflated the price of TVN's media products beyond their worth. Foreseeing this problem from the start, Reese Schonfeld, TVN's Vice president of operations, wanted to make TVN a entirely satellite-based network (Sherman, 2014: 101–107). Fatefully, TVN's 1973 birth was a few years premature in relation to satellite and cable's commercial development and by the time these technologies had become marketable, the network had dug a financial hole from which it could not climb out.

2016). The failed networks of the 1990s were no exception.[46] Fox News' "Fair & Balanced" rhetoric and the marketing rhetoric of the conservative television contemporaries shared the same strategy of using a journalistic rationale to justify their partisanship – in essence, reframing their political bias *as* balance. This strategy carried weight because it laid bare a hard truth about journalism's professional ideology. The "fair" political center is in fact a floating concept open to interpretation. Every editorial attempt to define it is unavoidably informed by subjective and ideological biases. This is how the "Fair & Balanced" marketing campaign defanged early attacks against Fox News, not by convincing the public that Fox was going to be politically neutral, but rather by hollowing out the very concepts of "balance" and "objectivity" themselves.

However, again, this hollowing out process began long before Fox News appeared on the cable dial. In *Messengers of the Right* (2016), Nicole Hemmer tells the history of the "first generation" of conservative media activists who, from the 1940s through the 1970s, helped forge a tradition of conservative media criticism that Republican President Donald Trump continued with his twitter attacks against "fake news." Figures like broadcaster Clarence Manion and magazine publisher William Rush advanced "an alternative way of knowing the world, one that attacked the legitimacy of objectivity and substituted for it ideological integrity. This was embodied in their notion of 'liberal media bias'" (14). They put the first chinks in the armor of the objectivity regime. And indeed, the wave of conservative media criticism they sparked, combined with the rise of a "counter-intelligentsia" in the form of conservative research networks and think tanks in the 1970s and 1980s (see Chapter 5), corresponded with the gradual decline in public trust in the press, "official sources" and experts.[47]

In their concept of "reflexive modernization," sociologists Ulrich Beck and Anthony Giddens maintain that the distrust of expertise was part of a

---

[46] For example, National Empowerment Television president Paul Weyrich said, "If we only present one point of view on this program, I think we will be doing exactly what everyone complains other media are doing." In another interview where a reporter asked Weyrich why liberals do not create their own ideological network, he snapped: "They don't have to. They've got CBS, NBC and ABC." See Kurtz (November 12, 1994).

[47] With the fall of a unitary epistemological system and the increased distrust of official sources, journalists have increasingly turned to unconventional, lay sources of knowledge and assumed more interpretative and judgmental approaches to official statements (Schudson, 2003: 112). For a statistical graph showing the historical decline of public trust in the media see Gallup (2016).

larger societal trend that extends beyond the discursive domains of politics and public affairs media. From the 1970s onward, credentials and expertise increasingly lost the nearly automatic credibility they once enjoyed as sources of authority (1994). Under Roger Ailes' stewardship, Fox News was not only quick to register these broader changes but was one of the first news networks to create and master new interpretative strategies around what journalism scholar Chris Peters describes as "the breakdown of the lay–expert divide" (2010: 853).[48]

The populist style of journalism that Ailes formulated was well suited for the increasingly politicized news environment of the 1990s, an environment where "facts" were losing their truth power as they were increasingly judged not by their internal merits and methodical soundness but rather by the partisan affiliation (perceived or actual) of the institution producing them. As my analysis of Fox's coverage of the Great Recession demonstrates, rhetorical appeals to cultural taste, "common sense," and "traditional values" have become exceedingly useful in the politicized informational space of today's media. Unlike formal expertise, these populist sources of legitimacy do not require institutional verification. What populism does require, however, is a deep knowledge of traditional moral discourses, an astute awareness of the key social cleavages (e.g., race, gender, and class) active in a given historical moment and, most importantly, an exceptional level of *performative* skill, enough to convincingly embody the cultural disposition of mainstream television audiences, the majority of whom are non-college educated.

Fox News undoubtedly benefited from the decades of media criticism its conservative predecessors waged against the "liberal media." In turn, the network's marketing and programming discourse expanded the reach of the conservative tradition of media criticism and, in so doing, drew even more attention to the relativistic aspects of professional news standards. This further loosened the conventional criteria of journalistic authority but, in contrast to its failed conservative TV projects of the 1990s, Fox actually did something with this opening. It introduced a decidedly *non*-professional, authority-type to the US news scene, a populist media persona Ailes especially cultivated in hosts Bill O'Reilly and Sean Hannity. The only thing Fox's early conservative television competitors seemed to offer was ideology.

---

[48] Journalism scholar Anthony Nadler describes this journalistic paradigm shift as the "postprofessional" turn (2016).

DIVERGENT CONCEPTIONS OF TV POPULISM: ORGANIZATIONAL VERSUS AESTHETIC

In addition to sharing Fox's ideologically centered audience strategy, the failed conservative networks of the 1990s also marketed their channels in explicitly *populist* terms. Like Fox, each of them said they would challenge the "elite," establishment press and give voice to "the people." Yet, as this section details, their institutional priorities led them to espouse a very different understanding of media populism than the one held by Fox's creative leadership. This guided how they adapted to the various currents of their historical moment. It is instructive to consider the factors that stifled these failed television projects. Such an exercise helps pinpoint the broader industrial, political and cultural developments that Fox News faced, managed, and – ultimately – exploited with great success. Three major societal developments converged in the 1990s to create hospitable conditions for Fox News' corporate strategy (highlighted further in Chapter 1). These include (1) technological advancements in communication and the subsequent proliferation of niche markets in the television industry, (2) the trend toward polarization in the political field and the revival of partisan identification in America, and (3) the trend toward entertainment-driven formats in the news field, a process journalism scholars have called "tabloidization."[49]

The failed conservative networks of the 1990s celebrated and embraced the first two trends, but they, like many of their liberal counterparts, decried the growth of sensational news styles and "infotainment." Instead, these failed networks chose to replicate the *aspirational* cultural style of conservative predecessors like William F. Buckley's *Firing Line*. Similar to public and nonprofit channels like PBS and C-Span, they branded themselves as stalwarts of civic culture standing against the tabloid media wave that was cresting in the mid-1990s. Fox News, in contrast, gladly rode this cultural wave, incorporating stylistic traits from "lowbrow" public affairs genres that Rupert Murdoch, Roger Ailes, and Bill O'Reilly had experience producing earlier in their careers.

What is critical to recognize about the various attempts at creating a conservative broadcasting network before Fox News is that, in the majority of cases, they were managed by politicians and activists, not business

---

[49] For a review on "tabloidization" see Sparks (2000). Introduction: Panic Over Tabloids News. In C. Sparks & J. Tulloch (eds.), *Tabloid Tales: Global Debates Over Media Standards*. Lanham: Rowman & Littlefield.

entrepreneurs and entertainment industry people. This fact helps explain not only their poor financial calculations, but also the extent to which they strategically thought about and invested in the presentational style of their programming.

In many ways, Rupert Murdoch had more in common with CNN founder Ted Turner than he did with his fellow conservative media producers like NET president Paul Weyrich. This is of course ironic in light of Murdoch and Turner's opposing political beliefs, intense personal rivalry (Turner challenged Murdoch to a fist fight at one point), and the fact that Fox News' brand identity was and is still built in contradistinction to CNN's. But, indeed, Murdoch's Fox News would follow the *institutional path* that Turner paved with CNN. In 1986, *Broadcasting* magazine called Rupert Murdoch an "Australian-born Ted Turner," because Murdoch, like Turner, took bold financial risks by aggressively acquiring large entertainment companies across various media platforms. Both Turner and Murdoch were skilled at leveraging the profit generated by the wide range of programming content of their respective media conglomerates in order to subsidize new projects and acquisitions (Holt, 2011). The conglomerated business structure of TBS (later merging with Time Warner) and News Corp. allowed these organizations to absorb the heavy financial losses they initially took on to launch their competing cable news channels. CNN did nothing but bleed money for its first five years on-air (Parson, 2008: 454). The same was true of Fox News, which did not turn a profit for News Corp. until 2001, also five years after its launch (Sella, 2001).

As opposed to ad-revenue, the failed conservative TV ventures of the 1990s received the bulk of their funding from conservative think tanks, political advocacy groups, and private foundations. These financial streams proved to be both inconsistent and insufficient. National Empowerment Television (NET), for example, was financed through Paul Weyrich's lobbying group the Free Congress Foundation (FCF). Like the conservative think tank the Heritage Foundation, FCF's funding came primarily from conservative business magnates and philanthropists such as Joseph Coors and Richard Mellon Scaif.[50]

Another revenue strategy was giving programming slots to conservative advocacy groups such as the National Rifle Association, Accuracy in Media and the American Life League, an anti-abortion organization.[51] In

---

[50] See Kurtz (February 10, 1994); Grann (October 27, 1997).
[51] See Williams (February–March, 1995).

1997, NET changed its name to *America's Voice* and re-launched as a for-profit company with another $20 million of seed money. However, by January 10, 2000, the network would fold in bankruptcy $23 million in the red.[52]

For its part, GOP-TV was directed and staffed through the Republican National Committee and, like NET, gained much of its financial support from elite private donors. Jay Van Andel and Rich DeVos, the co-founders of the multilevel marketing company Amway donated $2.5 million to build GOP-TV's broadcast studios and provided another $1.3 million to air GOP-TV's coverage of the 1996 Republican National Convention on the Family Channel.[53]

The tens of millions of dollars these nonprofit conservative media ventures spent (or planned to spend[54]) seems quaint when one compares such figures to the estimated *half a billion* dollars Murdoch ended up spending to establish Fox News.[55] Lacking News Corp.'s titanic financial

---

[52] See Morahanb (July 7, 2008). Yet another way Weyrich sought to fund NET was to air tobacco-friendly news-talk programs like *Freedom's Challenge* in exchange for donations from tobacco industry giants such as Phillip Morris. See National Empowerment Television (April 5, 1995).

[53] See Marcus (July 26, 1996). Johnson (August 15, 1996). Rich Devos is the father-in-law of President Donald Trump's Education Secretary, Betsy Devos.

[54] The Conservative Television Network (CTN) estimated the network would need $45 million before turning a profit, a number that approximated what NET actually spent before going under. However, CTN's awkward idea to have cable subscribers pay an entirely separate $3.95 monthly bill for CTN programming dissuaded investors and as a result the network never raised enough capital to launch. See Kurtz (November 12, 1994). The amount Alexander's RESN raised from "private donors" is difficult to ascertain. However, the political grounding of Alexander's fund-raising methods and the donor base was not. Much of RESN's funding came from $1000-a-plate dinners for Washington lobbyists and longstanding Republican Party donors. See DeParle (April 16, 1995).

[55] In total, News Corp. spent over $500 million to launch Fox News (Chenoweth, 2001: 189). In *Inside Rupert's Brain* (2009), Paul La Monica claims an even higher estimate and cites an October 2007 shareholder report by News Corp. that shows the company had invested up to $900 million on Fox News since its 1996 launch (83–84). In a 1996 *USA Today* interview, Fox CEO Roger Ailes described the challenge of gaining a mainstream slot on the cable guide as akin to "breaking into Fort Knox" (Lieberman, 1996; Collins, 2004: 72). Thankfully for him, Rupert Murdoch, his boss, was willing to go to extreme lengths to overcome this challenge. Murdoch made a financial offer to the nation's top cable operators they could not refuse. Instead of trying to sell Fox News programming to them for the standard rate of ¢.25 per subscriber, Murdoch, in an unprecedented move, assumed the role of buyer and offered to pay cable companies $10.00 for each subscriber they gave Fox News access to. Subsequently, News Corp. dished out over $200 million just to give Fox News access to a 17 million subscribers on the day of its launch, a meager potential audience considering its competitor CNN had 60 million subscribers at the time. Just to gain access to ten million subscribers, Murdoch paid TCI, John Malone's cable

clout, the failed conservative networks of the 1990s adopted a nonprofit-to-commercial distributional strategy. The nonprofit status allowed them the maximize the capital they could raise from private conservative donors. Like a stepping stone, they would use these donations to fund their news operations long enough to build an audience. Once established, they would sell this audience to advertisers and transition into a mainstream commercial network.

This nonprofit-to-commercial strategy was not unprecedented for conservative television programming. After all, the most successful conservative television show up until that point was William F. Buckley's *Firing Line* (1966–1999), a program that – ironically in light of Buckley's anti-government politics – gained national distribution and visibility by broadcasting on PBS, a publicly funded network (Ledbetter, 1997). *Firing Line*'s "highbrow" cultural style contributed to PBS' reputation as what one 1971 *TV Guide* article dubbed "upper-class TV." And indeed, as PBS' own audience research showed, PBS was mostly ignored by the masses of Americans and was only watched by a "very special" minority of affluent and educated citizens.[56] *Firing Line*'s patrician sensibility hindered the show's attempt to branch out from public television and gain access to the "mass" audience of commercial television.

In the mid-1990s, Newt Gingrich was both Speaker of the House and the star anchor of NET's flagship program *Progress Report*. In 1995, he rallied congressional support to defund PBS, the very network that provided *Firing Line* – the first major conservative television talk show – a national platform. Intriguingly, Gingrich used a class-based justification for doing so. Why, Gingrich asked, should working-class taxpayers be forced to subsidize a culturally elitist network they never watch?[57] This was a fair enough question, but considering the type of programming content Gingrich was promoting for his own channel NET at precisely the same time, one wonders if Gingrich's conflict with PBS had less to do with

---

distribution, over $200 million (Sherman, 2014: 185). After settling a bitter court battle with Time Warner, in 1997, News Corp. reportedly paid CNN's parent company $200 million to gain 8 million more subscribers. One million of these subscribers were located in the all-important New York City market, the advertising capital of the world (Collins, 2004: 106; Sherman, 2014: 227). With each year, Fox News' subscriber base grew. By 2002, Fox had achieved a level of parity with CNN reaching nearly 80 million subscribers (Levere, 2002). More impressively, Fox News started beating CNN in ratings by this juncture. From the beginning, Murdoch would settle for nothing less than access to a mass national audience and he was willing to use the blunt force of News Corp.'s enormous economic capital to attain it.

[56] Ouellette, *Viewers Like You?*, p. 181.   [57] Ibid., p. 58.

the network's highbrow cultural orientation and more to do with its status as a *public* institution.[58]

Ultimately, Gingrich agreed with PBS' reformist mission to make "good culture" accessible to the masses. This was reflected in the bourgeois cultural content that Gingrich proposed for NET's program offerings. It included educational shows such as a televised college history course program called *Renewing American Civilization,* taught by Gingrich himself, which was "paired" with other high-minded viewing options such as *The Vine Line,* a show for wine connoisseurs.[59] As shown in NET press releases and business proposals, "the PBS crowd" that conservatives like Gingrich supposedly despised was in fact the market he and NET were targeting.[60]

In 1997, NET would change its name to America's Voice and re-launch as a for-profit news organization. This commercial trajectory separated it from PBS and C-Span. However, in seeking to capture the same affluent, educated audience segment that these nonprofit channels tended to attract, NET adopted a similar marketing approach, pitching itself as a refuge from the tabloid inanity of commercial television. In one 1994 *Washington Post* article, Gingrich described NET as an, "antidote to sensational television coverage that devotes more air time to Lorena Bobbit and Tonya Harding [stories published by two iconic tabloids in

---

[58] Former PBS host Bill Moyers said that Gingrich's opposition to PBS was primarily political. The deregulatory policy arguments advanced by Gingrich and so many other conservatives on C-Span, Moyers explained, served the corporate interests of the very cable industry C-Span received its funding from (Carmody, 1995). NET, it could be argued, played a similar propagandistic function for the cable industry that Moyers accused C-Span of playing. In December of 1994, Gingrich had John Malone, the CEO of Telecommunication Inc. on his show *Progress Report.* TCI was the biggest cable operator in the country at the time. In this program, Malone argued that deregulating the media industry would unleash more technological innovation and broaden consumer choices. This broadcast, it is important to note, took place as Congress was gearing up to debate what would become of the 1996 Telecommunications Act. Shortly after Malone's guest appearance, TCI rewarded NET with the gift of distribution, granting the network access to over 11 million viewers. See National Empowerment Television (December 13, 1994). *The Progress Report.* C-Span [Video file]. Retrieved from: www.c-span.org/video/?62168-1/national-empowerment-television. Also see Goetz (July–August, 1995). Cable: Who's Connected? *Columbia Journalism Review,* 34(2), 17–18.

[59] For an overview NET's program offerings, see Brown, November 15, 1994. NET Channel: C-Span with a spin. Broadcasting & Cable, p. 34. *Youngbloods* was one exception to NET's general middlebrow programming orientation. This was a youth-driven program pitched as a "Gen X version of the *McLaughlin Group* and other *Crossfire*-like political debate shows." See Grann, October 27, 1997.

[60] National Empowerment Television (September 1994).

the 1990s] than to toxic waste and health care." "One reason," Gingrich posited, "we've [conservatives] been losing is we've not engaged the *intellectual side* [my emphasis] enough ... Network news takes 9 to 12 second sound bites. Here's a chance to be in a person's living room for an hour in a non-confrontational mode."[61]

We see a similar anti-tabloid positioning in GOP-TV's first promotional ads and press releases. For its January 29, 1994 debut, GOP-TV recruited former Republican presidents Ronald Reagan and George H. Bush to endorse the network. "There are a lot of choices on TV," Reagan told the camera, "But my choice is GOP-TV." In a profile about GOP-TV, *New York Times* writes that Reagan "does not tune in to *The Simpsons* at 8:00PM on Thursdays. He says he watches the Republican Party's new show." Reagan's jab at *The Simpsons*, the most successful program on Rupert Murdoch's Fox Broadcasting network, repeated something George H. Bush had said two years prior.[62]

In waging these media critiques, Gingrich and GOP-TV stood as strange bedfellows with many of their liberal contemporaries, such as network anchors Dan Rather and John Chancellor. In a 1993 speech to the Radio-Television News Directors Association, Rather criticized what he called the "showbizification" of the fourth estate.[63] At the duPont–Columbia Awards forum that same year, Chancellor decried how broadcast news, in the name of profit, was reducing "the dialogue to the lowest common denominator." He warned the audience of journalists about the grave dangers that this "populist" trend posed.[64] Differing from Chancellor's pejorative conflation of populism with tabloid journalism, Gingrich and other conservative media producers embraced the term "populism." This disjuncture in definitions of journalistic populism is worth dwelling on for a moment.

Political theorist Francisco Panizza argues that there are two main ways to conceptualize populism: (1) as a *mode of organization*, and (2) as a *mode of representation* (2000, 2005).[65] By referring to the cheapening of "dialogue" on television news, Chancellor is defining populism more in the latter sense, as a "low" cultural *style* of public

---

[61] Lamar Alexander also distinguished his network RESN from mainstream television news with the same "non-confrontational" descriptor. See Mannies, November 3, 1993. Conservatives Rushing to Be New Limbaugh. *St. Louis Post Dispatch*; Gingrich made the same distinction when discussing NET's presentational style, see Kurtz (February 10, 1994).

[62] See Berke (January 30, 1994).   [63] See Viles (1993).

[64] See Brown (February 1, 1993).   [65] Also see Arditi (2005).

affairs programming associated with adjectives like "sensational," "confrontational," and "infotainment." While Chancellor is using populism – a term conventionally applied to politics – to describe styles within the journalism field, political theorists such as Margaret Canovan have, conversely, used the journalistic term "tabloid" to describe the "simple" and "direct" communication styles of populist politicians (1999: 5).[66]

The failed conservative networks of the 1990s expressed concerns about the spread of tabloid culture. But, they – unlike the network news departments and prestige newspapers – happily took on the populist label. When C-Span reporter Susan Swain asked NET vice-president Brian Jones (a man who would at one time serve as vice-president of Fox News), "Do you have a political point of view?" "Yes," Jones responded, "it's called populist. . .our view is the point of view of our viewers and callers."[67] NET president Paul Weyrich described this as placing the "[media] megaphone in the hands of the people."[68] Haley Barbour of GOP-TV used similar language. In one interview, he maintained that satellite and cable technologies provide "a mechanism for people to get information unfiltered." Conservatives can now "leapfrog the media elites" and "talk directly to the people."[69]

How do we make sense of the inconsistency between identifying as populist while rejecting "low" popular cultural styles?

Returning to the populist political theory outlined above, the answer lies in the way NET and GOP-TV spokespeople repeatedly used "populism" as synonymous with *organizational* descriptors like "grassroots" and "bottom-up." Note how Barbour's reference to the "mechanism" and Weyrich's "megaphone" metaphor place the emphasis on the technological conduit of communication as opposed to their programming style. This technology-centered, organizational conception of media populism mirrored the rhetoric of the left-leaning "public journalism movement" that was gaining steam at precisely the same historical

---

[66] Also see Moffit & Ostiguy (2016).

[67] National Empowerment Television (December 13, 1994).

[68] Williams (February–March. 1995). Before Jones took over, former NET vice president Burton Pines framed NET the exact same way in a 1993 interview with *USA Today*. When the reporter asked about NET's ideological orientation, Pines claimed that network's "slant" was more "populist" than conservative. Lee (1993).

[69] Seplow (October 3, 1995). CTN executive Floyd Brown repeated similar rhetoric telling *Insight on the News*, "technology is moving us to a point where gatekeepers in the traditional mainstream media are going to have less and less power." Rust (May 22, 1995).

moment. "Don't hate the media, become the media," the movement's main slogan declared.[70] Replicating the popular democratic discourse of both the public journalism movement and Brian Lamb's C-Span, the failed conservative TV networks of the 1990s depicted themselves as civic-minded enterprises that – by using call-ins, online forums and other "interactive" platforms – would facilitate more public participation in the production of news.

This organizational understanding of media populism was explicitly articulated by Lamar Alexander when called RESN's main program, *The Republican Neighborhood Meetings*, a "grass-roots organizational tool" for "party activists."[71] Imagined as an "electronic town hall," Alexander's show was broadcast over satellite and on a few local public access stations. To watch the show viewers had to own a satellite dish (a burdensome and expensive commodity at the time) and "downlink" the channel's coordinates. While Alexander viewed RESN as "the most important grassroots movement in the Republican Party,"[72] the television reviews of his experiment in teledemocracy were less inspiring. *The Sacramento Bee* called his show "Wayne's World for policy nerds."[73] "As television," another critic wrote, it was "certainty no threat to '*Nightline*'."[74]

The reviews of Fox News' October 7, 1996, debut could not have been more different, as its programming was critiqued for being *over*-stylized, not under. One negative review from the *Denver Post* was entitled "Fox News Channel so busy it might make you dizzy" (Ostrow, 1996). While more neutral, a *New York Times* review offered a similar take, writing, "Fox producers appear to be going for a youthful look, a brisk pace and a direct approach: young reporters, fast-moving pictures, colloquial comments."[75] "Youthful," "hip," and "modern"? These are not the adjectives that naturally come to mind when imagining the conservative audience Fox News was attempting to target. Yet, founding CEO Roger Ailes seemed know something about the conservative audience that these reviewers and prior conservative media activists did not, which was that conservative TV viewers were no less responsive to the style and attitude of mass entertainment than other segments of the national television audience.

---

[70] For an overview of the public journalism movement, see Anderson (2011).
[71] Kurtz (February 10, 1994).
[72] Conservative Political Action Conference (February 12, 1994).
[73] Kurtz (February 10, 1994).   [74] DeParle (April 16, 1995).
[75] Goodman (October 10, 1996).

While Fox News' programming rhetoric praised Christian morality and old-fashioned American values, the presentational style it introduced in the mid-1990s was anything but past-oriented, which is to say, anything but small "c" conservative. Instead of attempting to catch up to the presentational look of established news networks like NET, RESN and GOP-TV desperately tried to do, Fox News was forward looking. It did not seek merely to match the stylistic quality of its centrist and liberal competitors. It would push the envelope. Ailes may have been just as politically motivated as Gingrich and Weyrich; however, unlike these figures, he had started his career in entertainment television, not politics, so he placed a far greater premium on visual communication. Ailes once described producing television news as "painting the Mona Lisa...every three seconds" (Chafets, 2013: 193). Reflecting these presentational priorities, he turned to entertainment professionals to build Fox News' original staff, specifically "all the tabloid shows" (Swint, 2008: 166).

As former consultant on *A Current Affair, Inside Edition* and *Hard Copy*, Ailes was well familiar with the talent of the tabloid television sector. From this pool, he hired producers Sharri Berg of *A Current Affair* and Jerry Burke of *Extra!* and anchors and correspondents Louis Aguirre, David Lee Miller, Jon Scott and Shepard Smith, also from *A Current Affair*. He recruited Bill O'Reilly from *Inside Edition* and, later in 2001, he helped recruit *the* prototypical tabloid host of the late 1980s and 1990s: Geraldo Rivera. In light of the composition of Fox's early production and journalistic team, Ailes biographer Gabriel Sherman maintains that Fox's "original blueprint was more tabloid and populist than baldly conservative" (2014: xv).

Just as the network news programs first criticized, then copied the hyper-stylized presentation of *A Current Affair* in the late 1980s, CNN and MSNBC chided Fox News for its tabloid style and then eventually adopted many of the presentational innovations Fox originated. These innovations include the stock ticker at the bottom of screen, breaking news "alerts," playing music and voice-overs in the segment breaks, using vibrantly colored set designs and backgrounds, and more. In a 2001 *New York Times* profile on Fox News entitled "The Red-State Network," Marshall Sella captures Roger Ailes' resentment about this. Ailes "talks energetically about how his competitors like to impugn Fox News' top-volume approach to presentation: the pun-driven titles, the vivid graphics, and visceral tone. But the phrase 'tabloid news,' Ailes asserts, has lost its meaning." Quoting Ailes directly, the Fox CEO defensively said, "There's no line. News is what people are interested in. You can watch *Dateline*

NBC [a network news program] and, arguably, every one of those stories was done by *A Current Affair* five years ago. We're just getting the same girls to dance around shinier poles."

In addition to foreshadowing the future sexual harassment cases that would lead to his downfall, Ailes' comments about *A Current Affair* and "girls" dancing "around shinier poles" hints at a contradiction that has been central to Murdoch's most popular and powerful news properties in his media empire, from his London tabloid newspaper the *Sun* to his US cable news channel Fox News, which is this paradoxical combination of a cultural-aesthetic transgressiveness (usually associated with the left) and conservative political ideology. Ailes' unique range of career experiences acquired before taking the helm at Fox News naturally intuited this contradictory formula. Ailes transitioned from producing the "hip" *Michael Douglas* talk show in the 1960s and theatrical plays in New York City in the early 1970s to working on Republican presidential campaigns in the 1970s and 1980s, and then, in the late 1980s and 1990s, returning once again to entertainment television, producing news-magazines like *A Current Affair* and *Inside Edition*. At an early stage of his career, Ailes learned how, biographer Gabriel Sherman writes, "television could harness [the] liberal culture [of show business] even as it was critiquing it" (2014: 70).

Rush Limbaugh was a master of radio, Ailes of television, and Murdoch of print; yet despite their different bases of media expertise, each man shared the same shrewd market-based definition of news as simply, to return to Ailes' prior quote, "what people are interested in."[76] This libertine evaluative posture toward the national media culture is one of the fundamental things that separated this cohort of "second generation" conservative media producers from the conservative media activists of the postwar era (Hendershot, 2011; Hemmer, 2016). Figures like Gingrich and Weyrich supported the economic deregulation and

---

[76] On several occasions, Rupert Murdoch and News Corp. journalists have expressed this same philosophy. In 1989, Murdoch said, "Anybody who, within the law of the land, provides a service which the public wants at a price it can afford is providing a public service." Paul McMullen, a former reporter for Murdoch's London tabloid *News of the World*, defended the paper's coverage of Prince Charles' affairs and sex life repeating the same words Ailes used in the 2001 *New York Times* article stating, "I think anything that the public is interested in is in the public interest" (Folkenflik, 2013: 28–29). At a 1991 radio conference in Seattle, Washington, Limbaugh echoed this same viewpoint telling the audience, "[p]eople turn on the radio for three things: To be entertained. To be entertained. And to be entertained." See Boss (June 9, 1991).

corporate consolidation of the US communications industry *on principle*, but, following the legacy of "first generation" conservative media producers, they were ultimately uncomfortable with the "cultural deregulation" (Carson, 2005) that was the logical byproduct of the unfettered commercialism that these types of policies unleashed. The failed conservative TV projects of the 1990s primarily saw television as a civic-educational tool for improving the intelligence and tastes of the citizenry. These networks may have railed against liberal media bias, but their programming still basically resembled mainstream journalistic outfits that performed the news in the much the same elitist register as those they opposed. They claimed to support "populism," but it was a grassroots form of organizational, small government populism, not the aesthetic populism of mass culture.

CHAPTER-BY-CHAPTER COMPENDIUM

This book consists of two main sections. The first chapters offer a historical perspective on Fox News' ascendancy and a theoretical framework for understanding its populist brand and programming style. The later chapters of the book transition from investigating the origins of Fox News' populist journalistic style to illustrating how it is deployed as a political tool for framing news events using the network's coverage of the late-2000s economic crisis as the book's principal case study.

"Chapter 1: Channeling America's 'tabloid soul': how Rupert Murdoch, Roger Ailes, and Bill O'Reilly remade television news" dives deeper into the conditions that led to Fox News' emergence. This chapter shows how the success of Fox relied on the development of technological infrastructures and deregulation that expanded the range of network options, increased polarization in the political field, and, crucially, content production that understood how to effectively use tabloid presentational strategies to formulate a populist news aesthetic. This chapter seeks to reveal the class-based roots that underlie Fox's counter-elite programming strategy by contextualizing the network's development within the broader history of the Anglo-American tabloid tradition.

"Chapter 2: Populism on cable news: a theoretical framework" sets up the book's interpretive model for analyzing Fox News' programming content. This model integrates theories of populism with theories of performance and cultural disposition. It also distinguishes between populism as narrative and populism as performance and then explains how these two core representational components work in tandem to produce Fox's overarching populist media brand. This chapter contrasts the conservative network to its main liberal competitors and adversaries (CNN, MSNBC and *The Daily Show*), considers the question of why liberal media organizations have shunned populist-styled media figures on the left, and explores to what extent this can be attributed to the existing racial and gender biases of populist forms of political communication.

"Chapter 3: 'I'm a blue-collar guy': How Fox News hosts imagine themselves and their audience as working class" seeks to explain how conservative pundits on Fox News have redefined class as a cultural identity, as opposed to an economic position. The rise of the postwar conservative movement occurred as the national economy was shifting from an industrial to a post-industrial model. This chapter demonstrates how conservative politicians exploited working-class apprehensions about the culture of a new college-educated class that stood to gain the most from the increasingly information-based labor market. It engages the question of whether or not Fox News' audience can be considered "working class" in the first place and uses textual examples from Fox News programming to illustrate two central aspects of how Fox News hosts attempt to symbolically embody the working class: (1) through aligning themselves with "lowbrow" cultural forms, and (2) lay bases of knowledge.

"Chapter 4: 'The makers and the takers': How Fox News forges a working class/business class political alliance," offers a close, multimodal analysis of the network's coverage of the economic crisis in the late 2000s. This analysis demonstrates how Fox News' political framing relied on the enduring moral narratives of *producerism*, a political discourse that has been recycled in American political culture ever since the Jeffersonian era. In labeling the wealthy and the business class as "job creators," Fox News' top programs reworked this traditional political discourse to include corporate managers in the moral community of producers along-side the long-venerated working class. At the same time as its pundits repeatedly blamed the crash on "undisciplined borrowers" and the Democratic policies, which aimed at increasing home-ownership among low-income citizens and racial minorities, Fox's recession narrative was able to tap longstanding racial stereotypes about welfare-dependency and public-sector parasitism.

"Chapter 5: 'The populist-intellectual tactic': How Fox News incorporates expert knowledge within its populist framework," analyzes the delicate maneuvers that Fox News programs use to disseminate conservative intellectual culture while maintaining their anti-elitist identity. In 2009, an unprecedented number of conservative authors and think tank researchers appeared on Fox News' top shows to lend "official" legitimacy to the network's critique of the stimulus bill. A striking component of these critiques involved revising the history of the Great Depression based on Amity Shlaes' 2007 book *The Forgotten Man: A New History of the Great Depression*. Pundits and politicians used the book's main argument that the New Deal prolonged rather than shortened the Great Depression served to demonstrate the folly of using government spending to lift the nation out of the late 2000s downturn. Fox News' promotion of this book highlights the institutional ties between conservative news outlets, free-market think tanks, and the Republican Party. A close examination of Shlaes' guest appearances on Fox's top programs shows how the network's populist hosts and expert guests embody different authoritative roles, a performative interplay I call the "populist-intellectual tactic."

The conclusion, entitled "Trumpian Populism: Fox News' respectable future clashes with its tabloid past," engages the multiple sex scandals that have rocked Fox News in 2016 and 2017 and explores the challenges the network faced when, in 2013, it attempted to attract a younger audience and rebrand itself as more "serious" and "straight" news organization. The dust up at the first debate of the 2016 presidential campaign between Megyn Kelly, the woman who was once considered Fox's future, and presidential candidate Donald Trump illustrates the contradictions that arise when a network built on an outsider ethos seeks establishment legitimacy. The following section engages recent debates on populism and, with several qualifications, offers a defense of this controversial rhetorical tradition. The final section addresses a set of reductionist analytical tendencies that have hindered the political left from taking something constructive from Fox News' success and proposes a path forward for future research on conservative media and partisan journalism.

I

Channeling America's "Tabloid Soul"

How Rupert Murdoch, Roger Ailes, and Bill O'Reilly Remade Television News

What do the barking heads of Fox News Channel and other Murdoch media have that CNN, Rather and Donahue don't? A true, virtuous, tabloid soul.

—Charles Pierce, 2002

The traditional media in this country is in tune with the elite, not the people...That is why we're [Fox News] not liked by the traditional media. That's not us.

—Rupert Murdoch, 2004[1]

In the early 1950s, a young Rupert Murdoch worked as a subeditor at London's *Daily Express* during his graduate years at Oxford. The *Express*, a leading tabloid in its time, was in the belly of the ferociously competitive Fleet Street. Lined with England's top newspapers, this London boulevard had long been a metonym for the British news market overall. Under the guidance of the *Express'* notorious chief executive, Lord Beaverbrook, Murdoch gleaned key lessons about "the black art of journalism" and how vital it was for a news executive to be a student of mass taste.[2] Murdoch would bring these insights back to his home country of Australia, transforming the newspaper he inherited from his father, *Adelaide News*, into a profitable tabloid. From this small, rural news outlet, Murdoch built what would become one of the largest and most politically influential media empires in world history: News Corporation.

[1] Strupp (September 22, 2004).   [2] Wolff (2008).

40

More than simply picking up on basic presentational characteristics of a good tabloid paper (e.g. punchy headlines, colorful layout, and sensational content), Murdoch gleaned a deeper understanding about the social logic behind the tabloid style. From the Fleet Street perspective, Murdoch biographer Michael Wolff explains that commercial news is, fundamentally, a "class business. Every Fleet Streeter knows which is his class" (2008: 72). Murdoch's philosophy on journalism would forever be colored by class or, at least, a particular cultural and normative conception of it that he and his news organizations expressed for decades through the anti-elitist tropes of the Anglo-American tabloid tradition.

In the 1960s, Murdoch returned to the UK and acquired two major London papers, *News of the World* and the *Sun*. His strategy was to direct these papers "downmarket" and go "mass." While the *Sun*'s scantily clad "Page Three girls" boosted circulation numbers, it also helped create Murdoch's seedy reputation as the "Aussie tit-and-bum king" (Mahler, 2006: 34).[3] Soon enough, he turned the *World* and the *Sun* into popular and profitable tabloids and, by 1978, Murdoch's *Sun* even exceeded the longtime leader *Daily Mirror* as England's top daily paper.[4]

Acquiring the *New York Post* in 1976, Murdoch believed he could execute the same working-class taste strategy in America's largest metropolis. For years, however, the *Post* yielded no profits at all. In her book *For Enquiring Minds: A Cultural Study of Supermarket Tabloids* (1992), historian Elizabeth Bird argues that with the *Post*, Murdoch "misread American tastes by assuming huge numbers of readers would accept the "sexy" and often self-consciously "working-class" British formula" (34). When a reporter asked Murdoch why the success he had achieved in London could not be repeated in New York City, the conservative news baron blamed the *Post*'s failure on Americans' lack of class consciousness. "This is a middle-class city [New York City]," Murdoch told one reporter, "Everybody in this country wants to get ahead, get a piece of the action. That's the fundamental difference between the Old World and the New World. There's not the self-improvement ethic in England that there is in this country" (Shawcross, 1997: 160). One could do worse than

---

[3] In 1970, the satirical British magazine *Private Eye* solidified this reputation with a front page that read "Rupert, 'Thanks for the mammaries,' Murdoch." Even though Murdoch faced a harsh backlash from cultural critics and politicians, The Page Three girls section boosted the *Sun*'s circulation from 1.5 to 2.1 million in just one year. Braid (September 14, 2004).

[4] By 1978, the *Sun*'s circulation numbers reached 4 million, overtaking the most popular newspapers in the UK, such as *The Daily Mirror*. Keeble (2009).

"self-improvement ethic" if one had to capture the essence of middlebrow taste with a single phrase.

Murdoch would eventually overcome the aspirational proclivities toward the US news market by shifting News Corp.'s energies more toward the television realm in the 1980s and 1990s. This chapter recounts the tale of Murdoch's tabloid victory in America, which, according to Wolff, Charles Pierce and many others, would come to its fullest fruition with the success of Fox News. The first section engages Fox's immediate history and explains how the industrial and technological transformations that frag- mented the US media landscape in the 1980s portended the rise of partisan journalistic styles in the 1990s and 2000s. The mass commercialization of cable and satellite technologies mark the beginning of the multichannel era. This new "high-choice media" (Prior, 2007) environment encouraged more entertainment-driven news formats and afforded the proliferation of niche news markets, particularly partisan ones. Much of the literature on Fox has emphasized the way its political branding strategy polarized the US journal- ism field along ideological lines. However, this approach often overlooks the equally profound way Fox polarized the US public sphere in terms of taste and aesthetics by reviving longstanding tensions between *aspirational* and *tabloid* market sectors. This chapter situates the *style* Fox News developed within the broader history of Anglo-American tabloid tradition, and then relates it to News Corp.-owned antecedents including the *Sun* in London, the *New York Post*, and *A Current Affair* (ACA), a pioneering television tabloid broadcast between 1986 and 1996.

In the United States, the word "tabloid" often conjures up the entirely apolitical newspapers and magazines that blare out sensational headlines in supermarket checkout lines about UFO sightings, celebrity love tri- angles, and gruesome murders. Journalism scholar Colin Sparks has argued that it is this "soft news" topical orientation (e.g. celebrity gossip, sports, sex scandals, sensational crimes) that primarily distinguishes tab- loid journalism from the "quality" press and "straight" news outlets.[5] But

---

[5] In the introduction of an edited volume entitled *Tabloid Tales: Global Debates Over Media Standards* (2000), Colin Sparks provides criteria for differentiating tabloid news outlets from more professionally styled ones. For him, the important question to ask is what kind of subject matter does a news organization mostly focus on? Does the media outlet primarily cover "hard news" topics such electoral politics, the economy and foreign policy, or "soft news" topics like celebrity gossip, sports, sex scandals, and sensational crimes? He maintains that tabloid outlets are oriented toward the latter and, adding another layer, gravitate toward the private matters and personal lives of newsworthy individuals as opposed to their public life.

when we turn our sights toward tabloid journalism's non-editorial, stylistic features, the connections between tabloid media formats and populist political communication become clearer.

Forged by activists and social movements, populism's recurring rhetorical themes center around *civic* issues such as democracy, institutional corruption and giving voice to the popular will. This is what populism scholar Cas Mudde calls populism's "thin-ideology." This "thinness" or vagueness is what allows a wide range of "full" or formalized political ideologies (right and left) to attach themselves to populist values and to claim the mantle of "the people."[6] The tabloid tradition, by contrast, is a species of *commercial entertainment* and as such has been historically more focused on spectacle, aesthetics, titillation, and melodrama. Like political populism, tabloid news also projects a normative, non-economistic imaginary of class conflict. However, unlike populism's political "insiders vs. outsiders" schema, tabloid media primarily represents class differences through the prism of high/low taste hierarchies. While it is important to acknowledge these differences, ultimately political populism and tabloid journalism are quite isomorphic – meaning many of the communicative traits of one tradition can be identified in the other. I group these traits into three categories: analytical disposition, presentational form, and public sphere imaginary.

Analytical disposition: Political populism and tabloid journalism more readily use subjective, personalizing modes of societal analysis, offer unambiguous moral conclusions, and treat individual experience and social background as equally authoritative to that of professional expertise.

Presentational form: Both political populism and tabloid journalism tend to give greater priority to affective forms of communication (e.g. visceral language, graphic images, colorful presentation, emotional embodied performance).

Public sphere imaginary: Both traditions project an antagonistic, "illiberal" conceptualization of the public sphere that resembles the political logic of populist movements as theorized by Ernesto Laclau and Chantal Mouffe (2001). "The official press," media scholar John Fiske explains,

---

[6] Mudde, 2007; Mudde & Kaltwasser, 2011. Benjamin Moffitt and Simon Tormey's article "Rethinking Populism: Politics, Mediatisation and Political Style" (2014) offers a nice overview of the "thin-centered" ideology approach to populism and compares its strengths and weaknesses to other theoretical approaches to populism, such as populism as "political logic," as "discourse," as "strategy," and as "style." Also see Canovan, 1999.

"strives to eliminate contradictions, difference and particularity in its quest for consensus." The tabloid news sector, by contrast, Fiske continues, "makes no attempt to smooth out contradictions in its discourse: indeed, it exploits them" (1992: 49–50). Capturing this blend of a hyper-stylized presentation with a blunt, confrontational news voice, the former editor of Rupert Murdoch's *New York Post* Frank Devine once said that a good tabloid paper gravitates around two things: "the shiny and the jagged" (Kurtz, 1988).

But while the programs that did the most to build Fox News' corporate identity –*The O'Reilly Factor* and *Hannity* – have exhibited all the communicative characteristics mentioned above, the main subject matter of these shows, like the majority of Fox's programming, is weighted toward "hard" news topics, such as electoral politics, federal governance, and the economy. It is in this way that Fox News greatly differs from what is commonly understood as tabloid news in America. To fully recognize Fox News' tabloid roots, one needs to move outside the national borders of the US news culture. For Fox News' style is to some extent of foreign import – ironic for a network known for its patriotic Americanism. News Corp., Fox News' original parent company, was founded in Australia and established its international presence in the United Kingdom. Indicative of the company's non-American origins, some of News Corp.'s first hit TV shows in the United States – *A Current Affair* and *America's Most Wanted* – were modeled after successful programs in Australia and the UK.[7] In addition to importing these reality entertainment genres to the Fox Broadcasting network, it is with Fox News that News Corp. would introduce the American public to a distinctively British formulation of tabloid journalism. Twentieth-century tabloid outlets in the United States had long exploited class differences based on taste and education; what Fox News added to the equation was to *partisanize* such differences.

THE RISE OF PARTISAN NARROWCASTING: "AFFECTIVE
ECONOMICS" MEETS "AFFECTIVE POLARIZATION"

In the 1970s, cable television had made great technological and infra-structural strides. On the consumer end of things, however, it would take another two decades for cable to reach mass adoption in American homes. In 1970, only 7.6 percent of Americans had cable. This number

---

[7] Lippman (January 24, 1990).

climbed to 33 percent by 1983. By 1997, one year after the launch of Fox News and MSNBC, the adoption rate had surpassed a majority threshold, with 70 percent of Americans subscribing to either cable or satellite television services (Prior, 2007: 94). The rate of cable and satellite market penetration now paralleled the growth of channel options. In the 1970s, Americans had access to only five or six television channels. By 1981, the early spread of cable television had catapulted the number of available channels to thirty-four. This number was nearly doubled by 1987 and, with the advent of digital cable in the early 1990s, channel options expanded even further, rising into the hundreds (Holt, 2011: 118).[8] Between 1994 and 1995 alone, fifteen separate cable networks had made their debut (Swint, 2008: 114). As evident by the names of these networks (e.g. Television Food Network, Home & Garden Network, History Channel), cable television's subscription revenue model allowed for specialized content and encouraged *narrow*casting over *broad*casting.

The revolutionary growth of channel options in these decades created what Markus Prior has called a "high-choice media" environment and this, as his research stresses, fundamentally altered the economic structure of the television industry (2007). Suddenly, television producers were no longer beholden to the financial imperative to reach a universal audience. The traditional broadcast networks, fearing the loss of advertising dollars, were producing programming that aimed to please everyone and offend no one. Industry insiders referred to this as LOP (least objectionable programming). *The Cosby Show*, a feel-good network sitcom centered on a fictional African-American family living in an upper-middle-class neighborhood in Brooklyn, New York, epitomized this LOP programming strategy. However, as former Comcast president Roger Clasen made clear, "cable isn't *Cosby*."[9]

As cable, satellite, and, later, Internet, platforms began to fracture the national audience into smaller and smaller market segments and niches, shear audience size was no longer the only economic measuring stick to consider. New audience characteristics pertaining to social differences and viewing behavior were becoming ever more important to television economics. In this new scattered media landscape, *passionate* audiences with clear, homogenous cultural identities were especially prized as they offered something that was, in a "high-choice media" context, now in

---

[8] For more data on cable/satellite expansion and channel options see Arceneaux & Johnson, 2013: chapter 2.

[9] *Broadcasting* (April 4, 1988).

scarce supply: a dependable target.[10] The financial structure of cable television enabled media companies to be profitable without having to attract large audiences with LOP content. This was a pivotal shift because it made the idea of a partisan television network a commercial practicality for the first time.

From a business perspective, partisanship was, in many ways, the perfect solution to the unprecedented marketing crisis that the television industry was just beginning to grapple with in the 1990s and 2000s. Unlike the "captive" reliable audience of the network era (1940s–1980s), the post-network audience was splintered and evasive. How would media companies and advertisers confidently target and maintain viewers who enjoy so much choice – viewers who can, with a flip of the remote, "zap" to the next channel if a program does not immediately catch their interests? The answer was to use what media scholar Henry Jenkins calls "affective economics" (2006: 61).

This new marketing theory had abandoned the conventional mass audience approach and instead would call on companies to target smaller but more "loyal" audience segments. If 80% of purchases are made by 20% of a company's consumer base, why not, this theory reasoned, invest your marketing energy toward the hard-core fans encouraging and amplifying the strong *emotional* attachments they have with the corporate brand?[11] Media scholar Jeffrey Jones makes similar points but connects

---

[10] See Mittell, 2010: chapter 2. Also see Jason Mittel's article (2016) "Donald Trump Doesn't Need to Broaden His Appeal. The Rise of Cable TV Explains Why." Additionally, Becker, 2006: chapter 3; Parson, 2008; Johnson, 2008: chapter 5; Baym, 2009: chapter 1; McMurria, 2017.

[11] In *Loudest Voice in the Room* (2014), Gabriel Sherman writes, "[t]he passion of Roger Ailes' audience [the Fox News audience] was something that had never before existed in TV news, a consequence of Fox's hybrid of politics and entertainment. Fox News did not have viewers. It had *fans* [my emphasis]" (291). Sherman's description of the Fox News audience as being "fans" presents a promising connection between the literature on partisan media and the scholarship on fan communities, a connection journalism scholar Oliver Jutel directly engages in his 2013 article "American Populism and the New Political Economy of the Media Field." Indeed, the "loyalty" and "intensity" of the Fox News audience's viewing behavior and the viewing behavior of audiences of fiction-based TV shows that have earned cult followings such as *Buffy the Vampire Slayer* are similar in terms of their suitability to post-network television economics. According to one report, the average Fox News viewer watches the network's programming 30 percent longer than CNN's average viewer. Battaglio, (September 16, 2003). New CNN Team Seeks a Long Run. *Daily News*. This longer viewing duration allows, Sherman notes, Fox to charge higher ad rates. As a 2011 Pew study put it, "[t]hough CNN has a larger pool of [unique] viewers from which to draw, Fox can boast a more dedicated audience." Pew Research Center (March 13, 2011).

them directly to the cable news field. He explains that in the crowded and competitive terrain of post-network television it had become "necessary for cable channels to craft intensive relationships with their viewers, connections that will encourage routine and repeated viewing" (2012: 180).

Few things in American public life are more emotionally charged than partisan politics. The 1990s was a particularly opportune time to exploit its "emotional capital" for branding purposes. This was evident not only because new communication technologies were making niche partisan news markets a technical possibility, but also because the 1990s marked a decade of partisan revival in America.[12] Political polarization spiked among the general voting public at this time and reached unprecedented levels among congressional elites, activists, and interest groups as well.[13] This polarization was found on both sides of the aisle but, with the historic 1994 midterm congressional victories ("the Republican Revolution"), conservatives in this era were becoming successful at pushing the political system and culture further to the right. The conjunction of intensified partisanship in the political sphere with the increased competitiveness in the television industry made efforts to create a television niche based on political conservatism an obvious move.

When Fox entered the cable news game, its marketing emphasis was on cultivating a "brand community," one that, media scholar Jeffery Jones argues, the network built using the powerful "symbolic material" of political ideology (2012: 181). Jones credits Fox News for recognizing how media businesses were changing from "content companies to audience companies" or, as television scholar Michael Curtin explains it, Fox moved "beyond the utility branding of a news network ... into a new phase of TV branding based on identity" (2009: 157). This stands in contrast to CNN and MSNBC's programming-centric promotional discourse. Although CNN had been vaunting the unmatched international scope of its reporting and its ability to be the first on the scene, and MSNBC had been promising to bring cutting-edge technology and big-name network anchors to cable news, neither of these networks was

[12] Bartels, 2000; Fleisher & Bond, 2000; Ceaser & Busch, 2005; Hetherington, 2010. For an overview of the politic science scholarship on polarization and its relation to media see Prior, 2013; Hmielowski et al., 2015.

[13] Some researchers emphasize the role that political elites have played in causing political polarization.
McCarty et al., 2001; Koger, 2010. Other researchers have focused on interest groups and activists. See Stonecash et al., 2003; Layman et al., 2006; Hetherington, 2010.

actually offering a coherent and compelling identity for its audience to rally around and emotionally invest in.

Dan Cooper, a former Fox News executive, confirmed Jones' point, saying that during Fox's launch period, "there was no talk about programming" and "it was all marketing strategy." However, Cooper stresses that Fox's brand community was created less through affirmative "performances" of conservative ideology, as Jones emphasizes, but was instead constructed mostly in negative terms; that is, as a marked contrast to the self-proclaimed "professional" culture of other news organizations and brand communities. In his memoir about working on Fox's launch team *Naked Lunch: Creating Fox News* (2008), Cooper references Al Ries and Jack Trout's marketing theory of "positioning" (1981) to explain the underlying logic of Fox's original 1996 "Fair and Balanced" campaign. According to Trout and Ries, the fundamental goal of positioning strategies is to differentiate the brand in the mind of the consumer; something that is achieved, in part, by embracing what the two men later termed, "marketing warfare" (1986). In practice, this means identifying the most recognized brand in a given product field and then relentlessly defining your own brand against it.

Many classic case studies in advertising history illustrate this strategy; for example, Avis Car Rental's 1962 "We Try Harder" campaign (positioned against Hertz), or, more recently, Apple's "Get a Mac" 2006 campaign (positioned against Microsoft's PC). Like these campaigns, Fox News' foundational slogans "Fair and Balanced" and "We Report, You Decide" were not, Cooper emphasizes, primarily designed to promote the quality of Fox's media product per se, but rather to differentiate Fox from other brands. Their main function was to "re-brand" their competition as something elitist and biased. In the case of MSNBC, this meant Fox's drawing attention to and ridiculing the network's "innate yuppiness," as Cooper phrased it (more on this shortly).

Interestingly enough, the formation of partisan identities is quite similar to the creating of a brand community vis-à-vis market "positioning" in that partisan identities, too, are primarily constituted by their contradistinction to an out-group or an Other. Stanford political scientist Shanto Iyengar and his colleagues maintain that "the mere act of identifying with a political party is sufficient to trigger negative evaluations of the opposition" (2012: 407). These scholars question the commonly-held assumption that today's partisan polarization is mainly the result of policy and principle-based ideological divisions among the voting masses. They cite research that demonstrates how average citizens, in contrast to the extreme positions expressed by political elites and activists, tend to have centrist views on most issues (406). "[The] vast majority of the public does not think about parties in ideological terms," they write. "[T]heir ties to [the] political world are instead *affective* [my emphasis] based on [a] primordial sense of partisan identity that is acquired very early in life and persists over the entire life cycle" (427). With their concept of "affective polarization," Iyengar and his colleagues argue that with social identity in particular, "how partisans view each other as a disliked out-group" (406) is a more consistent indicator of mass polarization than attitudinal differences about policy and political philosophy. Reflecting this insight about the nature of partisanship, Fox News' market positioning strategy has been and continues to be as much about associating CNN and MSNBC with a despised social group as it is about painting the two of them as ideologically-biased.

So, who was this despised group, the foil against which Fox News built its partisan news brand upon?

In *Gay TV and Straight America* (2006), Ron Becker discusses how, with the breakdown of the mass audience approach, television marketing in the 1990s started to become increasingly geared toward young, educated consumers living in big cities. This was referred to this as the "slumpy" demographic, an acronym that stands for "socially liberal, urban-minded professionals." Slumpys, as Becker explains, were not "just the 'genuinely affluent' but also [the] 'selectively affluent'... [TV networks] envisioned this audience to be 'hip,' 'sophisticated,' 'urban minded'" (95). Although Becker's book primarily considers the influence that the "slumpy" profile had on the development of entertainment programming – particularly in how it made way for gay-themed television shows like *Will & Grace* – the same marketing construct also had an impact on the marketing strategies of the cable news environment. The branding strategy of Microsoft and NBC's joint venture, MSNBC, was clearly trying to reach the same slumpy market. In his biography on Roger Ailes, Gabriel Sherman nicely characterizes the social and cultural imaginary of MSNBC's original brand:

From the very beginning, MSNBC spoke, very deliberately, to the coasts. MSNBC's specific concept was to re-create on camera the vibe of an espresso bar in downtown Seattle, the home of NBC's new corporate partner [Microsoft]...Exposed faux redbrick walls and industrial lighting transformed the America's Talking studio in Fort Lee, New Jersey into a loftlike space where urban twenty- and thirty-somethings chattered about the news of the day, like characters from *Friends* or *Seinfeld*.

(2014: 187)

In the months leading up to Fox News' launch, Roger Ailes said little about Fox News' own "distinguishing characteristics" but had plenty to say about MSNBC. Moreover, Ailes' jabs at MSNBC tended to focus more on the network's target demographic and cultural style than its political bias. For example, in a 1996 September interview just a month before Fox News' launch, Ailes explicitly mocked the urban-hipster aesthetic of MSNBC's set design. At Fox, he remarked sarcastically, "[W]e'll put drywall up on our set so we don't have any brick."[14] Ailes ridiculed other dimensions of MSNBC's cosmopolitan, professional class appeal, such as the network's on-set display of cutting-edge laptop computers and its claim to revolutionize television news by making it web-based and "interactive." "We're not going to consider ourselves in the business of having to sell computers every five minutes. Nor will we have to be in the business to tell people to turn off their television set and go to their computer to get more information."[15] Lastly, Ailes undercut MSNBC's central selling point about drawing from NBC's *established* network names, such as Tom Brokaw and Brian Williams, to cable news. At a 1996 September press conference, Ailes described this star-based strategy as prioritizing "hair spray" over gritty reporting.[16]

While CNN and MSNBC drew its on-air talent from network news departments and prestige newspapers, the talent pool Ailes tapped to build Fox News' top names mostly came from *outside* the reputable sectors of the journalism field. Sean Hannity, for example, came from the world of conservative talk radio, while Bill O'Reilly and Shepard Smith had previously worked as anchors on syndicated tabloid TV shows like *Inside Edition* and *A Current Affair* (ACA) – shows that Ailes helped produce and, in the case of *ACA*, Fox's parent company News Corp. owned. Ailes believed the outsider career trajectory of these anchors gave them a relatability that the network anchors lacked.

As a television producer, Ailes particularly prided himself on his ability to discover "authenticity" in people and to accentuate it on air (Collins, 2004: 140). In *Creating Country Music* (1997), Richard Peterson demonstrates how the country music industry has historically used the term "authenticity" as a stand-in for regional and class-based social traits that country singers either exhibit or do not exhibit. Ailes' usage of

[14] Levin (September 9–15, 1996).   [15] Taylor (July 19, 1996).
[16] Lafayette (September 9, 1996).

the term carries similar social and cultural connotations. It is no coincidence that the most visible and enduring names in Fox News' history that Ailes recruited each embody distinct forms of ethno-regional whiteness and/or cultivate "blue-collar" on-air personas. Shepard Smith, or "Shep," as he prefers to be called, hails from the deep Southern state of Mississippi, a background he exudes with his colloquialisms, with his personal and informal interview style, and with his unmodulated Southern drawl. Meanwhile, both O'Reilly and Hannity, having been raised in Irish-Catholic families in Long Island, New York, were encouraged by Fox to play up rather than mute their Northeastern, white ethnic backgrounds (the "Long Island edge"[17] as O'Reilly has called it). As I demonstrate in later chapters, the pillars of Fox News' cultural populist brand – class, region and whiteness – would become more pronounced in the Bush and Obama years. However, Fox News' top creative figures hinted at these themes prior to the 2000s and 2010s, and even before Fox News was launched.

Rupert Murdoch's tabloid papers in Australia had long pitted the "true" Australians from "the bush" (rural Australia) against the liberal "cognitive elites" from urban areas (Sawr & Hindess, 2004). In 1984, Murdoch described the US media field using similar anti-elitist rhetoric. At a panel sponsored by free-market think tank American Enterprise Institute entitled "Is there a Liberal Media Elite in America?" Murdoch claimed that the US journalism establishment disregards "the traditional values of the great masses."[18] Oxford-educated and raised by his wealthy family in Australia, one might say Murdoch himself lacked a personal knowledge of "the great American masses" he was speaking so highly of. However, in making Roger Ailes chairman of Fox News, Murdoch knew enough to recruit a man who undoubtedly did. Ailes had grown up in a small, blue-collar town in Ohio, a background he has referenced throughout his career as a way to confirm his self-presentation as a journalistic outsider.

In the years before joining Fox News, Ailes had been the network president at CNBC and America's Talking (A-T). At A-T, Ailes would remind his staff to not ignore the "flyover states" in the South and Midwest – the "NASCAR audience," as he referred to them.[19] Moving somewhat in parallel with these populist themes was Bill O'Reilly, who

[17] Kitman, *The Man Who Would Not Shut Up*, p. 137.
[18] McKnight, *Murdoch's Politics*, p. 71.
[19] Sherman, *Loudest Voice in the Room*, p. 151.

was cultivating a "regular Joe" on-air persona prior to becoming the number one host and face of Fox News. In 1994, O'Reilly proudly told one reporter that at *Inside Edition*, "we tap into the sensibilities of the middle class, the working class...We speak to the heartland of America."[20] O'Reilly would, of course, carry his "common man" self-presentation to Fox News in 1996. And while many of the first television reviews of Fox News would conclude that its 24-hour news format was little different from those of CNN and MSNBC, according to one 1996 *USA Today* article, O'Reilly's program was the one exception to this "bland sameness." Columnist Matt Roush wrote that O'Reilly's "confrontational irreverence" offered a "blast of originality."[21] Thus, seeing greater potential in *The O'Reilly Report,* Ailes moved O'Reilly's program from 6:00PM to a primetime slot at 8:00PM in 1998 and renamed it *The O'Reilly Factor.* With this switch, *The Factor*'s ratings immediately spiked upward. In a July 1998 interview, O'Reilly would attribute the success of his new Fox show and his other media endeavors to his ability to "*speak for* [my emphasis] blue-collar America...my confrontational style is what people want."[22]

Ailes' emphasis on the "NASCAR audience" and O'Reilly's reference to "blue-collar America" were as much a product of the 1990s and 2000s marketing culture as MSNBC's slumpy strategy had been. As Victoria Johnson demonstrates in *Heartland TV* (2008), these two consumer appeals were deeply entwined and mutually constitutive. She writes, "The top-ten urban markets, clustered on either coast in part depend upon the 'mass' older, rural, square Heartlander market to define their tastes and sensibilities as contrast[ed to the] young, urban, and hip." While slumpy appeals were, she explains, "organized to promise socially progressive market diversity, urbane mobility, and place-transcendence through consumption," flyover appeals rested on "social continuity, tradition, and recovery of place-bound identity in a fast-moving era" (150–151).

With all the competition geared toward the most populated urban markets, a handful of channels went in the other direction and adopted a "flyover" *counter*-programming strategy. This included networks such

[20] *Norfolk Virginian-Pilot* (May 3, 1994). This quote and citation can be found in Hart (2002). *The Oh Really? Factor: Unspinning Fox News Channel's Bill O'Reilly.* New York: Seven Stories Press: 17.

[21] Roush (October 8, 1996). Fox News Channel: Not Crafty Enough. *USA Today.*

[22] Bark (July 13, 1998). Journalist Writes About What He Knows: TV News' Cutthroat World. *St. Louis Post-Dispatch.*

as PAX, United Paramount Network (UPN), Outdoor Life, Country Music Television (CMT), and the Family Channel, a network in which News Corp. bought a large stake in 1997. To appeal to this "flyover" market, the networks mentioned above returned to a "mass" cultural address that had long treated rural and Midwestern tastes as plain, homogenous and culturally conservative. Although the "mass" approach had been adopted as the standard in the network era, in the 1990s and 2000s it had become an outlier and thus presented itself as yet another way to create a television niche.

In line with the "flyover" entertainment networks, Fox News would concoct a similarly paradoxical "anti-niche" niche cable news strategy. Fox News programs hail their audience as unhip, white, and majoritarian – characteristics that, in conservative media culture especially, signify "authenticity," or, to use former vice-presidential candidate Sarah Palin's terminology, "real Americanness." The regional dimension of Fox News' populist representation of its audience became especially solidified in the 2000 presidential election with the introduction of the "red-state" vs. "blue-state" political-geographic terminology and, to date, the Fox News audience has in fact been overrepresented in the Southern states (Levendusky, 2013: 12).

Empirically speaking, however, the Fox News audience is far from comprising the majority. Like the cable news audience as a whole, it represents a small percentage of the national television audience. As Kevin Arceneaux and Martin Johnson point out in their book *Changing Minds or Changing Channels* (2013), the combined audience of the top four cable shows only amounts to about 7.5 million people. The evening network news programs on NBC and CBS are still triple the size of primetime cable programs, and this size disparity was even more pronounced in the 1990s. The cable news audience seems especially tiny in relation to the size of the voting public, which is around 130 million (Arceneaux & Johnson, 2013: 4–5). Regardless of the empirical size of the cable news audience, however, *inside* the world of cable news, Fox's corporate strategy strove to occupy a "mass" positionality, both in terms of achieving the largest audience and in terms of cultural taste.

From 1998 to 2001, Fox grew its ratings in the 25–54 demographic by 430 percent. This took place while CNN's had declined 48 percent.[23] The next year, Fox would surpass CNN as the ratings leader. Accepting this as

---

[23] Sella (June 24, 2001).

a permanent trend, in 2003 CNN adopted a new revenue model that shifted away from the "mass" ratings game in favor of garnering premium advertising rates by attracting the cable news audience's most affluent and educated segments; that is, the cosmopolitan slumpy demographic that had been MSNBC's target from the beginning. In a *New York Times* interview, CNN president Jim Walton hearkened back to the Victorian appeals for decency in nineteenth-century print journalism and stressed why it was important to resist the temptation to go partisan and tabloid. "The important thing for CNN is to understand who it is and how it defines winning. It's not," he clarified, "just about chasing the higher number. Quality matters." Defending his choice to roll back some initial attempts by CNN to copy Fox News' tabloid presentational elements and combative partisan address, Walton said, "One might say I have a little bit of an understated style, and we may see some of that. Whatever CNN does across any of its businesses, I want the word *class* [my emphasis] associated with it."[24]

CNN's new elite-oriented branding strategy also involved engaging in forms of media criticism that sought to define Fox News as standing outside the news field altogether. "I honestly think they do something quite different from what we do," CNN's lead anchor Aaron Brown told the *New Yorker*, "I don't want to create a sense that they're in the same business we're in ... There's room for conservative talk radio on television. But I don't think anyone ought to pretend it's the *New York Times* or CNN" (Auletta, 2003). However, each time CNN and other news organizations excluded Fox News from the circle of "serious" news organizations, they unwittingly helped affirm Fox's narrative about liberal bias and, equally important, strengthened a *symbolic* association that Murdoch found immensely desirable: the association between right-wing politics and working-class taste. CNN and MSNBC's decision to market themselves as the more cosmopolitan, tasteful and professional news sources assisted and concretized Fox's populist branding strategy. In turn, Fox's uncivil, combative style and tabloid aesthetic provided CNN and MSNBC with a well-suited counter-audience against which they developed what TV critic Walter Goodman calls a "boutique programming" appeal (Hallin, 2000: 234).

Fox News' assumption of a populist-tabloid positionality in the US media field was not without risks, however. Such a media strategy has

---

[24] Rutenberg (February 24, 2003).

historically invited intense criticism from the journalism community. The brilliance of Murdoch is that rather than seeing the negative judgments – that predictably came when he tabloidized a news property – as a threat to its public legitimacy, he viewed it as an added benefit. The criticism from established news organizations and "prestige" journalists enlivened and legitimated the very anti-elitist narratives that News Corp. outlets like Fox News used as a badge of working-class credibility.

TABLOID!: THE DEBATE OVER "BAD" JOURNALISM AND ITS CLASS-BASED ROOTS

In 1880s and 1890s, Joseph Pulitzer's *New York World* and William Randolph Hearst's *New York Journal* achieved unprecedented circulation numbers each hitting the million mark by end of the nineteenth century. These papers attracted massive readerships with various editorial and presentational innovations such as using larger headlines, putting photos on the first page, adding sports stories, comic strips, and lifestyle sections for women. Pulitzer and Hearst's papers were fiercely condemned for promoting "yellow journalism," a pejorative term that critics coined to describe a set of now-familiar journalistic sins: placing style over substance, emotion over reason, entertainment over education, and advocacy over accuracy (Peck, 2014b).

A great wave of tabloid TV shows emerged in the late 1980s and cable news gained influence in the 2000s. In their wake, complaints about "bad journalism" became as common as they were a hundred years ago. As former ABC *Nightline* anchor Ted Koppel said in 2011, newscasts "no longer give you what you need to know but what you want to know – and that can be mindless trash."[25] Two media properties of News Corp. founder Rupert Murdoch, *A Current Affair* and Fox News, stand at the center of not one but two of the major *media panics* (Drotner, 1992) in US journalism at the turn of the twenty-first century. If concerns about "tabloidization" predominated public debates about the news media in the late-1980s and 1990s, the "partisanization" American journalism has been the central preoccupation of media criticism in the 2000s and 2010s.

Let us begin with the media panic surrounding *tabloidization*, which, for the sake of clarity, is a concept journalism scholars use to describe the process whereby the commercial–entertainment values of the tabloid

---

[25] Plummer (September 10, 2011). Also, see Koppel (November 14, 2010). Additionally, see Peck, 2014b.

news sector begins to takeover and supplant the professional–institutional values of mainstream news organizations.[26] Carl Bernstein – a veteran journalist whose "hard news" cache for breaking *the* investigative story of the century, Watergate, is second to none – pictured this process far more colorfully. In a 1992 essay entitled "The Idiot Culture," he described tabloidization as "the ravenous celebrity-and-sensationalism-scandal machine that is consuming decent journalists" and, it is note-worthy to add, he singled out the "sleazy, cynical standards" of Rupert Murdoch's News Corp. as one of the main culprits behind making "the weird and the stupid and the coarse ... our cultural norm, even our cultural ideal."[27]

With stories about killer dolphins, "Preppie Killers," and celebrity sex tapes, Murdoch's syndicated newsmagazine *A Current Affair* was tabloid incarnate. And, to the horror of Bernstein and other respected investigative journalists, the show's breakout ratings success invited imitation, spawning a slew of copycat shows such as *Inside Edition* (1988), *Hard Copy* (1989), and *Extra!* (1994). In this period, two other public affairs genres – talk radio and daytime talk shows – were causing similar kinds of uproar and, as such, were often clumped in the "tabloid" media category. "Shock jocks" like Howard Stern and Rush Limbaugh flourished on talk radio, establishing a mold for a provocative interviewing style and mas-culinist, "jerk" persona that O'Reilly and Hannity would later hone on television as Fox News anchors. At the same time, the number of daytime talk shows skyrocketed. By the mid-1990s, there were more than twenty daytime talk shows on network television.[28] Maintaining ratings in such a crowded field pushed the content and themes of daytime television toward evermore scandalous spectacles. Panel titles such as "I'm Pregnant by a Giant Transsexual" and "I was Ugly, Now I'm a Stripper!" prolifer-ated on notorious talk shows such as *Jerry Springer* and *Ricki Lake*.

In a 1999 end-of-decade retrospect entitled "The Tabloid Decade" (1999), *Vanity Fair* columnist David Kamp believed that this trend was the defining feature of the 1990s. The era produced several of the most iconic tabloid stories in media history, dishing up what he called "a Mondo Trasho of low-life extravaganzas ... Amy Fisher and Joey

---

[26] Sparks (2000).   [27] Both of these Bernstein quotes are found in Ehrlich (1996).
[28] Watching the great success of the *Phil Donahue Show* in the 1970s and 1980s, followed by *The Oprah Winfrey Show*'s even greater success in the mid-1980s, network television executives in the 1990s would launch an unprecedented amount of daytime talk shows, so much so that by the mid-1990s –when Fox News was launched – there was roughly two dozen daytime talk shows on air (Grindstaff, 2002: 50).

Buttafuoco, Lorena and John Wayne Bobbitt ... Michael Jackson's child accuser, the Branch Davidian inferno, and Kurt Cobain's suicide ... the O. J. Simpson epic."

As these "low" public affairs genres started to capture increasingly larger shares of the network news programs' audience, the more "respectable" network news programs like *60 Minutes*, *48 Hours* and *Nightline* started to adopt both the "soft news" editorial agenda of tabloid TV shows and their flashier presentational aesthetic. Academic content studies of this period show that, indeed, in the late-1980s and 1990s there was a discernable shift in the national press away from "hard news" topics like economics, national security and public policy toward "soft news" about celebrity gossip, human interest stories, and salacious scandals.[29]

Mathew Baum and other communication scholars such as Robert McChesney attribute this stylistic and editorial shift to political economic forces, namely, the Reagan administration's deregulation of mass media industries in the 1980s. Reagan's free-market–friendly FCC appointee Mark Fowler lifted longstanding federal mandates on broadcasters to serve the "public interest" with informative, educational programming. For Fowler, television should be treated no differently than any other commercial product; it was, he famously said, just a "toaster with pictures." The Democratic Clinton administration of the 1990s shared Fowler's free-market philosophy and pushed his deregulatory approach, further dismantling laws that prohibited media cross-ownership. Rolling back these anti-monopoly measures led, quite predictably, to the historic "mega-mergers" of the 1990s. In a relatively short period of time, the concentration of media ownership in America (and the world) went from being spread across hundreds of companies to being controlled by six massive, multinational conglomerates: Viacom, Disney, Sony, Bertelsmann, Time Warner, and News Corporation (McNair, 1998; McChesney, 1999). In this new hyper-commercialized, corporate media culture, television news became more profit-driven and ratings-based. This encouraged cable and network news organizations to adopt more eye-grabbing formats and, in an effort to decrease overheads, to use low-cost opinion-based talk formats in favor of more expensive investigative reporting (Hmielowski et al., 2015).

Many in the journalism community perceived the growth of "infotainment" as a full-blown epidemic. This alarm was formalized by a

---

[29] Patterson, 2000; Baum, 2003: 37–39; Jaramillo, 2009: 21–40; Berry & Sobieraji, 2014: 66–94.

1998 conference comprising 250 journalists, media executives, and opinion leaders who gathered to discuss "a much longer running crisis – the *rise of the tabloid* [my emphasis] and the trivial on our pages and screens, and the increasing pressure to conform to the values of our corporate owners" (Sparks, 2000: 1).

On the surface, the rising influence of cable news in the 2000s seemed to spark a different kind of moral media panic. Journalistic laments about cable news seemed less about the "vulgarization" of the national culture than about the political polarization of news organizations and audiences. Ted Koppel, an old-guard journalist who anchored ABC's *Nightline* for 25 years, has become one of cable news' most prominent critics. In a 2012 special report that he co-produced with MSNBC entitled "War of Words: Partisan Ranting is 'Marketing of Fear'" that aired on *Rock Center with Brian Williams*, Koppel paints a narrative of broadcast journalism's decline from the golden Cronkite years of the postwar era. The documentary places special blame on cable news for American journalism's fall from grace, specifically to the foundational role that Fox News' longtime number one host Bill O'Reilly played in inspiring a whole host of partisan news imitators. "If we tried a paternity test," he tells O'Reilly in a sit-down interview, "there would be a lot of [media] folks out there who would look upon you as their ideological dad."

In the introduction of the special, host Brian Williams articulates one of Koppel's central critiques. "News media that agree with you when you wake up in the morning, right or left, that is the subject of Ted Koppel's reporting tonight. He and others feel it is corrosive and does nothing to help compromise in this country." Koppel's argument that cable news partisanship is fostering political-democratic dysfunction is reinforced throughout the documentary and its consequences are framed as increasingly grave as the special report moves to conclusion. In an interview with *New York Times* columnist David Carr, Koppel asks, "What is the impact of people only hearing echoes of what they already believe?" Carr soberly responds, "I think it's an existential threat to our perfect union."

In many ways, Koppel's "War of Words" special mirrors the main critiques that political science literature on partisan media and "selective exposure" had been voicing since the early 2000s. Kathleen Jamieson and Joseph Cappella's *Echo Chamber* (2008) stands as one of the most extensive and prolific of these selective exposure studies. In line with Koppel's conclusions, the book's main normative concerns focus on how partisan media "echo chambers" discourage political compromise and consensus-building; things that are essential to the proper functioning of a democratic government (246–247).

In their novelty, the "selective exposure"-styled arguments heard in MSNBC's 2012 "War of Words" special seem to be fundamentally different than the ones Carl Bernstein, Dan Rather and John Chancellor waged against tabloid television in the 1990s. However, upon closer inspection, we see how Koppel and other voices featured in the documentary critique cable news partisanship, not merely in terms of its political effects but also in cultural terms that are reminiscent of the anti-tabloid critiques of previous generations. For example, Koppel bemoans cable news for lowering "the bar of civility" and "coarsening the dialogue in America," transgressions that have less to do with ideological reporting than with violating mannerly conventions of public discussion and debate. It is telling that Koppel's biggest charge against Bill O'Reilly in his one-on-one interview with the Fox News host deals with social etiquette. O'Reilly asks Koppel if it "offends" him when he is "rough on his guests." Koppel answers, "It offends me when you're *rude* [my emphasis]."

Another way in which "War of Words" recycles the typical "laments" (Langer, 1998) against tabloid journalism is by framing cable news's partisan qualities as a breed of sensationalism. This emphasis on cable news' unthinking emotionalism is made clear in the special's subtitle: "Partisan Ranting is 'Marketing of Fear.'" Like the crime stories and sex scandals of the 1990s, partisanship is treated as a new commercial device for stirring up emotion, boosting ratings and making profit. Steny Hoyer, a Democratic congressman featured in the documentary, tells Koppel, "Today's journalists too often, because it's profitable to do so and it builds audiences, see their job not to inform but to incite, to get people riled up, to get their juices flowing." In line with Hoyer's analysis, *Times* journalist David Carr argues, "People tune in for the warfare. They're not interested in the fruits of peace. It's bad television. Who would want to watch that?" Koppel ties all these points together in the final moments of the special. Regretfully, he tells Brian Williams, cable news programs "have discovered that the more irascible, more partisan, the nastier they are, the bigger audience they get." With the voice and demeanor of a disappointed father, Koppel suggests the viewing public clean up their act. "The only the way things are going to change," he intones, "is if the audience says you know something I'm tired of it."

The tale of journalism's corruption by the twin evils of commercialism and sensationalism is a remarkably old one. It goes at least as far back as the 1830s, when the first cheap, mass-circulation papers appeared. These "penny papers" were accused of lowering journalistic standards for including human interest stories and for conducting, of all things, interviews. While interviews are the staple of contemporary journalism, in the 1830s the practice was seen by the established papers as intrusive and tactless (Schudson, 1978).

Why do we see the same century-old rationales being used to distinguish "good" journalism from "bad"? Because class tensions have surrounded the commercial news industry in America since its inception. The American news market has long been divided into two sectors – one "serious," one tabloid – that serve as a proxy for deeper social antagonisms. Moreover, these divergent news markets and antagonisms have, at times, been aligned with different political camps and ideologies (Peck, 2014b).

Popular journalistic styles co-evolved with the rise of mass political parties and, as such, populist political rhetoric and tabloid marketing discourse have, since the Jacksonian era forward, shared strong recursive relationships. For example, the founder of the first penny paper, Benjamin Day, maintained in 1833 that he created the *New York Sun* to give a voice to the "common man" (Örnebring & Jönsson, 2004: 288), a phrase President Andrew Jackson used in his signature political slogan: "Faith in the Common Man." Attacked by the dominant, "gentlemen" class papers for their emotionalism and ineloquent writing style, early tabloid papers used populist counter-critiques and cited their commercial clout as alternative bases of journalistic authority. In so doing, they set the foundation for a self-consciously "non-elite public" in the US media field (Örnebring & Jönsson, 2004).

These changes in journalism were part and parcel of broader class-based polarizations that were beginning to take shape in the mid and late nineteenth century. Historian Andreas Huyssen refers to the splitting of the national culture into "high" and "low" camps as the "Great Divide" (1986). In *Freaks Talk Back: Tabloid Talk Shows and Sexual Nonconformity* (1998), Joshua Gamson describes the formation of this class-cultural hierarchy in terms of two opposing traditions of public culture. These traditions, he stresses, created an enduring stock of class-based stereotypes and cultural styles that entertainment industries, particularly television talk shows, would draw upon and reconfigure in the twentieth- and twenty-first centuries. Gamson describes the contrast between the "propriety" and "rationality" of the upper- and middle-class forms of public leisure, such as literary circles and the lyceum and the "irreverence" and "emotional directness" of working-class forms of entertainment, such as the carnival, the cabaret, the popular theater, and the tabloid newspaper (30).

While partisanship was a common trait of both elite and non-elite newspapers for most of the nineteenth century, by the end of the century it started to be seen through the prism of high/low cultural values. In the 1870s, education-minded social reformers and political groups like the Liberal Republicans (later called the Mugwumps) pushed newspapers to break from their political tribalism and partisan patronage in favor of a more "principled," "independent journalism" (McGerr, 1986). The views of these reformers, Michael McGerr summarizes, "reflected the liberals' faith in empirical social science and in their hopes in a less emotional, more intellectual public life" (58). In spite of their efforts, however, non-partisan news approaches were not well received by the deeply partisan American public for some time. According to journalism scholar Richard Kaplan, the political chaos that the 1896 presidential election between William McKinley and populist Democrat William Jennings Bryan was the key "epochal" turning point. This watershed election, combined with the burgeoning Progressive Movement's crusade against "party machines," put the existing system of political alignments in disarray. It is in this context, Kaplan argues, a moment where partisan identifications among the public were confused and dislodged, that "professionalism" could rise to become the new cultural base for journalism's public authority (2002).

The *New York Times*, arguably more than any other national news-paper, helped catapult this new professionally styled journalism into the twentieth century. In 1896, Adolph Ochs acquired the *Times* and repack-aged it as an "upmarket" paper. Its new motto, "All News that's Fit to Print," was an early example of "market positioning." In rejecting the ethos of Pulitzer and Hearst's massively popular tabloid papers, the slogan worked to establish the *Times'* reputation as the anti-tabloid. Interestingly, the *Times'* definition of journalistic "fitness" was as much about exuding "decency" as it was about fairness and accuracy,[30] which points to the moral and social dimensions underlying journalism's emerging professional ideology and culture.

In his classic book *Discovering the News* (1978), Michael Schudson argues that the opposing journalistic styles and consumer appeals of the

---

[30] Schudson, *Discovering the News*, p. 109.

late-nineteenth-century news market often served as "cover for class conflict" (118).[31] The tabloid papers of the era were geared toward what he describes as *story ideal* – a news style that prioritizes narrative form and presentation over factual purity. Prestige papers like the *Times*, by contrast, centered their public identity on an *informational ideal*. This informational mode of address imagined its readership as a rational, knowledge-seeking subject unswayed by partisan factionalism and unamused by lurid, mass entertainments. While this schema divided the reading public "morally in ways that are related to class," it did not, Schudson clarifies, "reflect it in any simple way."

Upper-class readers indulged in the "guilty pleasures" of the tabloid, for example, and, conversely, working and lower-middle-class citizens read prestige papers as a means of "self-cultivation" and, by extension, upward mobility. Out of commercial necessity, papers like the *Times* had to attract readers outside its elite base targeting, Schudson explains, "not just the wealthy but the aspirationally wealthy." With this social climbing reader in mind, one 1898 *Times* advertisement read: "To be seen reading the *New York Times* is a stamp of respectability" (1978: 112).

By acknowledging the aspirational dimension of the *Times'* marketing discourse, Schudson complicates attempts to draw one-to-one matches between the class-inflected styles of late-nineteenth-century newspapers and their audiences. This insight is important, as I demonstrate later, to understanding the class-cultural politics underlying the branding strategies of cable news channels at the turn of the twenty-first century. In the next section, I formulate and historicize what I call the *aspirational* journalistic address, and trace how this middlebrow sensibility would come to dominate American news culture until the 1980s and 1990s, when Rupert Murdoch and other conservative media pioneers introduced a *cultural populist* style to rival it.

THE "ASPIRATIONAL" NEWS STYLE: ANTI-TABLOID
JOURNALISM IN THE TWENTIETH CENTURY

In *The Making of Middlebrow Culture* (1992), Joan Rubin challenges the conventional belief that the "genteel," high cultural tradition of the late nineteenth century died out with the rise of mass entertainment industries such as film and radio. Instead, she shows how this cultural tradition

---

[31] Also see Conboy, 2002: 51–54.

survived well into the twentieth century, as it was successfully adapted to and distributed as commercial entertainment, creating what she terms *middlebrow culture*. This started in the 1920s when producers of "high" art and literature transitioned from merely trumpeting the virtues of gentility within their own insulated social circles to adopting an activist, civic-oriented project to share "good culture" with the American masses. Educational radio programming like classical composer Walter Damrosch's *Music Appreciation Hour*, Harvard President Charles Elliot's "Harvard Classics" book club, popular lecture circuits, and newspapers and magazines were some of the notable "instruments of diffusion" that these genteel reformers used to forge an aspirational cultural sensibility in the United States.

Literary critics played a special role in shaping the core ideals of the genteel tradition. Rubin specifically points to transcendental philosopher Ralph Waldo Emerson as a key figure who defined what it meant to be a "cultured" person in America. Emersonian gentility, Rubin explains, rested on ideas about building "character" and mastering the "inner self," all of which are achieved through formalistic aesthetic training and through rejecting base, materialistic impulses. Rubin also highlights the role that news industry played in this endeavor, giving special attention to the advent of the "book review section" in newspapers such as the *New York Herald* and the *New York Times* and in magazines such as *The Nation*, the *Atlantic Monthly* and *The New Republic*. As she notes, the proliferation of book review sections marked a shift from papers merely reporting on the release of new books to a "higher journalism" that provided the public with literary guidance and aesthetic instruction.

The literary editor's mission to reform public tastes dovetailed with the "public service" discourse at the center of journalism's professionalization efforts in the early decades of the twentieth century, representing two prongs of the same genteel-grounded, middle-class marketing strategy. The book reviewer's efforts to save the American public from what *North American Review* founder Charles Elliot Norton called popular entertainment's "paradise of mediocrities" was similar in cultural logic to the newly professionalized journalist's commitment to replace the emotional drives of partisanship with independent, rationalistic reporting. Both the news and lifestyle elements of the prestige paper's aspirational address articulated a desire for self-control and intellectual autonomy, the ultimate purpose of genteel refinement.

Another commonality between literary editors and professionalized journalists was that both groups conceptualized the newspaper as a vehicle for disseminating expert knowledge. In the early twentieth century, especially in the years following World War I, public intellectuals and Progressive reformers increasingly supported the professionalization of journalism, which would entail formally training journalists to parse and process information in a way that emulated the disinterested analytical approach of the scientific method. This embrace of "objectivity" corresponded with the rise of science as the dominant epistemology for making truth claims in public debate (Hallin, 2000). The invention of the *social* sciences (e.g. sociology, psychology), which modeled themselves after the quantitative methods of the hard sciences, were particularly influential to journalism. The epistemological victory of science was punctuated by the secularization of America's top universities in the 1910s and the highly publicized defeat of religious authority in the 1925 Scopes "Monkey" Trial.[32]

The most prominent advocate of the "objectivity ideal" during this era was journalist and public intellectual Walter Lippmann. In *Public Opinion* (1922), a text James Carey has called "the founding book of modern journalism" (1987), Lippmann envisioned journalists as a "specialized class" who use "trained intelligence" to not only curate the information the public receives but to interpret it as well. The "objective" lens of the journalistic professional would debunk erroneous information skewed by "primitive instincts" and "stereotypes" (a term Lippmann coined) and, in so doing, fix one of democracy's greatest liabilities: allowing charismatic demagogues access to mass media through which they could speak directly to the fears, superstitions, and "prejudices" of "the masses."[33]

Lippmann's emphasis on science and technical expertise seemed quite different from the humanistic orientation of *New York Herald*'s "books" editor Stuart Sherman. Disciplinary tensions did exist between literary-minded editors and scientific-minded reporters. For example, genteel reformers viewed journalists' support for vocational, technical training as a threat to the universal liberal arts education they revered. Setting these differences aside, the humanistic and social scientific legs of the middlebrow news appeal worked together to project what sociologist Pierre Bourdieu calls the "general culture" of higher learning (1984: 25). In an "educated" taste culture, the display of a cool, "disinvested"

---

[32] This conflict had its roots in the battles that took place between the "modernists" and the "fundamentalists" in 1910s and 1920s as documented in sociologist Robert Wuthnow's 1988 book *The Restructuring of American Religion*.

[33] See Schudson, 1978: 127–129; Steel, 1980: 180–185.

evaluative disposition is taken as the normative analytical posture for assessing any cultural object, be it a piece of art or scientific report. The disinterested cultural style of professional journalism that was established in print during the early years of the twentieth century would be carried over to radio and then later to television news. The "space-transcending qualities" (Hilmes, 1997: 16) of these new electronic forms of mass media would propel the "objectivity regime" and its aspirational cultural appeal to levels of national hegemonic dominance not seen before.

However, there were a few bumps on the road toward this news style becoming the broadcasting industry's standard that deserve mention. For one, even with the advent of electronic media like radio, tabloid print papers such as the *New York Daily Mirror* and the *New York Daily News* continued to garner massive readerships in the early twentieth century. As V. Penelope Pelizzon and Nancy Martha West document in *Tabloid Inc.* (2010), the *News* and *Mirror* innovated melodramatic narrative forms and masculine, "hard-boiled" archetypes that, in a recursive manner, informed and were informed by popular crime-themed movies and novels of the 1920s and 1930s. The working-class styles of masculinity and melodramatic narrative structures of tabloid newspapers influenced the representational strategies of radio hosts and, later, television pundits, especially on Fox News.

The first challenges to middlebrow journalism in the broadcast arena came from populist radio hosts that rose to fame in the 1920s and 1930s. The most notorious of these firebrand broadcasters was Father Charles Coughlin, nicknamed the "radio priest." Coughlin claimed to understand, "the pulse of the people" better than professional media experts, an assertion echoed by his other radio populist contemporaries, such as Dr. John Brinkley and William Henderson.[34] These figures utilized the sonorous qualities of the radio medium to add emotion to their coverage of politics and public affairs.

While most contemporary articles and academic studies have drawn parallels between Coughlin and Fox News hosts, Derek Vaillant's historical analysis of Henderson presents, arguably, a more suitable precursor (2004).[35] For example, in order to cultivate his folk hero on-air

---

[34] For scholarship on Father Coughlin see Brinkley, 1982; Kazin, 1998: chapter 5. For work on William Anderson Jr., see Vaillant, 2004. For work on Dr. John Brinkley, see Lee, 2002; Frank, 2004: 196–199.

[35] For a comparison between Fox News and Father Coughlin, see Conway, Maria, & Grieves, 2007: 197–223. For a comparison between Glenn Beck and Father Coughlin, see Harris (February 02, 2011).

personality as "old man Henderson," he, like Fox host Bill O'Reilly, downplayed his educated background and self-consciously transgressed the genteel "cult of respectability" by using vernacular speech and regional slang. Foreshadowing Sean Hannity's Fox program, Henderson played country music as opposed to the standard orchestral musical introduction used by the major broadcast networks. The educated professional class these radio populists railed against was ultimately the community that forced them off-air. Coughlin's overt anti-Semitism, sympathy for Nazi fascism, and later-career opposition to President Franklin Roosevelt's New Deal inspired federal legislation to ban opinionated, ideological programming in the form of the Fairness Doctrine (a policy that would remain intact until the dawn of talk radio in 1987) (Hendershot, 2011: 16).

As the advent of radio eclipsed print journalism's influence, the advent of television in the 1940s would, by the 1950s, surpass radio as American's preferred source of news. Thanks to favorable government regulations, three major networks – ABC, CBS, NBC – shared a monopoly over American television broadcasting. In exchange for this market advantage, the "Big Three" were federally mandated to provide "culturally uplifting" programming that served the "public interest." One way the networks answered this call was by creating robust news divisions and public affairs programming. As Michael Curtin (1995) argued, investigative TV journalism like Edward Murrow's hard-hitting *See It Now* documentary programs worked to "redeem" the network's "lowbrow" entertainment offerings, the popular game shows and sitcoms that made up what FCC Chairman Newton Minow famously called the "vast wasteland."

Though critically acclaimed, Murrow's films were not particularly popular with working-class audiences (Curtin, 1995: 9, 217). However, because the networks were, to a degree, insulated from market competition and the demand for ratings, they could afford to support programs that prioritized "hard," empirical realism over "soft," feel-good entertainment. The coupling of field camerawork amid dramatic events with expert commentary featured in *See It Now* programs influenced many of the most successful and long running news programs, including *60 Minutes*. Overall, however, television journalists of this era viewed visual stylization, pop culture, and the display of emotion – things that could *engage* a popular audience as opposed to merely *inform* them – as impediments to factual reporting. Newscasts tended to feature austere subject matter delivered with flat affect, "discourses of sobriety" to match the dispassionate anchoring style epitomized by CBS's Walter Cronkite (Nichols, 1991: 3–4).

Following the vision Lippmann articulated in the 1910s, network news anchors in the 1950s through the 1970s saw themselves as informational experts who served the public by translating the "official" knowledge of intellectuals and government authorities into a popular language that the lay viewing audience could understand (Baym, 2009). This was the zenith of what communication scholar Daniel Hallin calls the "high modern" era of journalism, when news was "dominated by a culture of professionalism, centered around the norm of objective reporting and rooted in the conviction that the primary function of the press was to serve society by providing citizens with accurate, 'unbiased' information about public affairs" (2006: 1). For many old-guard journalists like Dan Rather and Ted Koppel, this was the golden era, a time when the news was driven by civic ideals rather than crass commercialism, when reporting was based on facts and expertise as opposed to partisanship and the cult of personality. The plain but intellectually grounded middlebrow voice of "Uncle Walter" seemed to transcend the high and low taste divisions that fractured the nineteenth-century news landscape as network news programs enjoyed a nearly universal audience that crossed social lines.

But before we praise this era for reaching some great class compromise, let us remember what middlebrow culture is. It is not, Rubin points out, a happy medium between working- and upper-class tastes; rather, it is a cultural style that seeks to democratize high culture for the masses. Middlebrow culture is egalitarian to the extent that it expresses the belief that all Americans – regardless of social rank – have the capacity for critical reasoning, informed citizenship, and cultural enrichment. It is ultimately elitist, however, in that it implicitly treats professional educated culture as the ideal and working-class culture as something that requires fixing. With middlebrow, the burden of cultural moral reform is weighted toward those on the lower rungs of the social ladder. Of course, the predominance of middlebrow styles in the US news market created a vacuum for a *cultural populist* brand of journalism, and it was only a matter of time before someone filled it.[36]

Enter Rupert Murdoch.

---

[36] For a shorter distillation of this argument, see Peck, 2014b.

THE UNMAKING OF MIDDLEBROW NEWS IN AMERICA

It is hard to understate the impact Rupert Murdoch has had on US journalism and the national popular culture more generally. Since appearing on the American news scene in early the 1970s, media products from Murdoch's News Corp. (now renamed Twenty-First Century Fox, Inc.) have consistently been at the forefront of several key national media trends. Murdoch purchased his first American newspapers in 1973, the *San Antonio News* and the *San Antonio Express*. Following the tabloid formula he used in Australia and the UK, these Texas papers ran sensational headlines such as "Midget Robs Undertaker at Midnight" and "Killer Bees Head North."[37] In 1974, Murdoch founded his first national newspaper in the United States, a tabloid magazine called the *Star*. In the 1970s and 1980s, supermarket tabloids grew to unprecedented levels of popularity and the *Star* was at the center of the American tabloid renaissance. By the late 1970s, the *Star* had become Murdoch's most profitable American media asset and – in reaching 3 million in circulation – was beginning to rival Generoso Pope's *National Enquirer*, the longtime tabloid leader (Bird, 1992: 30).

The circulation numbers of the *Star* and the *National Enquirer* would expand even more in the 1980s. These papers, however, despite the immense size of their readerships, were not taken seriously by American politicians and the broader journalism establishment due to their strict soft news orientation and willingness to circulate rumor. This political toothlessness stood in contrast to their tabloid counterparts across the pond. The tabloid news sector in the UK during the same period was, Michael Wolff writes, "the most powerful media, breaking stories, setting the agenda, electing politicians, changing the culture" (2008: 205). Of course, soft news stories about sports, celebrities and sex scandals are defining characteristics of British tabloids, but, as comparative journalism scholars such as Daniel Hallin and Paolo Mancini have noted, so is partisanship and political editorializing (2004: 210–211).

By the 1970s, Murdoch's *News of the World* and the *Sun* had become some of the most important mouthpieces of the British Right. They were particularly vital in generating what Stuart Hall called the "authoritarian populism" of the conservative Thatcher administration (Gilroy et al., 2000: 321). It wasn't just that Murdoch's British tabloids juxtaposed

[37] Mahler (May 21, 2005).

the pop cultural and the political, "soft" news with "hard" news. By the late 1960s, local news stations in the United States had already discovered the financial benefits of such an editorial mix. More than simply enticing readers with the honey of entertainment in order to feed their readers "hard news" vegetables, the *World* and the *Sun* actively *rationalized* connections between the more palpable cultural politics of celebrity and sports and the distant, formal politics of government. Much in the same way historian Michael McGerr describes the "style" of partisan journals in the United States during the nineteenth century, the partisan British tabloid of the twentieth century rendered a comprehensive social universe for its readers, one that is both culturally familiar and politically meaningful.

Unlike his early US papers which mostly conformed to the apolitical, celebrity-driven format of the supermarket tabloid, Murdoch fashioned the *New York Post* in the image of the partisan tabloid of the London newsstand. Recognizing the special political clout that comes with owning a major daily newspaper in the world's biggest media capital, Murdoch and his editors almost immediately injected the *Post* into the New York political scene by supporting Ed Koch in the 1977 mayoral election. Though Koch was a Democrat, he ran to the right of his liberal opponents, Mario Cuomo and Bella Abzug, with Nixonian "law and order" campaign themes. Like the *Sun* and other Anglo-Australian predecessors, the *Post* seamlessly fused pop cultural events with political events, as evident in one 1985 issue celebrating Koch's third mayoral electoral victory. The headline read "Triple Crown Winners." Below the headline there were three checked boxes which read: "Koch: ✓, Yanks: ✓, Mets: ✓" (Cannato, 2013). Here, Koch's political victory is represented as something that elicits the same everyday gratification as a win from New York City's widely followed baseball teams.[38]

Measured as an individual commercial asset, the *Post* was a revenue drain for News Corp. However, the local political influence it gave Murdoch's company would ultimately yield net financial benefits. Through political favors and/or political threats, Murdoch's New York

---

[38] This discursive strategy plays out today even at the conglomerate level, where in Twenty-First Century Fox, Inc. (Fox News' parent company) is attempting to outcompete ESPN, the longtime leader in cable sports news, by painting it as liberal, politically correct, and overly serious and, at the same time, by depicting its own cable sports news channel, FS1, as being more irreverent, macho, and conservative. See Barrabi (June 26, 2017).

tabloid helped News Corp. evade anti-trust and cross ownership laws.[39] This policy-for-publicity tradeoff was most apparent when Republican Mayor Rudy Giuliani, a politician the *Post* vigorously supported, used the power of his office in 1996 to pressure a recalcitrant Time Warner to allot Murdoch's new cable news network, Fox News, a channel spot in the all-important New York City cable market.

This power play and the tight political web between Murdoch, Giuliani and Fox's founding CEO Roger Ailes has been well-documented and much written about. What deserves equal attention with regard to the role the *Post* played in Fox News' development, however, is the stylistic, editorial and, yes, even intellectual blueprint that the *Post* provided for Fox. The *Post* was using the *New York Times* as an elitist foil for building the paper's populist self-image long before Bill O'Reilly's bromides against the *Times* on Fox. As I illustrate in Chapter 3, in turn, the guest and topic selection of Fox News programming symbolically blends blue-collar tastes with political ideology in much the same way the *Post*'s editorial framework had been doing since the Murdoch takeover. Lastly, the *Post* provided one of, if not *the* most important popular outlets for the budding neoconservative intellectual movement of the Reagan era. Norm Podhoretz, the editor of *Commentary*, a hub of neoconservative thought, is one of the leading conservative intellectuals who frequented the editorial pages of the *Post*. Of course, this was often overlooked due to the paper's notoriously graphic front page images and sensationalist headlines (e.g. "Headless Body in Topless Bar").[40] As I show in Chapter 5, Fox News followed the *Post*'s model tactically guarding its high-cultural, intellectual elements (as opposed to wearing them on the sleeve as a middlebrow outlet would tend to do). Akin to the *Post*'s colorful layout and sensationalist front page content, Fox News' flashy graphics, leg-revealing women pundits, and partisan emotionality has worked to execute a similar populist-intellectual sleight of hand, which encourages its critics to underappreciate the network's role in promoting conservative intellectual culture.

---

[39] Governor Cuomo gave Murdoch a federal waiver to own the *New York Post* and TV stations at the same time in the 1993. This was mostly done not out of favor but fear as Murdoch's *Post* had positioned politicians like Koch against Cuomo on multiple occasions and attacked Cuomo's candidacy. Gottlieb (March 24, 1993).

[40] David McKnight stresses this point and documents how the *Post* "included commentary and opinion pages written by some of the leading figures of the intellectual Right, a matter of some significance since they were the distinctive and crucial heart of the Murdoch package but have been almost entirely ignored by critics" (2013: 74).

For all the political leverage it afforded Murdoch, the *Post* was still a local New York newspaper that most Americans did not read or had never heard of. Eventually, Murdoch came to realize that in the suburban world of America the television set reigned supreme, not the newsstand.

TABLOIDS FOR TELEVISION: *A CURRENT AFFAIR, INSIDE EDITION*, AND BILL O'REILLY BEFORE BILL O'REILLY

By the mid-1980s, Rupert Murdoch would venture beyond print and purchase a film company in Twentieth Century Fox and a broadcast network in Fox Broadcasting Company. With these daring acquisitions, Murdoch turned News Corp. into a multimedia conglomerate almost overnight. Murdoch's Fox Broadcasting network, which was launched in 1986, earned the distinction of becoming the first successful attempt to break the CBS–NBC–ABC triopoly. By the late 1980s and 1990s, the "fourth network" was, as Daniel Kimmel and others have argued, "reinventing" American television (2004). With programs such as *In Living Color* (1992) and *Martin* (1992), Fox was the first major broadcast network to innovate narrowcasting strategies that targeted youth and African-American subcultures (Zook, 1999). In addition, Fox redefined the family sitcom genre with breakout shows like *The Simpsons* and *Married ... with Children*. In contrast to the "respectable" upper-middle-class Huxtable family of the *Cosby Show*, the Simpsons and the Bundys of *Married with ... Children* were comically dysfunctional and unapologetically working class in taste and lifestyle. Fox Broadcasting also played a pivotal role in ushering a new era of low-cost, "reality"-based programming with sensational, ratings-grabbing shows like *America's Most Wanted* (1988) *COPS* (1989), and *When Animals Attack!* (1996).

Political and media discourse from the late 1980s through mid-1990s was characterized by complaints about the vulgarization of American national culture and the programming of Fox Broadcasting was repeatedly referenced to symbolize the nation's descent into the gutter. In the name of "family values," it was mostly Republican politicians, not Democrats, who vigorously condemned Fox's top shows. By the early 1990s, *The Simpsons* had become a bona fide national phenomenon and was, in 1992, starting to draw larger audiences than NBC's longtime ratings leader the *Cosby Show*.[41] During his 1992 presidential campaign,

---

[41] *Broadcasting* (March 2, 1992).

President George H. Bush criticized *The Simpsons*. "We need a nation closer to *The Waltons* than *The Simpsons*," he told the audience at the National Religious Broadcasters convention (Turner, 2004: 225–226). His Vice President Dan Quayle and even First Lady Barbara Bush attacked *The Simpsons* as well, painting the popular animated sitcom as symptomatic of the nation's cultural and moral decline.

By the early 1990s, both Fox Broadcasting's daytime and primetime programming was taking off and with this, its advertising rates and profits spiked upward. News Corp.'s television assets in the United States suddenly made up the company's largest revenue stream.[42] Murdoch, a newsman at heart, was ready to turn his American television network into more of a "journalistic operation," a "full-service" network that provided a complete slate of entertainment and news programming, seven days a week.[43] Until the early 1990s, Fox Broadcasting's program offerings were limited by "fin-syn" broadcasting regulations. This Federal Communications Commission (FCC) law barred television broadcasters from being *both* producers and distributers of content. Fox Broadcasting, a subsidiary of News Corp., circumvented this rule by airing no more than 15 hours per week of primetime programming so as to evade the official FCC definition of a "network."

However, federal communication regulations were not the only thing that potentially hindered Murdoch's attempt to expand Fox Broadcasting's programming with a "Fox News" division. Murdoch's tabloid background and the political moral panics surrounding the "lowbrow" entertainment content of Fox Broadcasting posed marketing challenges for attaching the "Fox" name to any "serious" television news department. "Every time some congressman cites *Married . . . with Children* as an example of trashy TV on the House floor," a January 1996 *Mediaweek* article writes, Murdoch's media rivals, such as *Daily News* owner Mort Zuckerman, "smile . . . for days." Editors at another Zuckerman outlet, *US News & World Report*, said the owner "loves seeing [Fox's] news division trying to overcome Murdoch's image."[44]

---

[42] *Broadcasting & Cable* (June 21, 1993).

[43] Coe (March 2, 1992). Also see Mahoney (March 2, 1992). The goal of being a "full-service network" is discussed in McClellan (June 1, 1992). Fox Fills in the Blanks. *Broadcasting*, pp. 18–19. For a comprehensive political economic analysis of News Corp. and Fox Broadcasting, see Alisa Heylay Perren's 2004 dissertation *Deregulation, Integration and a New Era of Media Conglomerates: the Case of Fox, 1985–1995*.

[44] Mundy (January 1, 1996).

According to New York University media professor Mark Crispin, the very name "Murdoch" had become "a byword for journalistic sleaze, for tabloidism at its worst; so the mainstream press likes to speak in fearful tones of the danger of Rupert Murdoch taking over a newspaper" (Kitty & Greenwald, 2005: 49). This "danger" and "fearful tone" was palpable from the very moment Murdoch stepped foot in the US media market in the late 1970s. In response to his aggressive acquisition of three major New York City publications in 1976 and 1977, the *New York Post, New York* magazine and the *Village Voice*, editorial cartoons in the late-1970s and 1980s depicted Murdoch as various monsters such as King Kong, Dracula and Dr. Frankenstein's monster (see Figure 1.1).

Very quickly, Murdoch gained a reputation among the prestige news institutions in the United States as "the Anti-Christ of Professional Journalism."[45] One *Columbia Journalism Review* article in 1980 went as far to call him and his New York City tabloid the *Post* "a force of evil."[46] The CJR article's condemnation of the *Post* was in part related to the anti-crime, race-baiting themes that the paper instigated and exploited. However, another point of critique had to do with News Corp.'s lack of deference to American journalism's public service tradition. Much of the journalistic team Murdoch brought in to work at the *Post* and *A Current Affair* were British, Australian and New Zealand expatriates. This group, tabloid TV producer Burt Kearns writes, were "cynical veterans of the world's most hardscrabble newspaper wars from Fleet Street to Hong Kong." For them, "news-telling wasn't the privilege of the elite. They didn't model the cloak of public service and were unapologetic in their quest for ratings" (1999: 21).

In the late 1980s and 1990s, thanks in part to the media properties News Corp. introduced to the American public, tabloid media culture was reaching unprecedented heights. Although the popularity of super-market tabloids had been growing in the United States since the 1970s, it wasn't until their irreverent style and sensational content appeared on television – the dominant medium of American culture – that tabloid journalism became a central object of public concern. By all accounts, News Corp.'s syndicated newsmagazine program *A Current Affair* was the American forerunner of what came to be called "tabloid television." *A Current Affair* is important to the specific history of News Corp. because it stands as Murdoch's first successful attempt at creating a

---

[45] Glynn (2000).   [46] *Columbia Journalism Review* (January–February 1980), 18(5), 22.

FIGURE 1.1. Murdoch's *Time* cover January 17, 1977

television news program in the United States, as his other televisual tabloid adaptations on Fox Broadcasting network such as *The Reporters* and *Front Page* quickly flopped.

The brainchild of Australian-born producer Peter Brennan, *A Current Affair* debuted in 1986 on Fox Broadcasting's local WNYW station and starred a gregarious up-and-coming anchor named Maury Povich, who was formerly at WTTG, Fox's Washington D.C. affiliate. The show also featured Steve Dunleavy, a former editor for Murdoch's *Star* and *New York Post* who was notorious for both his jingoistic right-wing politics and his pompadour hairstyle. After producing strong ratings performances in the New York and Boston markets, *A Current Affair* was nationally syndicated in 1987. The program's rapid ratings growth immediately inspired imitations, most notably *Inside Edition*, the place where future Fox News star Bill O'Reilly first established a national name. A King World product, *Inside Edition* was not under Murdoch's News Corp. umbrella, but the show stole such a large amount of production talent from Murdoch's *A Current Affair* that industry insiders nicknamed it "*A Current Affair* II" (Kitman, 2007: 135). Again, future Fox News CEO Roger Ailes did media consultant work for both *A Current Affair* and *Inside Edition*.

In the 2012 "War of Words" special cited earlier, O'Reilly explained to Ted Koppel in the simplest terms possible the basis of the populist news persona he had developed. "I just have taken my *presentation* [my emphasis] from Levittown, New York, that the nuns used to scorn, and I've made millions and millions of dollars." Now, this notion that O'Reilly's anchoring style derived organically from his early Irish-Catholic upbringing in blue-collar Levittown is not altogether false, but it is not completely true either. This direct leap from his childhood background to Fox News stardom glosses over several evolutionary steps along the way; namely, it overlooks how significantly O'Reilly's time at *Inside Edition* changed his original reportorial style.

What many forget about O'Reilly is that before joining *Inside Edition* and then Fox News, he worked for decades as a reporter and columnist. In his heart and mind he may have been conservative all along but he did not hail from the activist world of the Republican Party, nor did he get his start in the politicized world of talk radio like many of the biggest names in conservative media (e.g. Sean Hannity, Rush Limbaugh, Glenn Beck). O'Reilly was a genuine product of the television journalism field. His professional career in journalism traces all the way back to 1975 when he was an "action reporter" at Channel 16, WNEP, in Scranton, Pennsylvania.

From there, he worked at a multitude of other local news stations from Dallas to Denver to Portland to Hartford to Boston. He even had a few stints on network programs such as ABC's *The World News Tonight*. From the very beginning, O'Reilly used "looking-out-for-the-little-guy" rhetoric (Kitman, 2007: 78) but this was more in the vein of consumer protection stories and typical journalism tropes about exposing fraud and rooting out corruption. The "tribune-of-the-people" (Peters, 2010) discourse he used at this career phase lacked both a partisan edge and the epic "culture war" scale that would characterize his "looking out for the folks" rhetoric on Fox News.

As an "action reporter" at local news stations in Scranton and Dallas, O'Reilly's investigative, ambush-style interviews with businesses who were "screwing over" consumers taught him about the entertainment value of on-air confrontations. Yet O'Reilly's *anchoring style* still conformed to the network news standards, the programs he, like every other television journalist of the 1970s and 1980s, aspired to anchor one day. By the late 1980s, O'Reilly had hit a career ceiling, so he opted to work in tabloid television.

In 1989, O'Reilly would replace British reporter David Frost as *Inside Edition*'s lead anchor. When *Inside Edition* launched, *A Current Affair* was at the height of its game; it was the "granddaddy of sleaze," as *Vanity Fair* dubbed it (December 28, 1989). A few years later, Maury Povich would leave *A Current Affair* to host his own daytime show *The Maury Povich Show*. Povich was the heart of *A Current Affair*; thus, his departure predictably led to the show's eventual demise and, conversely, to *Inside Edition*'s rise to the top. But, at least in the media culture of the late 1980s and early 1990s, Povich stood over O'Reilly as a master does a pupil. With coaching help from producers Peter Brennan and Roger Ailes, Povich set the mold for what it meant to be a great tabloid TV anchor and, in being positioned in direct competition with Povich, there is no doubt O'Reilly took notes. It was Povich, not O'Reilly, who first demonstrated how a television anchor could connect with an audience through affect and body language. *A Current Affair* producer Burt Kearns said that Povich had the "most expressive eyebrows in the business" and marveled at the way Povich could dispense judgment about any given story with a "simple shake of the head" (1999: 20).

Kearns' assessment of O'Reilly's television performances during this period was far less flattering. "When O'Reilly was cast as the new host [at *Inside Edition*]," Kearns recalls, "He was like a doofus, 180 degrees from what he is today ... He was very, you know, sickening and polite."[47] Bill O'Reilly, "sickening" and "polite"? This description is, of course, the polar opposite of Ted Koppel's critical assessment of O'Reilly in the 2012 interview ("it offends me when you're rude"). At *Inside Edition*,

---

[47] Quoted in Kitman, *The Man Who Would Not Shut Up*, p. 138.

O'Reilly was still transitioning from the straight anchoring style of his early professional training to the populist style he would adopt at Fox News; his body language, regional accent, and overall emotional disposition were more restrained, so much so that his anchoring style did not completely fit *Inside Edition*'s tabloid format.

In an August 3, 1993 episode on James Douglas Pou, an Air Force sergeant who faked his own death, we see the disjuncture between the melodramatic, punny writing of *Inside Edition* and O'Reilly's "serious" mode of address. The voice-over says, "those who know him say Doug Pou is many things: hero, husband, father, deserter, bigamist, liar." The segment cuts to the studio anchor desk, where O'Reilly reports "Pou is currently awaiting trial on charges of desertion, escape and bank robbery and if it were against the law he'd also be charged with" – O'Reilly pauses and then says with a straight face – "breaking hearts" (August 3, 1993).[48]

It is doubtful Povich would have let such a sappy line roll off his tongue without a smirk or one of his signature eyebrow raises. Through both body language and verbal rhetoric, Povich connected with his audience by mocking the tabloid genre itself. O'Reilly, at least at this stage of his career, was far less reflexive of the cultural politics of the news field – quite a difference from his self-description as a news "barbarian" that he would proudly adopt at Fox News years later (see Chapter 2). On *A Current Affair*, Povich repeatedly expressed a media meta-sensibility about *A Current Affair*'s "low" cultural status in the US public sphere. A May 31, 1989 episode of *A Current Affair* went *full meta*, producing a humorous, mock news story complete with a dramatic reenactment (a classic tabloid news-telling device) about a reported dispute between Povich and his wife Connie Chung, who was, at the time, a rising network news anchor. The comedic tension of the skit is grounded on Povich's supposed jealousy over Chung's "prestigious" position as a network anchor.

CONNIE CHUNG: Now when I used the word sleazebag I was referring to the serial killer on your show, not you.
MAURY POVICH: That is not the word I objected to!
CONNIE CHUNG: What, the word tabloid just means a little newspaper with a lot of pictures!
MAURY POVICH: And I guess they don't use pictures in network news, do they?
CONNIE CHUNG: I never said there was anything wrong with syndication. At least we don't do those tawdry dramatizations!

---

[48] MightyFalcon2011 (January 26, 2014).

In a reflexive manner, this fake story plays with the tabloid news genre as it reports on a rumored marital fight between a celebrity power couple. But the true purpose of the segment is to engage in a type of "media metacommentary" (Jacob & Townsley, 2011); specifically one that comments on and draws attention to the very *real* high/low cultural antagonisms that divide and structure the US news industry.

Another key way in which Povich would portend O'Reilly's performative traits on Fox was the way the host of *A Current Affair* would use a personal mode of address, injecting his own voice and feelings into the story. At the time, this was a fairly transgressive thing to do in journalism, as it broke with the conventional, detached anchoring style of network news programs. In a celebrity segment about a physical altercation between television star Roseanne Barr and the paparazzi, Povich not only expressed emotion, but also took a clear side in the incident, saying to the audience, "Somehow I think I want to *nail* [my emphasis] those guys [the paparazzi], not Roseanne" (July 17, 1989). In another episode, which was covering religious broadcaster James Dobson's interview with serial killer Ted Bundy, the viewer sees Povich visibly saddened. Speaking *directly* to the audience, he says in a somber voice, "I've been watching it with you. For some reason my thoughts are with the families of all those innocent victims" (January 24, 1989).

O'Reilly, like every other major news anchor at the time, covered the Bundy interview on *Inside Edition* as well. The difference between his treatment of the story and Povich's is subtle but important. With little to no emotional display, O'Reilly tells the audience, "the pain that Ted Bundy created for so many families across this country and *we* [my emphasis] should never forget that." As opposed to his personal feelings, O'Reilly situates his analysis of Bundy in terms of his career history, noting how he covered Bundy's murders as an investigative reporter when the serial killer was at large. O'Reilly concludes the segment by saying, "for all of *us* [my emphasis] there should be sadness that anything like this could happen in a civilized society" (January 24, 1989). Notice how O'Reilly opts to speak to the audience in the more detached terms of the *societal* "we." This universal mode of address follows the conventional high-modern style of network news but differs from the personalized tabloid address we see exemplified by Povich ("watching with *you*," "*my* thoughts"). One can easily imagine the future, Fox-News–Bill-O'Reilly expressing personal outrage and framing Bundy's execution as the just comeuppance for a "scumbag."

The final way *A Current Affair* and *Inside Edition* influenced the evolution of O'Reilly's journalistic style and, by extension, the cultural politics of Fox News is by exhibiting what Leon Hunt calls "permissive populism," a term he coined to describe a strategic form of sexual vulgarity that came to characterize British comedy (e.g. *The Benny Hill Show*) and tabloid news culture in the 1970s. This discourse, Hunt explains, repurposed the sexual liberationist ethos of the 1960's counter-culture into "low" cultural politics that stands in opposition to Victorian sexual propriety and middle-class tastes.

As journalism scholars Anita Biresse and Heather Nunn point out, "permissive populism" was a central ingredient of Murdoch's most powerful London tabloids such as *News of the World* and the *Sun* (2008: 14). But I would argue it was no less important to News Corp.'s early television properties in America. In examining an April 28, 1989 episode of *A Current Affair* and a promotional ad for the Fox sitcom *Married ... with Children* that precedes the episode, we see how this permissive populist discourse circulated across News Corp.'s television offerings. The ad begins showing the mesmerized face of Al Bundy (played by Ed O'Neil) staring eye level at a young blonde woman's breasts. Standing over Bundy, the woman says, "Oh Mr. Bundy, you're so magnificent." Next, the viewer sees the annoyed face of Bundy's wife "Peg" (played by Katey Sagal) as a laugh track plays in the background. The commercial break concludes, and *A Current Affair* begins. Then host Maury Povich gives the customary breakdown of the night's topics. In line with the raunchy sexual themes of the *Married ... with Children* promo, Povich introduces one of the top stories: "In the TV show *Diff'rent Strokes*, Dana Plato was the wholesome teenage girl next door. Now she's done it all for *Playboy*. And baby, take a look at her now!" On *A Current Affair*, these kinds of racy topics were par for the course as the program ran stories like the "new" breast implant trend, the opening of Frederick's of Hollywood's lingerie museum (March 7, 1989), and rumor-based reenactment stories like one *A Current Affair* aired about British royalty visiting an American sex shop (March 2, 1989).[49]

In comparison to its main competitors, *A Current Affair* and *Hard Copy*, Bill O'Reilly's *Inside Edition* was the least tabloid of the "big three," as it offered more of a balanced proportion of "hard" and "soft" news stories (Ehrlich, 1996). As Kearns has noted, *Inside Edition* still

[49] See *Forty-eight Hours* (March 2, 1989).

covered stories about "school buses with defective axles in Ohio" (Kitman, 2007: 138) and O'Reilly's coverage of the 1992 L.A. riots on *Inside Edition* was particularly notable[50] (and strikingly more progressive in its tone than the way O'Reilly would cover the Black Lives Matter protests of 2016). Nevertheless, *Inside Edition* frequently featured the same type of sexually driven stories as its tabloid peers. We need search no further than the previous episode about Dobson's Ted Bundy interview. O'Reilly's final, morally righteous comments about how a civilized society should be sad it could create a person like Bundy is awkwardly segued by a voice-over that previews the next episode of *Inside Edition* saying, "Tomorrow ... the million dollar battle for the superstar model and custody of her nude test pictures, how nasty will it get."

For all their stylistic influence, the crass use of sexualized content and "soft news" editorial thrust of *A Current Affair* and *Inside Edition* undercut their public authority and limited their potential political influence. If the programming content of the failed conservative networks of the past was under-stylized and overly ideological, the content of Murdoch's *A Current Affair* and O'Reilly's *Inside Edition* was deplete of political – moral significance – something Fox News would add by appropriating the populist class narratives of the postwar conservative movement. This is why CEO Roger Ailes' decision to appoint former *Time* magazine columnist John Moody and former ABC White House correspondent Brit Hume as executive and managing editors at Fox News was so important. Moody and Hume were conservatives, but they were also veteran news professionals. As such, they functioned as a check on the tabloid editorial instincts of Fox's production staff (Sherman, 2014: 192).[51]

The romantic affair between Democratic President Bill Clinton and intern Monica Lewinsky that surfaced in 1998, roughly one year after Fox News' launch, was a godsend for the young network as it unified the opposing tabloid and prestige wings of Fox News' staff. The sexual

---

[50] See Wdshelt (July 7, 2012).

[51] In *Loudest Voice in the Room* (2014), Gabriel Sherman recounts an incident that occurred in 1999 where Jerry Burk, a man Roger Ailes recruited from the celebrity tabloid show *Extra!*, attempted to run a story on Fox News about the romantic relationship between basketball player Dennis Rodman and model Carmen Electra but was prevented from doing so by Brit Hume. Hume, a managing editor at Fox and anchor of the network's "straight" news program *Special Report with Brit Hume*, sought to protect Fox News' journalistic reputation (242–243). Sherman cites Fox's firing of Matt Drudge, founder of the conservative aggregator site The Drudge Report, as another early example of when Fox News toned down its tabloid, sensational qualities in order to strike a better balance between its professional and tabloid elements (243).

nature of the story firmly fitted within the tabloid genre and, because it involved a sitting US president (better, a Democratic one), it also satisfied the news worthiness standards of Fox's "serious" journalists. With such a story, Fox could provide its viewership with two contradictory pleasures. Its anti-liberal narrative framing of the scandal worked to elicit feelings of moral righteousness while the graphic, personal details of the relationship between Clinton and Lewinsky worked to intrigue and titillate at the same time. This formula would be repeated on *The O'Reilly Factor* throughout the 2000s and 2010s with recurrent stories about the moral depravity of college Spring Breaks and hip-hop videos. On one hand, these kinds of stories gave O'Reilly the pretext to advance a conservative *political* narrative about how 1960's liberalism had created a sexually licentious culture divorced from "family values." On the other hand, these same stories provided an occasion to use background imagery of scantily clad young women and men designed to arouse and entertain.

This contradictory formula followed a template Murdoch had long established with his British tabloid in the 1970s. Within Murdoch's London tabloid the *Sun*, the "Page Three Girls" coexisted with editorials that championed Thatcher's "authoritarian populist" themes of "family, duty, authority, standards, and traditionalism" (Hall, 1988a: 48). Journalism scholars James Curran and Jean Seaton wrote that the *Sun* "was both hedonistic and moralistic, iconoclastic and authoritarian, generally conservative in its opinions and radical in its rhetoric."[52] According to Michael Wolff, Fox News exhibited Murdoch's same "odd combination of mischief and sanctimony." The editorial formula of the *New York Post* used the same "odd" mixture, but it was the wrong medium. *A Current Affair* was a popular television show that had plenty of mischief but little sanctimony – at least none that was taken seriously. Yet with Fox News, Wolff writes, "all the lessons are combined and they all work ... [Murdoch] produces, finally and successfully, his American tabloid" (2008: 282).

"PARTISANSHIP NEEDS TO BE PRODUCED"

When Fox News debuted on October 7, 1996, it had to meet the challenge no previous conservative broadcasting project had been able to overcome. Since Richard Nixon's fateful loss to John F. Kennedy in the

---

[52] This quote was found in Anita Biresse and Heather Nunn's *The Tabloid Reader* (2008: 9).

1960 presidential election, conservatives had been dreaming of establishing a countervailing media system that could challenge the stranglehold they believed liberals held over the journalism field. Yet, every previous attempt to launch a conservative television network had failed miserably. So why did Fox News succeed?

This chapter relied on insights and evidence from three primary bases of research to demonstrate how Fox News' ascendancy was enabled by a confluence of *multiple* factors. The first body of literature derives from the biographical books and columns written by those popular writers and academics who have focused on the individual talents of Fox's key creative figures: Murdoch, Ailes, and O'Reilly.[53] This biographic research provides rich details about Fox's corporate leadership that reveal the thinking behind the design and development of the network. A bonus feature of this literature is in its tracing of the shared personnel and institutional ties between Fox News and those earlier *tabloid* media ventures that Fox's top executives and top talent directed or took part in.

A second place from which one can find an explanation for Fox's rise in the 1990s and 2000s is among the group of analysts – mostly mass communication and television scholars – who have looked to the economic and technological transformations that fragmented the American media industry in the late 1970s and 1980s. This is important as it was the mass commercialization of cable and satellite technologies that helped expand channel options, which, in turn, allowed for the existence of niche television markets based on political identity.[54]

A third place where one might find what has made Fox News' corporate brand and programming content so forceful is in its ability – perspicacious or not – to anticipate historical trends. So rather than putting their focus on the *creators behind* Fox News, many political scientists have zeroed in on the Fox News *audience* and have particularly debated the degree to which the audience's political predisposition facilitated the success of Fox's partisan news model. This is useful because what is often overlooked in the rush to blame Fox News for today's politically polarized environment is the fact that the resurgence of partisanship in America, already underway from as far back as the late 1970s, had particularly intensified in the early to mid-1990s *just before* Fox's 1996 launch. This calendar tracking lends support to a "weak media effects" perspective on Fox News, meaning that advocates of this perspective will argue that Fox

[53] Swint, 2008; Wolff, 2008; McKnight 2013; Sherman 2014.
[54] Turow, 1997; Prior, 2007; Curtin & Shattuc, 2009; Stroud, 2011.

did not create today's partisan culture: it merely exploited existing political divisions for its own commercial purposes.

There is, however, a significant body of research that challenges this
notion by showing the various ways in which Fox News has indeed
driven, and not simply mirrored, political and media trends. Economists
Stefano DellaVigna and Ethan Kaplan's ground breaking 2005 study
entitled "The Fox News Effect" demonstrated how the introduction of
Fox programming in a select group of cable television markets had altered
the voting patterns in those geographic areas in favor of Republicans. The
insight sparked a whole branch of "effects" research that would measure
Fox's impact on a range of things from voting behavior,[55] audience
attitudes,[56] public knowledge,[57] and congressional legislation.[58] While
the chicken-or-the-egg debate remains unsettled, scholars from both sides
concur that the relationship between partisan media and partisan audiences is – to varying degrees – dynamic and co-constitutive. Journalism
scholar C.W. Anderson captures the circular relationship between the two
nicely, writing that "partisan media feed polarization in the electorate,
which increases demand for partisan media and so on ..." (2016: 162).

Each of these three literatures provides critical pieces to the puzzle that
is Fox News. However, an explanatory resource that has been largely
overlooked is the very media product that Fox has created. To date, there
have been relatively few in-depth textual studies of the network's programming. This tendency to avoid conducting "thick," (Geertz, 1973)
close readings of Fox's content is no doubt related to preconceived
notions about why Fox is appealing. After all, if one believes that the
viewers' media choices are completely predetermined by their political
views and social backgrounds, there is little reason to invest energy in
considering the quality of Fox News' presentation and messaging. But, as
sociologist Matthew Norton critically asks, "Would it be enough for a
[Fox News] presenter to sit in front of a camera and read off a list of
events and explain how they confirm the audience's political and social
prejudices? It is hard to imagine three million people tuning in for this
performance." There is a *performative* distinction, Norton stresses,
"between the partisan hack and a media hero defending the borders of
the sacred." Sure, Fox is partisan, but Norton's crucial insight is that
"partisanship needs to be produced" (2011: 317).

[55] DellaVigna & Kaplan, 2007; Hopkins & Ladd, 2012; Martin & Yurukoglu, 2017.
[56] Morris, 2005; Jamieson & Cappella, 2008; Levendusky, 2013.   [57] Cassino, 2016.
[58] Clinton & Enamorado, 2014; Bartlett, 2015.

As I asserted in the Introduction, textual-stylistic analysis and hegemony theory are useful approaches for studying Fox News because these analytical modes offer a way to engage the relationship between the network's political ideology and its sociocultural address without requiring one to abandon an attempt to explain how Fox programs seek to *persuade*, and not merely pander to their audience's preset attitudes and beliefs. Drawing from Norton's hermeneutic model, the following chapter offers a multi-modal, interpretive framework that enables one to see how Fox News attempts to produce compelling television through the use of populist political *narratives* and through the working-class *performances* of its top opinion hosts. This framework also seeks to elucidate the central differences between Fox News' partisan mode of address and that of liberal news sources such as MSNBC, CNN and *The Daily Show*.

2

Populism on Cable News

A Theoretical Framework

The elite media ... has lost enormous power. Meantime, Fox News
continues to rise.

—Bill O'Reilly, 2010[1]

In the November 15, 2010 episode of *The O'Reilly Factor*, Bill O'Reilly
and his guests responded to veteran network anchor Ted Koppel's
scathing op-ed on cable news. "I don't understand Koppel's beef,"
O'Reilly huffs. Guest panelist Ellis Henican responds, "Nobody gives
up a monopoly willingly. It's a whole lot more fun when you run
the whole street." With his references to "monopoly" and running "the
whole street," Henican suggests a power struggle to control the journalistic field, a struggle that old-guard journalists, like Koppel, in the liberal
media are now losing after decades of dominance, thanks to Fox News.
The other guest panelist, Tammy Bruce, used more histrionic language.
"Look, this is about the elitist snobbery, the monarchy have [sic] to
realize, and not liking the fact that barbarians and peasants have taken
over. We're the commoners, you guys. That's a thing they can't stand."
With a smirk on his face, O'Reilly responds with a tongue-in-cheek tone,
"If there ever were a barbarian taking over you are looking at him." "It's
the Irish," Bruce retorts.

In one textual study that compared MSNBC and CNN's programming
to Fox News, the author, Terry McDermott, concluded that this kind of
rhetoric is "peculiar to Fox and it derives from its origin narrative as the

[1] O'Reilly (March 12, 2010).

85

network for the unrepresented, for the outsiders" (2010: 8). One way to make sense of how Fox News represents itself as a network for "commoners" and "outsiders" is through the tools of populist political theory. When Bill O'Reilly describes his mission as "looking out for the folks," he does not mean the same "general public" that venerable news anchor Walter Cronkite had in mind during the network era. Rather, O'Reilly uses "the folks" as a *populist signifier* and thus refers to a particular (not universal) faction that is represented as both a popular social bloc on one hand and a group that is disenfranchised and perpetually under siege on the other (Laclau, 2005a, 2005b, 2007).[2] The Fox News audience – O'Reilly and other top hosts have long inferred – is not just another interest group or news niche among a myriad of others (even though empirically speaking it is). Instead, Fox pundits have hailed their audience as the "real Americans," not the actual numerical majority, but rather what is suggested to be the *ideal* majority of the nation, its authentic moral core.

As detailed in Chapter 1, Fox News' populist identitarian branding was indicative of a broader trend toward narrowcasting and niche television strategies that started in the 1980s and 1990s. This shift toward identity, as journalism scholar Geoffrey Baym has explained, also transformed the way television journalists presented the news and addressed their audiences. In contrast to the disembodied voices of network news anchors during the high modern period (1940s–1980s), from the late-1980s onward news anchors increasingly used a socially *situated* voice, presenting the news "from somewhere," that is, from a particular social background and perspective (2009).

Baym uses the example of how African-American anchors on Black Entertainment Television (BET) ground their voice within the "black community" by representing their reporting as a continuation of the civil rights political tradition and aligning their taste politics with hip-hop culture. In like manner, he shows how MTV's news department recruits anchors who use teenage vocabulary and don edgy, informal styles of dress (e.g. piercings, tattoos, colorfully dyed hair) as a way to present news from the perspective of America's youth (something more recent outlets like *Vice News* have replicated). Newsmagazine programs like *Aquí y Ahora*, on the Spanish-speaking network Univision, use language itself to draw social affinities to Latinx Americans (Rodriguez, 1999;

---

[2] This was made explicit in one episode where O'Reilly said that a "populist is not a bad thing, it just means you're looking out for the folks" (February 15, 2010).

Dávila, 2001). While Fox News emphasizes different axes of identity, the network's star pundits have used the same *situated* mode of address. And like Univision, BET, and MTV, Fox has claimed, since its founding, to serve an underrepresented group of citizens that has been ignored by the "establishment media." Fox, O'Reilly declared in 2001, "gives voice to the people who can't get on other networks."[3]

This, however, is where most of the similarities end. Fox News' dualistic conceptualization of the US public sphere differs from Univision, BET, and MTV's pluralistic, "postmodern" vision, with its "montage of publics" (Hauser, 1998; Baym, 2009). Instead, Fox's populist rhetorical framing radically simplifies the US "journo-political" terrain, splitting it into two dueling media systems: one for "the liberal elite" and one for "the folks," a term that is synonymous with white working-class conservatives. As the writing of Argentinian political theorist Ernesto Laclau has emphasized, the populist signifier of "the people" is politically useful, as it provides a singular identity or *nodal point* around which the various social factions of a political movement coalesce. But, Laclau stresses, appeals to "the people" have no meaning independent of the relation of antagonism. The "us versus them" rhetorical framing of populism glosses over the internal differences and ideological contradictions of the political community wielding the discourse.

It is tempting to reduce Fox's "us versus them" representation of the media field to plain old partisanship. But, as I show in the following sections, the way Fox News represents political reality is quite different from its partisan media counterparts on the left. Laclau's dichotomy of *equivalential logic* versus *differential logic* provides a helpful schema for explaining the differences between Fox News and recognizably liberal outlets such as MSNBC and the satirical news program *The Daily Show*. It also helps illustrate how Fox has used populist discourse to cohere the identity of the conservative political subject and to elicit an *affective* response from Fox viewers.

However, by overemphasizing how populist identities are constructed by macro-ideological structures and grand realignments in political history, Laclau and other populist political theorists often overlook the equally important role that hegemonizing techniques play inside the

---

[3] This quote comes from the *Philadelphia Inquirer* (April 10, 2001) and the citation can be found in Hart (2002).

political text. In a highly *mediatized*[4] era of politics where the public's primary interface with policy and democratic elections happens mostly through video representations, these ideological techniques involve visual-aesthetic modes of expression and on-air performance tactics. As Benjamin Moffit and Simon Tormey have pointed out, Laclau's linguistic-centric model does not properly account for the aesthetic and performative elements of televisual populism (2014), nor, as I show in the final sections of the chapter, does it adequately address how the *embodied* race, gender, and sexuality of political media figures facilitates or hinders their ability to execute populist communication strategies. To address these shortcomings, this chapter builds a framework for decoding cable news programming that synthesizes political theories of populism with theories of performance and cultural disposition.

FOX NEWS VERSUS MSNBC: "LOGIC OF EQUIVALENCE" VERSUS "LOGIC OF DIFFERENCE"

MSNBC's 2010 "Lean Forward" campaign advertisement entitled "Declaration of Forward" illustrates the deeper political logic that distinguishes MSNBC's partisan mode of address from Fox News. In this ad, the viewer is given a montage of festive scenes: a wedding, a marching band, a birthday party, and a child sledding. The voice-over recites lines from the Declaration of Independence: "We hold these truths to be self-evident, that all men and women have certain unalienable rights." Then, breaking from the founding document, the ad says, "We are the United States of come-as-you-are. Our differences are what unite [sic] us. Starting today, may the ideas that advance our country, no matter who or where they come from, win." While the line "no matter who or where they come from" is being said, the camera rapidly flips through various headshots of Americans from all age groups, genders, and ethnicities.[5]

In MSNBC's "come-as-you-are" nation, the tie that binds the progressive community is the universal right of its members to advance their mutual differences and express their individuality. Like the Democratic

---

[4] Mediatization describes the process whereby media organizations come to usurp the traditional duties of political parties and where the economic and stylistic imperatives of commercial entertainment increasingly shape the priorities and practices of political systems. Nick Couldry's article "Theorizing Media as Practice" (2004) is a foundational text in the literature on mediatization. For a contemporary definition of the term, see Strömbäck (2016).

[5] Brandingm3 (October 27, 2010). MSNBC: Lean Forward [Video file]. YouTube. Retrieved from: www.youtube.com/watch?v=4CQAcewckXo.

Left writ large, MSNBC programs celebrate diversity and multiculturalism and valorize the "politics of difference" ("Our differences are what
unite us") something that corresponds with the *logic of difference* that
Laclau argues is the heart of "small-l" liberal democracy. In contrast,
Fox's populist representational strategy favors the politics of sameness,
Laclau's *logic of equivalence*. Unlike the left's political culture, conservatives have far fewer intellectual qualms about embracing the usable fiction
of a *singular* political identity.

MSNBC may be partisan like Fox, but it still maintains a pluralistic
understanding of the political public sphere. Consistent with liberal
democratic theory, the MSNBC ad suggests social turmoil should be
solved through deliberation ("may ideas that advance our country ...
win") and by reforming political institutions, making them more func-
tional, responsive, and inclusive. The populist political narratives of Fox
programs suggest that only by vanquishing the elite social bloc that
corrupts such institutions can communitarian fullness be achieved. Where
the group bond for political liberalism is established by the equal inclusion of *all* individuals and minoritarian voices into the institutions that
grant political sovereignty and representation, Fox anti-establishment
politics brings the conservative coalition together by stressing its
members' common (imagined or real) *exteriority* to those same political
institutions. In short, Fox's conceptualization of the public sphere is
fundamentally "illiberal," to use journalism scholar Oliver Jutel's description (2015: 1131–1132).

For Fox's populist imaginary of the news landscape to be complete,
it needs an establishment to rebel against, the journalistic "monopoly"
hinted at in the opening example of this chapter. Taking a page from
Murdoch's print tabloid *New York Post*, Fox News has frequently
cast the *New York Times* to play this role. In a segment about the
Times, O'Reilly and his guest, author William McGowan, discuss the
paper's recession-era financial troubles. McGowan affirms that, even
with the paper's economic woes, the *Times* is still "the most important
media outlet in America." "More important than Fox News?"
O'Reilly asks in disbelief. "In certain policy circles, yes," McGowan
responds. Still skeptical, O'Reilly says, "Are you talking about the
Democratic Party ... politicians, business people? Because they're not
the folks. The folks don't care about the *New York Times*" (November 15, 2010).

Since overtaking CNN in ratings in 2002, Fox News has become, by all
objective measures, a media powerhouse, and this success threatens its

self-presentation as a journalistic underdog. This is why McGowan's assertion that the *Times* is still "the most important media outlet in America" and the *Times'* own marketing claim to have "the best journalists in the world"[6] is so important. These statements reestablish the power/threat of the antagonistic media camp, thus allowing Fox to continue to present itself as the "little guy." The uncertain, haphazard fashion in which O'Reilly tries to locate the *Times'* base of influence ("Are you talking about the Democratic Party ... politicians, business people?") works to present the *Times'* source of social legitimacy as dubious, esoteric, and inscrutable: characteristics of elite political influence itself. In contrast, O'Reilly is completely definitive in stating the social community with whom the *New York Times* has no legitimacy: "the folks." In this way, Fox News can be both a victim failing to earn the approval of prestige journalists and other cultural elites, and a media champion dominating ratings and winning the battle for the hearts and minds of the working-class majority.

Through its use of populist media frames and narratives, Fox News programs have helped *articulate* the various political positions and identity groups of the conservative movement onto what Laclau terms a "chain of equivalence" (2001, 2005a; 2005b). One sees how Fox's top program *The O'Reilly Factor* performs this quilting function in a "talking points memo" segment entitled, "Why the far left thinks America is a dumb country." Host Bill O'Reilly says to his guests, "The far left elitists portray any populist as a bumpkin ... If you are pro-choice, you're a bumpkin. Okay? If you go to church, you're an idiot." Reinforcing this frame, guest panelist Naomi Wolf ties gun ownership to religion, stating: "On the far left ... there is an instinct to talk down to people." O'Reilly interjects, "That's right." Wolf continues, "You know, if you have a gun, if you go to church, there's this assumption you're not smart" (July 30, 2009). In a *Hannity* segment on the "Bittergate" controversy[7] that emerged during the 2008 presidential campaign, host Sean Hannity suggests that Obama "sounds like a snob" and then says, "[President Obama] is saying to small-town America that they are a bunch of gun-toting, bible-thumping bigots" (November 4, 2008). In these quotes,

---

[6] nytimers (February 25, 2009).

[7] "Bittergate" refers to a gaffe that candidate Obama made during the 2008 presidential campaign where he told an audience at a San Francisco fundraiser that the working class are "bitter" and "cling to their guns or religion or antipathy to people who aren't like them."

some of the core identity groups that comprise the imagined conservative community are coupled together and discussed in a manner that presents their political unity as a given.

The same equivalential logic is apparent in Fox's representation of the liberal Other as well. In a segment debating the "unfair" coverage by the "establishment media" of vice presidential candidate Sarah Palin, Hannity asks rhetorically, "Is this about the inside-the-beltway mentality? The New York–Hollywood mentality?" (July 6, 2009). Here, the recurring stock of elite factions that comprise Fox News' vision of the liberal power bloc – the political class, the media, coastal elites, and the hip and trendy – are sequenced side by side to recreate their symbolic correspondence.

While the mere coupling and sequencing of rural, working class, pro-choice, gun-owning Americans on a nightly basis is powerful in itself, the key to how these identity groups become semantically glued together is through being commonly positioned against an antagonistic elite. Hannity and O'Reilly's rhetorical moves involved more than simply inundating their viewers with slick associations (something propaganda analysis emphasizes). These hosts did in fact give their audience a *rationale* for why the various factions of the conservative movement are socially and politically alike: they are equal objects of the "far left's" derision and condescension (e.g. that people are "bumpkins" or "bigots"). As populism theorist Francisco Panizza explains it, "The oppressor simultaneously renders all of them 'the same'" (2005: 6). In addition to a rationale or political logic, however, such anti-elitist statements work to elicit an affective response among the Fox News audience as well.

French philosopher Gilles Deleuze has developed specific theories around the concept of *affect*. My application follows affect theorist Ann Cvetkovich's more "generic" definition as a "category of that encompasses affect, emotion and feeling and that includes impulses, desires and feelings that get historically constructed in a range of ways" (2012: 4). Cvetkovich's key insight is recognizing how "feelings" like depression or anger are not limited to individual cognitive processes but instead manifest themselves in social and public ways. Following Cvetkovich, feminist scholar Sara Ahmed has stressed how "feelings" do not simply exist in the vacuum of our minds, but instead serve a crucial cohering function in the formation of group identities. She writes: "How we feel about others is what aligns us with a collective, which paradoxically 'takes shape' only as an effect of such alignments. It is through how others impress upon us that the skin of the collective takes shape" (2014: 54).[8] One can debate whether conservatives are truly oppressed or discriminated against by society's leading cultural institutions, as they so often claim. But what is key here is how Fox News' consistent emphasis on liberal intellectual condescension ("The media elite think they're smarter than the rest of those stupid bastards, and they'll tell you what to think") is an affective strategy conservative media producers have used to create an emotional pull, which, in turn, ties the conservative political community together. The emotional responses that partisan media elicits has mostly been viewed from the cognitive psychological lens of the "limited effects tradition."[9] The genealogies of populism that are featured in Chapters 3 and 4 suggest that such emotion also derives from the *historical* rootedness of the enduring political themes and narratives that Fox News and other conservative outlets use in their news coverage.

A FOX NEWS HERMENEUTICS: NARRATIVE AND PERFORMANCE

When examining a contemporary cable news program, the analyst faces a media text overflowing with semiotic content. All at once, the viewer's eyes and ears are struck by the verbal speech and body language of the hosts and guests, the multiple video windows recycling footage over their shoulders, the glittering set design and desk within which they sit, the colorful computer-generated patterns mesmerizingly fluctuating behind the pundits as background, a tickertape shuttling information across the bottom of the screen, the brand icon or "bug" at the corner of screen, and more. How does one begin to analyze such an unwieldy bulk of information?

In his article "A Structural Hermeneutics of *The O'Reilly Factor*" (2011), sociologist Mathew Norton develops a useful heuristic for making the first incision into the textual corpus of a Fox News program. He distinguishes the *simplistic* binary structure of Fox News' core political narratives (e.g., "the people" versus "the elite," "conservative media" versus "liberal media") from the *complex* and subtle performance techniques that Fox News hosts deploy to cultivate a relatable media

---

[8] I credit Laurie Ouellette's talk at the 2017 ICA preconference on populism for directing me to these references. See Ouellette (2017) "#Notokay: Trump as an Affective State" at the "Populism, Post-Truth Politics and Participatory Culture: Interventions in the Intersection of Popular and Political Communication."

[9] Sunstein, 2001; Tsfati & Cappella 2003; Prior, 2007; Bennett & Iyengar, 2008; Cappella & Jamieson, 2008; Stroud, 2011; Arseneaux & Johnson, 2013; Levendusky, 2013.

"persona." We can think of this "simplicity–complexity" dynamic in cinematic terms. A movie script provides the basic plot and identifies the heroes, the villains and the nature of the conflict. However, "deep acting,"[10] proper staging, close-up camera shots and other production techniques are required to dramatize and add meaning to these roles and relationships.

Let us begin by clarifying the general role that narrative plays in journalism. News organizations have long relied on narrative structures to cohere disparate pieces of information about a given event. The clutter created by the greater inclusion of sound bites, video imagery and graphics in television newscasts beginning in the 1970s and 1980s only heightened television news' reliance on the cohering function of narrative (Hallin, 1994). However, narrative structures do more than make information intelligible. They carry tacit moral ideas and normative assumptions about how the world *should* be (White, 1981, 1987). In this way, they are quite similar to communication scholar Robert Entman's conceptualization of "media frames" (1993). Connecting narrative theory to journalism and political communication, Jill Edy argues that media outlets gain "cultural authority" and, thus, a degree of power, by framing news events within familiar and resonant story structures (2006).

It is telling that Fox News' most formidable opponents mention the network's use of narrative when describing its greatest strengths. Former *Daily Show* host Jon Stewart became a liberal hero and major national figure during the Bush and Obama years by satirically skewering Fox News. When asked to explain Fox's prominence in the US news landscape, Stewart said, "Fox News is the most passionate and sells the clearest narrative of any news organization."[11] In turn, Media Matters, the media watchdog group that has devoted much of its existence to exposing Fox News' conservative bias and propagandistic qualities, explains Fox's success as due to the "ideological clarity" it offers news consumers, a clarity that is the end result of its marketing and programming narratives (Rabin-Havt & Brock, 2012: 58).

The way Fox's reigning number one program, *The O'Reilly Factor*, covered the passing of the Affordable Care Act (ACA) on March 24,

---

[10] In his analysis of *The O'Reilly Factor*, Chris Peters mentions this acting technique to shed light on the persuasiveness of host Bill O'Reilly's on-air persona (2010: 845).

[11] O'Reilly (March 22, 2010). The O'Reilly Factor [Video file]. New York: Fox News Channel. Retrieved June 23, 2011, from UCLA Communication Studies Archive, University of California, Los Angeles.

2010 – the most significant piece of legislation passed by the Democratic Party in generations – seems like an appropriate place to begin exploring how Fox has used narrative in its framing of political events. In one sense, the *Factor*'s coverage offered the usual type of information that one would expect to encounter in a news segment about a major policy event. Statistics were cited, other news analyses were referenced, and members of congress were interviewed to discuss the policy. However, departing from traditional news coverage, in this episode all these different bits of information were placed within the context of an overarching, if not epic, *social* conflict. Beginning the episode with his customary introductory segment, "Talking Points Memo," host Bill O'Reilly addressed the audience with a direct gaze:

When you cut through all the baloney, the controversy in America today is over freedom. Those lined up against the Obama administration believe the federal government is becoming too intrusive...On the left, the pro-Obama people say there is unfairness in America that needs to be corrected by the Feds. Thus, the battle lines are drawn. "Talking Points" believes the freedom issue is crucial. In the *New York Times'* lead editorial today, that far-left paper celebrates Obamacare and urges the president to continue spending billions of dollars to protect individual Americans from just about everything. In addition, the *Times* wants the Feds to take over the education system, the energy industry, and control the banking system. This is what many Americans fear, that the USA will become a top-down society.

Here, the news event – the passage of the health care bill – has a secondary role in the program's presentational priorities. It is more of a peg or a segue for the real focus, which is the dramatic *story form* O'Reilly uses to explain the policy event, the "battle" narrative about "the Feds" and their elite media allies' efforts to establish a "top-down society" that "many Americans" oppose in order to defend their "freedom." O'Reilly's narrativization of this event was, in turn, preceded and primed by similar framing done in the months leading up to the enactment of the ACA. In one healthcare-related segment on August 13, 2009, O'Reilly declared, again, that, "the battle lines have been drawn, as the nation is deeply involved in the most intense political debate in years. President Obama has the power of his office. And most of the media squarely behind him. The folks have the folks. We'll see who prevails."

In these examples, O'Reilly strategically positioned the issue of healthcare policy within a set of moral binaries: freedom versus tyranny, "the folks" versus the elite, fair conservative media versus biased liberal media. These rhetorical oppositions comprise what Mathew Norton calls the program's "deep meaning structure." This structure allowed host Bill O'Reilly to make snap, unequivocal judgments about a range of diverse issues and events night in and night out. In the heat of debate, he could plug ideas, issues or a person of interest into the show's preset value system. And this structure persists, Norton stresses, "outside the rapid flow of news cycle and events." "The more closely an issue conforms to the moral logic of one or more of these binaries," he continues, "the more likely it will be covered, perhaps on multiple occasions" (2011: 327). Other content studies of Fox News programming have observed this as well, noting how Fox's editorial logic is more strongly organized around the network's founding narratives and long-term programming themes.[12] In contrast, CNN, like the traditional network news programs, is more readily directed by the short-term editorial agenda of the "breaking news" approach.

Fox's greater emphasis on narrativity parallels the higher importance the network has placed on embodied *performance*. At CNN, founder Ted Turner used to say, "News is the star," meaning the anchors and reporters should be secondary to the breaking news event. This approach couldn't be more different from the personality-driven one of Fox News' founding CEO Roger Ailes, who once said frankly, "[Y]ou may get better ratings if you just have two people sitting in chairs, if you have the right two people."[13] In *Crazy Like a Fox: The Inside Story of How Fox News Beat CNN* (2004), Scott Collins described the "guiding principle" of Ailes' programming philosophy: "[G]reat television," Collins wrote, "meant great *performances*, whether from a politician, an executive, or a talk show host. People were the essence of the medium, the reason viewers watched in the first place" (140). The host-centered format of the cable newsmagazine genre was especially conducive to Ailes' television philosophy, as it enabled his on-air talent to accentuate their personalities.

In the mold of talk show legend Oprah Winfrey, Fox News' top hosts consistently personalize discussion topics by framing them in relation to their own biographies and current personal relationships. "[M]y father who died from melanoma" said O'Reilly in one segment, elliptically referencing his own father's plight while discussing actor Patrick Swayze's fight with cancer (July 7, 2009). In an episode of *Hannity*, where a

[12] See Jamieson & Cappella, 2008; Peters, 2010; McDermott, 2010.
[13] Collins, *Crazy Like a Fox*, p. 141.

discussion panel had been weighing in on the sex scandal of professional golfer Tiger Woods and the circumstances of Woods' marital relations, Hannity cited the "authority" of his own wife's opinion and opined to the panelists "[M]y wife says that his [Tiger Woods'] wife is not staying with him" (December 9, 2009).

In addition to their Fox News program, Fox's top pundits are encouraged to use other media platforms, such as their websites, radio programs, speaking tours, and published books to elaborate the image of their social pasts and/or their current friends and family network. This follows the model of what has been central to the construction of what Norton calls the "O'Reilly persona," but is a model that equally applies to the "Hannity persona" and "Glenn Beck persona." These hosts constantly share details about their upbringing as a way to create a "para-social relationship" with their audience, a "mediated intimacy" that strives to make their viewers feel as if they personally know these media figures (Horton & Wohl, 1956; Norton, 2011).

While the commercial entertainment benefits of creating a relatable television persona are obvious, it is an equally vital aspect of Fox's political communication strategies. The familiar and recognizable "persona" that O'Reilly and other Fox News pundits created provided the viewer with, Norton writes, "a relational point of access to the show" which primes their assessment of O'Reilly's political arguments and claims. "[I]f we know a party to a dispute," Norton elaborated, with the "we" referring to the Fox viewing audience, "it matters to us much more" (325). While Norton and others scholars, such as Jeffrey Jones (2012) and Chris Peters (2010), have discussed the way in which O'Reilly's performative style encapsulates Fox's conservative political ideology, less attention has been given to the way his performance helped build the working-class sensibility at the heart of Fox's populist news brand.

In *Women without Class* (2003), sociologist Julie Bettie provides a theoretical framework for conceptualizing class as a performance. She distinguishes Judith Butler's concept of *performativity* (1990) from Erving Goffman's concept of *performance* (1959). Class performativity, she explains, re-instantiates an individual's objective class position. From this conceptual posture, public performances of class are less a form of strategic social maneuvering, as Goffman might suggest, than they are an outcome of the material class structure. In most cases this material class structure dictates the type of symbolic resources and *cultural capital*

(Bourdieu, 1984) one has at one's disposal. Bettie contrasts this to "class performance," which she describes as an attempt to emulate a class-based style of identity that is not of one's inheritance or upbringing. While it is more typical that "class-origin-equals-class-performance," this is not, Bettie reminds us, always the case. There is a slippage between the objective and subjective moments in the reproduction of class differences – a slippage that creates a space for "class performing" and, thus, "class passing" (49–56). Bettie's ethnographic study of one California high school shows that, at least in the public setting of school, not only are some upper-middle-class teenage girls able to simulate the cultural disposition of working-class identities, but also that some working-class girls are able to simulate the cultural disposition of their peers' upper-middle-class identities.

No matter how guileless or "real" someone perceives themselves to be, everyone relies on "scripts" and "performance techniques" to build their social identity and manage their public reputation. The point of using dramaturgical metaphors like "stage," "performance," and "script" is not, Erving Goffman has argued, to separate what is "fake" about people from what is "true"; rather their purpose is to draw attention to the symbolic aspects of routine face-to-face interactions (1959). At the level of everyday life, people are mostly oblivious of the "class scripts" that guide their self-presentation. But in the rarefied world of television, the script-like character of class identity is far more apparent. As Laura Grindstaff shows in her study of daytime talk shows (2002), television producers actually coach hosts and guests to deliberately perform working-class cultural dispositions – what producers call being "ordinary" or "authentic." And from an entertainment standpoint, for guests to perform these class scripts in the most spectacular (and stereotypical) ways possible is in fact ideal.

In the history of American broadcasting, there have been numerous examples of speakers who had come from upper-class backgrounds but had still been able to effectively create populist public personas through their ability to perform the "social scripts" of the working class. In the 1920s, William Henderson, a man *Radio Digest* deemed "the most popular broadcaster in the South," fashioned the folksy on-air persona "Old Man Henderson" even though he himself was highly educated and had come from a wealthy Northern Louisiana family (Vaillant, 2004). Moving on to a more contemporary case, in the late 1980s, the television talk show host Morton Downey Jr. had become a ratings hit by combining a jingoistic right-wing nationalism with misogynistic vulgarity – even once telling a female guest to "sit down you fat bitch" (October 28, 1988).[14] In 1989, at the height of his popularity, Downey sought to capitalize on his television success by cutting a pop country album (Hilburn, 1989). The lead track was entitled "Blue Collar King," a self-designation that belied the fact that he was the son of the 1930's radio singer Morton Downey Sr., and had grown up in a mansion located right across from the Kennedy family compound in Hyannis Port, Massachusetts. While Downey's enemies and critics had frequently attempted to expose the artifice of Downey's working-class image by pointing to his elite background, such rhetorical attacks did little to diminish the affection given to him by the raucous studio audience at News Jersey's WWOR, a collective that Downey endearingly called "The Beast."[15] Bob Pittman, the head producer of *The Morton Downey Jr. Show* and the founder of MTV, has stressed that the key to Downey's appeal was not his background but rather how he "understood performance, how to turn everything into something theatrical" (Kogan, 2015).

Defined strictly in terms of genre, *The Morton Downey Jr. Show* had been much closer to the *Jerry Springer*-type "freak show" side of the talk show spectrum (Gamson, 1998) than it was to the current newsmagazine talk format of Fox News' major opinion shows. However, in terms of Downey's own "working-class" self-branding, the "Blue Collar King" provides a better precursor to Bill O'Reilly than do the waspy pundits of early conservative television talk shows on PBS, like *Firing Line* and *The McLaughlin Group*. In 2004, Fox News' official bio of Bill O'Reilly on the channel's website read: "From humble beginnings from Long Island, New York, Bill O'Reilly has risen to become the 'the new pope of TV journalism.'" The final line of the bio reads, "Bill O'Reilly continues to live on Long Island where his best friends are guys with whom he attended first grade."[16] However, the most important platform O'Reilly has used to reinforce his working-class self-brand was not FNC's website, his speaking tours or even his many best-selling books. It was the news program that carried his namesake, *The O'Reilly Factor*. "I'm a blue-collar guy," he told one guest in an October 6, 2010 episode, "even

---

[14] D. Oom (May 29, 2013). Morton Downey vs Stripper for God!! [Video file]. Retrieved from: www.youtube.com/watch?v=JM45bTgmoog.

[15] See the 2012 documentary film *Évocateur: The Morton Downey Jr. Movie* (directors Seth Kramer & Daniel A. Miller). Producer Daniel Miller, Magnolia Entertainment.

[16] Fox News Channel (April 29, 2004). Bill O'Reilly's Bio [Web page]. Retrieved from: www.foxnews.com/story/2004/04/29/bill-oreilly-bio.html.

though I'm wearing a green [dress] shirt tonight and I'm a rich guy, but I'm still that *sensibility* [my emphasis]. You know me. All of my friends who are all blue-collar, most of them say the same thing. 'He [Obama] doesn't understand me and he doesn't care about me'" (October 6, 2010).

In saying President Obama was out of touch with ordinary Americans, O'Reilly made a typical statement one would expect from a political commentator. However, what distinguishes this kind of rhetoric from conventional journalism and marks it as populist is that in this quote O'Reilly claims, on the basis of a common class-cultural "sensibility," that he is on the same social level as his audience. Traditional journalists have long claimed to serve the people and *represent* their voice in a liberal democratic way. However, they tend to recognize (and even brag about) their special status as journalists. They are cognizant of the *re-* in representation; that is, how their relationship with the public is one-step removed (Arditi, 2005).[17]

This traditional view was apparent in a 2011 MSNBC promo showing correspondent Chuck Todd driving through the White House gates. He says in the voice-over, "Our leaders need to be held accountable. I have *unique access* [my emphasis] to the President and Congress. I better use that access for a greater good."[18] Although Fox News hosts are, by all accounts, political insiders like Todd, they downplay their own "unique access" and instead stress their exteriority to the political and journalism establishment. Following the logic of populism, the purpose of performing this exteriority is to stress Fox's moral purity, a purity that is established in terms of a *distance* from the corrupting force of political and media power centers.

FOX NEWS VERSUS *THE DAILY SHOW*: PERFORMING SINCERITY VERSUS IRONY

If there is one media figure on the left who was able to match Bill O'Reilly in popularity and political stature in the late-1990s and 2000s, it was the

---

[17] In his essay "Populism as the Internal Periphery of Democratic Politics" (2005), Benjamin Arditi points out that the *re-* in representative democracy alludes to the fact that the relationship between speaker (the political representative) and audience (the represented) is one-step removed. In contrast to traditional political modes of representation, a populist mode of address denies the "representational relationship all together" and seeks to express the notion of a "joint presence without representation," that is, a sense that the populist speaker is both a political leader and a member of the audience (82–83).

[18] Jennocuse (September 8, 2011).

former *The Daily Show* host, Jon Stewart. On *The Daily Show* (now hosted by Trevor Noah), Stewart had a special knack for skewering Fox News and exposing the class-contradictions of O'Reilly's populist self-image. As a frequent guest on *The O'Reilly Factor*, Stewart even waged these critiques during face-to-face debates with the Fox News host. In one episode, when O'Reilly had been accusing President Obama of "separating himself from regular folks ... the people are going 'come on, you're the leader of the country. You have to comment,'" Stewart took on O'Reilly's rhetorical assumption of "the people's" voice and groused back, asking O'Reilly, "[W]hat people?" O'Reilly's dissociating response – "The folks, regular people. The people who watch me. Not *you*. [emphasis added]" – gave Stewart the opportunity to highlight the great social distance between O'Reilly, himself an exceptionally wealthy TV star, and the current denizens of O'Reilly's beloved working-class hometown. "When was the last time you visited Levittown, Bill?" countered Stewart sarcastically (September 22, 2010). In another episode, when O'Reilly had been attempting to promote Glenn Beck, Fox's newest rising star at the time, Stewart raised similar illogicalities. O'Reilly had just finished telling Stewart that Beck is "everyman ... he sits on bar stool ... he doesn't shill for any party. He just spouts." Stewart interrupted O'Reilly, and snapped, "Everyman has got a show?"

This sort of critical reflection on the theatricality of political news is a signature trait of *The Daily Show*. From its beginning in 1996, *The Daily Show* had been a comedy program that mostly satirized the television news genre. It became far more political when Stewart took over as host in 1999. Along with Bill Maher's *Politically Incorrect* (1993), Stewart's *Daily Show* innovated a whole new hybrid genre of political journalism, which would come to offer a comedic presentation of "hard news" topics. Its success inspired a sub-industry of liberal news shows headed by comedians. These included *The Colbert Report* (2005), *Last Week Tonight with John Oliver* (2014), *Late Night with Seth Meyers* (2014), *The Nightly Show with Larry Wilmore* (2015), and *Full Frontal with Samantha Bee* (2016). Notably, most of the programs cited here were, or are, hosted by former *Daily Show* "correspondents."

These programs have used satire and parody as interpretive tools for dissecting, exposing, and critiquing the deceptive techniques of modern political communication. In highlighting the absurd qualities of contemporary political news, they have indirectly supported the idea of public media sphere driven by *rational* discussion and facts as opposed to being pushed to favor commercially motivated spectacle or emotional partisanship (Baym, 2009; McClennan & Maisel 2014). Geoffrey Baym argues that these comedy shows represent a "neomodern" paradigm of journalism that uses pop culture, entertainment and "the style of post-modernism to pursue the high-modern ideals of public information and democratic accountability that motivated news of the network age" (20). In *From Cronkite to Colbert* (2009), Baym convincingly shows how *The Daily Show* and *The Colbert Report* provided the kind of "critical inquiry" that a liberal, deliberative democracy necessitates. However, Baym offers less consideration regarding the class-cultural politics and sarcastic news styles of Stewart and the numerous *The Daily Show* offshoots.

There are affinities between the ironic mode of address of news-based comedy shows and the "disinvested" gaze of high cultural products and texts. As Pierre Bourdieu's research demonstrates, the cultural bourgeoisie (i.e. artists, intellectuals, educated professionals) find "nothing more naive or vulgar" than texts that take themselves too seriously, or texts that expect the viewer to fully invest their identity in them. While a big budget Hollywood film invites its viewers to lose themselves in the lives of the characters onscreen, with bourgeois cultural texts the pleasure derives from exposing and depreciating the "theatrical fiction," not from whole-heartedly identifying with it (Bourdieu, 1984: 33). Reflecting this, *The Daily Show* and *The Colbert Report* hail their audiences as viewers who can see through mass media's "easy seductions" and "art of illusion." In political media particularly, this means recognizing the contrived elements of populist political performances – the "fighting for the little guy" rhetoric, the photo-ops of politicians "having a beer" with "everyday Americans," and the activity of doing other "folksy" ventures at county fairs or rodeos.

I am not arguing here that ironic or satirical criticism is *exclusively* enjoyed by educated professionals, nor am I suggesting that *The Daily Show* under Stewart did not have its own class-based critiques against "the elite." However, in terms of cultural style, *The Daily Show*'s mode of address is clearly designed with the professional-class viewer in mind. The show has been heralded by advertising trade magazines as the go-to program to "reach an educated audience that reads political non-fiction."[19] In contrast to Fox News' top programs – which seldom, if ever, earn critical acclaim from prestige-granting organizations like the

---

[19] Quote found in Baym (2009), *From Cronkite to Colbert*, p. 116.

Emmys – *The Daily Show* and *The Colbert Report* have received numerous awards by such cultural institutions. While Baym attributes the "antirealist skepticism" expressed on *The Daily Show* and *The Colbert Report* to an epochal postmodern sensibility, I would argue that their detached, ironic mode of address and aversion to "realist" sincere performative news styles operates, *in part*, as a professional class, aspirational appeal.

If comedy-based news programs engage the "dramaturgy of politics," using Baym's language, only to denounce its conventions, artistic effects, and performances, Fox News has strived to produce better theater. Catering to a "popular gaze," Fox News programs work from the expectation that the viewer will approach the performances of Fox's top hosts with what Bourdieu calls a "good-natured credulity" and a "*deliberate* naivety." The assumption is not that the Fox News audience will be duped into believing the millionaire celebrity Fox host is just like them; the *real* assumption is that the Fox News viewer, like the blockbuster movie-goer, has a "desire to enter into the game" (Bourdieu, 1984: 33) – that is, has a willingness to identify with the narratives and performances of Fox News pundits. Like the entertainment wrestler who stays in character during a "match" (something known in the wrestling fan community as "kayfabe"[20]), the Fox News host's emotionally invested journalistic style invites the viewer to assume a good faith interpretive approach when reading their working-class performances. This is a charitable evaluation that is undoubtedly easier to encourage when the host shares and supports the viewer's partisan worldview.

The sincere class performances of Fox News hosts do not always run smoothly, however. Good television requires a degree of authentic, spontaneous reaction. To capture this, producers must accept a level of unpredictability when thinking through how the guests they book will interact with the Fox News host. Not having full assurance that a given guest will "play along" with the host's performance poses risks for the host and the news brand. We are given an example of a failed class performance in one episode of *Glenn Beck*, where Beck was hosting a "small business forum" for companies that had been impacted by the economic recession. Somewhat rhetorically, Beck queried Brett Parker, a co-owner of a New York City bowling alley, "You think your business would be doing well right now because you're not going to uber-elite; you're going to the average everyday schmo, are you not?" Parker

---

[20] Litherland (2014).

responded with a smirk on his face, saying, "Well, we cater to a little bit more upscale than your normal bowling alley audience. But we've really been hurt [by the recession]." Caught slightly off-guard by the response, Beck defended his assumption that bowling is a lowbrow leisure activity for "everyday schmos," declaring, "I bowl!" But contradicting Beck's self-depiction as one of these "schmos," Parker reminded Beck (and the audience) of the TV host's exceptional wealth and averred, "Yes, you're pretty upscale" (August 17, 2009).

Acknowledging the great affluence and status of Fox News hosts threatens to create a what Bourdieu calls a "social break" between them and their audience. As a result, they deploy various representational tactics to prevent or repair such breaks. One such tactic is to remind the audience of their working-class origins. We see this in a March 24, 2009 episode of *Hannity* that featured country music artist John Rich as a guest panelist. Following the *economic populist* themes of his newly released anti-bank bailout anthem "Shuttin' Detroit Down," during the panel discussion Rich expressed outrage about the bonuses AIG's corporate executives were receiving using government bailout money. However, when in the course of his bromide Rich's anger shifted to media elites, it suddenly seemed his charges were actually meant to be indicting Hannity and his fellow panelists, since Rich was repeatedly addressing *them* as "you guys":

You guys [my emphasis] living in D.C. and New York, hey, good for you. I tour all over the United States, and we are really seeing what is going on out there. I grew up in a trailer park in Amarillo, Texas. I didn't go to college … [everyday Americans] are watching *you guys* [my emphasis] give these grandiose explanations as to why we can give hundreds of billions of dollars to companies that abuse, disrespect, and spit in the face of taxpayers.

These statements having come at the end of the allotted time for that particular discussion topic, Hannity was left without time to directly respond. However, once there was an opening in the topic rotation, Hannity returned to Rich's comments. "I want to come back to something," Hannity said, indicating Rich's previous comments had been preoccupying the host's thoughts:

You really touched a nerve here and that is the America *we* [my emphasis] grew up in. My father grew up poor. My father had to work and did paper routes to pay and help with his family growing up. When he came out of World War II after fighting four years for his country, it was a proud moment to get a 50 by 100 lot in Franklin Square, Long Island and raise his kids in a better situation than he had. Are people at home relating to, you know, trillions and trillions [of bailout money]?

Considering Fox News' populist brand, it is no coincidence that many of
the network's top hosts as well as deceased CEO Roger Ailes all depicted
their lives as a Horatio Alger tale. Through scattered but repeated statements about their working-class upbringings, Fox News hosts have
labored to nullify their wealth and media status.

Noting this as a central rhetorical device in the Fox News pundit's
toolkit, liberal critics like Michael Kinsley, Al Franken, and Peter Hart
have questioned the authenticity of Bill O'Reilly's working-class pedigree. O'Reilly took these charges very seriously and devoted several
segments to presenting counter-evidence that sought to prove his
humble background. To a degree, all of this misses the point. As former
News Corp. sports writer and *Salon.com* columnist Charles Pierce has
said, "[I]t doesn't matter if Bill O'Reilly is really a blue-collar hero as
long as he can play one on television" (2002). Establishing that Archie
Bunker, Rocky Balboa, or Al Bundy are fictional characters from
television and film does not diminish their iconic status as symbols of
working-class identity. Fox News pundits like Bill O'Reilly have, from
the beginning, staked out a working-class positionality in the symbolic
terrain of television journalism, a positionality, I would stress, Fox's
liberal media competitors have been mostly uninterested in trying to
contest and assume themselves. Rather than poking holes in O'Reilly's
working-class self-biography, a more fruitful endeavor may be to
seek to identify and explain the characteristics of the Fox pundit's
performance that are not empirically accurate or wholly representative
of the American working class per se, but are evidently effective at
producing a compelling representation of a working-class disposition
and mentalité.

THE COLD SHOULDER: NO PLACE FOR POPULISTS
IN LIBERAL CABLE NEWS

When we look at the few examples of hosts that have adopted populist
language and/or performed a working-class anchoring style on CNN and
MSNBC, these media personalities have often been ridiculed by their
liberal peers and/or have been marginalized, even despite generating solid
ratings. For example, CNN's short-lived show *Rick's List*, launched in
January of 2010, was hosted by Rick Sanchez. Sanchez was born in Cuba,
grew up in Florida in a Spanish-speaking home and then studied journalism at Minnesota State University by way of a football scholarship. At
CNN, the wide-shouldered, square-jawed Sanchez had a presentational

style that prioritized personal relatability over wittiness and erudition. He was roundly mocked as a buffoon in *The Daily Show* segments. Clearly hurt by this, he lashed out in a radio interview in October of 2010, accusing *Daily Show* host Jon Stewart of being a classist "bigot." He said, Stewart "can't relate to a guy like me...he can't relate to somebody who grew up poor." Then, in the course of the interview, Sanchez's criticism turned anti-Semitic as he suggested CNN and other news networks were controlled by Jewish people like Stewart. This racist suggestion prompted CNN to cancel his show.[21]

In the case of Sanchez, there was a clear, incident-based reason for his firing. However, MSNBC demoted key hosts on its network because the management viewed their *style* as off base with the network's branding goals. For example, in 2011, Turkish-American anchor Cenk Uygur was bumped from his 6:00PM timeslot to the weekends because, according to him, MSNBC president Phil Griffin did not like his "aggressive style." Griffin reminded Uygur, the co-founder and star of a successful online news webcast called The Young Turks (TYT), that the cable news audience and online audience "require different manners of speaking."[22] While MSNBC spokespeople denied Uygur's claims that MSNBC wanted to censor his anti-corporate views, they did confirm that the crux of disagreement between Uygur and MSNBC management was over communication style.[23] In contract negotiations, Uygur rejected MSNBC's offer to host a weekend show (a veritable no-man's land for cable news programming). Instead, Uygur left cable news and concentrated his focus on TYT. In the years since, he and his Armenian-American co-star Ana Kasparian have used a decidedly *leftist populist* branding strategy to turn The Young Turks network into one of the most successful online news organizations in the world as it currently garners more YouTube subscribers than CNN and many other major news networks.[24]

Moving MSNBC host Ed Schultz from primetime to the weekends in 2013 was arguably an even more puzzling case. Unlike Uygur, *The Ed Show*'s ratings were clearly trending upward at the time of his demotion.

---

[21] Stelter, B. (October 1, 2010). CNN Fires Rick Sanchez for Remarks in Interview. *New York Times*. Retrieved from: www.nytimes.com/2010/10/02/business/media/02cnn.html. Shea, (October 1, 2010).

For Jon Stewart and *The Daily Show*'s response to Sanchez, see Stewart, October 4, 2010.

[22] Stelter (July 20, 2011).   [23] See *Politico* (July 21, 2011).

[24] Weigel (May 27, 2016).

In 2013, "Big Eddie," also, interestingly enough, a Minnesota State University alumnus who got his degree via a football scholarship, had the second highest rated show on MSNBC. In fact, his show was beating all CNN's top programs, nearly doubling the numbers of his direct 8:00PM CNN competitor Anderson Cooper, and, most impressively, was surpassing the ratings of MSNBC's top show, *The Rachel Maddow Show*, on various occasions.[25]

This programming reshuffling made even less commercial sense when one considers the cross-promotional benefits Schultz uniquely offered MSNBC. Like several Fox News commentators, Schultz started his broadcasting career on talk radio. In 2013, *The Ed Schultz Show*, the radio analog to Schultz's MSNBC program, was ranked within the top 6 in *Talkers Magazine*, just under the likes of Limbaugh, Hannity, and Beck. "Overall," *Politico* reporter Mackenzie Weinger writes, "conservative hosts far outweigh liberal talk radio hosts on the list, and Schultz makes the left's highest showing."[26]

If Schultz's *leftist politics* made him standout in talk radio environment, his presentational style made him an outlier in the *liberal taste culture* of MSNBC. Schultz, like Fox pundits, framed American media and politics in morally stark, populist terms. In the rhetorical system of *The Ed Show*, "corporate America" and the "millionaire establishment media" were named as the power elite, however, not intellectuals and professors à la Fox News. Always using a direct, personal address, he referred to his audience as "middle-classers" and he, like O'Reilly, socially *situated* his news analysis in terms of this classed social bloc's interests.

Following Fox News' "activist" journalistic approach to (and entertainmentizing of) the 2009 Tea Party protests, Schultz broadcasted several live shows at the Wisconsin Labor protests of 2011, something no other MSNBC primetime show was willing to do. Surrounded by firefighters, nurses and teachers, Schultz roused the crowds during these protest broadcasts by calling out conservative media figures like Glenn Beck and Rush Limbaugh for slandering unions and public sector workers as "freeloaders."[27] Another unique feature of *The Ed Show* is that the program did not merely use labor leaders as interview subjects; instead, it treated union organizers as television pundits and news

[25] *Mediaite* (August 10, 2012); Sareen (March 13, 2013); Rothman (May 23, 2013).
[26] Weinger (March 13, 2013).   [27] VampiressOnDaProwlq (February 20, 2011).

analysts, thereby tapping a talent pool of *dispositionally* working-class communicators underutilized by most liberal news shows.

At the level of performance and embodied affect, Schultz spoke with his hands (like O'Reilly), used working-class slang and sports references (like Sean Hannity) and frequently leaned close into the camera for emotional effect (like Glenn Beck). These communicative elements are displayed in a June 9, 2009 episode, when Schultz responded to conservative media figures like Hugh Hewitt and Rush Limbaugh who had called on their listeners to boycott American car manufacturers Chrysler and General Motors to protest the government aid that these so-called "socialist" companies were receiving. Rather than calling Hewitt's boycott "problematic" as his colleagues might say, Schultz slammed it as "un-American garbage." Adopting an overtly "ethical disposition" (Bourdieu, 1984), Schultz looked into the camera and asked rhetorically, "Do you know how many Americans have lost their jobs in manufacturing? Do you know how many American families are being affected, their livelihoods are being drilled because of this recession ... what do you say we just kick the American worker in the teeth?" he shouts, while physically performing this violent act with his leg.[28]

This kind of charged, emotional performativity invited jeering criticism from centrist and liberal media outlets. In 2011, *Gentlemen's Quarterly* (GQ), a male fashion magazine for business professionals, mocked Schultz by putting him on its satirical "25 least influential people alive" list. As part of a developing feud between Schultz – the populist performer – and CNN's Anderson Cooper – the prototypical news professional – Cooper's program *AC360* drew attention to the prestige-denying GQ article on Schultz in one of its "RidicuList" segments.[29] By the early 2010s, Schultz had become one of the mainstream media's go-to "left-wing" examples of the decline of journalistic "civility." The video montage at the conclusion of Jon Stewart and Stephen Colbert's 2010 "Rally to Restore Sanity" event, which was broadcasted by Comedy Central and C-Span, juxtaposed confrontational highlights of Schultz's show with similar highlights from *The O'Reilly* and *Hannity* in order to draw left–right stylistic equivalences across the media. The montage, in line with the event's central theme, condemned cable news for catering to the most "extreme" and "irrational" segments of the American public. Ted Koppel's 2012 "War of Words: Partisan Ranting is 'Marketing of Fear'"

---

[28] NBCnews.com (June 10, 2009).   [29] Yazakchattiest (December 4, 2011).

special cited in Chapter 1 used highlights of Schultz's show for a similar purpose. This is not to suggest all the criticism surrounding Schultz's "incivility" was unwarranted. In May of 2011, he was temporarily suspended from MSNBC for his misogynistic attack against conservative talk radio host (now at Fox News) Laura Ingraham, whom he called a "talk slut" on his radio show.[30]

All this bad press undoubtedly informed MSNBC's demotion of Schultz in 2013. Writing about the network's move to diminish Schultz's visibility, one Huffington Post article read that Schultz's "barnstorming, Midwestern, labor-friendly brand of populist liberalism has come to look more and more at odds with the increasingly wonkish tone taking hold on the rest of MSNBC."[31] Embodying this wonkishness is Chris Hayes, the host who would replace Schultz at the 8:00PM slot. *All in with Chris Hayes* went on to set record lows for ratings and has long been on the verge of cancellation, that is, up until the 2017–2018 Trump–Russia scandal, which boosted the ratings of MSNBC's entire primetime line up.

The momentary success of *The Ed Show* and subsequent success of Uygur's online news network TYT demonstrates how a programming strategy *stylistically* geared to working-class segments of MSNBC's audience *could* have been commercially effective, or even politically effective. Yet similar to CNN's shift in marketing strategy in 2003, MSNBC's corporate leadership *chose* to invest its promotional energy in the opposite direction. This inflexible commitment to its original "slumpy" (socially liberal, urban-minded professionals) target demographic and attendant taste culture has prevented MSNBC's executives from considering the possibility that the "wonkish tone" they culturally prize may be "at odds" with the network's actual audience, let alone a larger segment of untapped viewers. According to the 2012 Pew study, only 26 percent of MSNBC's viewers have a college degree. While this is more than Fox's 24 percent, such a number is actually lower than the national average of 30 percent.[32]

Yet the network still generally rejects a populist programming strategy in the mold of Uygur, Schultz and civil rights activist Al Sharpton, another working-class-styled MSNBC host whose program *Politics Nation* was bumped to weekend programming in 2015 and then cancelled. MSNBC executives continue to attribute Fox's competitive edge to

---

[30] Farhi (May 26, 2011).   [31] Sareen (March 13, 2013).
[32] Pew Research Center (September 27, 2012); United States Census Bureau Public Information Office (May 19, 2016).

its conservative ideology and not its populist *style*. As such, MSNBC has recently recruited more conservative pundits; notably, Hugh Hewitt, the very person Schultz once called upon the MSNBC audience to boycott.[33] This is an especially odd move to make in the first years of the Trump presidency. When Obama officially took office in January of 2009, Fox News did not recruit more liberals and "tone down" its oppositional programming themes. It did the very opposite and as a result generated some of the highest ratings in network's history, and, more importantly, drove the national debate over how the government should respond to the economic crisis.

Charles Pierce maintains that it is simply not in MSNBC's corporate culture – a politically liberal culture – to embrace tabloid representational techniques and promote populist media performers. In a prescient 2002 article, "Fox Populi," Pierce describes the TV performances of Fox News hosts as "authentically artificial," by which he means the network's top stars fully and unapologetically embraced the performative nature of news and politics. They, following the history and culture of Fox's parent company News Corp. (now Twenty-First Century Fox, Inc.), have what he calls "a true, virtuous, *tabloid soul* [my emphasis]." This is in contrast to liberal news organizations who continue to hold onto an *informational* conception of news (Schudson, 1978), and only half-heartedly and guiltily accept how it functions as entertainment and cultural discourse. "I don't know when progressive politicians in general lost touch with the tabloid soul," Pierce ponders. He posed this question to Marcy Kaptur, still the longest serving Democratic congresswoman in the House of Representatives. Kaptur is a Midwestern Ohioan from an auto-union family whom Pierce describes as a "stalwart foe of NAFTA and a proudly untriangulated old Democrat." Kaptur clearly knows something about populism as she defeated the media darling of the right, Samuel Wurzelbacher (aka "Joe-the-Plumber"), in a 2012 congressional election. Kaptur agrees with Pierce that Democrats have lost the working-class cultural politics that once defined her political camp. When he asked why, she ventured, "[I]t might have been educated out of the party" (2002, para. 38).

It is vital to remember how, in the media culture of the 1930s, all these relationships had been understood in the reverse. In this era, commercial country music was, if anything, politically-coded towards the left, with socialist country artists like Woody Guthrie leading the "hillbilly" music

[33] Vyse (May 1, 2017); Grim (May 2, 2017).

scene in Los Angeles, at that time a central peformance hub for country music before the rise of Nashville (La Chapelle, 2007). The Popular Front, the most energized political movement of the New Deal era, launched a consciously tabloid, lifestyle-centric newspaper called *PM* which featured anti-fascist political cartoons by Theodor Seuss Geisel – or, as he became known, Dr. Seuss (Denning, 1998). In the 1930s and 1940s it had been the Democratic Left who had more readily embraced "lowbrow" culture, tabloid news styles, and "performance" as political communication tools. Meanwhile, the "objective" prestige sector of the news media of the era was dominated by conservative voices.

In the 1940 presidential election, for example, Democratic President Franklin Delano Roosevelt (FDR) had garnered 55% of the popular vote but was only endorsed by 25% of the daily newspapers and 33% of the weekly newspapers (Winfield, 1994: 128). As conservative media historian Richard Viguerie acknowledges, FDR was able to counter the influence of the dailies – the dominant medium of political communication at the time – by using the new technology of radio. But, what was equally important about FDR is how he understood the political importance of performance, particularly the performance of sincerity. In contrast to the cold, technocratic style of his Republican predecessors Herbert Hoover and Calvin Coolidge, FDR spoke to the American public with a personal voice that resembled the authorial address of the tabloid news sector. With his "fireside chats," FDR was able to take advantage of, rather than shun, the emotive possibilities that radio's sonic quality presented. In so doing, FDR effectively created an intimate, "para-social" relationship with the American public.

In a limited sense (emphasis on limited), FDR can be thought of as an early-twentieth-century liberal version of Republican presidents such as George W. Bush and Donald Trump. Like Bush and Trump, Roosevelt gained the trust of large swathes of the American public by transgressing the communicative norms of his own patrician, Ivy League background (it is notable that FDR and his team worked assiduously in this pre-television era to hide the fact that he used a wheelchair). For one thing, Roosevelt's rhetoric was melodramatic and morally loaded, which stemmed from his belief that the presidency "is more than an engineering job efficient or inefficient. It is preeminently a place of moral leadership" (Schlesinger, 2002: 483). Secondly, like Bush's television appearances, FDR's radio performances were characterized by his emotional availability, which worked to convey of sense of cognitive transparency. Thirdly, like Trump, FDR was not afraid to use confrontational rhetoric. Roosevelt called the corporate elite and the wealthy of the era "economic royalists" and vowed, using biblical metaphors, to run these "money changers" out of the temple (March 4, 1933). Responding to "organized money's" political retaliation, he famously said he "welcomed their hatred" (October 31, 1936). This type of confrontational tone and rhetoric is something one seldom hears from modern "establishment" Democrats like Barack Obama, Hillary Clinton, and Democratic National Committee chair Tom Perez.[34] Lastly, and most importantly, FDR shared another critical factor that aided his populist performance strategies. He was *white and male.*

MSNBC and, by extension, the Democratic Left's unease with populism cannot be wholly explained by its professional class cultural bias, especially in a post–civil rights, post-Nixon political landscape. MSNBC's failure with populism must be evaluated in context to the network's relative success at appealing to nonwhite audience segments. Among the top three cable networks, MSNBC has consistently garnered the highest number of African-American viewers. In 2013, this racial group made up an impressive 30 percent of the network's 25–54 demographic.[35] The next section explores why it is far more complicated, and risky, for people of color and women political figures to use populist media styles than it is for their white, male counterparts.

POPULISM'S RACE AND GENDER PROBLEM

Let us return to a quote that was cited earlier where Bill O'Reilly told Jon Stewart that President Barack Obama was "separating himself from regular folks." The Fox host repeated this charge throughout Obama's two terms. In an October 6, 2010 episode, which I will examine more

---

[34] The rhetorical differences between the populist and establishment factions of the Democratic Left couldn't be more starkly illustrated than in a joint April 17, 2017 interview with former presidential candidate Bernie Sanders and DNC chair Tom Perez on MSNBC's *All in with Chris Hayes.* In this interview, Sanders stressed the need for Democrats to adopt more of a populist, confrontational style. "We [as a party]," he said, "need to have the guts to point the finger at the ruling class of this country, the billionaire class and Wall Street, and say 'your greed is destroying this country and you know what we are going to take you on.'" Hayes asked Perez if he agrees with Sanders that Democrats need to identify a villain: "Do you have to say," Hayes directly says to Perez, "these are the people that are screwing you." Perez, following Obama and Hillary consensus-oriented rhetorical style, calls for "hope" themes over anti-establishment ones saying, "well listen, when we put hope on the ballot, we win. When we allow our opponents to put fear on the ballot, we don't do so well."
Stein (April 19, 2017).

[35] Chariton (January 2, 2014). Also see Wilstein (December 15, 2014).

closely in the next chapter, O'Reilly claimed that Obama did not understand and in fact "looks down on working-class Americans." In this episode, O'Reilly had pointed to specific Democratic policies that he believed reflected this class disconnect. However, the primary reason he had given for Obama's not being "in sync with the white working class" was the President's "cultural disposition." Then in a November 8, 2010 segment entitled "Who exactly is President Obama?" O'Reilly complained that Obama "is not going to reveal himself to the American people ... the American people sense [again channeling the "people's" voice] [that] Barack Obama is distant from them, and that is a major problem for the President." Nodding his agreeing with O'Reilly was fellow Fox anchor Brit Hume, who confirmed that "Obama is not outwardly emotional and thus is inaccessible." These two pundits, both white men, went on to also criticize Obama's lack of "toughness" and the fact that he tended to style himself as a calm, deliberative professional. The poetic quality of Obama's speeches was also a point of criticism on Fox News as well as from talk radio hosts like Rush Limbaugh. Even populist-minded liberals like Bernie Sanders, though seldom critiquing Obama based on his oratorical eloquence or on his background as a professor, as these conservatives did, similarly expressed frustration with Obama's cool-headed, non-confrontational approach to both Wall Street and the conservative opposition.

Obama's cultural disposition as an educated professional has been a central part of his public image since his early days as an Illinois senator. Stylistically, Obama's 2008 and 2012 presidential campaigns differed from the more working-class targeted approach of Jesse Jackson's 1984 and 1988 campaigns, which stood as the most successful presidential bids by an African-American politician up until Obama.[36] By no stretch of the imagination did Obama's two presidential victories usher in a "post-racial America." However, scholars of racial stereotyping maintain that it did amplify the visibility of an existing professional class "subtype" for Black Americans (Fisk et al., 2009). Surely, the educated style that Obama embodies stems in part from his background. His mother, Ann Dunham, was an accomplished scholar who had a Ph.D. in Anthropology, and his absentee father, Barack Obama Sr., earned his Master's degree at Harvard. Before his own activist-political career, the bulk of Obama's early adulthood had been spent in the academic world

---

[36] For a historical analysis that ties Jesse Jackson's presidential campaigns to the populist rhetorical tradition, see Kazin, *The Populist Persuasion*, pp. 270–280.

serving as a professor and editor of one of the most prestigious journals in the world: the *Harvard Law Review*.

However, an educational pedigree does not dictate the self-presentational choices of a politician or media figure. As already illustrated, the history of American media and politics is flush with examples of white men from elite schools performing working-class identities and playing the role of populist. Franklin Roosevelt and President Theodore Roosevelt, his distant cousin, are two obvious examples.[37] One cannot understand Obama's cool, professional style without considering the quality that separates him from every previous president for the last two-and-half centuries – that being the fact of his embodied *blackness*.[38] Obama's racial identity denied him the kind of leeway and range of representational options that white presidents and media figures had long been given.

Social psychologists have used the concept of "status fragility" to describe the way people of color and white women who attain leadership positions, when compared to their white, male counterparts, are more intensely chastised for having the same character flaws and making the same mistakes (Dawson et al., 2008). In fact, something like the inverse of "status fragility" seems to apply to white, male conservative populists like the Fox hosts. As a political style, *cultural populism* requires adherents to wear their social flaws on their sleeve. As Donald Trump's 2016 presidential campaign so spectacularly demonstrated, lacking credentials, expressing rage, having poor taste and "bad manners," and following one's gut can be positively spun as signs of "ordinariness" and "authenticity."[39] However, from another vantage point, these same exact presentational traits can signal one's "incompetency" and "impropriety." These opposing interpretative outcomes cannot be analyzed merely in terms of how well politicians and journalists execute their respective media performances. The *embodied* race, gender, and sexuality of the speaker is paramount.

When Bill O'Reilly pounded his fist and famously yelled at Democratic Senator Barney Frank at the top of his lungs, "You're a coward!" on national television, he was celebrated by the right as a "fighter."

---

[37] For an excellent analysis of how President Theodore Roosevelt created his masculine, working-class public image through film, see David Gerstner's 2006 book *Manly Arts: Masculinity and Nation in early American Cinema*.

[38] Walters, 2007; McIlwain, 2007.

[39] Moffitt & Tormey, 2014; Moffit & Ostiguy, 2016.

Meanwhile, if Obama had adopted anything but a polite, middle-class disposition, he would have run the risk of being labeled a "black militant." Indeed, Fox News programs unsuccessfully attempted to brand him this way during the 2008 presidential campaign, when they routinely affiliated him with the fiery pastor at his Trinity United Church of Chicago, liberation theologist Jeremiah Wright. Likewise, when former First Lady Michelle Obama adopted a confrontational rhetorical style on the campaign trail in 2008, conservative pundits depicted her as an "angry black woman," a gendered version of the same "black militant" stereotype. Her anger was a race-specific attitude problem, not an authentic expression of her sense of morality or deep personal concern for her own vision of "the folks." Michelle Obama had a "chip on her shoulder," or so Tucker Carlson and other conservatives insisted.[40]

In the next chapter, I illustrate how Fox News hosts build their populist media personas by displaying their affinity for things like sports, country music, and chain restaurants, but before doing so let us explore how race factors into political performances of working-class taste.

The working class in the United States is culturally segmented by race in much the same way it is by economics.[41] This fact means that nonwhite politicians face difficulties in performing a working-class identity through taste-based appeals. As much as any president before him, Obama engaged popular culture to increase his likability; most notably, he reached out to artists in the hip-hop industry, an African-American influenced sector of mass entertainment for which none of his predecessors had ever shown an appreciation. On Fox News, such moves were not treated as signs of Obama's down-to-earth nature. Instead, Bill O'Reilly and other conservative pundits harshly criticized Obama for supporting what they deemed to be "over-sexualized" and "harmful entertainment."[42] From Fox News' white conservative gaze, hip-hop was mostly read as "ghetto" – or to use O'Reilly's language, as "gangsta" – meaning that for the Fox gaze, hip-hop's "menacing" racial codings completely overwhelmed and erased its class cultural qualities.[43]

---

[40] Zieber (January 12, 2012).   [41] Cosgrove, 1984; Kelley, 1996; Alvarez, 2008.

[42] USAhistorywriter (March 11, 2014).

[43] In Bill O'Reilly's long tenure at Fox News, hip-hop culture and hip-hop artists were recurrent objects of O'Reilly's moral outrage. He has a storied career of going after hip-hop artists from Ludicrous to Eminem to Nas to Cameron to Jay-Z, just to name just a few. His on-air battles with rap artists have been chronicled by various hip-hop magazines and blogs. See Berry (April 19, 2017); Ozzi (January 23, 2015); Soundbitten (December 20, 2002).

The white liberal view of black music, while "positive" in being read as "hip," still complicates attempts by African-American politicians to use black culture as a populist political resource. Too often white liberals treat hip-hop as a "distinction"-oriented (Bourdieu, 1984), trend-driven musical form, one which follows a long historical pattern whereby bohemian whites (i.e. "hipsters") use black music to be transgressive and to *distinguish* themselves from other white groups that they perceive as less culturally savvy (e.g. "yuppies," "rednecks," older Americans).[44] Hence, neither the liberal nor conservative white gaze imagines hip-hop as "ordinary" or "traditional," even though this sample-based musical form is *literally* built on nostalgia and homages to past musical generations.[45] Meanwhile, country music, because of its white racial orientation, is given the type of *traditionalist* cultural cache that is so vital to political populism, even though musicologically-speaking, modern country music shares as much with its 1920's "hillbilly" ancestor as hip-hop does with blues and jazz from the same era.

When evaluating the gendered dimensions of political communication, we find equally striking double-standards. For example, when former Republican House Speaker John Boehner cried on-camera, which he did on various occasions, conservative media depicted it as a demonstration of his compassion, and, at a deeper level, his *moral leadership*. But when a liberal female politician has done the same thing, it was more often read as weak or manipulative, as was the case when Hillary Clinton was accused of "fake crying" at a campaign stop in New Hampshire in 2008.

Or consider if an aspiring woman news anchor introduced herself the same way Glenn Beck (another conservative figure known for crying in public) did in one of his first episodes on Fox News. Beck told the audience, "I'm not a journalist. I'm just a dad. I'm a guy who loves his country. And I think you are very much the same with me" (February 6, 2009). Ten days later, Beck *situated* his journalistic authority in the same

---

[44] For a historical perspective on the connection between white bohemia and black culture, specifically, white appropriation of black styles of masculinity, see Eric Lott, *Love & Theft* (1993), chapter 2, specifically Lott's critical analysis of Norman Mailer's famous 1957 essay "The White Negro" (56–57).

[45] Victoria Johnson argues something similar in her analysis of Midwestern-themed sitcoms like *Roseanne* and *The Ellen Show*. Her analysis insightfully problematizes how the white, culturally "square" characters in these shows consistently treat black culture and queer culture as "hip," and, thus, as something that exists outside or apart from rural, working-class communities in the Midwest. See "chapter 5: There is no 'Dayton Chic'": Queering the Midwest in Roseanne, Ellen and the Ellen Show in *Heartland TV* (2008).

way. Casting his eyes downward to one side, he began to scratch the back of his neck as if to suggest both deep contemplation and nervousness typical of anticipating one's personal and difficult disclosure: "I'm just a dad. I'm a schmo," Beck confesses. "I was a deejay in 2000. I didn't [graduate college] ... I'm a self-educated guy. So take everything I say with a grain of salt" (December 16, 2009).

The power of Beck's statement rests on the gendered stereotype that, as a man and TV host, Beck is *not* "just a dad." He is a political leader and breadwinner (Lorber, 1994). As Liesbet van Zoonen writes, "male politicians may show their private lives to suggest that they are complete human beings combining caring and working responsibilities" (2006: 298). However, as van Zoonen explains, citing one's personal life to enhance one's public persona – something critical to populist political styles – carries far more hazards for women politicians than it does for men. If women public figures do not reveal their sensuality and/or "private" domestic life enough, they risk being painted as cold, uncaring, and careerist – think Hillary Clinton or Germany's Prime Minister Angela Merkel. On the other hand, if women emphasize their physical beauty and roles as mothers, they risk not being taken "seriously" as political leaders – public service roles that are dispositionally and structurally precoded as masculine.

THE FEMININE POPULISM OF CONSERVATIVE WOMEN

No matter how circumscribed the range of acceptable political styles may be for women politicians and media figures, women pundits on Fox News, and now beyond, have demonstrated that the technocratic, "professional class" style Democratic women tend to prefer is not the only option. Pundits such as Ann Coulter, Michelle Malkin, and Laura Ingraham, and rising stars such as Tomi Lahren, Dana Loesch, and Fox's Judge Jeanine Pirro all exhibit the same confrontational rhetorical style as their male counterparts in the conservative talk industry. Paradoxically, these women pair this aggressive style with an always present but unacknowledged hyper-feminine appearance (low-cut dresses, shoulder length hair – usually blond, hourglass figures, expensive jewelry, subtle but intensive makeup, bright and soft lighting, etc.). This illusion of effortless beauty plays into a conservative aesthetic politics.

In other words, female Fox hosts look the part of the conservative ideology they promote, an ideology that champions "traditional" patriarchal marriage and stresses the naturalness (i.e. rightness) of gender differences. "We're [men and women] not biologically the same," the former co-host of Fox's *The Five* Andrea Tantaros writes in her anti-feminist book *Tied Up in Knots: How Getting What We Wanted Made Women Miserable* (2016), but, she insists, "this should be a source of strength" (2016: 231). Sadly ironic, just after Tantaros published her book, she, like many other women at Fox, filed sexual harassment charges against Fox executives Roger Ailes and Bill Shine. Having a more feminist institutional culture could have guarded against such behavior, but this butts up against a very long tradition whereby conservative women attack feminism as a way to prove their ideological bona fides within the movement.

As Elinor Burkett recounts in her book *The Right Women* (1998), the 104th Congress of 1994 (the "Republican Revolution") toasted talk radio host Rush Limbaugh at an event broadcasted on C-Span. This congressional class included seven freshman Republican woman – up until that point, the highest number ever elected in a single year. Representing the seven women, Rep. Barbara Cubin of Wyoming presented Limbaugh with a honorary plaque, which read: "Rush was Right." She assured him and the crowd, "There's not a femi-nazi among us," using the radio host's notorious slur for liberal feminists. Of course, the anti-feminist politics of conservative women has a long history that goes back to the grassroots conservative women activists of the Barry Goldwater for President movement in Orange County, California during the 1960s (McGirr, 2001) and to Phyllis Schlafly's crusade against the Equal Rights Amendment and Anita Bryant's fight to save traditional family values from the "scourge" of homosexuality during the 1970s.[46] Yet the ideology of conservative women pundits on Fox News does not entirely explain their gender performance strategies.

Most commentary about the notorious short skirts of Fox News' female pundits and the significant number of former models and beauty pageant contestants that Fox has employed make the obvious point about how this functions as "eye candy" for the male segments of Fox's audience. However, few have considered how this programming tactic operates as a *feminine* representational mode for communicating Fox's

---

[46] There is a significant body on literature on the role that women activists have played in the postwar conservative movement. For a good introduction, see Spruill, 2008. Gender and America's Right Turn. In B. J. Schulman & J. E. Zelizer (eds.), *Rightward Bound: Making America Conservative in the 1970s*. Cambridge, MA: Harvard University Press. Other notable references include: McGirr, 2001; Critchlow, 2006; Moreton, 2010.

lowbrow cultural politics, one that is directed at the network's women viewers, who are, in fact, the dominant audience segment according to a Pew 2012 study. As Sarah Banet-Weiser's analysis of American beauty pageants demonstrates, women who "*overdo* [my emphasis] their performance of femininity: 'they' wear too much makeup and clothes that are garish and too tight" are often stereotyped by other pageant contestants as being working class or as a part of a nonwhite subculture, social groups who are "presumed to lack both taste and style" (1999: 82). Sociologist Pierre Bourdieu has gone as far to argue that body image is in fact "the most indisputable materialization of class taste" (1984:190), and taste, as I stress in Chapter 3, is inexorably entangled with social constructions of intelligence, something muscular "meat head" men and "girly girl" women are perceived to lack.

Laurie Ouellette's analysis of Helen Brown's editorial takeover of *Cosmopolitan* magazine in the 1960s provides yet another way to understand the class logic underlying the hyper-feminine style of women pundits on Fox. On the surface, the magazine's politics in the 1960s and 1970s was anything but conservative. It supported women working outside the home, questioned compulsory motherhood, promoted the use of birth control, and, most notably, it challenged Victorian taboos against premarital sex and female sexual pleasure. On these grounds, liberal feminists applauded the magazine. What they took severe issue with, however, was how the magazine counseled women on how to use their "looks" as a means of upward mobility. This discourse, Ouellette makes clear, inevitably "legitimated sexism and the capitalist exploitation of women's labor" (1999: 360). Nevertheless, she astutely recognizes Helen Brown's advice on how to *strategically* use one's feminine sexuality resonated with working-class woman in a way the mainstream feminist movement and upscale women's magazines like *Ms.* did not. "[T]o women who found themselves taking on new roles as breadwinners, but who lacked the wages, education, professional skills and social opportunities to recognize themselves in more conventional, male-oriented upward mobility narratives," the "success myth" of the Cosmo Girl, Ouellette writes, "seemed more attractive and even more feasible" (377).

On Fox News, both the hedonist and class-based elements of its female pundits' sexual performative tactics are often paradoxically reframed as a religiously inflected affirmation of "traditional" demarcated gender roles (i.e. patriarchal heteronormativity). However, this same performance trait implicitly works, I suggest, as an attempt by Fox News to create a *feminine* point of identification within its political narratives about class and liberal cultural elitism. The former Alaska governor and 2008 vice presidential candidate Sarah Palin may be the best modern archetype of this feminine brand of conservative populism. Palin, a onetime Fox News contributor, was also a beauty pageant contestant in the mid-1980s.[47] This background is reflected in her ultra-feminine dress and body image, a femininity she reinforces by rhetorically stressing her role as a mother, as she has described herself as a "mama grizzly" who, like all strong conservative women, voraciously "protects her cubs." And like other conservative woman populists, Palin has combined this assertive femininity with a confrontational rhetorical style and white working-class taste politics. Hunting, snowmobiling and country music comprise some of her favorite cultural reference points.

From a strictly stylistic perspective, Sarah Palin and current President Donald Trump are quite similar. Recognizing the compatibility of their respective political brands and shared political constituencies, Trump made a public appearance with Palin in New York during her failed 2011–2012 presidential campaign (the "One Nation" tour). Returning the favor, Palin shared a stage with Trump in January 2016 to endorse him on the eve of the Iowa Republican primary. Palin and Trump have both used a free-flowing speaking style that, in departing from conventional, highly scripted political speech, carries a colloquial feel. Both of them have moved between the political field and reality television field and have shrewdly used the sensational qualities of this "low" TV genre to garner political publicity. Lastly, with both figures, their populist political performances critically involved exaggerating their gender identity. Yet, supporting the larger point of this section, Trump was politically rewarded for this whereas Palin was ultimately punished.

As a politician, Palin was no more ineloquent, unknowledgeable, or gaffe-proof as Trump. Yet the Republican Party has mostly treated her as a feminine, working-class token. The same party, by contrast, nominated Trump as their figurehead. Palin's *embodied femininity* undeniably skewed how the public, including members of her own political community, assessed her "legitimacy" as a presidential candidate. Hillary Clinton's wonkish political style may have hurt her likability and

---

[47] In the 1984, Palin competed in the Miss Alaska pageant placing third. In 1989, former *Fox & Friends* co-host Gretchen Carlson was crowned Miss America. Carlson was the first major Fox News employee and star to break silence about sexual harassment within the Fox News workplace, harassment primarily, but not exclusively, perpetrated by Fox's founding CEO Roger Ailes.

Obama's educated disposition may have diminished his appeal with the white working class. Nevertheless, the professional-class performance strategy they mutually shared helped ensure they would at least be treated as "serious" candidates, a baseline prerequisite for political competition. By not having to work against historic stereotypes, white, male political communicators do not have to invest so much energy in proving their institutional "competence" and middle-class "propriety." This frees them up to elaborate and display their personal, emotional self and cushions them when they break the normal rules of political "respectability," rules Trump has transgressed in historically unprecedented ways (e.g. "pussy-gate").

3

"I'm a Blue-Collar Guy"

How Fox News Hosts Imagine Themselves and Their Audience as Working Class

The language of the *Daily Mirror* is neither a pure construction of Fleet Street "newspeak" nor is it the language which its working-class readers actually speak. It is a highly complex species of linguistic *ventriloquism* in which the debased brutalism of popular journalism is skillfully combined and intricate with some elements of the directness and vivid particularity of working-class language.

—Stuart Hall, 1981[1]

The October 6, 2010 episode of *The O'Reilly Factor*, host Bill O'Reilly made his often-repeated charge that President Barack Obama does not understand the white working class. O'Reilly had begun the program citing recent poll numbers showing how white workers without college degrees favored Republicans over Democrats. The rest of the segment was spent positing why this was so. O'Reilly said that one could explain the poll numbers by the economic downturn. He notably added, however, that "minority workers [who support Obama] are apprehensive as well, so there must be more to this." O'Reilly continued:

"Talking Points Memo" believes it is a *class factor* [my emphasis]. President Obama and the Democrats are simply not in sync with white working-class values ... Now the liberal media would have you believe that white working-class Americans are opposing Mr. Obama because of his skin color. That is a blatant lie. While there are bigots in every group, it is the cultural disposition of the president. That is his problem now ... the liberal media ignores the cultural aspect of Mr. Obama ... Now, the liberal media is going to overlook the cultural aspect of Obama's declining poll numbers because it, itself, looks down on working-class Americans.

[1] Hall (1998).

With the line about the "liberal media" looking "down on working-class Americans," we see how Fox programs thread and articulate their "liberal media bias" stories with populist themes. But how do we make sense of the claim that "class" had been the main "factor" driving the white working-class' alienation with the Democrats and Obama, when at the same time O'Reilly was offering a counter-intuitive argument that by "class" he had not been referring to economics but to a "cultural aspect"? What was O'Reilly actually referring to when he talked about working-class "wisdom," "values," and "cultural disposition"?

Looking at some of the political positions O'Reilly associated with working-class culture in the course of the episode – positions such as illegal immigration and the ground zero mosque – one might conclude that O'Reilly was really talking about *white* culture when he championed working-class culture. This episode, as well as many other episodes O'Reilly would host, gives plenty of support for an interpretation that he constructs the identity of the white working class in contradistinction to racial minorities and those whom he would target as foreign threats. For this reason, an "intersectional" lens (Crenshaw, 1989) is indispensable for analyzing Fox News' representation of class. Indeed, as discussed in the previous chapter and in subsequent chapters, Fox's populist imagination of its audience is fundamentally entwined with race and gender-based identifications. However, an analysis treating the appeals of O'Reilly or other Fox pundits to "class" as being either a *complete* stand-in for whiteness or masculinity or being just a symptom of "false-consciousness," abdicates a genuine attempt to understand how conservative media figures represent the working class *in terms of class* rather than merely serving as a mask or substitution for another identity. It is, I argue, this constant invocation of class that gives Fox News' political narratives their bite and moral power.

Now, a liberal or leftist reader may scoff at this idea. If anything, they might say, Fox News, like conservative political thought itself, downplays, if not completely denies the existence of class inequality in the United States. Rejecting this position, some leftist critics, most notably Thomas Frank, have argued that the populist rhetoric of the right is, indeed, an attempt by conservatives to speak the language of social class. In *What's the Matter with Kansas?* (2004) (WMK), populism is the central answer to Frank's core question about why the white working class predominantly votes Republican even though, he argues, it is a vote that works against their own economic interest. In WMK, Frank details how conservatives in the W. Bush era reinvented populism as a political discourse that exploited cultural wedge issues based on region, religion and taste. This *cultural* mode of populism encourages, Frank writes, "class hostility and simultaneously denies the economic basis of the grievance" (113).

I applaud WMK for breathing new life into questions about class and politics and for acknowledging how class is a *felt* category of identity for many Americans, including conservatives. It is not enough, however, to identify the classed dimension of conservative populism. *How* one approaches it once identified is as important as whether or not one approaches it in the first place. WMK mostly overlooks the racial and gendered aspects of conservative populism even though such characteristics are, to say the least, vital to understanding how conservative political discourse imagines the working-class majority. WMK also lends support to the "false consciousness" arguments that Stuart Hall and other Gramscian scholars have vigorously problematized (Grossberg, 1992; Bérubé, 2009). False consciousness is a Marxist concept that describes how workers buy into the values and mythologies of capitalism. This leads them to misrecognize their own economic class interest and to identify politically with the business class and the wealthy instead. Hence, they vote not as workers but as future business owners and *pre*-rich citizens. This frame of analysis has informed leftist explanations for working-class conservatism from as far back as Werner Sombart's 1905 essay "Why is there no socialism in the United States?"

To be fair, Thomas Frank has always placed far more blame for the conservative capture of the white working class on the Democratic Party's lack of a pro-working-class agenda than on the mystified political thinking of conservative voters. This is a particular point in his most recent book *Listen, Liberal* (2016). Nevertheless, WMK's culture-for-economics substitution thesis has helped perpetuate a false dichotomy whereby economic distinctions are treated as "real" class factors and cultural distinctions are seen as "fake" ones. Or the latter are, at least, treated as window dressing when compared to the "hard" economic factors of wealth and property. As a result, many liberals continue to believe that a full-throated support of "economic populist" *materialist-distributive policies* is all that is needed to defeat the cultural populist *identity politics* of the right.[2] This line of thinking underappreciates both the stylistic-

---

[2] For a good overview of the debate concerning distribution-based critiques of neoliberalism verses identity-based critiques, see the Introduction of Lisa Duggan's 2003 book *Twilight of Equality?: Neoliberalism, Cultural Politics, and the Attack on Democracy.*

performative dimension of populist social movements and the significant ways in which class identity *is* shaped by culture.[3]

As Pierre Bourdieu's work has shown, the cultural aspects of class are far from sociological fluff. His foundational book *Distinction* (1984) challenges the narrow, economistic class schemas of orthodox Marxism and provides a comprehensive theory of class that illustrates how taste and labor, education and income, and subjective identity and objective condition represent different moments of the same overarching process of class differentiation. Without the cultural components of class, Bourdieu explains, the fluctuations and recurrent crises of capitalist economies would make it difficult to maintain familial dynasties and class patterns across generations. Cultural and educational inheritance, or what he calls "cultural capital," is what gives economic inheritance a longer lasting power than it would have otherwise.

Bourdieu's research shows how class domination does in fact occur through the educational system, through expertise and credentials, through aesthetic self-presentation and other symbolic practices, all things Fox's anti-elitist programming discourse highlights and politicizes. "There are people who really, really despise [Fox News]," Bill O'Reilly told one guest in an episode of *The O'Reilly Factor*, "and they do what?" he asks. "Most of them are television critics. You know, there are a lot of academics, a lot of professors, high-school teachers, things like that" (October 7, 2009). Though high school teachers and professors have drastically different socioeconomic positions than Hollywood celebrities and powerful politicians, Fox's programming accentuates their common association with *cultural prestige* in order to represent them as members of the same elite social group.

Drawing upon Bourdieu and the work of other cultural sociologists such as Michèle Lamont, the textual examples I provide in this chapter strive to show how Fox News' populist representation of society does express *some* meaningful class differences. If it did not, it would be hard to imagine how Fox's most familiar names like Bill O'Reilly and Sean Hannity could have been so effective at building working-class media personas. The true ideological maneuver of Fox News' populist strategy is not to swap "real" class grievances with "fake" ones, but rather to offer a strategically limited conception of class hierarchy in America that

---

[3] See Bourdieu, 1984; Gans, 1999; Lamont, 2000; Bettie, 2003; Skeggs, 2004.

foregrounds *real* class-cultural inequalities in order to obscure *real* economic ones. While Fox News' representation of class is deceptive for concealing the market's role in creating social inequalities, liberals and Democrats should nonetheless pay close attention to the aspects of Fox News' populist media style that do make compelling class identifications.

THE SOCIAL LOGIC OF ANTI-ELITISM

Bourdieuian concepts such as "disposition" and "gaze" elucidate the underlying social logics that guide how different classes evaluate each other's cultural practices and consumer choices. While professional class taste is geared toward what Bourdieu calls a *principle of distinction*, working-class taste is guided by a *principle of conformity* – meaning it is oriented toward cultural products that *conform* to the "popular aesthetic." This aesthetic, he writes, favors "homogeneous experience and social collectivity" over individualism. In working-class communities, Bourdieu explains, there is no greater sin than for a member to act, dress, and speak as if he or she were something special. Attempts to distinguish oneself through cultural markers are seen as a repudiation of one's class-familial background. "[T]he son of a bourgeois who breaks with his family is favourably regarded [i.e. praised for being an individual], whereas a worker's son who does the same thing is condemned" (381).[4] Bourdieu's "conformity" versus "distinction" schema offers a useful analytical framework for grasping the slippery, non-economic vision of class that Fox News' anti-elitist rhetoric propagates.

Bourdieu gleaned his insights about the connection between class and taste from the empirical research he conducted in his home country of France. In *The Dignity of Working Men* (2000), Michèle Lamont demonstrates how similar class-cultural dynamics exist in the United States. Like their French counterparts, American workers tend to adhere to the *conformity* principle, seeing attempts to dress and talk uncommonly as something "fake" or "pretentious." Moreover, Lamont shows how the expression of anti-elitist attitudes and the very act of rejecting

---

[4] Conversely, as Stephanie Lawler's research has shown, bourgeois, middle class identity is centrally constructed through expressions of "disgust" for working-class tastes (2005). For an excellent Bourdieusian overview and analysis of American taste politics, particularly in regard to music, see Nadine Hubbs' 2014 book *Rednecks, Queers, and Country Music*, pp. 15–18.

distinguishing cultural practices functions, in itself, as an important way to signal one's working-class membership and reinforce "class homophily" overall (108–109).

But there are limits to the applicability of Bourdieu's Franco-centric class analysis to the US context. As Lamont points out, Bourdieu's model does not account for the way in which national *moral* discourses particular to American culture shape how workers conceptualize social hierarchy (2000: 9). The deeper cultural penetration of market ideology in the US predisposes the American working class to more readily accept market-based definitions of meritocracy, which in turn leads this class to be less critical of the business class and of the wealthy. French workers, by contrast, express greater hostility toward the rich and a deeper solidarity with the poor. However, while French workers tend to be more skeptical of market-based inequalities, they are more likely to accept class inequalities based on "cultural distinctions and cultural capital" (220). American workers, by contrast, refuse to see themselves as intellectually inferior to those who surpass them in "high" cultural knowledge, education and credentials. As such, the American working class more vigorously *contests* the merit of cultural class markers. Lamont attributes the relative absence of anti-cultural elitist discourse among French workers to the French higher educational system, attributing its greater presence among American workers to the national "cultural repertoires" she associates with "populism."

Two of the most predominant populist rhetorics of class that Fox News has appropriated are *cultural populism* and *producerism*. While Chapter 4 spotlights the latter, this chapter will engage the former. The following section offers a genealogy of cultural populism that illustrates how this substrain of the populist rhetorical tradition has historically expressed the *conformity principle* of working-class taste cultures. The subsequent textual analysis sections strive to show how cultural populism entails more than the simple praising of popular culture's democratic virtue and the repudiation of highbrow culture as scholars such as cultural studies theorist Jim McGuigan (1992) and historian Michael Kazin (1998) have suggested. These sections highlight how this discourse involves the embodied performance of particular aesthetic and epistemological dispositions. I argue that cultural populism, at least as it is used by conservative media figures, is better understood as an elaborate *political* discourse that articulates, in a variety of representational forms, an informal theory of class as a cultural identity.

THE "SILENT MAJORITY" VERSUS THE "NEW CLASS": HOW THE CONSERVATIVE MOVEMENT REDEFINED CLASS IN AMERICA

The term "populism" originally derived from the third-party movement called the People's Party or Populist Party, which was formally established in 1892. This movement was primarily known for its anti-monopoly political economic themes (see Chapter 4). However, the Populist movement also had a class-cultural politics that is often forgotten. This politics becomes apparent when we contrast the People's Party to another political movement that was ascendant in the late nineteenth century: the Progressive movement. Partly a political response to the ills of industrial capitalism, the Progressive movement and its reformers expressed many of the same societal critiques against political corruption, corporate power and wealth inequality that had been so central to the Populists. But while the Progressives believed their "hopes for social progress lay specifically in advanced formal education," the rank-and-file farmers and artisans of the Populist movement, as historian William Hogeland has argued, "deemed advanced formal education and its resulting expertise [as] tools for keeping ordinary people out of the halls of power" (2010). "[O]ne of the hottest blasts of populist rhetoric," Hogeland stressed, "was directed less at specific policies than at elites' dismissal of ordinary people's judgments" (para. 16). This is the essence of what I'm calling *cultural populism*.

At its most basic level, cultural populism is a type of political discourse that champions the common wisdom, taste, and intellectual capacities of everyday people, and denounces justifications for power based on credentials and elite cultural knowledge. Like all forms of populist rhetoric, this discourse presents a narrative of societal conflict between the controllers of the dominant institutions and those being marginalized *by* them (Canovan 1981). What distinguishes cultural populism from the economic and religious strands of the populist rhetorical tradition is how the former also specifically targets and vilifies social groups and institutions associated with high educational capital and/or cultural prestige.

William Jennings Bryan, the leader and figurehead of the Populist Party, was known for his religious, "Social Gospel" politics and his bromides against corporate monopolies. Yet while he passionately condemned the unchristian nature of "plutocratic wealth," he also expressed weariness about what he called "the aristocracy of learning." During the

Scope's "Monkey" Trial in the early twentieth century, Bryan took a more belligerent position toward formal education and credentialed expertise (Bryan, 1913: 362), after which his populist themes got an added boost in the age of electronic media with the help of populist radio personalities such as Father Coughlin, William Henderson Jr., and Dr. John Brinkley. In a mixture that seems quite strange to modern eyes, this cohort of populist radio broadcasters renewed Bryan's rhetorical blend of religious conservatism and leftist anti-corporate politics, with each, like Bryan, taking a hostile stance against educated professionals. This hostility was not simply an effect of what historian Richard Hofstadter might call their "paranoid style"; these populist radio hosts would actually be forced off the airwaves by professional associations such as the Federal Radio Commission (FRC) and American Medical Association.[5]

While cultural populist forms of political discourse were a significant part of nineteenth-century and early twentieth-century political discourse, for the most part this brand of populism had been overshadowed by producerist and Evangelical, religious strains of populism (Kazin, 1998: 4). However, the postwar period did turn out to be one of the most generative moments of anti-cultural elitist discourse in American political history. By the mid-twentieth century, the word "elite" had started to take on a new set of meanings. In his etymology of the word, cultural theorist Raymond Williams traced how "elite" would gradually move away from its previous association with "natural leadership" toward a more pejorative connotation. He stressed that not only did "elite," "elitist," and "elitism" become associated with snobbish attitudes and social practices, but simultaneously it had also started to suggest a hostility toward those educational *institutions* seen as producing and guaranteeing the existence of social elites (1985: 112–115). From the 1950s to the 1970s, key developments, such as the unprecedented explosion of higher education, the transition from an industrial to a post-industrial economy (Bell, 1973), and the rise of knowledge-producing occupations (notably, in the field of information technology) would facilitate this discursive shift.

Before World War II, only 14% of college-age Americans were enrolled at a university. By 1961, this number had shot up to 38% and by 1970 the percent of college-aged youth attending college reached an

---

[5] For scholarship on Father Coughlin, see Brinkley, 1982; Kazin, 1998: chapter 5. For work on William Anderson Jr., see Vaillant, 2004. For research on Dr. John Brinkley, see Frank, 2004: 196–199; Lee, 2002.

astonishing 50% (Burner, 1996: 136).[6] According to sociologist Robert Wuthnow, the partial massification of higher education in the postwar era shifted "the very basis of the social order" by making higher education, more than ever before, a major means of "stratifying the society into different *subcultures*" [my emphasis] (1988: 163).[7] The rapid growth of higher education and the increased importance of a college degree in the labor market significantly altered the patterned distribution of educational capital in the United States. All these developments would create deep cultural wedges within the broad middle class. As such, the growth of the professional class and the *middlebrow* sensibility (see Chapter 1) that had defined its taste culture predictably became an object of class resentment and, by extension, a useful target in the political arena.

It is in this period where a new populist breed of conservative politician emerges. In the 1950s and 1960s, figures like Senator Joseph McCarthy and Alabama governor George Wallace would help fashion an anti-government brand of populism that would transform the meaning of "the elites" and "the fat cats" from the "economic royalists" embodied by FDR's version of the private sector to the "twisted intellectuals" embodied by McCarthy's version of the bureaucratic state. During the Red Scare of the 1950s, McCarthy had placed educated elites at the center of his communist conspiracy. Along with his purging the socialist intellectual camp from the Democratic Left (leaving only a social scientific and Keynesian one in its place), McCarthy's anticommunist crusade laid the groundwork for conservative populism's cultural-educational vision of the elite.

In the 1960s, Alabama governor and third party presidential candidate George Wallace picked up where McCarthy left off and described the elites as "pseudo-intellectuals." Like McCarthy, Wallace was skilled at using electronic media and interviews to create confrontational exchanges with network journalists to gain notoriety. By playing the role of the straight-talking common man who says what is on his mind in the face of polished Northeastern journalists, Wallace would endear himself to many Americans and gain a national visibility (Kazin 1998: 232). Rightfully known for his racist, segregationist politics, Wallace's astute sense of

---

[6] In *New Industrial State* (2007), John Kenneth Galbraith cites another interesting statistic that tracks the growth of the professoriate in these years. In 1960, there were 381,000 professors in America; by 1972 there were 907,000 (350).

[7] From 1960 to 1970 the enrollment rate increased 139 percent and government expenditure rates altogether grew from only 5.6 billion in 1960 to 23.4 billion by 1970. For this data, see Wuthnow, 1988: 155–156.

class resentment based on taste and educational differences was another important feature of his political style. Wallace often interlaced white supremacist appeals with attacks on cultural elites and was able to wed these different types of politics together in an articulation that persists today. Historian Michael Kazin writes:

[Wallace's] main targets were powerful judges, "bureaucrats," and "theoreticians" who wanted to foist "absurd" blueprints for change on average men and women. That many of those blueprints were attempts to aid black people was an essential element in the resistance mounted against them. But so was a widening cultural gulf between European-Americans that had as much to do with differences of class and with moral judgments as it did with their opinion about the rights of African-Americans.

(1998: 233–234)

Wallace's notion of "foisting" over-intellectualized, "utopian" schemes onto ordinary people offered a useful rhetorical frame for subsequent conservative populists. Differing from the anti-corporate focus of radio populists like Coughlin and Henderson, this rhetorical combination rationalized anti-elitist cultural politics with free-market ideology. In the New Deal era, the Progressive idea of a "positive state" was seen as a necessary corrective to the inhumane, uncaring quality of the market. In contrast, by wielding the newly acquired weapon of populism, the postwar conservative movement became increasingly successful at presenting government intervention as an act of elitism itself, an affront to traditional knowledge and common sense.

McCarthy and Wallace's story of a captured government directed by an educated elite would establish conservative populism's central story line. As Nicole Hemmer shows in *Messengers of the Right* (2016), the intellectual strata of the conservative movement was as invested in this narrative as their populist counterparts were. The specter of the intellectual statist formed the foundation of their "elite populist" alliance. The analysis of power put forth by top conservative intellectuals such as Friedrich Hayek, William F. Buckley, Irving Kristol, and Milton Friedman all commonly hinged on the notion of a "New Class."[8] Ironically, conservatives had taken this term from left-leaning scholars concerned with

---

[8] For an overview of leftist critiques on the New Class, see chapter 3 in Stanley Aronowitz's 1992 book *The Politics of Identity: Class, Culture, Social Movements*. Also see Barry Briggs-Bruce's chapter "An Introduction to the Idea of the New Class" in *The New Class?* (1979). Additionally, Alvin Gouldner's *The Future of the Intellectuals and the Rise of the New Class* (1979).

how a growing professional-managerial class was using technocratic methods to discipline workers. Of course, conservative thinkers would take *out* the anti-corporate element of the term and instead emphasize those professional groups who wielded influence through government and major cultural institutions, such as the media and higher education. As histories on conservative think tanks document, the 1970s and 1980s was a crucial building period for the conservative knowledge establishment. This intellectual project would share populism's oppositional consciousness – meaning the picture it painted was mostly defined in negative terms, as a struggle *against* what historian Alice O'Connor refers to as the liberal "philanthropic-government-academic establishment" (2007: 75).

This elite–populist compact, however, has been and continues to be precarious. At times, its class contradictions bubble to the surface and threaten to undermine the intellectual–populist coalition. In the same way the *National Review* had opposed both the cultural populist candidate Donald Trump in the 2016 presidential election and vice presidential candidate Sarah Palin in the 2008 election, so too had this longstanding hub of conservative intellectual thought vigorously opposed George Wallace during the Nixon years. The paper's founder William F. Buckley and his colleagues had feared that Wallace's appeal to working-class taste could mutate and grow into larger, economic class resentments (Williamson, 1978).

Nixon advisor Kevin Phillips, however, unlike Buckley, valued Wallace's populist style and understood its importance to the advancement of the conservative movement. Wallace, Phillips recognized, was able to do what most conservative politicians had been incapable of doing up until that point, which was to forge cultural bonds between the white working class and the Republican Party. Phillips believed that if Wallace's cultural-political style could be replicated by mainstream Republican candidates, the Republican Party could shed its country club image and blunt its reputation as the party of the rich, a reputation that had been repelling workers from the party for decades.

As part of their attempt to capture the working-class base of the Democratic Party in the 1968 and 1972 presidential elections, Richard Nixon, Kevin Phillips, and other key Nixon strategists, such as Pat Buchanan and future Fox News CEO Roger Ailes, would incorporate Wallace's cultural populist narrative and style into Nixon's representational strategy. The combined strategic elements only needed some fine tuning to better suit mainstream politics. On the one hand, Nixon's representational strategy could occlude the extreme qualities, like McCarthy's conspiratorial anticommunism and Wallace's *overt* racism (while taking advantage of the civil rights movement's accompanying white backlash to masquerade Nixon's state's rights arguments with "law-and-order" rhetoric and pro-segregationist positions). On the other hand, the strategy would still be able to accentuate the most popular aspects of these early conservative populist prototypes.

One distinctive element the Nixon administration added to its cultural populism was its featuring of journalists as central players in the imagination of the cultural elite. They became the "nattering nabobs of negativism," as Nixon's combative Vice President Spiro Agnew would famously cast them. A second innovation of the Nixon administration was in its aligning of its populist *political* strategy with the *culturally* populist sectors of the entertainment industry. Like Wallace, the Nixon administration found it could appeal to white working-class tastes by reaching out to, and campaigning through, the country music industry.[9] For example, not only had Nixon been the first US president to visit the Grand Ole Opry, which is country's music's most hallowed institution; in 1973, Nixon would invite country star Merle Haggard to perform his anti-"counter-culture" anthem "Okie From Muskogee" at the White House itself.

Country music's systematic exclusion from the coastal-dominated pop music market in its formative early years had already burned an anti-elitist cultural politics into the genre. The name "Grand Ole Opry" was itself a tongue-and-cheek jab at bourgeois taste in its playing with the term *Grand Opera* (Malone, 2002: 75). When the Republican Party aligned itself with the country music industry in the late 1960s and early 1970s, conservative politicians were largely adopting, rather than creating, the cultural enemies that the country music industry had been contesting since its commercial inception in the 1920s ("enemies" being media executives, academics, urbanites, and cultural critics). As country music historian Diane Pecknold has written, "Country music did not so much shift to the right as the right shifted to country, consciously seeking to transform an established marketing demographic into a political one" (2007: 219).

Through these representational practices, the Nixon administration and the Republican Party were able to construct a conservative populist identity they would christen the "Silent Majority." So while the descent of

---

[9] Kazin, 1998; Malone, 2002; Wilman, 2005; Feder, 2006; Pecknold, 2007; La Chapelle, 2007; Hubbs, 2014.

the labor movement and the rise of the New Right have often been interpreted by leftist critics as the absolute decline of class consciousness in United States (with Ronald F. Inglehart and Pippa Norris describing this as a turn toward "post-materialist" politics (2016), I would argue instead that the rise of conservative populism in this period would signal not the end of class consciousness in the United States but rather its transmutation into a cultural-educational formation. This transmutation was being made possible by the restructuring of the national economy and the growing culture and belief system of an expanding professional-educated social class who stood to *materially* benefit the most from the new high-tech, information economy and who, over time, had begun to *politically* think of itself as a class (Frank, 2016). As historian E.P Thompson has stressed, class must be understood as a relationship and not as a stand-alone social station. The identity of each class is fundamentally constructed through a struggle for position and status with other classes (1963). The introduction of a "New Class" such as this one, thus inevitably altered how other class factions in the United States would come to see themselves.

However, these conditions alone did not create this new cultural understanding of class. It was significantly *constructed* by conservative populists in discursive fields of media and politics. Conservative political actors made sense of the post-industrial economy by developing a compelling narrative of class conflict and with it, a theorization of class as a cultural identity. And the cultural populist strategy that had been freshly imagined by McCarthy and Wallace and refined by the Nixon administration has had an enduring impact on American political discourse, as evidenced by the fact that the practice of painting one's political adversary as a cultural elitist remains to this day a hallmark of American politics. While the cultural populist narrative and conceptualization of class would become important for future Republican political leaders, such as President George W. Bush, vice presidential candidate Sarah Palin and, most recently President Donald Trump, it would become the master codex for Fox News and the conservative talk media industry overall.

IS FOX NEWS' AUDIENCE WORKING CLASS?

The partisan audience strategies of the cable news field are undoubtedly informed by partisan–demographic alignments in the electorate, but they do not reflect them perfectly by any means. For example, the Fox News audience is actually more white than the already exceptionally white

Republican Party.[10] In terms of socioeconomic demographics, there is a fairly close parity between Fox News' audience and rank-and-file Republican voters. In the 2016 presidential election, Republicans outperformed Democrats in the middle-income group ($50,000–$99,000) while Democrats performed better among lower-income Americans ($30,000–$49,999) and the poor (less than $30,000).[11] The Republican slant of middle-income voters without college degrees in 2016 repeated a long historical pattern.[12]

This same socioeconomic group happens to be the heart of the cable news audience, whose median income approximates $62,000 (Pew, 2007).[13] According to Nielsen Media Research's third quarter analysis of 2009, the median household income of Fox News viewers is $53,000 a year.[14] In a 2010 Pew study, 61% of Fox's audience made *less* than $75,000 a year and 71% lacked a college degree.[15] A 2012 Pew study yielded similar findings with 64% making less than $75,000 and 76% without a college degree.[16] The socioeconomic demographics of CNN and MSNBC generally mirror Fox's. Thus, their audiences tend to be older and wealthier than the average Democratic voter, but, reflecting the Democratic political coalition, both networks have audiences that are more racially diverse and more educated than that of Fox News.[17]

The most recent Pew data indicates that MSNBC seems to be losing college-educated viewers, hence closing the historic education gap between its audience and Fox's (something I explored in the previous chapter). However, when one combines different Pew Research data sets

---

[10] Using Nielson's demographic statistics, in 2010, *New York Times*' Brian Skelter showed that a meager 1.38% of FNC's viewers are African American. In contrast, African Americans make up 20.7% of CNN's audience and 19.3% of MSNBC's. In the 2016 election, Trump received 8% of the African American vote and 29% of the Hispanic American vote, while Hillary received 88% of the African American vote and 65% of the Hispanic American vote. See Luhby & Agiesta (November 9, 2016); Shea (July 26, 2010).

[11] Huang et al. (November 8, 2016).

[12] In *The Tea Party and the Remaking of Republican Conservatism* (2012), Theda Skocpol and Vanessa Williamson document that the majority of the Tea Party movement was compromised by middle-income Americans (23). Also see Wallsten & Yadron (November 3, 2010).

[13] Pew Research Center (January 6, 2007).   [14] See Berr (January, 2011).

[15] Pew Research Center (September 12, 2010).

[16] Pew Research Center (September 27, 2012).

[17] In the 2016 presidential election, Republican candidate Donald Trump won every major demographic category of white voters save one glaring exception: college-educated whites. Cohen (March 1, 2018). For more data on the educational divide between liberals and conservatives, see Smith (April 26, 2016).

across several years, a clear pattern emerges. Of the three major cable news outlets, Fox News has consistently attracted the lowest number of viewers with college degrees.[18] Other studies, such as the 2008 National Annenberg Election Survey (NAES), have revealed a similar educational gap but refined the analysis by using "professional degree" as a way to measure how many professionals with postgraduate educations watch cable news. Liberal MSNBC outperformed Fox in this category by nearly a double digit margin (15% vs. 24%) (Levendusky, 2013: 13).

Several major "regression analysis" studies that have more thoroughly parsed the available audience data on cable news have consistently singled out "education level" as the demographic trait that distinguishes Fox's audience from MSNBC's and CNN's. A 2008 study by Barry A. Hollander uses cable news audience data ranging from 1998 to 2006 to show that "education was a negative predictor of exposure to Fox News but a positive predictor of exposure to CNN, broadcast television news, and news off the Internet" (2008: 32). A more recent 2017 regression study conducted by Gregory Martin and Ali Yurukoglu offers the most robust data sets on the cable news audience to date. Their study considers audience information that spans almost a decade of viewership (2000–2008) and synthesizes a highly diverse mix of sources from

---

[18] Here is a timeline of data on the percentage of college-graduates among the cable news audience. I took this data primarily from Pew surveys. Some surveys include audience demographic information on all three of the major cable networks and some only include Fox News and one other competitor.

> Year 2012: Fox News 24% vs. CNN 29% vs. MSNBC 26%
> Year 2010: Fox News 29% vs. CNN 34% vs. MSNBC 34%
> Year 2007: Fox News 22% vs. CNN 30%
> Year 2004: Fox News 21% vs. CNN 27% vs. MSNBC 28%

Fox News had consistently attracted the least number of college-educated viewers than CNN and MSNBC. The educational gaps between the three cable networks have varied over time and seem to be closing, especially between MSNBC and Fox News. In 2009, Fox News received a great deal of criticism for its full throated support of the conservative Tea Party protest movement. In response, the network started to tone down its populist style and began to more heavily foreground its "straight news" anchors such as Shepard Smith, Bret Baier and Chris Wallace (Sherman, 2014: 343–344). This attempt to shift to a more professional news style was especially evident with the incorporation of Megyn Kelly in the primetime lineup in 2013, which may help explain Fox's slight increase in college-educated viewers. However, as I discuss in the conclusion, Donald Trump's presidential campaign has complicated any attempt by the network to tone down or move away from its foundational tabloid-populist formula. For the demographic data featured in the timeline, see Pew Research Center (September 27, 2012); Pew Research Center (September 12, 2010); Johnston, 2008; Pew Research Center (April 15, 2007); Pew Research Center (June 8, 2004).

commercial ratings agencies like Nielsen and Mediamark to government and non-profit sources like Pew, NAES and Cooperative Congressional Election Study (CCES). Martin and Yurukoglu write that while "some attributes move viewership in the same direction for all [cable news] channels [MSNBC, CNN, and FNC]: older viewers, for instance...Other attributes have differential effects: *college education* [my emphasis] increases viewership of MSNBC but decreases it for FNC" (2587).[19]

In 2008, Fox News anchor Brit Hume said, "We [Fox News] appeal to white working-class voters."[20] Is this statement true in light of what we've learned from the audience data? The answer, of course, all depends on one's definition of the "white working class." When Hume made these comments, the national median income was $52,000.[21] While some like statisticians such as Nate Silver treat median income as a threshold for determining who is and who is not *economically* "working class," others such as Thomas Frank and University of California law professor Joan C. Williams vigorously dispute this class line as an overly narrow definition of the working class.[22]

---

[19] Lending more support to the findings of the Hollander (2008) and Martin & Yurukoglu's (2017) regression studies, an earlier regression analysis of Fox News made similar observations. Political scientists Stefano DellaVigna and Ethan Kaplan's groundbreaking 2005 study "The Fox News Effect" analyzed marketing demographic data on Fox News from the year 2000 and concluded that "the regular Fox News audience is significantly less educated than the rest of the population" (14). DellaVigna & Kaplan (May 10, 2005).

[20] Stelter (May 2, 2008).   [21] United States Census Bureau (September 2009).

[22] For example, this is the criterion that statistician and writer Nate Silver used to refute the common belief that Republican Donald Trump enjoyed significant support among the white working-class in the 2016 presidential election. In an article "The Mythology of Trump's Working Class' support" (2016), Silver cites polling data showing the median income of Trump supporters during the primaries to be $72,000. Because this number stands above the $56,000 national median of 2015, Silver maintains that Trump's base cannot be considered working-class. In her 2017 book *White Working-class: Overcoming Class Cluelessness in America*, University of California law professor Joan C. Williams challenges Silver's assumption that a household making $72,000 a year is excluded from the working class. According to her and economist Heather Boushey's socioeconomic schema, this number is actually "a bit below the median working-class income assuming the term to refer to 'working class' as neither rich nor poor ..." or "those with household incomes above the bottom 30% but below the top 20%." Silver (May 3, 2016); Williams, 2017.

In a 2016 American Political Science Association presentation entitled "What's the Matter with *What's the Matter with Kansas?* (2006), Larry Bartels challenged the claims of Thomas Frank's popular book *What's the Matter with Kansas?* (2004), namely the notion that the Democratic Party has a white working-class problem. He offers data that shows how white working-class voters are increasingly voting Democrat, not Republican. But this claim is only true if one accepts Bartels' quite narrow definition of the working

Measured strictly in terms of income, the working-class status of Fox's audience (many of whom are Trump supporters) is debatable. However, if one defines "working class" as the non-college educated, as many political scientists, sociologists and pollsters tend to do, then the majority of Fox's audience easily fits within this class group.[23] Of course, education level is not a perfect measurement of class. There are people with humble incomes who are highly educated, and wealthy people who never went to college. However, *in general*, there is a strong causal link between education and wealth (OECD, 2016). Moreover, unlike tax bracket measurements, which only gives a snap shot of an individual's income at one moment in their life-career stage, educational attainment tends to be a better predictor of both class origins and long-term life chances (Keister & Southgate, 2012). It also happens to be the strongest factor in determining marriage-partner selections in modern America,[24] a trend

class as those at the bottom third of the national distribution scale or who make less than $35,000 a year. In a rejoinder to Bartels entitled "Class is Dismissed" (2006), Frank writes sardonically, it is "well-known to poll-readers everywhere – that society's very poorest members tend to vote Democratic – [Bartels] simply switches the labels, claims that those poorest Americans are "the working class," and – hey presto! – declares the problem [of white working-class conservatism] solved" (3). Frank goes on to argue, "When white voters are broken down by income into quintiles *rather than thirds*, it becomes plain that the Republican Bush won [in 2004] every quintile except the very bottom, as an August, 2005 study by the Pew Research Center demonstrates." This included the "middle-income quintile" of $35,000–58,000. Bush won this group by an 8 point margin (36%–28%). See Bartels, Larry (September 1–4, 2005). What's the Matter with *What's the Matter with Kansas?* Prepared for presentation at the annual meeting of American Political Science Association. Washington, D.C. This presentation was converted into an academic article published in 2006 at *Quarterly Journal of Political Science*. 1(2), 201–226. For Thomas Frank's rejoinder see Frank, T. (2005). For the 2005 Pew study Frank cites in his rejoinder to Bartels, see Pew Research Center (August 5, 2005).

[23] Both political scientist and Brookings Institute scholar Ruy Teixeira and Harvard sociologist Michèle Lamont use this metric to define the working class. See Lamont, 2000; Teixeira & Rogers, 2001.

[24] In their 2005 study, "Trends in Educational Assortative Marriage from 1940 to 2003," Christine Schwartz and Robert Mare show that in the last sixty years, who Americans end up marrying has become increasingly determined by educational level. At present, educational level has become a greater predictor of marriage selection than religious denomination and has even, according to some studies, surpassed race as a factor for determining marriage choice (that is, depending on select types of interracial marriages) (Qian, 1997). In a 2012 *New York Times* article, Sabrina Tavernise engages the issue of growing wealth inequality and asserts that the increase in educated-based marriage homogamy strongly reinforces it. Tavernise, S. (February 2012). Codifying the trend of educated-based marriage homogamy in web form, in 2014, a German-based company named Affinitas launched an online dating service, geared for people who want to date other professionals, called EliteSingles.com.

that in itself echoes much older notions of "good breeding" that have informed American class perceptions as far back as the colonial period, as Nancy Isenberg's book *White Trash* (2016) historically documents.

To the dismay of many on the left, class designations by income often lack the same popular register as stratification schemas based on cultural status.[25] Since the 1940s, Gallup polls have demonstrated how citizens from widely divergent socioeconomic backgrounds commonly think of themselves as "middle class." This was even the case in the Great Recession period, a time when millions of Americans were experiencing rapid downward mobility due to the financial crisis. One recession-era poll showed that 40% of Americans making less than $20,000 a year described themselves as middle class, while one-third of those making $150,000 defined themselves in the same way.[26]

The history of American political discourse has contributed to the nation's "middle class mythology." In the nineteenth century, American politicians started to use what historian Kenneth Cmiel calls a "middling rhetoric" (1991). Though seldom radical, this rhetoric has not been void of class politics either. Since Thomas Paine's revolutionary pamphlet "Common Sense," political writers and orators have used anti-aristocratic themes and populist terminology distinguishing the "people" from the "elites" to add class edges and accents to US middle-class social imaginary.

As sociologist Craig Calhoun has pointed out (1982), class struggle in the United States has more often been waged in the name of the "people" – a populist signifier – than in the name of the working class. In turn, while the working class is often at the center of the populist conception of the people, the popular social bloc that is implied in populist discourse seldom refers to an exact, objective definition of the working class and instead more often includes various class groups from within and without the proletariat.

Populist class critiques in the United States have historically been more *normative* than empirical (Kazin, 1998: 13) and this partly explains populism's great malleability in serving highly divergent political agendas and economic groups. Political theorist Ernesto Laclau, and longtime collaborator Chantal Mouffe, have particularly emphasized this contingency. The theoretical framework they built highlights the *constructive* role that populist political discourse plays in the formation of social blocs

---

[25] See Vanneman, R., & Cannon, L. W. (1987), chapter 3: Class Divisions and Status Rankings: the Social Psychology of American Stratification. Also see Lamont, 1992, 2000.

[26] Pew Research Center (April 9, 2008).

(i.e. loose conceptions of class groupings).[27] This helps explain why colloquial monikers of class such as "the people" and "the producers" can be assigned to an array of different "objective" classes and social groups in different historical moments.

In light of their ideological inconsistency and sociological imprecision, populist class critiques have often been dismissed as irrational, incoherent, or not really class critiques at all (Hofstadter, 2008). This dismissal often assumes that class identities are, or should be, direct reflections of economic conditions. However, over-materialist class analyses miss the crucial way in which class identities are expressed through, and constructed by, partisan social loyalties (Wilentz, 1984), kinship and familial ties (Bettie, 2003), taste and aesthetic preferences (Bourdieu, 1984; Gans, 1999), national moral discourses (Lamont, 1992, 2000; Sayer, 2005), and, last but not least, the mass media and popular culture (Aronwitz, 1992; McRobbie, 1994).

Chapter 1 documented how the commercial news industry has been structured around two opposing journalistic styles and market addresses, one culturally "populist," the other culturally "aspirational." These opposing media styles invoke different class-based groups; but, to stress again, they do so in complex and subtle ways. In the history of American media, there has seldom been a clean sociological match between media brands and media audiences; this relationship has always entailed a degree of cultural slippage and subjective identification. For more than a century, working-class news consumers have sought to embody the stereotypical "learnedness" of educated professionals and, conversely, professional class consumers have yearned to exude the stereotypical "authenticity" of the working class.

The symbolic interplay and mutual mimicry that occurs between and across social classes complicates attempts to *empirically* deny or confirm the classed identity of any given media organization. "[C]lass," as Russian semiotician Mikhail Bakhtin explained,

does not coincide with the sign community, i.e. with the community that is the totality of users of the same set of signs for ideological communication. Thus, various different classes will use one and the same language. As a result, differently oriented accents intersect in every ideological sign.

(1973: 23)[28]

---

[27] Laclau & Moufee, 2001; Laclau, 2005a; 2005b; 2007.
[28] See Voloshinov, V. N. (1973) *Marxism and the Philosophy of Language*. While officially attributed to Bakhtin's colleague Valentin Nikolaevich Voloshinov, many argue that Bahktin was the book's true author.

In addition to whiteness, country music carries a working-class "accent," as Republican politicians are all too aware.[29] But rather than approaching country music as the exclusive possession of one class group or another, it is better to approach this kind of pop cultural symbol as, historian Eric Lott writes, "sites in which class struggles are fought out" (2007: 51). The primary purpose of this chapter, then, is not to *prove* that Fox News has captured a working-class audience. Instead, it is to elucidate the cultural populist strategy Fox News uses to stake its claim on white working-class identity.

"I EAT AT RED LOBSTER": PERFORMING WORKING-CLASS TASTE

Fox News programs frequently intersperse "soft news" items about celebrities, sports and pop culture within their coverage of "hard news" topics. In some cases, pop culture is built into a program's format. In one episode of *The O'Reilly Factor*, for example, a discussion on Obama's tax policy was followed by a reccurring segment called the "Great American Culture Quiz," where fellow pundits are tested on questions like "What was the second biggest hit off of Elvis Presley's *Jail House Rock* album?" But Fox is far from unique in this respect. To varying degrees, all modern news shows – whether cable or network, conservative or liberal, serious or comedic – juxtapose "hard news" stories about economics and politics with pop cultural references and lifestyle topics.[30] Fox News' competitors have light-hearted, pop culture-oriented segments included in their formats as well. MSNBC's Rachel Maddow has her "Cocktail Moment" segment and Anderson Cooper of CNN has his "Ridiculist" one.

Moreover, nearly every modern news program has adopted the hypervisual, aestheticized broadcasting look that Fox News, and *A Current Affair* before it, helped innovate. In *Pretty Package Ugly War* (2009), Deborah Jaramillo shows how *both* CNN and Fox News exude the "high-concept" presentational style of big budget Hollywood films. From this perspective, Fox News shares more aesthetic and topical similarities with the rest of the news field than differences. Yet these superficial likenesses overlook the deeper class-cultural logic that distinguishes Fox

---

[29] For a forceful argument explaining why country music is a decidedly *working-class* genre of music, see Hubbs, 2014: 12–15.
[30] Baum, 2003; Zoonen, 2005; Baym, 2009; Jones, 2012; Nadler, 2016.

News' aesthetic style and pop cultural repertoire from its competitors and also misses the specific *dispositional* posture that Fox News hosts take toward popular cultural forms.

Maddow's presentation of "low" pop culture still carries an air of intellectualism and connoisseurship. Maddow doesn't just enjoy popular culture; she "nerds out" on it. In her "Cocktail Moment," a segment title that itself communicates a certain tastes politics, she seeks the "expert" guidance of comedian Kent Jones, a self-titled "Pop Culturalist." CNN's use and integration of pop culture similarly carries a tongue-in-cheek quality. In one episode of *AC 360*, host Anderson Cooper announces that his favorite reality show star is "Snookie" from *Jersey Shore*. The smirking expression on his face as he says this indicates the insincerity or, at the very least, the "guilty pleasure" nature of this declaration. While pop culture has a presence in CNN and MSNBC programing, the two networks often engage it in a quaint or playful manner.

This playful approach shares resemblances to the semi-detached, sarcastic style of liberal comedy-based news programs like *The Daily Show*. When *Daily Show* pundits said in a former segment called "Pantry of Shame" that they enjoyed highly processed food products like "Bacon-naise" and a "pancake wrapped sausage on a stick," they did so ironically. As I demonstrate in greater length in Chapter 5, when Fox News hosts adopt ironic, distancing modes of address, their sarcastic gaze is often aimed upward toward their own or their audience's highbrow pretensions (this has been a key comedic device in both country music and "blue-collar comedy"). This stands in contrast to the *sincere* style in which O'Reilly and other Fox pundits had used when discussing lowbrow taste. When Hannity said, "I played *The Best of Alabama* in my car. My kids know the songs by heart" (November 17, 2008) and O'Reilly said, "I eat at Red Lobster. I like Red Lobster. And they give you lots of shrimp for free. I eat there" (November 23, 2009), these hosts – regardless of how contrived one may believe these statements to be – are endeavoring to perform an *effusive*, non-ironic adoration for working-class cultural products and practices.

Moreover, the various references to popular taste on Fox News are rationalized within an overarching narrative of anti-cultural elitism; each performative declaration for loving this or that working-class cultural form interlocks with a myriad of other complementary representational tactics for performing "cultural ordinariness." Lacking this comprehensive approach, Cooper and Maddow's appeals to lowbrow cultural forms seem random and eccentric, and therefore less grounded and meaningful.

On *Hannity*, now Fox News' top rated show, everything from the program's guest selection, its graphics, and its music to Hannity's embodied performance seek to exude cultural ordinariness, or, using Bourdieusian terms, the aesthetic *principle of conformity*. Rather than the suspenseful orchestral music that CNN news programs use in their program breaks, on *Hannity* the viewer hears electric guitar licks played with distortion and timbre as if catching the end of a Southern rock song. In addition, contemporary country music hits are frequently played in the segment transitions. At the close of every broadcast, Hannity postures like a quarterback and throws a *Nerf* football to an unseen person off set. During discussion panels, Hannity frequently mentions sports-related events, uses sports analogies, and, like every "Joe-six-pack," goads guests who support or play for rival teams. Hannity's tie to sports culture, and by extension, a working-class masculinity, is further reinforced by his physical appearance, which, with his thick neck and square jaw, makes him appear like someone who may have played football in his younger years.

This working-class taste politics is also expressed through *Hannity*'s visual graphics as well. Unlike the international and high-tech iconography displayed on CNN, *Hannity*'s graphics during the Great Recession period resembled interstate road signs. This "graphic inclination" (Caldwell, 1995) plays on icons of Americana, car culture, and the mythologies tied to Route 66 and the Interstate Highway System (see Figure 3.1). Like something one might find in a sports bar or at an Applebee's restaurant, a recurring program-break graphic the show used in this period was a mosaic of state license plates.

The choice to use an interstate road sign and license plates as the show's central symbols – par excellence objects of banality and public life – highlights the *Hannity*'s representational priority to align its visual aesthetic with the culturally unexceptional. The hyper-patriotic quality of *Hannity*'s graphics also works to communicate the program's working-class taste politics. Like other Fox News programs, the *Hannity* set is saturated with American flags, white stars, and red and blue color schemes, something that was ruthlessly parodied by the liberal comedy news show *The Colbert Report*. Obviously, this patriotic visual branding supports the hyper-nationalistic nature of the Fox News' politics (especially in the buildup to the Iraq War), but it also serves to distance the show from the taste culture of educated professionals who tend to see such fulsome displays of patriotism as "tacky."

FIGURE 3.1 *Hannity* segment transition graphic

In today's entertainment-driven news environment, the relevant question is no longer whether or not news programs integrate pop culture into their programming. The more pressing questions are to what *systematic extent* do news organizations incorporate popular cultural references in their news coverage and *which* sectors of mass entertainment do they align their corporate brand and politics with? Both country music and the Academy Awards are forms of popular culture, which is to say neither of these mass media products could be accurately defined as "high art." Yet the Oscars gesture, in an *aspirational* way, toward "the high," "the hip" and "the modern," while country music, having a *cultural populist* value system, celebrates the "square" and the "ordinary." The conventional "high culture" versus "popular culture" dichotomy fails to account for these nuances. Divisions exist *within* the popular cultural arena that correspond with taste-based tensions within the working and middle class.

Because celebrities make up an important faction of Fox News' despised "liberal elite," and because the very concept of celebrity works against the logic of cultural populism in conveying – by definition, a social apartness from everyday people – Fox News' top programs are highly selective in picking the celebrities and popular cultural genres they claim a cultural alliance with. The celebrities that most frequently appear on Fox News tend to be ones that are mutually preoccupied with embodying the "culturally ordinary" and who also espouse narratives of media marginalization. In this way, Fox News programs extend the network's anti-elitist institutional narrative beyond the political media field, thereby thickening its cultural texture and broadening its social meaning.

It is not uncommon for Fox News hosts to prime or encourage celebrity guests to share stories about discrimination at the hands of cultural elites in the entertainment industry. In an interview with Jeff Foxworthy, a Southern comedian who rose to fame with his "you might be a redneck if . . ." line of jokes, Glenn Beck was telling Foxworthy that media critics depict Fox's audience as a "bunch of idiots." Beck then asked the comedian, "Do they attack your audience as well? Because, you know, you're just a hick. You've got no talent too." Foxworthy responded, "Oh yes . . . We caught the same thing on the 'Blue Collar [Comedy]' tour" (June 16, 2009). Along with comedians, pro-athletes and military heroes, country music singers represent a recurring type of celebrity that appears on Fox News' top-rated programs, both as performers and as panelists (see Figure 3.2).

The presence of country singers on Fox News programs – their physical build, clothing style, and plainspoken, usually Southern, voices – serves a symbolic purpose, as they add a working-class feel to the stuffy, suit-wearing professional class environment of television news. In a reciprocal fashion, these singers utilize Fox News to associate their "country music personas" with Republican partisanship, a political badge that affirms both their rural identity and white working-classness.

A December 1, 2008 episode of *The O'Reilly Factor*, where host Bill O'Reilly was interviewing country singer Trace Adkins, reveals how Fox News programs applied the same populist-partisan framework to map the entertainment field as they used to map the journalism field. "You're a conservative, traditional guy," O'Reilly told Adkins, "And many country music performers are there. And then you go to Hollywood, where you were, and then New York where the music industry [is], and you see very liberal people. Why the split?" Adkins responds in his gruff, baritone voice, "You know, there is a split. But I would have to say, too, though, that I know a lot of guys in the rock/pop world that are conservative. It's just that they can't really be that outspoken and out front with it." Here,

FIGURE 3.2 Trace Adkins on *The O'Reilly Factor*

Adkins is repeating a familiar story that conservative celebrities commonly recount on Fox News about having to censor their political views in the "liberal" entertainment industry.

O'Reilly asks Adkins if it is annoying when singers use their music platform to "preach" their political philosophy. "It is," Adkins affirms, "because I think that there are a lot of people that buy into that *artist thing* [my emphasis]." Assuming the perspective of a country fan, Adkins then elaborates, "I just want to hear tunes ... I don't to hear you puke up your ... liberal stuff on me." Pushing Adkins a little, O'Reilly asks, "Aren't you an artist? ... You're [an] actor. You're a writer. You're a singer." Distancing himself from the term, Adkins replies, "You know, I'm a singer man, I sing country songs ... I write some, yes. But I think that some of the artists start thinking that they're more enlightened than you and I ... I don't consider myself ... Picasso." Like every celebrity, country musicians like Adkins are highly self-conscious of their public image. What distinguishes them from other celebrities, however, is the immense effort they devote to *avoid* coming across as exceptional or socially distinct from their fans. In *Rednecks and Bluenecks: The Politics of Country Music* (2005), *Rolling Stone* contributor Chris Willman says that, in the country music industry, no word is dreaded more than the "E" word (4–5). The fear of being branded an "elitist" is equally palpable in the conservative talk industry. For the same reason Adkins rejects the "artist" label, conservative hosts like Hannity, Beck and Limbaugh have rejected the label of "journalist"; both titles imply a social break with their fan base.

But, as we will see in the next section, appeals to cultural taste are not the only representational means through which Fox News pundits attempt to perform a working-class cultural disposition. One's membership in a taste culture conveys more than food and entertainment preferences; it says something deeper about one's intellectual mentality. Put another way, social evaluations about "good taste" are inexorably tied to social evaluations about "smarts." In the network era, the cerebral world of television news had been stringently separated from matters of taste and lifestyle. However, in a contemporary news environment that is far more aestheticized and dialogic with the entertainment media sector, modern news programs are constantly drawing connections between types of taste and types of intelligence.

"I'M NOT AN EXPERT, BUT I AM A THINKER": PERFORMING WORKING-CLASS INTELLECTUALITY

Fox News host Glenn Beck began one segment standing in front of a colorful blackboard and before a table of assorted groceries. After he finished his argument about the interconnection between the devaluation of the dollar and the rise in food prices, he leaned closer to the camera. "Look," he said with a slightly frustrated exhale, "I'm not an economist. I'm a high school educated guy. And maybe that's why I can see things that other people can't, because I don't have that big ol' head [that's] been filled by the so-called experts ... I try to figure it out myself" (November 4, 2010). Rather than regarding his lack of a college degree as a shortcoming, Beck was asserting that this gave him an insight that other, more credentialed political analysts do not have. Formal erudition (i.e. getting a "big ol' head"), he suggests, hinders one's ability to think independently and practically about the world. This type of anti-credential-educational rhetoric is something one simply doesn't hear from political liberals.

Thus, unlike liberal journalists, conservative media figures either downplay their elite educational backgrounds when they have one (e.g. Bill O'Reilly) or treat their *lack* of credentials and a college degree as a badge of honor. In addition to Glenn Beck, other conservative media heavyweights such as Sean Hannity and Rush Limbaugh have touted the fact that they never graduated from college. In doing so, these pundits are making a powerful claim about their capacity to share contemporaneously (as opposed to anachronistically) a class-cultural likeness with the majority of the television news audience who also do not have college degrees. Conservative figures like vice presidential candidate and former Fox News contributor Sarah Palin have learned to anticipate liberal criticism about their educational inadequacies and seize upon this criticism as proof of both liberal elitism and their own working-class authenticity.

Yet this is only the most obvious way Fox News hosts try to depict working-class intellectuality. A college degree, they seem to intuit, stands for more than an occupational competency or discipline-specific knowledge set; it marks one as being a member of a particular knowledge community, or of what Karin Knorr-Cetina terms an *epistemic culture* (1999). As Knorr-Cetina demonstrates in her ethnographic study of various scientific disciplines, displaying learnedness is as much about expressing *how* one thinks as it is about the content of *what* one knows.[31]

As part of the broader cultural populist strategy of Fox News, Fox's top pundits do more than appeal to working-class tastes; they attempt to pose as representatives of a working-class epistemic culture by performing what I term a *popular intellect*.[32] An example of this can be seen in a June 6, 2010 episode of *Hannity* about the British Petroleum (BP) oil spill in the Gulf of Mexico, then seen as the worst oil spill in world history. In keeping with his partisan argument about the incompetence of the government and President Obama's response to the catastrophe, host Sean Hannity groused, "It's frustrating, because, I'm looking at, look, I love fishermen. I have friends of mine that fish for a living. They clam out in

---

[31] In *Professional Powers* (1986), Eliot Freidson maintains that one of the defining characteristics of the professional class is a tendency to possess specialized forms of knowledge and gain their legitimacy by the approval of professional peers and educational credentials. However, the professional class is not synonymous with experts because professionals are not only characterized by *what* they know, but *how* they know what they know, and how they *display* competency. In *The Future of the Intellectuals and the Rise of the New Class* (1979), Alvin Gouldner maintains that professionals, whether the humanistic and technical intelligentsia, share what he calls a common "culture of careful and critical discourse" (47), meaning they share a similar tendency toward hyper-formalized language, detached modes of analysis and justification.

[32] Paul Saurette and Shane Gunster's 2011 article "Ears Wide Shut: Epistemological Populism, Argutainment and Canadian Conservative Talk Radio" describe something similar with their term *epistemological populism*.

the bays of Long Island. I have people that I know. They work hard. Their livelihoods may be interrupted for generations" (June 14, 2010). By using trades lingo that fishermen in the area of Long Island would use ("clam out"), Hannity is able to socially ground his voice in covering this particular news event, the spill. In a previous era of journalism, the notion of bringing up one's personal ties ("I have people I know") and emotional attachments ("I love fishermen") to a news item would have been seen as a professional liability, but in the culture of Fox News it adds valued credibility to the anchors' journalistic interpretations.

In contrast to the network era, when anchors wanted the viewer to see their statements as coming "from nowhere" (Baym, 2009) – that is, from no particular social point of view or bias – Hannity and other Fox pundits are constantly situating their statements *exactly* in terms of "from where they come." Drawing from Bourdieu, this *invested* interpretive stance approaches nearly all public statements and informational products as commodities driven by social and political interests (1984: 34–50).[33] Thus, within Fox's populist public sphere model, the choice being offered is no longer between disinterested and interested journalism, but between different types of interested analysis. Arguing from an openly *self-interested* position is not really an option because this would present the speaker as someone who is, at best, power-seeking and morally baseless. Therefore, Fox News hosts embrace an overtly *ethical disposition* of the working-class cultural gaze, standing in contrast to the morally agnostic expressive style of both a scientific epistemic culture and bourgeois taste cultures (Bourdieu, 1984: 44–50). This means that Fox News pundits, having consistently foregrounded the moral stakes of each news topic, seem to be showing how their analytical point of view is guided by communal values that transcend their own self-interest. If the game of legitimation in the high-modern era of journalism had been based on performing objective distance, the game of legitimation on Fox News'

---

[33] The *invested* brand of news analysis we see in Fox's top opinion shows mirrors working-class schemas for evaluating objects of everyday consumption. Commenting on the ways in which workers approach artistic photographs, Pierre Bourdieu maintains that "the image is always judged by reference to the function it fulfills for the person who looks at it or which he thinks it could fulfill for other classes of beholders" (1984: 41). Unlike the detached, bourgeois gaze that evaluates art as an autonomous product that "has no referent other than itself," the popular evaluative stance measures the text's value by its assumed social uses and affiliations or, as Bourdieu puts it, by the assumed "interest [behind] the information it conveys" (43).

most popular shows is meant to be based on performing one's personal investment and moral concern.

We see this *ethical disposition* on display in a September 16, 2008 episode of *The O'Reilly Factor*. This episode is particularly useful for demonstrating how such a style of analysis has no natural ideological orientation because host Bill O'Reilly – typically a defender of the business class and a promoter of deregulation – actually criticizes the oil companies here for their greed and calls for more "oversight." (This of course is a viewpoint more commonly expressed by the left). The segment shows O'Reilly engaging with Neil Cavuto, the host of a Fox News Business program. Their heated debate was about whether or not the banks and oil companies were harming "everyday Americans" in the pursuit of greater profits.

In the lead-up segment to this debate, O'Reilly had said of the two presidential candidates in the 2008 election that "both guys need to be very specific when it comes to what they want to do to protect Americans from irresponsible corporations." Then, self-referentially citing an example of corporate irresponsibility, O'Reilly observed, "By the way, as I pointed out yesterday, the price of oil has declined about 33 percent in two months. But the price of gas at the pump has declined seven percent. The oil companies strike again and nobody is watching them." With a smirk on his face, O'Reilly now offered his Fox News business host up to his audience, his tongue-in-cheek introduction serving to taint his network colleague with the ills of the oil industry: "Now for the top story tonight, another view of this. Fox News business anchor Neil Cavuto, always a defender of corporate America." Cavuto, already anticipating this kind of introduction, merely shook his head and replied in a pleading tone:

You got to stop this ... 18 months ago, when a barrel was at $50, gas was at $2.22 a gallon, right, so we got up three times that rate on oil, right? Why didn't gas prices go up three times that way to be almost $7? Why didn't – you can pick and choose your date range, Bill. You criticize politicians for playing fast and loose with the numbers. So why do you pick a period that suits your argument[?]

Interestingly, Cavuto was using an *evidence-dependent* line of critique to challenge O'Reilly's claims by citing first a flurry of alternative sets of numbers that, in trying to give the viewer a broader temporal scope of price ranges, seemed to present self-evident proof that oil companies are not raising prices for selfish reasons. Moving on, in an attempt to undercut O'Reilly's own statistics, Cavuto then suggested that his host had not objectively evaluated the evidence, instead manipulating it to "suit his argument."

When expressed in the frenetic pace of a cable news talk show, though, Cavuto's argument can come across as slightly dizzying because he relies so heavily on numbers. Sensing this convolution, O'Reilly countered with his characteristic "straight talk" and shifted the entire mode of analysis. Rather than debating Cavuto's numbers or bringing in additional statistics, O'Reilly tried to reframe the truth of the oil companies' culpability. "Let me ask you a very simple question," O'Reilly inquired of Caputo. "Do you believe the oil companies are NOT maximizing ... their profits at every turn? ... Do you think they're being fair with the American people?" O'Reilly had turned the issue to a matter of what one intuitively *believed* about oil companies' interests and what those interests say about the companies' intentions, not about what the evidence itself revealed.

Now Cavuto was forced to challenge not only O'Reilly's "evidence" but also the *popular* belief that oil companies care more about profit than about everyday consumers.

Uncomfortable with O'Reilly's "in-the-folk's-interest" or not-evaluative criteria, Cavuto decided to bring the discussion back to O'Reilly's statistics, accusing him of a glaring inconsistency. He said to O'Reilly, "You just said a statistic ... By your definition then, they should be gouging us with $7 gasoline now. And it's a lot less than that." The viewer begins to sense that Cavuto is becoming increasingly frustrated. Abandoning the discussion about "data," Cavuto charged O'Reilly with deceptive beguilement. "You push this *populist* [my emphasis] nonsense that doesn't make sense. And you get people to believe it." But O'Reilly stubbornly repeated his previous question about whether Cavuto truly believed the oil companies were not trying to maximize profits through price gouging. By this, O'Reilly suggested that Cavuto had not yet disclosed his true, personal beliefs about the issue. Finally, Cavuto answered no. The door was now open for the populist O'Reilly to snap back with his retort, "No[?]. And I do!" (August 16, 2008).

Here, truth ultimately rests not in evidence, but in the Fox News host's deeply *felt* beliefs about the issue (Peters, 2010) and their ability to *perform* emotional concern for the social groups involved.

The legitimating power of this "invested" mode of news analysis makes more sense when one understands how Fox News conceptualizes the US public sphere. On Fox, the media has not only been one of the most predominant topics of discussion; it has been treated as a powerful political actor in its own right and identified as one of the main villains in Fox's populist imaginary of the political field (Conway et al., 2007: 207–210). This idea remains central to contemporary conservative political media in the online sphere. Republican-aligned online outlets like InfoWars and Breitbart News applauded President Donald Trump's infamous February 17, 2017 "tweet" when Trump branded the media as "the enemy of the American people" (Grybaum, 2017). Like Trump, Fox News' hosts have attributed immense causal power to journalistic interpretations in determining political outcomes (Cappella & Jamieson, 2008: 51). In light of this, Fox's top opinion hosts have strived to demonstrate how their news analyses are indeed biased – precisely *because they are invested in the interests of* "the folks" and other groups that are deemed morally righteous (e.g. soldiers) or innocent (e.g. children).

POPULIST JOURNALISM: AN ENEMY OF FACTS OR OF CULTURAL ELITISM?

Long conceived of as a media form for the mind, political news has played and continues to play a special role in the social construction of intelligence. In accordance with the conventional format of this "serious" mass media genre, Fox News' top opinion programs have a predominantly "hard news" editorial orientation. As such, they, like all political news programs, hail their audience as subjects who *think* about larger societal problems, political debates and ideological differences – that is, the stuff of intellectual culture. What distinguishes the Fox News' mode of address from those of prestige newspapers and cable news competitors is that it does not particularly address its viewers as culturally aspirational subjects seeking to approximate the intelligence of experts and professionals. In a 2001 *Newsweek* interview, CEO Roger Ailes touches on this difference. "The media elite," he tells the reporter, "think they're smarter than the rest of those stupid bastards, and they'll tell you what to think. To a working-class guy, that's bulls—t" (Wolcott, 2001). In contrast to the mainstream media, Fox News, Ailes suggested, validates the capacity of *non*-professionals to deliberate about the political world, thus affirming that "common sense" is all one needs to assess matters of public importance.

Critics have often interpreted this populist analytical posture as an indicator of Fox's anti-intellectualism. However, a Fox host's hostility to someone's educational credentials and display of high culture does not reflect an anti-intellectual bias tout court. Drawing such a conclusion could lead one to overlook how Fox News programming makes the case for a *lay* brand of intellectualism, a *popular intellect*. Moving beyond the content of the Fox News stories, the very act of turning to one's personal experience or family history in the midst of a political discussion can convey class identifications that will associate the speaker positively with a working-class epistemic culture.

Of course, Fox's populist mode of argumentation marks a significant departure from the high-modern era of American journalism. In the traditional paradigm, the credibility of a given statement was evaluated by how well it measured up to empirical facts; whether the statement served a particular social group or political camp should be irrelevant to its truth-value. Practitioners of the objective style of journalism treat methodologically sound pieces of evidence (e.g. a government report, a set of statistics, a historical event) as non-intentioned, *self-contained* units of truth. The traditional anchor's performance of distance from the information surrounding a news event gives the facts he or she reports a sense of autonomy – that is, a bias-free integrity.

Today, in the Trump era, media critics have raised concerns about the rise of a "post-truth" or "post-fact" national press; something that echoes the same concerns liberal pundits raised a decade prior in the Bush era using political comedian Stephen Colbert's term "truthiness." Writing about Fox News, journalism scholar Chris Peters described the heart of this concern most succinctly. When, he writes, "the beliefs of the host are both the starting point for debate and evidential proof for assertions...the threshold demanded under journalism's traditional rules of truth" are drastically lowered (2010: 842).

I do not want to downplay the gravity of Peters' point here or suggest that the concern many have voiced about the depreciation of "facts" and professional, peer-reviewed knowledge is not serious and warranted. I share the same concerns. However, as someone who has dwelled in the culture of conservative media for a decade, I can't help but wonder if this "post-truth," "postmodern" diagnosis is less a universal societal malady as its often depicted by liberals and is more a feeling and anxiety that is specific to liberal media culture. It is telling that CNN's current attempts to counter-program to pro-Trump media like Fox explicitly centers on assuaging this anxiety: "This is an Apple," its 2017 #FactsFirst ad campaign states simply. "Some people might try and tell you it's a banana. They might scream banana, banana, banana over and over and over again ... You might even start to believe that this is a banana. But it's not," the ad assures, "this is an apple."[34] Of course, some conservative commentators have also raised concerns about "epistemic closure" and

---

[34] Steinberg (October 23, 2017).

the politicization of empirical knowledge.[35] But taking the conservative media sector as a whole, one does not hear the same level of alarm on this issue as one hears from the left. For conservatives, the cultural elitism of the journalism community is of greater importance.

This chapter has strived to show how Fox's taste-based appeals and the presentational priority its programming gives to lay forms of knowledge and analysis is not simply tied to a profit motive, nor is it the product of a postmodern zeitgeist that took hold of the news industry. Rather, it is, I argue, a representational choice that is directly connected to Fox's larger populist branding strategy, a strategy that interlocks with and is reflective of the ongoing hegemonic project of the postwar conservative movement. It must be noted, however, that Fox News' praise for popular taste and intelligence can be both racially and ideologically selective.

In one of his many on-air disputes with hip-hop artists, O'Reilly chastised the lyrics of guest Lupe Fiasco, which had been critical of Obama's (not Bush's) "War on Terror." Lecturing the rapper, O'Reilly said, "You go out there and talk to a lot of younger people, your constituency are not exactly political science PhDs, okay, they're impressionable kids." "Well," Lupe responded, "I don't think that matters, I don't think you need to have a political PhD to understand politics" – interestingly, a line that O'Reilly, Sean Hannity and Glenn Beck had each uttered in some form or fashion themselves. O'Reilly nevertheless insisted that the hip-hop audience – a community that is imagined to be young and black – needed formal education before deliberating about politics. This assertion stood in stark contrast to the immense faith O'Reilly places in his own predominantly white audience to use their "common sense" (June 2, 2011).[36]

One circumstance that *does* seem to diminish O'Reilly's faith in the white working-class majority appears when their views contradict his free-market ideology. In yet another discussion with Fox pundit Neil Cavuto about "the disconnect between average folks and Wall Street folks," O'Reilly contrasted the financial sector's opposition to Obama's tax policy with the fact that "sixty-six percent of Americans like the idea of raising taxes on those earning more than $250,000 a year." O'Reilly's conclusion was that "while the financial markets oppose President Obama, most of the folks are still with him." Cavuto responded matter-of-factly, "The Wall Street folks and their view eventually become the

---

[35] Cohen (April 27, 2010).   [36] Fox News Insider (June 20, 2011).

Main Street folks' view." Instead of playing his typical role as the defender of "ordinary judgment," then, O'Reilly affirmed Cavuto's condescending statement and responded, "It takes them [Main Street folks] a little time to catch up" (March 5, 2009). This segues to the next chapter, which details how Fox News pundits use the rhetoric of producerism and "job creators" to represent the expertise and skill set of the business class as different from the "elitist" knowledge of professors and intellectuals and as something closer to the non-abstract, "practical" thinking of everyday workers.

4

"The Makers and the Takers"

How Fox News Forges a Working-Class/Business-Class Political Alliance

Explain ... why other people on this planet deserve the fruits of my labor.
– Bill O'Reilly

A liberal is somebody who thinks he has a right to my hard-earned money
– Sean Hannity

In a "special" episode of *Glenn Beck* that aired March 13, 2009 entitled "You Are Not Alone," Glenn Beck captures the essence of the "forgotten man" narrative that appeared across Fox News programming during the Great Recession. In Beck's reinterpretation of Franklin Roosevelt's famous phrase, it is the small business owner, not the rank-and-file industrial worker, who is the central protagonist and economic victim. In this episode, Beck announced the launch of his Tea Party–affiliated organization, the "9/12 Project." As a sort of dress rehearsal to Fox News' more expansive coverage of the national Tea Party protest on April 15 (see Introduction), the program starts by showing all the "viewing parties" and rallies across the nation that are linked to the broadcast through live video feeds. The viewer hears the cheers of the live studio audience in the background as Beck leans very close into the camera and assumes an unconventional distance and angle that became a signature feature of his short-lived show on Fox. Visibly shaky, he pauses to laugh at himself indicating that he is about to tear up. Gathering himself, he proceeds with his speech. At this point, the camera transitions into a documentary with Beck's narration:

Our companies faced new union mandates and global cap-and-trade and the second highest corporate tax rate in the world. All the while, politicians wonder why jobs are going overseas ... Meanwhile, over 4 million friends and neighbors have lost their jobs in the last four months alone ... Yet 70 percent of all jobs are created by the small businessman and nobody seems to even notice him. What happened to the country that loved the underdog and stood up to the little guy? What happened to the voice of the *"forgotten man"*? The *"forgotten"* man is you!

As Beck stresses, small business owners are people of moral virtue, as they stand for economic productiveness ("70 percent of all jobs are created by the small businessman"). The visual images that accompany Beck's narration plays on the slippery, class dualism of the small business owner. On the one hand, the interests of small business and big business are seen as essentially equivalent. Like big business, the small business person is positioned against policies such as "union mandates" and "cap-and-trade" (policies that have a remote relationship with truly *small* businesses). On the other hand, the small business owner is still just a "little guy" – particularly in relation to Wall Street.

The documentary juxtaposes images of stock tickers and shiny building plaques that bear the names of the major banks that were bailed out by the government (Citibank, Morgan Stanley, JPMorgan Chase, AIG) with a sequence of images of worn-down, small business establishments. One image shows a small store in a strip mall; another shows a house that was converted into a corner store; the last shows a store that appears to be located on a main street of a small town. Cued with the line "and nobody seems to notice him [the small business man]," the viewer is given a sequence of shots showing a small bakery, a man working at a car wash, and an older couple tending a produce stand, the proverbial "mom and pop." The sequence bills the small business owner as an Everyman or Everywoman through the locations, building appearance and size of the stores, and by the mundane and unglamorous character of the types of businesses that are featured. These images present business owners as living in and being from the same working-class social world as most Americans.

By constantly celebrating the managerial skills and duties tied to mom-and-pop businesses and by simultaneously associating the labor of these businesses with forms of work that have been the most celebrated in the history of American political culture – namely, the artisan, agricultural, and industrial forms of manual work – Fox News programs were able to champion policies that served the business class while claiming to represent the recession's "forgotten man." But the deployment of Fox's pro-business class brand of populism also carried the risk of inciting the audience's resentment toward managers and bosses. So Fox used a *moral* version of class identity to hold the political alliance together.

This chapter illustrates how Fox News' claim to represent the downtrodden of the Great Recession was established less by advocating policies that directly supported working-class economic interests and more by presenting Fox hosts as the protectors and advocates of a "moral economy" that honors hard work and productivity. While Democrats were asserting the cost-benefit arguments about the details of the countercyclical spending measures they were proposing to recuperate the economy, Fox News pundits questioned the very *principle* of state intervention and government assistance. This was the most important feature of Fox News' interpretive strategy; how its energy was invested in defining the moral stakes of the economic crisis.

In their news analysis, Fox hosts drew on enduring moral-economic principles from the American populist rhetorical tradition, and particularly from an old discursive strain called *producerism*.[1] This discourse draws an opposition between "producers" and "parasites" and argues that a moral society rewards those who produce. Thus, the economy should favor the interest of the industrious, not the idle. While producerist archetypes and moral logics have been recycled by American politicians and social movements as far back as the Jeffersonian era, it was during the Great Recession that Fox News was able to rework this tradition to both protect and strengthen the hegemonic hold of free-market ideology in the face of crisis.

On Fox programs, pundits repeatedly suggested that the financial collapse was the result of "undisciplined" borrowers and Democratic policies aimed at increasing homeownership among low-income citizens and racial minorities. In this way, the network's framing of the crisis played into preexisting racial stereotypes about welfare dependency and state-based parasitism. In one episode of *Hannity,* the second highest-rated show on Fox at the time, British politician Daniel Hanna, a

---

[1] Burke, 1995; Kazin, 1998; Huston, 1998; Berlet & Lyons, 2000; Peck, 2014a, 2017. Few political analysts and critics use the term "producerism" to describe the conservative populist discourse of the Recession era. However, two prolific columnists have used the term to describe the rhetoric of the Tea Party movement. *The New Republic's* John S. Judis (2010) and *New York Times* columnist David Brooks (2009) have used the term and they both trace this rhetorical tradition's historical roots back to the Jeffersonian and Jacksonian political movements of the nineteenth century.

recurring guest, proclaimed, "You cannot carry on forever squeezing the productive bit of the economy in order to fund an unprecedented engorgement of the unproductive. You cannot spend your way out of recession or borrow your way out of debt" (May 19, 2009). Echoing this more succinctly, a guest on *Glenn Beck* similarly claimed, "Stimulus forwards the indolent at the expense of the productive" (November 10, 2009).

In contrast, Fox's top hosts celebrated producers, including among them the business elite. Fox hosts passionately proclaimed that business owners and the wealthy were the ones who shouldered the biggest tax burden and thus contributed the most to government and all that it provided for the entire population. For it was this group, the hosts stressed over and again, who produced the most value in society. This is the hallmark of what I call *entrepreneurial producerism*. This discourse advances the supply-side economic theories and the familiar "trickle-down" arguments of the right, all of which generally oppose regulatory restraints on the business class and taxes on the wealthy. But Fox's use of entrepreneurial producerism offered not so much an economic argument as a moral rationale for supply-side policies as a way of rewarding hard work.

Fraught with profound contradictions, the successful deployment of entrepreneurial producerism had been no easy task for Fox News programs. They had to use elaborate rhetorical strategies to conceal, redirect, and manage the core contradictions of this discourse. Fox programs claimed to speak for "the many," while suggesting that the producing class was an embattled "few." And Fox News had to frame the producing class as an economically "successful" group that was simultaneously victimized and marginalized. Noting these contradictions, one progressive blogger described Fox's recession era rhetoric as "rich-guy populism," and liberals in general have wondered how the rhetoric could be taken seriously by anyone (Reed, 2009). But I argue that it was populist moral rhetoric, not economic reasoning that prevailed, allowing Fox pundits to defend economic policies geared for the wealthiest citizens at the very moment when middle-class Americans were descending into poverty in record numbers.

FROM TRADITIONAL PRODUCERISM TO
ENTREPRENEURIAL PRODUCERISM

Michael Kazin, a leading historian of American populism, maintains that from the nineteenth century and well into the twentieth, the "producer ethic" has been "the central element in populist conceptions of 'the people'" (1998: 13). Kazin stresses that producer populism is first and foremost a moral discourse, albeit one that has been particularly used by mass orators and political parties to either critique *or* justify wealth inequality. Like all populist discourses, producerism dichotomizes society into two opposing camps: the "producers" and the "parasites." During the recession, Fox pundits referred to these groups as the "makers" and the "takers."

In this tradition, the government is seen as having been captured and controlled by an elite social class that enriches itself by expropriating the wealth of the producing classes. Historian James L. Huston refers to this story structure as the "political economy of aristocracy" (PEA). In his book *Securing the Fruits of Labor* (1998), he documents how, from the 1760s all the way through the nineteenth century, American politicians relied on PEA theft narratives to explain the maldistribution of wealth and "unnatural" forms of class hierarchy. Huston identifies two core theoretical streams that establish the foundation of producerist moral reasoning. One is John Locke's "republican theory of property distribution," which asserts that truly just societies distribute resources on the basis of the labor each citizen contributes.[2] Huston locates producerism's other core tenet in the "labor theory of value" of classical political economy, whereby all wealth is the result of productive human labor.[3] In revolutionary era parlance, these two tenets were joined and expressed by the phrase "the fruits of labor." This phrase, and the producerist moral logics it carries, was embraced and popularized by farmer and artisan political groups in the Jeffersonian and Jacksonian eras (Foner, 1970; Wilentz, 1986).

As a testament to its ideological flexibility, producerist rhetoric was used to justify both the "Indian Removal" policy of President Andrew Jackson (Saxton, 1990) and the abolition of slavery by President Abraham Lincoln (Foner, 1970). Likewise, urban, working-class organizations like the Knights of Labor (1880s) relied on producerist tropes as did the radical agrarian movements of the 1860s to the 1880s; movements that eventually culminated in the establishment of the Populist Party in 1892. Whereas as the producerist discourse of the antebellum period primarily promoted laissez-faire ideological positions, at the end

---

[2] For more on republican theories of property, see Shapiro, 1991, and Katz, 1976.
[3] For comprehensive overview of the labor theory of value, see Meek, 1976.

of the century producerist political narratives started to be modified in unprecedented ways.

The Populist Party, for example, used producerist rhetoric to protest the advancement of industrial capitalism, or at least its most deleterious consequences, such as the spread of the wage system, the managerial administration over labor and the polarization of wealth.[4] While keeping to individualist, Lockean theories of property, Populist activists rejected laissez-faire ideology. Instead, they pushed for a stronger state involvement in the economy, even calling for the nationalization of major industries such as the railroads, the telegraph, and the banks.[5] These Populists believed that such nationalization was the only way to return the economic system back to the meritorious rules of a "simple market society."[6]

Nonetheless, producerism's articulation of republican ideology with the labor theory of value was – as the Populists discovered – problematic for making critiques of the new corporate political economic order. Increasingly the national economy would be controlled by firms whose scope, size, and complexity would become greater than anything ever seen before. The Lockean theory of property that had underpinned producerist critiques against wealth concentration had only been able to explain how the plutocratic tendencies in the social order were just the result of political graft and government favoritism. How wealth inequality originated from within the capitalist system itself went beyond nineteenth-century populist analyses of power.

However, in the 1930s, the labor movement and the New Deal coalition would attempt to take on this conceptual problem. In the depths of the Great Depression, President Roosevelt and the Democratic Party fashioned a new brand of producer populism which presented government, for the first time, not as the enemy of economic egalitarianism but

---

[4] As many great historical studies on American populism have shown, one of the strongest impetuses for artisan producer movements in the United States in the nineteenth century was the threatening prospect that the industrial, wage-system dominating the English economy would take root in the United States. For American artisans, the fundamental moral and political problem of British style industrialism and labor relations was that it robbed the small producer of his economic independence – a core tenet of American republicanism – making him/her subject to the wage system and managerial judgment. Under an industrial-managerial structure, the worker's individual labor was no longer measured and valued by the meritorious market; rather, it was judged by other people. See Pollack, 1966; Foner, 1970; Goodwyn, 1978; Palmer, 1980; Montgomery, 1981; Noble, 1985; Wilentz, 1986.

[5] Pollack, 1966; Schiller, 1996: 4–20.

[6] For more on the term "simple market society," see Palmer, 1980: 12.

instead as its main agent and ally (Wilentz, 2002: 77). Roosevelt's attempts to reverse producerism's original anti-statist orientation is evident in his speech at the 1936 Democratic National Convention:

> For too many of us the political equality we once had won was meaningless in the face of economic inequality. A small group had concentrated into their own hands an almost complete control over other people's property, other people's money, other people's labor _ other people's lives ... Against economic tyranny such as this, the American citizen could appeal only to the organized power of government.

Here, Roosevelt explains why, in an age of corporate gigantism, one cannot simply blame economic inequalities on corrupted actors within the political system. In the middle lines, when Roosevelt mentions "other people's property," "money," and "labor," we see how Roosevelt took rhetorical themes directly from the most militant labor organizations of the era such as the Nonpartisan League. Steve Fraser writes that the years of 1936 and 1937 marked the height of Roosevelt's "reform zeal," a moment when "the language of labor and the language of executive power were indistinguishable" (1989: 71). One of the most central rhetorical attacks from labor organizations of the 1930s was aimed at "the manipulators of other people's money and exploiters of other people's labor" (70–71). During the Great Recession of the late 2000s, Democratic politicians largely stayed away from this type of morally loaded rhetoric about economic theft. Tea Party activists and Fox News pundits, on the other hand, completely embraced it. However, when the New Dealers were targeting the "exploiters of other people's labor,"[7] the parasites and vampires they were singling out were not the mere bureaucrats manipulating the economy from their own government perches. Rather, they were the very bankers and industrialists comprising the "private power[s]," actors indigenous to the market.

Yet, relative to the New Deal's broader history, this rhetorical posture was short-lived. By the end of the 1930s, the New Deal movement had transitioned from what historians Gary Gerstle and Steve Fraser refer to as "social Keynesianism" to that of "commercial Keynesianism" (1989: xiv). In addition to foreclosing the New Deal movement's more radical policy approaches, this transition would mark a shift in rhetorical style as well. The oppositional, anti-monopoly politics of the early New Deal and

---

[7] New York State Labor Non-Partisan League, "Declaration of Principles," July 16, 1936. (Fraser, 1989: 70)

the "venerated ideology of productive labor" underpinning it would now be abandoned in favor of technocratic arguments and social scientific bases of authority (Fraser, 1989: 56). This rhetorical shift, Fraser insists, is what drained the New Deal of its "moral preeminence, its political threat, and its elemental social significance" (1989: 57).

It wouldn't be until the "conservative backlash" of the 1960s and the rise of the "Silent Majority" during the Nixon era that producerism and the labor theory of value would return to mainstream politics. In addition to his "law and order" messaging, a key theme in Richard Nixon's speech at the 1968 Republican Convention was his pledge that he "would not rob [Americans] of the fruits of their success" (Wills, 1970: 310). In a later Labor Day message that same year, Nixon opined, "In a time when the national focus is concentrated upon the unemployed, the impoverished and the dispossessed, the *working* Americans have become the *forgotten Americans* [my emphasis]" (311). Similar to Jeffersonian–Jacksonian producerism, Nixon's "Silent Majority" rhetoric advanced laissez-faire economic positions but, unlike the artisan and farmer groups of the nineteenth century, it expressed little concern for banks, monopolies or wealth concentration. In the "Silent Majority" version of the producerist theft narrative, government welfare was presented as the principal mechanism for stealing the productive majority's wealth and property, with racial minorities being portrayed as society's chief parasitic menace.

Indeed, over the course of American political history, populist attacks have been aimed downward at nonwhite citizens and the poor as much as they have been directed against groups at the top of the social ladder (Berlet & Lyons, 2000; Lowndes, 2005). This is to say that while the postwar conservative movement may have taken advantage of populism's racial dimension, by no means did it invent it. The image of the American producer has almost always been a white, masculine persona (Roediger, 1991; Kazin, 1998). This was true even of the New Deal coalition's leftist articulation of producerism. In fact, the New Deal coalition's inability and unwillingness to incorporate the types of occupations that were predominantly held by women and people of color into the benefit structure of the New Deal, mirrored, as historian Elizabeth Faue has stressed, the exclusion of these groups from the movement's *symbolic construction* of the producing class.[8]

---

[8] Commenting particularly on the New Deal coalition and the Popular Front, historian Elizabeth Faue maintains that, "Women remained in a marginal and subordinated

It wasn't until these exclusionary measures came back to haunt the Democratic Left that the postwar conservative movement would, decades later, invert the political meaning of the working-class symbolism the New Deal activists had done so much to revive and reshape (Denning, 1998; Lipsitz, 2001: 47–50).

During the 1960s and 1970s the US class structure would go through profound changes as the national economy shifted from an industrial to a postindustrial model. Women workers flooded the ranks of the growing service sector and increasingly female-headed households started to replace the traditional lunch pail, blue-collar father figure of the postwar era (Stacey, 1990). Because President Lyndon B. Johnson's Great Society sought to accommodate – to an extent – the political demands of the civil rights and feminist movements, women and minorities became aligned with political liberalism. In the name of these different factions of the working class, the Democratic Party raised issues that had been traditionally associated with producerist values, such as establishing *fair pay* for women and minority workers and, as a corrective for its historical discrimination, creating an employment environment truly organized by *hard work* and *merit-based* advancement.

Civil rights leaders like Martin Luther King Jr. attempted to frame the nonwhite workers as an *underpaid* bloc of the working class whose low wages afforded the high living standard of middle-class whites by giving them cheap services (2010: 7). Still, conservative populists like Vice President Spiro Agnew and Alabama Governor George Wallace were more effective at framing the same group of workers as shirkers being coddled by government and showered by its largesse – an idea that was crystalized years later by President Ronald Reagan's mythology of the Cadillac-driving "welfare queens." In turn, while the second-wave feminist movement had attempted to highlight how women workers were in

position in the movement excluded both from the arrangements of power *and* [my emphasis] from the symbolic system of [productive] labor" (1991: 20). Sociologist Julie Bettie maintains that because women and people of color had been systematically excluded from industrial and union activity, claiming the category of productive labor was, she writes, "the exclusive domain of white working men." Thus, she continues, "The historic 'making of the American working class,' as well as its representation in culture, makes it difficult to envision white women and people of color as working class. Because [the] working class is identified with industrial labor, nonindustrial [and] nonunionized jobs, held largely by white women and people of color, appear to be outside the working-class category [and I would add the category of producer]" (1995: 134).

essence "double-producers" carrying an added economic load, given that they were both laborers in the paid workforce and laborers in the unpaid sphere of the home, this perspective, too, could be countered by conservatives questioning the commitment of these second-wave feminists to motherhood and blaming the so-called moral decay of society (a precursor term to "family values") on the decline of stay-at-home mothers. Conservatives were able to accentuate the gender of this new bloc of women workers, which, in effect, downplayed their class identity (Duggan, 2003). The conservative backlash that swiftly followed the policy gains women and minorities had made in the 1960s and 1970s could not be easily combated. With no countervailing leftist vision of who the producing class is, from the Great Society all the way to the Trump era, conservatives have consequently succeeded in politically positioning white, male workers against women and minorities.

The conventional story about the evolution of producer populism usually ends here. Gender and race-based scapegoating had disbanded the New Deal coalition, thus allowing the Right to capture the white working class and, in so doing, remake the waspy social image of the Republican Party into a working-class image. Political scientist Joseph Lowndes typifies this kind of historical analysis when he says, "Antistatist populism [became] attractive when race became the key issue to be managed by the liberal state" (2005: 171). But arguments like this are not so much wrong as they are incomplete. They only explain how conservative populism was able to construct a political–social alliance between the white working class and business elites through making a mutual contradistinction to nonwhite Others. This overlooks and underappreciates the enormous amount of intellectual work the postwar conservative movement had already devoted to constructing this link in positive terms by promoting the *productive-worthiness* of entrepreneurs, business owners, and those otherwise wealthy groups whose status as producers had been suspect within the populist tradition for centuries.

Thanks to "Chicago School" thinkers like Milton Friedman in the 1970s and thereafter, neoclassical and monetarist free-market theories started to dominate the academic field of economics and the policy circles of Washington (Harvey, 2005; O'Connor, 2007; Van Horn & Mirowski, 2009). At same time, we see outside the academy the explosion of free-market think tanks such as the Heritage Foundation (1973), the Cato Institute (1977) and the Manhattan Institute (1984). Using these new knowledge infrastructures, conservative activists more ardently committed themselves to translating free-market ideology into the populist moral language of producerism.[9]

As discussed in Chapter 3, the discursive work of conservative think tanks in this era was assisted by the new material realities of the postindustrial economy. Deindustrialization had reduced blue-collar, mid-skilled jobs to jobs of lesser status, and this in turn polarized the sociotechnical hierarchy of the labor market, thereby creating a situation whereby a few "high-skilled," IT related jobs occupied the top rung and a massive bloc of "low-skilled," service-sector jobs comprised the bottom. This created a symbolic vacuum for the producerist claims that conservatives usurped. Larry Grossberg writes that, in the shift to a service-sector–oriented labor market, "The welfare of workers ... declines almost directly in proportion to the increasing status of entrepreneurs, who, through their willingness to take risks, are now seen to produce the real wealth of the nation" (2005: 123).

"THE JOB CREATORS": FOX NEWS' REINTERPRETATION OF THE LABOR THEORY OF VALUE

On April 12, 2012, Fox News' founding CEO Roger Ailes gave a rare public lecture to an audience of journalism students at the University of North Carolina. As Zev Chafets chronicles in his biography of Ailes, the dean of the school requested that Ailes stay clear of politics in his talk. But with the 2012 presidential election on the horizon, Ailes couldn't help himself. Predicting that Obama would be running on a platform to raise taxes on the wealthy, Ailes told the students, "Every time I needed a job, I had to go to the rich guy. I love the poor guy. He had no job. I got a job, I tried to help the poor guy ... But I'm not going to let anybody divide me against the people who actually gave me the jobs" (2013: 227).[10]

---

[9] It is during the 1970s that, as historians Steven Fraser and Gary Gerstle write, one sees, "the startling recapture of the mind and soul of the Republican party by an old orthodoxy: the moral and commercial axioms of the nineteenth century's free market ideology" (1989: 296), i.e. the moral rhetoric of producerism. Supporting this, in his book *The Republican Noise Machine* (2004), David Brock highlights conservative intellectual William Rusher's 1975 book *The Making of the New Majority*. In this book, Brock writes, Rusher "concocted a theory of class conflict that pitted the struggle for political power as one of the 'producers' – manufacturers, blue-collar workers and farmers – against the 'non-producers," "chiefly members of the knowledge industry, the major news media, the educational establishment, the federal bureaucracy, the foundations and research centers and a semi-permanent welfare constituency" (81–82).

[10] For the full talk, see Ailes (April 12, 2012).

This talking point was nothing new. It's been echoed by conservatives since the 1970s. However, it was especially reiterated on Fox News' top shows during the Great Recession. In a June 17, 2009 episode of *Glenn Beck*, Beck read a letter from a viewer by the name of Janet Contreras, who had written:

Redistribution of wealth: No, I work for it. I work for my money. It's mine. I've always worked for people with more money than I have, because they gave me a job. That's the only redistribution of wealth I support. I never got a job from a poor person. And let me ask you another question, why do you want me to hate my employers? What do you have against shareholders making a profit, and charitable contributions?

This defense of the wealthy was even advanced on *Hannity* the day after America's largest financial institutions collapsed. In this September 16, 2008 episode, Hannity reminded his audience about the "luxury tax" in the early 1990s and groused, "They were going to tax yachts ... and guess who lost their job? The people who made their yachts and washed their jets. The really rich people didn't get hurt. I never got a job from a poor person."

Throughout Fox News' coverage of the recession, hosts across its leading programs equally referred to the rich as "job creators." This term is very important because it is what is used on Fox to redefine businessmen as part of the laboring class. In another episode of *Hannity*, one in which former (and now disgraced) Democratic congressman Anthony Weiner had asked host Sean Hannity, "Do we really need to give millionaires and billionaires a tax cut?" Hannity responded, "[Y]ou use this word millionaires and billionaires, it sounds pejorative to me ... [Y]ou say rich, let me use another term for rich: job creator, taxpayer" (December 14, 2010). Recognizing how Weiner's income-based descriptions of the rich had highlighted their extreme class difference from Fox viewers, Hannity was attempting to reinstate the moral standing of the rich by stressing their identity as "job creators" and as economically productive people.

The concept of "job creator" and its association with the rich, however, poses a set of problems for Fox News because having the ability to give or deny job positions is not so obviously productive work. In its long history, producerist discourse has associated social value with laboring. In fact, the very term "working class" is etymologically linked to its nineteenth-century predecessor, "the producing class" (Williams 1985: 64). Contrasting colonial American enterprise to aristocratic idleness in the Old World, Benjamin Franklin once called the United States "the land of labor," and for hundreds of years the "hard worker" has been considered the ideal civic subject. In contrast, wealth by birth has often been disparaged. So in echoing these cultural values, Fox News programs constantly reiterate that the wealth of the *worthy* rich is the product of individual effort, not that of nepotism or cronyism.

In another *Hannity* episode, his guest, former college football coach Lou Holtz, had complained that by raising taxes "we're trying to punish ... people that are most successful. Like, if you're successful, man, you must have done it illegally rather than with hard work" (April 13, 2010). As is evident here, in Fox programs the term "successful" is regularly used to describe the worthy rich. Unlike the term "rich," the term "successful" treats affluence and market dominance as merited. One encountered this rhetoric on *The O'Reilly Factor* as well. In an episode where guest Marc Lamont Hill had argued that Democrats "want to reward hard work" by providing better healthcare, education, and housing to the ninety-five percent of Americans who, Hill stressed, "go to work everyday," O'Reilly responded by claiming, "Rewarding hard work is when you succeed" (March 10, 2009). In other words, it is the market that determines the value of producers. And when translated into these moral terms, the privileged position of most elites becomes reconfigured as a product of the labor value of their work. In Fox News' social imaginary, all actors whose worth is defined by the market share a solidarity as both "workers" and "producers." In this way, Fox News commentators can emphatically argue that the wealthy are workers, too. In fact, the wealthy are often framed as the *hardest* workers, as the "super-producers," to use a term from conservative novelist Ayn Rand.

Fox News' constant emphasis on the hardworking personalities of "job creators" thus aligns them with the working class by defining them as members of – to use one Fox pundit's own words – "the productive people of the private sector," which, in turn, defines them against those of unearned privilege or the idle, something that is regularly associated with workers in the public sector. But businessmen do not fit this labor theory of value. So how can "job creation" and mere business ownership be said to create value? To address this, Fox News programs must construct the job creator's economic activity as that of useful, value-creating labor. And exactly what kind of labor is it that "job creators" do in the world of Fox News?

Job creators mainly amass capital, organize personnel, and live by the rules of the market. This is illustrated in an episode of *Glenn Beck*, where

Beck had compared the US federal government to "one company," which he sarcastically named "Evil Capitalism, Inc." In Beck's depiction, this company does not live by the market, and cannot govern in the face of its collapse. Beck suggests that the key to getting the "American engine" to "start-up" is to put to work the skills and insight of the CEO, which he equates with "common sense." Beck explains:

This one company, '[E]vil [C]apitalism Inc.' has these four [product] divisions ... What you do as a good CEO is you'd see these [underperforming] divisions and say, you suck! Do what this [successful] division is doing ... As a CEO, if you had one division consistently outperforming others, you wouldn't punish it. But that's exactly what America's CEO [President Obama] is now doing.

(August 11, 2010)

The essential skill that Beck identifies with the CEO is an ability to recognize the productivity and market performance of workers and products, and a willingness to distribute financial resources and organizational support accordingly. In Fox News' programming, the term "CEO" stands for effective leadership, and "running a business" stands for good governance. As a result, the managerial skills of the business class are consistently juxtaposed with the supposed incompetence of government officials and regulators. For example, in a different episode of *Glenn Beck*, guest pundit John Tamny declared, "Regulators are never equal with the very people they want to regulate. If they had these kinds of skills, they certainly wouldn't work for the federal government" (June 29, 2009). In yet another interview segment of *Hannity*, his guest, former vice presidential candidate Sarah Palin, questioned the leadership ability of President Obama and other Democrats by saying, "I don't know when they have run a business. I don't know when they have been a CEO of anything where they've had to look out for the bottom line and they've had to make payroll and live within their own means with a budget" (April 10, 2010). Here Palin represented the CEO as embodying fiscal discipline and responsibility, in contrast to the "reckless" misuse of money that she says is exemplified by Obama and other Democrats.

Frequently, the wise money management of a CEO is equated with what is done in frugal families – the kind who understand how to budget and "tighten their belts" in hard times – or by small business owners who, like CEOs, are accountable to market forces and understand the workings of the economy. In another episode of *Glenn Beck*, guest Mark Sanford, the Republican Governor of South Carolina, challenged polls showing that most Florida citizens supported taking federal stimulus money for infrastructure projects. Sanford asserted instead that, "There is a silent majority out there who doesn't fit ... with those polls ... who overwhelmingly are hardworking small businesspeople, who know what it's like to meet the bottom line, who had to actually make adjustments in their small businesses, who've actually had to make real world sacrifices" (June 8, 2009).

In Fox News programming, an equation is regularly made between big and small businessmen, suggesting that all private sector actors have – as evidenced by their superior fiscal self-discipline – a greater sense of economic realism than those working in the public sector or those receiving public aid. When depicting the business world, Fox News programs often use a discourse of what could be called *market empiricism* – that is, a notion that the market is an institution that most accurately reflects the conditions of empirical reality (i.e. "the real world"). In turn, the public sector is represented as a sphere of distorted reality that has been created by those who want to selfishly and irresponsibly insulate themselves and others from the moral obligation of work.

One sees the discourse of market empiricism in *The O'Reilly Factor* episode cited earlier, when O'Reilly had explained the nature of the economy in the lead segment. It is notable how O'Reilly sought to legitimate his economic analysis by aligning it with the views of a famous former CEO, Jack Welch, and other Wall Street traders. O'Reilly stated:

Welch is echoing what Wall Street believes that all this social engineering Barack Obama is promoting has little to do with getting the economy on track. Until the President understands that Wall Street is not buying into his western European vision for America, the economy will remain at risk. Ideology and capitalism are not a good mix. Free markets are tough places where the strong survive and the weak go under. Big government cannot dictate a vibrant marketplace.

(March 10, 2009)

Here, the business world is represented as a pragmatic, and even naturalistic sphere of action. When O'Reilly comments about "ideology and capitalism" not mixing, he treats government figures, namely President Obama, as ideologically driven proponents of social engineering who only have political, overintellectualized knowledge. Unlike public-sector workers and politicians, business figures are driven by practical concerns and rely on *apolitical*, utilitarian modes of reasoning.

In another episode of *The Factor*, where it was O'Reilly who was interviewing Sarah Palin, the value of producers was again constructed against the public sector's supposedly false standards of merit. In this interview, O'Reilly asked Palin to respond to critics who had challenged her intelligence and capability by posing his own question, "Do you believe that you are smart enough, incisive enough, intellectual enough to handle the most powerful job in the world?" Palin responded:

I believe that I am because I have common sense. And I have … the values that are reflective of so many other American values. And I believe that what Americans are seeking is not the elitism, the kind of a spinelessness that perhaps is made up for with some kind of elite Ivy League education and a fat resume that's based on anything but hard work and private sector, free enterprise principles.

(November 20, 2009)

The sexist undertone of O'Reilly's question about Palin's "competency" harkens back to points made in Chapter 2 concerning the differential treatment that Palin, a woman populist, received from her male conservative peers, which stood in contrast to the immense confidence O'Reilly, Hannity and others placed in Donald Trump's leadership abilities. But here, let us focus on Palin's own rhetoric. In her response, we see how she asserts that educational credentials are not as good a measure of worth as living by "private-sector, free enterprise principles." So producers are to be defined not only against government workers, but also against educational elites who do not measure worth in market terms. Because the market is constructed as the fundamental apparatus for measuring merit, educational credentials – a standard of worth assumed to be most valued in the public sector – are viewed as inflated or altogether illusory indicators of capability and work ethic.

In these ways, Fox News' leading programs work to naturalize the association between utilitarian intelligence, the practical world, and the free market, emphasizing social affinities between the business class and the working class. From this position, Fox News is able to present reasons to politically oppose Obama's stimulus spending and healthcare reforms and to support greater privatization of the public sector. The result of privatization is portrayed not as a loss of services or opportunity for workers, but rather as a gain that expands the realm that most recognizes their work ethic, brand of intelligence, and skill set.

During the Great Recession, talk of "socialism" versus "capitalism" saturated Fox News programming. These terms did not so much describe different economic systems but rather emphasized their divergent moral systems and the social divide between producers and parasites. They were useful shorthand for Fox News' more elaborate construction of socioeconomic conflict. On Fox News, the term, "capitalism," and its corollary, "the private sector," signify the traditional moral world and the meritocratic strategies of producerism: hard work, personal discipline, and practical know-how. These strategies imagine capitalism as consistent with working-class morality and culture. While liberal critics had been smugly pointing out that Fox News pundits were misusing the word socialism, Fox pundits were making this term and its corollary, the public sector, a tool for shaping the producerist ethic with its own special conservative meaning. Socialism became a useful way for Fox programs to signify the opposite of producerism, by adapting the term and using it to mean an immoral strategy of personal gain based on social maneuvering and cronyism rather than on *real* labor and merit.

Still, Fox's management-friendly interpretation of the producer tradition marked a fundamental break with nineteenth- and early twentieth-century conceptions of the producing class. While Jeffersonian–Jacksonian producerism of the nineteenth century had defined producers as artisans and farmers and had asserted a laissez-faire economic ideology, early twentieth-century Progressives and the New Deal coalition focused on the industrial-proletariat and supported a more interventionist state. Despite their differences, though, these versions of producerism emphasized the value created by direct labor – that is, the value created by the people closest to the point of production. But Fox News was now defining entrepreneurs as producers because they were "job creators," even though they were still a step removed from providing a product or service. And while the entrepreneurial producerism on Fox News was attempting to represent managerial activity as exemplary of utilitarian intelligence and skills, the types of utilitarian skills that have been most lauded by the working-class political movements of the past – the skills that physically and directly lead to the making of stuff. To explain this discrepancy away, Fox News started equating all entrepreneurs with small business owners who seemed similar to the otherwise disappearing small producer artisans or farmers of Jeffersonian America. Now, these people were both owners and manual laborers, entrepreneurs and skilled craftsmen.

Joseph Wurzelbacher's overnight transformation into a conservative media celebrity during the 2008 presidential campaign provides an especially poignant example of how conservative populist representational strategies strive to link business ownership to manual forms of labor. At an Ohio campaign stop, Wurzelbacher approached then-candidate Barack Obama and criticized his proposed tax policies because they would, from Wurzelbacher's perspective, hurt his dream to become an owner of a plumbing business. After this exchange, Wurzelbacher was nicknamed

"Joe the Plumber" and was immediately booked on several Fox News programs and talk radio shows. This gambit was then given further ballast through the verbal rhetoric of the McCain campaign and conservative pundits, all of whom said they were embracing Joe the Plumber because he represented the average American's aspiration to become a business owner. However, on a visual level, Joe the Plumber was a useful political symbol because he – a tall, white, brawny tradesman – at least residually embodied the manly image of the industrial working class, an image that stood in contrast to the feminized labor of service sector workers, which is the sector that actually employs the majority of the present-day working class.

As Jefferson Cowie's book *Stayin' Alive* (2010) demonstrates, in the 1970s, the Nixon administration's "blue-collar strategy" effectively wedded white union workers to the Right through calculated cultural appeals. Since then, the image of the construction worker has effectively been tied to conservative politics. This symbolic link between blue-collar labor and political conservatism gives conservative populism a deep cultural bearing. However, while the producerist class-coding of construction-related labor remains, since the 1970s many unionized, blue-collar jobs have disappeared and been replaced by nonunion contracting jobs. Contractors in the residential construction trades like plumbing, electrical, drywall, and framing might therefore be technically seen as "business owners," but what this label obscures is how often their incomes fluctuate and their ownership statuses remain tenuous – as Joe the Plumber's own personal story exemplifies. Certainly, self-employed contractors evade the necessity of having a boss in the traditional sense of the word, but the financial institutions they rely on to purchase supplies and fund operational costs often enact similar kinds of managerial supervision and discipline.

Nevertheless, for many workers small business ownership is perceived as a more attractive and/or likely route to upward mobility than higher education.[11] Echoing long-established ideas from "consensus" historians

---

[11] Michèle Lamont (2000) shows how white workers in the United States more readily identify with those who have higher incomes than those with higher educations. She posits that one reason workers are drawn to avenues of achievement defined by wealth over education is because, she writes, "the former is perceived as more within reach than the latter and can help workers to locate themselves above the college-educated" (104). For scholarship that illustrates the strong aspirations workers have to become business owners, see Chinoy, 1955; Palmer, 1957; Robinson & Kelley, 1979; Jackman & Jackman, 1985; Vanneman & Cannon, 1987.

such as Louis Hartz, David Potter, Daniel Boorstin, and Richard Hofstadter, some leftist critics attribute working-class aspirations to become business owners to the hegemony of possessive individualist values in America and a subsequent misidentification with the upper-class. What this "you-too-can-be-a-capitalist"-type of analysis tends to overlook, however, is how small business ownership also represents a moral-utopian view of labor and the economy that is particularly appealing to social groups who endure the most intense managerial supervision. Business ownership is seen as a way to achieve freedom from administrative evaluation and imagines a working context where one's intelligence and ability are judged principally by the quality of one's products or services as opposed to one's educational credentials or social connections. In short, wage workers identify with small business ownership not despite their class position but because of it.[12]

RACIALIZING THE STIMULUS ACT: THE PRODUCERIST NARRATIVE OF THEFT

In a March 10, 2009 segment of *The Factor* entitled "Socialism and the Economy," Bill O'Reilly confronted liberal guest Marc Lamont Hill with the dictate, "I want you to explain ... why other people on this planet *deserve* [my emphasis] the fruits of my labor?" Hill's response is interesting in that it questions O'Reilly's assumption that his wealth and success are merely the product of his *individual* labor. After some discussion O'Reilly maintains that he does not mind paying taxes, but, he argues:

Income redistribution is something else other than taxes ... it's basically above and beyond your fair share, which I'm willing to pay, all right, and I'd say 40 percent to 50 percent of my paycheck is fair ... Above and beyond that, Barack Obama and you and others say no, you have more of an obligation to then social engineer people who hadn't gotten educated, who don't work hard, who maybe were addicted for 30 years of their life, maybe they're clean now. Okay?

So while technically all forms of progressive taxation are redistributive in nature, we can see that O'Reilly's distinction between "socialist," "redistributionist policies" and regular tax policy is a moral one. He is suggesting that the former aid those without work ethic and self-discipline, and the latter description serves worthy individuals and programs.

[12] See Vanneman & Cannon, 1987: 83–87; Norell, 1990.

Later in the segment one sees how O'Reilly is articulating this framework of "deserving" and "undeserving" hardship within a highly personalized story of theft, stating:

The one percent pays more than 50 percent in income to the Feds. That's way skewed, but it's all right because we have the money. And I love my country. What I don't want is when I die you coming into my house, taking the stuff I've already paid taxes on out of my house to give it to somebody I don't know who may not deserve it.

But Hill smirks as if in disbelief that the Estate Tax is the policy O'Reilly would cite to make a point about economic fairness. Hill says, "First of all, the death tax [aka the Estate Tax] affects such a small slice of American people." O'Reilly, raising his voice, interjects, "It affects me!" This exchange demonstrates how O'Reilly is able to take a policy that exclusively benefits the wealthiest "slice" of the American population – something one might assume would be a liability for populist economic arguments – and turn it into a clear and compact example that captures the central lines of producerist moral reasoning.

O'Reilly compares taxation to home intrusion and burglary – after one's own death no less – and in doing so creates a vivid image of tyrannical government. The immorality of this act is heightened by stressing the unworthiness of the assumed recipients of government assistance (i.e. the "somebody I don't know"; "people ... who don't work"). Making this transfer of wealth even more immoral, O'Reilly frames Obama's "redistributionist" policies as victimizing the most virtuous members of the national community. In framing the debate over Obama's potential (albeit not actual) tax policy in terms of how it personally would impact his own life ("It affects me!"), O'Reilly becomes a stand-in for top-income earners and thus represents them as a meritorious group who come from the same humble background as does O'Reilly – and implicitly the viewer – but who, like O'Reilly, rose to wealth solely through their own talents and hard work. As a final hammer, O'Reilly amplifies the immorality of increased taxation on the rich by suggesting that it is they who carry the biggest economic burden for the national community ("the top one percent pays more than 50 percent in income").

Interestingly, this moralistic posture was largely absent in Fox News' coverage of the 2008 financial collapse. In this programming period, Fox News pundits asserted, over and over again, that the recession was caused by ill-conceived Democratic policies that "forced" banking institutions to lower lending standards to in order to help minority and low-income communities attain mortgages. The policies that were particularly blamed were the Community Reinvestment Act of 1977 and the more recent policies of government-sponsored mortgage companies like Freddie Mac and Fannie Mae, all of which were designed to extend access to home loans for the traditionally discriminated against, economically disadvantaged groups.

In essence, Fox News' causation narrative was a story of how government elites and their base supporters ruined the economy due to, at the top, a blind commitment to liberal statist ideology and, at the bottom, the unintelligent and "undisciplined" character of subprime borrowers. Though not explicitly calling it welfare, this causation narrative racialized these policies by frequently describing them as "redistribution" and "affirmative action." These anti-welfare rhetorical frames dovetailed with Fox News' coverage of Obama's presidential campaign and his political ascendancy as well. For example, in a September 1, 2008 episode of *The Factor*, O'Reilly suggested that if Obama won it would be because of Hollywood support and because "he'll win among minority voters. And his *entitlement* [my emphasis] message is powerful" (September 1, 2008).

While Fox News' causation narrative blamed the recession on the liberal opposition, it faulted them primarily in terms of their incompetence and ignorance as opposed to their immorality and aggression. However, once Obama officially took power and the Stimulus Act, the largest most affirmative response to the crisis, was moved forward, one sees how Fox News began to increasingly structure its interpretation of the late-2000s recession around a singular moral transgression: theft. Theft narratives convey a sense of victimization and evoke visceral image of assault. Fox News' adoption of this story structure in early 2009 did what the network's 2008 causation narrative failed to do: it provided a justification for Fox News hosts and pundits to approach recession-related stories using an emotional, populist mode of address that was so crucial to both the network's brand identity and, on a political level, to its ability to channel the discontent of rank-and-file Republicans.

A February 18, 2009 episode of *Hannity* exemplifies the tonal and narrative transition from Fox News' 2008 causation narrative to its 2009 anti-stimulus narrative. Aired the day after the Stimulus Act was officially passed, host Sean Hannity told his guest:

For the average American sitting back here tonight . . . you know, people who get up every morning, shovel coffee down their throat . . . work fourteen hours a day, they obey the laws, they played by the rules . . . Now they're going to pay the bill for the mortgages of people who are not responsible. And these banks were forced to make these loans by government because of redistribution policies. . .They're on the hook to pay other people's mortgages?

On February 19, 2009, the very next day, a far more famous exchange occurred on *Squawk Box*, the CNBC morning business news program. In what became known as the "rant heard around the world," financial analyst Rick Santelli half-jokingly called for a "Chicago Tea Party" protest and, in so doing, unintentionally coined the name of the already growing conservative protest movement that, up to this point, had been describing its events as "porkulous protests." Santelli's Tea Party defining speech echoed almost exactly the narrative Hannity had expressed on Fox News the night before. Standing among fellow stock traders on the floor of the Chicago Stock Exchange, Santelli angrily suggested first that "people vote on the Internet as a referendum to see if we really want to subsidize the losers' mortgages; or would ... like to ... reward people that could carry the water instead of drink the water." Santelli then turned from addressing the *Squawk Box* host through the video feed to addressing the applauding day traders around him and asked, "How many of you people want to pay your neighbor's mortgage that has an extra bathroom and can't pay their bills? Raise [your] hand. President Obama, are you listening?"

Both Hannity and Santelli would give variations of the "forgotten man" narrative that would be repeated across various conservative media outlets during the recession – the story of an "average," economically productive citizen (e.g. a "they work fourteen hours a day," or "carry the water"-type) who is coerced by the government to financially support irresponsible and unproductive citizens (e.g. those who only "drink the water"). As evident in this language, this variation of the forgotten man narrative relies on the same producer/parasite binary and theft narrative of the PEA outlined in the previous historical section. However, unlike the nineteenth-century political narratives, which focused on corporate–government collusions, Hannity and Santelli emphasize how the state funnels wealth to an undeserving, parasitic class who dwell below in exchange for partisan loyalty and political patronage.

Even in the stimulus bill's prospective form before it was brought to Congress, Fox News' top programs were framing it not as something designed to kick start economic activity but as, to use the words of Dick Morris (a recurring guest on *The Factor*), a "Trojan horse" for trans-forming America into a "welfare-oriented society," or, as O'Reilly put it in the same conversation, a "hyper-Sweden" (January 29, 2009). By framing the progressive economic policies used to address the crisis as essentially nothing but a Democratic ploy to expand government welfare

programs, these policies, like Fox News' framing of the subprime mortgage crisis, took on the racial connotations of welfare.

In an episode of *Hannity*, Joe the Plumber told the host, "I don't
pretend to be an economic wizard here, but the stimulus package he's
[Obama] talking about sounds like a handout to me" (January 19, 2009).
Days later, Hannity attacked Obama advisor Robert Reich for his suggestion that the jobs programs in the stimulus bill should ensure that
women and racial minorities equally benefit from the package. Hannity
framed Reich's comments as proof that the bill was designed to favor
minorities (January 22, 2009). Beck's and O'Reilly's programs followed
this trend of framing the stimulus bill as nothing but a ruse to increase
"nanny state" welfare.

However, the racial dimensions of Fox News' rhetorical framing of the
Great Recession involved much more than simply presenting the Stimulus
Act as welfare by another name. This policy, Fox News pundits stressed,
symbolized a deeper, cultural break with traditional values and the
American past. In the months leading to the passing of the stimulus bill
in early 2009, Fox News pundits made grand warnings about the growing
distance between the current generation and the moral–economic principles of traditional America. In an episode of *The O'Reilly Factor*, Bill
O'Reilly questioned whether or not "Americans – some, not all, of
course – are willing to sell out the capitalistic system for Big Brother
government to *give* [as opposed to earn] them money" (January 5,
2009). Parroting O'Reilly, Hannity himself asked, "Has the average
American maybe lost touch with our founders and our framers? Do you
think most Americans have been conditioned to think that the government is going to be the answer to every problem they have? (February 20,
2009). Though Fox hosts use terms like "Americans," having long
addressed the conservative base as the "traditionalist" bloc of the US
political field, Fox hosts and the audience are implicitly claiming to be
part of the "not all" hinted at by O'Reilly, the ones standing against the
cultural trends of the moment.

As memory studies scholar Barbie Zelizer stresses, the notion of a
"stable past" is fundamental to the "establishment and maintenance of
political identity" (1995: 227). It is the past, quoting Jean Chesneaux,
that "enables us to know what is worth defending and preserving in
[society], and what should be overthrown and destroyed" (227). Paul
Taggart notes how populist political movements are particularly reliant
on "past-directed" concepts like "tradition" and "heritage," and they

often present their cause as an effort to "bring back ancient values into the contemporary world" (2000: 16).

Too often critics assume that Fox News pundits' repeated references to "traditional values" is always a watchword for culture war issues (e.g. God, guns, and gays). However, it is also deeply tied to the notion of the traditional "work ethic," namely, producerist moral-economic principles. As Franklin Gilliam and Shanto Iyengar's research shows, the "new racism" of today's news environment is most often expressed through the language of "traditional values" (2000: 566), with the issue of welfare being at the heart of this language, since it is a political topic that is in fact a stronger wedge issue with the low-income whites than are religious topics like abortion and school prayer (Bartels, 2008: 83–93).

The comparison between the late-2000s crisis and the Great Depression of the 1930s was one of the most persistent, widespread media themes in the national media during 2009 (Pew, 2009). In their framing of the Great Recession, Fox News programs would make similar historical analogies, but their analyses went beyond making mere economic comparisons. Fox pundits consistently proclaimed a *cultural kinship* with the Depression generation and strove to present their audience as its modern standard bearers. This rhetorical strategy involved shifting modes of analysis when treating past and present crises. On the one hand, the principles of the stimulus bill and Obama's popular base were presented as antithetical to the "producer ethic" of the Depression generation. On the other hand, this same generation's historical ties to FDR (Franklin D. Roosevelt Sr.) and the Democratic Party and their reliance on New Deal policies were depoliticized and turned into an amoral, technical question about the efficacy of Keynesian policy solutions. Fox News pundits executed this delicate double-move to imply that the recipients of stimulus aid in the Great Recession were fundamentally different than the Greatest Generation.

"WHO HAVE WE TURNED INTO?": THE STIMULUS ACT AS A SIGN OF GENERATIONAL TRANSFORMATION AND MORAL DECLINE

In his 1935 annual address to Congress, President Roosevelt famously condemned the free-market principle of possessive individualism. "Americans must forswear the conception of the acquisition of wealth," he had proclaimed. During the stimulus debate, Fox pundits criticized contemporary American culture along the same greed-condemning moral lines but reversed FDR's policy analysis. In a segment devoted to the Depression's history, guest Mike Huckabee told Hannity, "The fundamental difference between the generation of FDR and my parents and this generation ... [is that t]hey really believed that they should make sacrifices so their kids would have a better life." By supporting stimulus spending and raising the national debt, he concluded, "We're sacrificing our kids for ourselves" (February 20, 2009). Following Huckabee's logic, it is government assistance that is acquisitive and self-centered, while it is a free-market policy that is guided by a communitarian ethic. In another episode, Hannity made similar generational distinctions: "My father grew up during the Depression, literally put cardboard in his shoes, because he couldn't afford it ... They didn't have healthcare, they didn't have college tuition, they didn't have a mortgage, or a house guaranteed. When have we taken on this entitlement mentality?" (February 24, 2009).

Here, we see how Fox pundits have turned the moral lessons of the Great Depression on their heads and have rescripted the Depression generation's story to be that of a bootstrap tale of self-reliance – even though this generation turned to government in unprecedented ways to achieve a middle-class life. In contrast, those seeking government aid in the Great Recession are depicted as acquisitive and immoral. Fox News' analysis of Depression era policies utilize a proportionally different mode of criticism; they tend to undercut New Deal policies more on empirical historical grounds. This analytical gear shifting allows Fox News pundits to discredit the New Deal's affirmative, interventionist approach without questioning the Depression generation's work ethic, self-reliance and manhood.

In a February 17, 2009 episode of *The O'Reilly Factor*, when the Great Depression is discussed, O'Reilly's guest Neil Cavuto denounced the efficacy of the New Deal with reference to the "empirical" historical record, telling Bill O'Reilly matter-of-factly, "They [financial experts] know the history on this stuff as you know the history on this stuff. Stimulus, heavy on spending does very little to help us out of a morass." Yet, when O'Reilly turned to the present crisis and asked Cavuto what the average American should be most "afraid of" in today's economic environment, ironically the financial analyst and "numbers guy" Cavuto insisted that Americans should be most worried about shifting cultural norms. He warned, "I would be very afraid of the precedent we're setting here, that if you can't pay your mortgage, someone's there to bail you out. If you're falling on tough times, the government's there to help you."

FIGURE 4.1 Fort Myers Town Hall

The February 11 and 12 episodes of *Glenn Beck* are particularly illustrative examples of how analytical approaches change with the era being addressed. In both episodes, discussions about the New Deal were directly preceded by segments focusing on the town hall meeting President Barack Obama held in Fort Myers, Florida, to stress the need for the stimulus package. In the February 11 episode, Beck began the segment by asking if the stimulus package would fix the economy. After some discussion with Stephen Moore, an economist and columnist for the *Wall Street Journal*, Beck segued to a video clip of an exchange between Obama and an audience member. The viewer sees an older African American woman standing in the audience with microphone (Figure 4.1).

She pleads, "We need something more than vehicles and parks to go to," indicating she is homeless. "We need our own kitchen and our own bathroom. Please help." Approaching her, Obama promises, "We're going to do everything we can to help you ... I'll have my staff talk to you after this town hall." As the topic of discussion segued from the stimulus package to the video clip, the mode of analysis shifted from Moore's economistic expertise to a moral evaluation of the woman in the clip. This individual exemplifies, Beck asserted, a "how do I get mine" mentality. He continued, with a tone of disbelief, "She just went to the president of the

United States and said, "I need a new house," and then she got one." Having the last word, Moore closed the segment saying, "You know what most Americans think of this? Get a job!" (February 11, 2009).

In the following day's episode, Beck and conservative pundit Michelle Malkin commented on three video clips from the same town hall event. The viewer was shown a clip of an African American man who asked the president about an easier way to maintain government assistance when facing sporadic fluctuations in monthly income. The second clip replays the video of the older African American women seeking housing. The last clip featured a white Hispanic teenager who said he works at McDonald's. This Millennial generation worker asks Obama how he would address the lack of job mobility and stagnant wages fast-food employees like himself face. The camera returned to a mid-shot of Beck. He cocked his head with a grimaced look and said, "Michelle, hmm . . . who have we turned into?" Malkin responded, "I'm appalled that the culture of entitlement has exploded so much that people don't think twice when these audience members go seeking absolution and all sorts of manna from heaven from the president of the United States." "My gosh," Beck responded, "I couldn't imagine asking that." "Yes," Malkin finished, "we've become a nation of moochers."

Threading together Beck's framing of the stimulus bill with previous framing used during Fox's coverage of Obama's 2008 presidential campaign, Malkin continued, "We saw a very similar video clip, which has been played on Fox News a lot, of another Obama supporter." "Here," Beck said, "we have the clip." The viewer is shown a video of a young, African American woman with her daughters in the crowd at Obama's victory speech. A reporter asks her why she was so moved by the moment. She responds, "Because I . . . won't have to worry about putting gas in my car. I won't have to worry about paying my mortgage . . . if I help him, he's going to help me." The camera returned to Beck shaking his head in disbelief. Malkin said, with a smile on her face, "That's right. Loaves and fishes multiply, pork and Kool-Aid falls from the sky!" Without acknowledging this racist comment, Beck segued by offering a historic quote that encapsulated the central tenet of producerism, "Thomas Jefferson said: [a quote appears on the screen] Democracy will cease to exist when you take away from those who are willing to work and give it to those who don't" (February 12, 2009).

A February 9 episode critiqued FDR's interventionist approach by using a historical comparison that contrasted the New Deal to President Coolidge's laissez-faire approach to the "forgotten depression" of

1920–1921. Statistical analysis, policy events and references to Hayekian economic theory were used to highlight the New Deal's supposed failure and the triumph of free-market policies at fixing earlier recessions. Beck's February 10 segment on the Depression shared the statistical orientation of the previous episode but instead focused on the theme of the New Deal's wasteful, ineffectiveness. Note again that Beck's focus was not on the immorality of New Deal policies or the people who relied on them.

In fact, in all these episodes Beck's program is careful *not* to describe New Deal policies using the language of idleness and dependency. In contrast, his analysis of the stimulus and Obama's popular base will predominantly focus on questions about moral integrity and work ethic. Through the juxtaposition of these segments and through the selective use of anti-welfare discourses, these Fox programs implied that the New Deal – despite its misalignment with free-market ideology – provided *deserved* assistance.

WHY MORAL DISCOURSES OF CLASS MATTER

In the middle of one of the most severe economic crises in recent history, Fox News, the most influential media source of the American Right, adopted the *forgotten man* narrative of the 1930s to explain the economic injustices laid bare by the Great Recession. But Fox's top hosts defined these injustices in a very specific and limited way. They were almost always presented as the result of corruption within the political system and biased government intervention. Capitalism bore no blame. In fact, Fox hosts presented the market as a liberatory, subversive force that counteracts political cronyism and the credential-education-based class system. This does not mean that Fox News programs presented the private sector as a classless domain; rather, the private economy was depicted as a "naturally classed" social space (Burke, 1995) where, to quote O'Reilly, "the strong survive and weak go under."

Gareth Jones described a similar conceptualization of social class in his examination of the British Chartist movement's populist rhetoric during the mid-nineteenth century.

The distinction was not primarily between ruling and exploited classes in an economic sense, but rather between the beneficiaries and the victims of corruption and monopoly political power. The juxtaposition was in the first instance moral and political, and dividing lines could be drawn as much within classes as between them.

(1983: 169)

Moral discourses of class are less effective at explaining the empirical causes of income inequality and the defining of class differences with precision. However, as Andrew Sayer has observed, such discourses are more effective than social-scientific ones in telling us why we should care about class in the first place (2005: 7). And, when used in service of a political movement or ideological project, moral discourses of class tell us which forms of social hierarchy we should oppose and which ones we should accept as normal or fair. Fox News' populist framing of the Great Recession was successful, I argue, because producerist moral rationales still inform, often in unrecognized ways, the underlying normative assumptions about class, work, and wealth distribution in the United States.

Cultural sociologist Michèle Lamont argues that, often, "conceptions of moral communities and cultural membership underlie policy choices." But she also notes that the political impact of moral discourses of social hierarchy in America "remains underexamined" (2000: 9). Linguist and cognitive scientist George Lakoff is arguably the most prolific scholar whose research addresses the role of moral rhetoric in American politics. Indeed, my analysis of Fox News' recession coverage reinforces two core claims that Lakoff has been making for decades (1996; 2004; 2008). First, my analysis confirms Lakoff's argument that, in the hierarchy of political modes of thought, moral rationales take primacy over rational logic and fact-based considerations. Second, I agree with Lakoff that American conservatives tend to be more adept at using moral language than liberals, partly because conservatives are more willing to embrace this mode of political communication.

Where I differ with Lakoff is on the question of why moral narratives resonate. His explanation is primarily neurological. Moral frames are powerful and even dangerous, he suggests, because they activate "neural circuits" and unconscious thought processes (2008). Social psychologist Jonathan Haidt describes something similar with his concept of moral "triggers" (2012). In contrast to Lakoff and Haidt, however, I attribute the influence of conservative moral narratives less to our evolutionary psychology and more to their deep, historical embeddedness in American political culture.

The moral narratives conservatives use have power not because they are exclusively tailored to the psychological dispositions of Republican voters and conservative audiences, as Lakoff and Haidt suggest. These narratives have pull precisely because their cultural currency transcends contemporary partisan lines and the discursive borders of the conservative media echo chamber. Fox's CEO Roger Ailes hinted at the extra-partisan, popular appeal of Fox's moral rhetoric in a 2010 interview with the Hoover Institute, a free-market think tank. "If you understand America," Ailes said, "people say well it's a center right nation and there is some truth to that [but], in the end, there are simple things the American people believe in ... Americans are simple but not simpletons."[13]

In this chapter, I demonstrated how populism, the producer ethic and "traditional values" are NOT inherently tied to conservative politics. Instead, these linkages are *constructed* by Fox News and other producers of conservative discourse. Historicizing the connection between producer populism and political conservatism reveals that the values and work-based sources of dignity that conservatives deeply identify with have been before and could again be realized through alternative political solutions. This same process of denaturalization shows liberals that the populist tradition is far more mutable than it appears to be and cannot be automatically reduced to authoritarian politics and the primitive, reactionary impulses of the white working class.

[13] Hoover Institution (2010).

5

The Populist-Intellectual Tactic

How Fox News Incorporates Expert Knowledge within Its Populist Framework

Fox News' top programs are unique in television news because they are more likely to embrace lay forms of knowledge such as personal experience in an attempt to perform (and construct) a working-class brand of intellectualism that I call the *popular intellect* (see Chapter 3). But because critics often emphasize this tendency of Fox News to separate itself from the epistemic culture of educated professionals (a culture, by the way, that had comfortably dominated the journalistic field for the greater part of the twentieth century), Fox has been frequently cast as an anti-intellectual news organization. The satirical news program *The Daily Show* in particular helped create Fox's anti-intellectual reputation by treating Fox News as its favorite comedic object. But the branding strategies of Fox's main competitors in the cable news market also helped create the Fox stereotype. For example, *Morning Joe*, one of MSNBC's most successful programs, once marketed itself as "the thinking viewer's choice," an implicit jab at Fox's morning show *Fox & Friends*. Yet a closer look at Fox News programming reveals that both the exaggerated quality of these negative representations of Fox and that network's own performed hostility to educated elites is, in fact, selective and, to an extent, contrived.

This contrivance was no more apparent than during Fox News' coverage of the stimulus debate of early 2009. In this period, an unprecedented number of conservative authors and think tank researchers had been appearing on Fox News' top shows to lend "official" legitimacy to the

FIGURE 5.1 *Hannity* presents Shlaes' book

network's critique of the stimulus bill.[1] A striking component of these critiques involves the concerted revising of the history of the Great Depression, with Amity Shlaes' *The Forgotten Man: A New History of the Great Depression* (2007) being the book that Republican politicians and Fox News pundits most often referenced for the grounds of their argument (see Figure 5.1).

Shlaes had contended that, contrary to conventional wisdom, it had been the New Deal itself that prolonged rather than shortened the Great Depression of the 1930s, and thus it was the New Deal that exemplified

---

[1] The year of 2009 marks a high point for the appearance of experts and researchers from the top five conservative think tanks on Fox News programming over a ten-year time span, according to Factiva's database of Fox News broadcast transcripts and its analytic tools for tracking phrase frequency (accessed December 7, 2011). The highest points where experts from these major think tanks appeared on Fox News' top-rated programs or were cited came in three marked periods: the early months of 2009, the months surrounding the stimulus debate and during August and September, and the months during the town hall protests over the healthcare bill. Hundreds of lesser-known think tanks also appeared on Fox News during this period but the most visible think tanks were the Heritage Foundation (1973), the Cato Institute (1977), the Manhattan Institute (1984), the Competitive Enterprise Institute (1984), the American Enterprise Institute (1943), and the Hoover Institution (1919).

the folly of using government spending to lift the nation out of the 2008–2010 economic downturn.

Taking the example of Fox News' elaborate promotion of Shlaes and her book, this chapter demonstrates how the network provides an exceptional publicity platform to the conservative intelligentsia. I argue that Fox News is better understood not as inherently *anti*-intellectual, but rather as a popular interface *for* conservative intellectual culture. With its programming serving as a vital translation function, I show how Fox News has been able to convert the theoretical knowledge produced by free-market think tanks into what Stuart Hall calls "a public idiom"– that is, into an accessible, popular language.[2]

While it is true that, during the recession, Fox News' top programs would continue to cover all its familiar celebrity scandals and sensationalistic phenomena like the "teenage 'sexting' epidemic," an equal, if not larger, part of Fox News' editorial agenda covered the "hard" news topics of government policy – and most notably that of economic policy. The two fields of knowledge that became central in the national news media in early 2009 – economics and economic history – have a strong quantitative orientation that necessitates expert-driven, empirical modes of argument. Difficult as it might seem to execute in a news environment saturated with the voices of economists and statistic-heavy, economic stories, Fox News' programming strategy was brilliant in the way it seamlessly folded expert bases of knowledge into the network's larger populist representational strategy, thereby enhancing its hosts' accompanying moralistic rhetoric with a shrewdness and distinction that can appear quite persuasive.

In addition to having think tank researchers as guests, Fox News' top shows regularly guided the viewers to the website of free-market institutes for "more information." For example, in one of the "recession-era" episodes, host Sean Hannity tells famed Republican strategist Karl Rove how he found all the information about the stimulus bill at the Heritage Foundation's website. "By the way," Hannity then says in an aside to his viewers, "the website is AskHeritage.org. I got a lot of information [from them]." Backing Hannity's suggestion, Rove notably follows up by echoing the name, "AskHeritage.org. Yes." Then plugging it one more time, Hannity

---

[2] In "The Social Production of News" (1981), Stuart Hall and his colleagues explain a process whereby experts, which they call "the primary definers," first produce the elite knowledge that *pre*-frames the agenda and ideological perspective of the news reports, after which journalists, or "the secondary definers," translate this official knowledge into a "public idiom" which makes the news products accessible for a lay audience (1981: 342–345).

repeats the site name again, "AskHeritage. All right" (January 29, 2009). The soft sell point is thus made, then made again, then made yet again.

Yet the citation of conservative think tanks and the on-air use of data points taken from the policy briefs they produce constitutes only one of the more simplistic aspects of how expertise is used on Fox News. To really grasp the complexity of this, we must look more closely at the appearance of experts on Fox News programs and probe the institutional affiliations behind the production and promotion of their work.

In order to create the new "consensus" about the New Deal – one seemingly shared in elite academic circles and by the commonsense-thinking Fox hosts – Fox programs borrowed from different class-based forms of knowledge and cultural authority. I refer to this performative orchestration of populist and technocratic modes of argumentation as the *populist-intellectual tactic* (PIT). When done successfully, PIT can be a powerful ideological tool. On the other hand, using this tactic also carries risks, particularly for Fox News, since relying too heavily on elite author-ities potentially undermines the working-class aesthetic and populist sens-ibility that Fox News programs had used to distinguish themselves from their rivals in the news industry. How are Fox programs able to continue to construct their populist brand when they frame it as being opposed to intellectuals, while they simultaneously deploy these same elite forms of credibility to validate their conservative revision of the Depression's history? An episode of *Hannity* that features Amity Shlaes and her afore-mentioned book, *The Forgotten Man*, shows how the inherent elitism of expert knowledge is kept at arm's length through the use of various representational maneuvers.

The first section of this chapter engages the history of conservative think tanks and draws upon scholarship that uses Bourdieusian field theories to conceptualize public intellectuals and think tank experts. The second section uses Amity Shlaes' career and the promotion of her book during the stimulus debate to highlight the interrelationships between the three major knowledge apparatuses of the conservative movement: their free-market research centers, the Republican Party and Fox News. Moving from this organizational perspective, the remaining sections provide a close textual analysis of a *Hannity* episode devoted to *The Forgotten Man*. Using the concept of the populist-intellectual tactic, I demonstrate how Fox's top programs did more than plug Shlaes' book and amplify her name recognition. They carried out the intricate and challenging *interpret-ive* work of adapting the historical content of the book to the cable news-magazine format.

According to Stuart Hall, the translation function that news programs like *Hannity* provides "not only makes [expert viewpoints] more 'available' to the uninitiated; it invests them with popular force and resonance, naturalizing them within the horizon of understandings of the various publics" (1981: 345). While the Fox News *organization* had helped realize the publicity strategies of Amity Shlaes, equally important was how Fox News *programs* had discursively reconfigured her research in a way that expanded her base of cultural authority beyond the narrow confines of the conservative intellectual community and its middlebrow consumer base.

In the last decade, a number of journalism scholars have applied field theory to elucidate the media-based strategies that experts like Amity Shlaes use to gain or secure status within their own intellectual communities (Benson & Neveu, 2005).[3] This literature has done much to reveal both the inter-field dynamics between social science, journalism and politics and the internal field logics that structure the rules of competition among experts within knowledge-producing institutions. However, less attention has been given to the *representational* dimension of field logics, how they are constructed and reinforced by and through media presentations that involve rhetorical strategies, aesthetic calculations and embodied performative styles.[4] One of the goals of this chapter is to address this gap and specifically show how media performances of expertise are enhanced when tactically paired with performances of non-professional, populist communicative styles.

CREATING THE "COUNTER-INTELLIGENTSIA":
UNDERSTANDING THE RIGHT'S CLOSE BUT COMPLICATED
RELATIONSHIP WITH INTELLECTUAL CULTURE

Fox News' skill in managing the tensions between the populist and intellectual elements of conservative political culture at the level of

---

[3] The foundational text in this literature is Rodney Benson & Erik Neveu's 2005 edited volume entitled *Bourdieu and the Journalistic Field*. Also see Jacobs & Townsley, 2011; Medvetz, 2012; Benson, 2013; Briggs & Hallin, 2016.

[4] Erica Robles-Anderson and Patrik Svensson (2016) demonstrate how "performative authority" has become increasingly more important with the proliferation of PowerPoint software. This software triggered the rise of what they call "a presentation culture," a culture that is epitomized by TED talks, a media organization that provides free online lectures designed for popular audiences.

representation is part and parcel of the conservative movement's historical success at reconciling the same tensions at an organizational level. With the rise of the "Chicago Revolution" and the rebirth of neoclassical economic theory in the 1970s, the conservative movement had produced one of greatest ironies of modern American politics. That is, while the movement was formulating its working-class populist image by attacking cultural elites, it was, at the same time, investing immense resources into building free-market research institutes and promoting members of its own intellectual class such as Milton Friedman. Stephanie Mudge identifies this paradox within the work of neoliberalism's most foundational thinker, Friedrich Hayek. "Given Hayek's critique of expert rule," she writes, "one of the ironies of neoliberalism's victory is the rise of economics [experts] as one of the most – if not *the* most – politically powerful professions in the world" (2011: 346).

In 1973, beer magnate Joseph Coors helped launch the Heritage Foundation. This organization would not only become one of the most influential think tanks in the United States, it would also, at a deeper level, redefine political expertise altogether. Historian George Nash's description of Heritage as "the nerve center of the Reagan Revolution" was not hyperbole (1998: 335). According to conservative activist Paul Weyrich, at Reagan's first cabinet meeting in 1980 the new President passed out Heritage's policy transition manual and said, "This is a blue print to run the administration. I want you to follow it."[5] Like other conservative think tanks that emerged around the same time, such as the American Enterprise Institute (revamped in 1972), the Cato Institute (1977), and the Manhattan Institute (1978), the Heritage Foundation was inspired by former Nixon Supreme Court nominee Lewis Powell's now infamous "Powell Memorandum." Addressed to the Chamber of Commerce and enthusiastically received by corporate leaders at Hewlett-Packard and Standard Oil (Phillips-Fein, 2009: 163–169; Medvetz, 2012: 102–105), the memo echoed an argument conservative intellectuals such as Irving Kristol and William Simon had already been making in their writing; this was a call for conservative activists and business leaders to go beyond an electoral-legislative-based political strategy and invest greater energy in building a "counterintelligentsia" that could challenge the Democratic Left's cultural hegemony in the arts, academia and the media (O'Connor, 2007: 73–75).

---

[5] Quoted in Medvetz, *Think Tanks in America*, p. 109.

Though the Democratic left had been quite successful in the heyday of the Progressive era and in the 1930s at developing "in-house" movement intellectuals, since the Nixon and Reagan eras they had failed to match the same kind of strong commitment the Right has more recently shown. Today's liberals have tended to attach their policy arguments to the non-partisan knowledge producers operating *outside* the political field.[6] While this strategy has allowed Democrats to secure more votes from professors, college students, journalists and other educated groups who pride themselves as being part of the "fact-based community" (Sherman, 2010), it has not been nearly as effective as that of their conservative counterparts in the mainstreaming of socialist or Keynesian, demand-side economic theories through popular media channels.

In his book *Think Tanks in America* (2012), Thomas Medvetz argues that part of the reason the conservative research institutes began to eclipse liberal and non-partisan think tanks such as the Brookings Institution relates to the former's greater ability at managing the contradictions and opposing pressures of the "field of expertise." Medvetz takes this concept from sociologist Gil Eyal (2002, 2006). Eyal's theoretical model defines this field in terms of two strategic dilemmas that expert groups find themselves continually facing:

(1) Are they to embrace "closure" strategies designed to achieve elite distinction among an insulated group of expert peers, or should they embrace "openness," media-centric strategies that elevate the value of their research through publicity?

(2) Should they be stressing their intellectual "autonomy" and creative independence, or should they accept their "dependency" on the consumers of their intellectual products and thus be shaping their work according to the audience's communicative and ideological preferences?

---

[6] In his article, "The Politics of Expertise in Congress and the News Media," Andrew Rich surveys the views members of congress have of think tanks to show that Democratic congresspeople view think tanks that do not identify with a political ideology as most credible, whereas conservative congress members hold that conservative think tanks are the most credible (2001: 586). This demonstrates how the congressional Left is still committed to the "end of ideology" liberal consensus of the postwar era, whereas their conservative counterparts are more likely to cite and support ideologically invested and self-identified knowledge-producing organizations. This study also demonstrates the significant uptick of sources from conservative think tanks that had been called to testify in Congress after the 1994 and 1995 Republican takeover (592). Rich notes similar differences between the two parties in "chapter 3: Political Credibility," in his 2004 book *Think Tanks, Public Policy, and the Politics of Expertise.*

As Medvetz explains, many of the activist-experts of the Left who cut their political teeth during the liberation movements of the 1960s were harbored by university institutions and gradually became "ivory tower" intellectuals, a type of expert enjoying high degrees of intellectual autonomy but low degrees of public engagement. The rules of career advancement within higher educational institutions encouraged left intellectuals to rely on "closure" strategies of cultural legitimation (to be fair, many leftist intellectuals adopted closure strategies to protect themselves from McCarthyist repression). While this type of strategy might be effective at achieving prestige, it also tends to isolate experts and increases the risk they will become politically and culturally irrelevant. Seeing American universities as *captured* by the Left, many conservative intellectuals went the opposite route turning to "openness," publicity-driven strategies. Yet this "openness" option would have lacked feasibility without organized business's concerted development of a think tank-based knowledge infrastructure in the 1970s and 1980s to back it up.

Medvetz describes think tanks as an "interstitial field," a semi-structured network of knowledge-producing organizations that operates *between* the more established fields of business, government, media and the academy (137–140). While think tanks have less of the professional legitimacy that academic institutions tend to have, their loose organizational structure and hybrid field logic gives their researchers a multi-field mobility that university intellectuals lack, enabling these think tanks to exploit the promotional opportunities of both news-based media and political parties. In the next section, I focus on Amity Shlaes' career and the promotion of her book during the stimulus debate as a way to exemplify the openness-orientation of activist-experts from think tank networks. The focus on the *Hannity* segment in the remaining sections turns my analysis of the discussion and Shlaes' place in it as an "activist-expert" to the other strategic dilemma of Eyal's model: the autonomy versus dependence one. Unlike ivory tower intellectuals, activist-experts experience more direct pressure to produce work that follows the political-ideological imperatives of their benefactors. This diminished autonomy hurts their intellectual credibility, because, after all, if the expert appears to be completely compliant to the demands of his or her consumers, he or she no longer embodies a special apartness from lay citizens, which is the very basis of expert authority. I will show how activist-experts like Shlaes seek to counter this credibility threat by performing, drawing from Pierre Bourdieu, a *disinvested* analytical disposition that seeks to demonstrate how activist-experts are able to achieve an autonomy and objective distance from their research topic.

AMITY SHLAES AND THE "OPENNESS" OF THE ACTIVIST-EXPERT

Amity Shlaes' research on US economic history has intersected at one moment or another with almost all the major nodes of the conservative intellectual establishment. In an effort to "open" her work up even more to the public, she has frequently appeared on, and has worked for, major news outlets across various platforms. In the world of print journalism, she has been an editor and/or columnist for key sites of free-market editorial opinion such as the *Wall Street Journal,* the *Financial Times,* the *National Review, Commentary,* and *Bloomberg News.* Shlaes has also appeared on radio (e.g. NPR's *Marketplace*) and television (e.g. Fox News, CNBC, Bloomberg Television), and has taught courses on the Great Depression at NYU's Stern School of Business. As a distinguished fellow, she has directed or contributed to various research centers, most of which openly advocate free-market policies (e.g. the International Policy Network, the Manhattan Institute, the American Enterprise Institute, the George W. Bush Institute). But she has also contributed to centers that present themselves as non-ideological (e.g. the Council on Foreign Relations). As evidenced by the warm obituary she wrote in 2006 for Milton Friedman in the *New York Sun,* Shlaes identifies herself and her work with the history of the conservative intellectual movement, and her peers place her within this tradition as well. In the preface of a 2004 edited volume of essays titled *Turning Intellect into Influence* celebrating the twenty-fifth anniversary of the Manhattan Institute, Shlaes is included as part of the new generation of conservative intellectual leaders and is compared to the likes of Charles Murray and George Gilder.

While Shlaes has published four national bestsellers on economic history, such as *The Greedy Hand* (1999) and, more recently, *Coolidge* (2013), *The Forgotten Man,* published in 2007 by HarperCollins, is by far her most successful book to date. HarperCollins, it is crucial to note, shared, at the time, the same parent company as Fox News: News Corp. News Corp.'s conglomerated corporate structure enables cross-promotional moves like this, a move that is one example among many of Rupert Murdoch's signature skill at aligning his political-ideological beliefs with his commercial interests.[7] Aided by News Corp.'s immense publicity apparatus as well as Shlaes' own undeniable talent as a writer and storyteller, *The Forgotten Man* was able to remain on the *New York Times* bestseller list for nineteen consecutive weeks, and over 250,000 copies have been printed. This is an exceptional number for a book on economic history. In addition, *The Forgotten Man* won Shlaes the Manhattan Institute's Friedrich von Hayek Book Prize in 2009, and she has also chaired the jury for this prize.

In his book *On Television* (1999), Pierre Bourdieu has described actors like Shlaes who shuttle between the intellectual field and the news media "journalist-intellectuals." These individuals use the skills they developed in research institutions to establish their status as speakers in the media field. Conversely, they can capitalize on the name recognition they garner from appearing on television to secure higher salaries and positions of authority in the academic field. Yet in this new multichannel, post-broadcast news environment, the play of forces driving the behavior of public intellectuals has become exceedingly complex. The explosion of think tanks in the 1970s and 1980s and the subsequent emergence of partisan news markets in the 1990s and 2000s has not only blurred the distinctions between the media and the intellectual field –which had been Bourdieu's chief concern in *On Television* – it has also blurred the lines between journalism and politics themselves.

So in this new media landscape where corporate and political strategies are increasingly entwined, it is not clear that all public intellectual content, in the end, submits to the logic of commercial entertainment in the way that Bourdieu suggests. The example of how Fox News used Amity Shlaes and her research to advance the network's interpretation of the Great Recession actually highlights the strong *political logic* underlying the deployment of expertise in contemporary journalism. The fact that the book received little fanfare when it was first published in 2007 and had only gained widespread visibility when Republican politicians and conservative media pundits began referencing it during the early months of 2009 – when the Stimulus Act was being debated and passed – speaks to how the book's rising cultural capital has been fundamentally tied to its political utility, as opposed its inherent intellectual merits, entertainment value, or news worthiness.

---

[7] For work that discusses how Murdoch balances and combines political and corporate strategies, see Arsenault & Castells, 2008.

While Republican politicians cited Shlaes' book during the 2008 financial crisis, they especially mined it for its talking points during the early stages of the stimulus debate.[8] In a December 2008 interview, then Indiana House representative and now current Vice President Mike Pence argued against the growing political consensus that a massive stimulus was needed to address the financial crisis by paraphrasing Shlaes' argument from *The Forgotten Man*. "Shlaes points out," he told a local Indiana reporter, "the spending and taxing policies of 1932 and 1936 that exacerbated the situation. That's why I say it's important for the Congress to act, but one of the lessons of the 1930s is we can't borrow and spend back to a growing economy" (Weigel, 2009).

On February 6, 2009, Republican Minority Leader Mitch McConnell implicitly invoked Shlaes' book, saying on the floor of the Senate, "One of the good things about reading history is you learn a good deal. And we know for sure that the big spending programs of the New Deal did not work."[9] That same month, during the confirmation hearing of Energy Secretary Steven Chu, Republican Senator John Barrasso explicitly referenced Shlaes by lifting a copy of it and presenting it to the committee and the press in attendance. He told the audience, "In these economic times, a number of members of the Senate are reading a book called *The Forgotten Man*, about the history of the Great Depression, as we compare and look for solutions, as we look at a stimulus package" (Chait, 2009). A February 3, 2009 *Washington Independent* article entitled, "The GOP's Anti-Stimulus Manifesto," discusses how Paul Ryan, the then-ranking Representative on the House Budget Committee, and Senator John Ensign, then the head of the Senate Republican Policy Committee, were recommending and distributing copies of Shlaes' *Forgotten Man* to congressional colleagues. One liberal commentator wrote that they were "carrying around *The Forgotten Man* like it's Mao's *Little Red Book*" (Leuchtenber, 2009: 304).

---

[8] In June of 2007, former Speaker of the House Newt Gingrich praised Shlaes' book for shedding light on the pre-New Deal era of "Whig-style free-market liberalism" that Gingrich suggested we should return to as a country. In September 2008, Senator John Kyl, the Republican whip, referenced Shlaes' book on the floor of the Senate to denounce comparisons being made between George W. Bush and Herbert Hoover. Kyl said, "In the excellent history of the Great Depression by Amity Shlaes, *The Forgotten Man*, we are reminded that Hoover was an interventionist . . . a strong critic of markets" (Weigel, 2009, para. 10).

[9] *RealClearPolitics* (2009).

During an April 2009 press conference about the stimulus bill, Alabama Representative Spencer Bachus delved deeper into the content of Shlaes' book and even elaborated on William Graham Sumner's 1883 "Forgotten Man" essay – Sumner being the late-nineteenth-century intellectual Shlaes quotes in the epigraph of her book (more on this in the following sections). Bachus told the audience, quoting Sumner directly, "He [i.e. the forgotten man] works; he votes; generally, he prays – but he always pays." Applying the quote to its present-day context, Bachus continued, "Now, the forgotten man today is the taxpayer ... It's discussed and it's decided that we are going to help this individual or corporation out, we propose a law, and guess what, it's the forgotten man today who always pays for someone else's mistake. He pays his mortgage on time, but he [also] has to pay someone else's mortgage." According to the *Politico* article that featured this quote, Mike Ference, the policy aide of Republican House Minority Whip Eric Cantor, invited Shlaes to join a select group of House Republicans for lunch at a Capitol suite in the early months of 2009.[10]

Paralleling this aggressive promotion of *The Forgotten Man* on Capitol Hill, from August 2008 to April 2009 Shlaes and her book were mentioned several times on Fox News across multiple programs. In contrast to the fall of 2008, however, where Shlaes had only appeared on the lower-rated daytime programs,[11] from January to April 2009 (i.e. the same time period when references to her book spiked among Republicans in Congress), Shlaes and her book were recommended and/or given full segments on Fox News' top three rated shows. For example, in a *Hannity* episode, former New York City Mayor Rudy Giuliani remarked to Hannity, "I hope he [President Obama] and his people have read *The Forgotten Man*, Amity Shlaes' book that came out last year. I think it's back on the bestseller list. Basically it points out why the recession of 1929, which was a bad one, became the Great Depression of eleven or twelve years ... the actions of the New Deal ... did not work from the point of view of solving the Depression" (January 26, 2009).

In the episode of *Glenn Beck*, guest Mark Stanford, the then Republican Governor of South Carolina, told Beck, "A lot of the same [policies] that are being pulled out of the pages right now were played in the 1920s

[10] Coller & O'Connor (2009).

[11] Such as the *Journal Editorial Report* (October 11, 2008) and *America's News Headquarters* (November 13, 2008; December 1, 2008) and on *Cavuto*, a program on Fox News' sister network, the Fox Business Network (August 21, 2008).

and 1930s and they did not work. We're talking about going down a road that is going to prolong, exacerbate and deepen the crisis that we're in." Closing out the segment, Beck told Sanford, "Governor, thank you very much," and then inserted, "By the way, if you have not read Amity Shlaes' book, *The Forgotten Man* ... have you read that Governor?" Sanford responded, "I have read it, fabulous. I highly recommend it" (February 2, 2009).

On an April 15, 2009 episode of *The O'Reilly Factor* – the day of the first national Tea Party protest – conservative comedian Dennis Miller used terms from Shlaes' book to describe Tea Party protesters and their cause. Explaining the theory Shlaes takes from Sumner, he told O'Reilly, "I'm reading an interesting book now by a woman named Amity Shlaes. It's a great book about the forgotten American and about the Great Depression. And she cites this Yale professor in 1883 in her foreword notes. And the speech he gives, the essence being 'A' discerns a problem with 'X.' 'A' consults 'B' and figures out how they can help 'X.' 'A' and 'B' tell 'C' what he's going to give 'X.' And today was a 'C' change [playing on the word "sea"]. I think 'C,' [the Tea Party protester] the forgotten man, as per Shlaes' book, has just had enough."

Soon enough, this coordinated publicity strategy had effects far beyond Fox News and the conservative media echo chamber. As William Leuchtenburg details in his book, *In the Shadow of FDR* (2009), conservatives pundits on network news programs like ABC's *This Week* were repeatedly bringing up and questioning FDR's (Franklin D. Roosevelt Sr.) record and, like Fox News pundits, invoking Shlaes' book as support for their matter-of-fact conclusions that the New Deal had failed (299–312). Eventually, all the critical discourse surrounding FDR's New Deal that Shlaes' book generated would be felt by President Obama himself. "[Obama] wondered why, at a time when he was attempting to cope with collapsing financial houses and a resurgent Taliban, were reporters peppering him with questions about the interpretation of events that had transpired long before he was born?" At one news conference, Obama complained that, "some Senators and House members are ... still fighting FDR" (2009: 306). In *Pity the Billionaire* (2012), Thomas Frank pondered the long-term historical consequences of the publicity campaign that propelled Shlaes' book. He wrote, "To Google nearly any aspect of the first two Roosevelt administrations is to encounter almost immediately the obsessive loathing for the New Deal felt by conservative entertainers and libertarian economists. You can find the works of scholars like Arthur Schlesinger or Irving Bernstein or Michael Denning or Robert

McElvaine down at the library if you wish, but if you begin your search on the Internet, the expert you will encounter first [is] likely to be Amity Shlaes" (135).

TRANSLATING INTELLECTUAL KNOWLEDGE INTO THE LANGUAGE OF CABLE NEWS

On January 26, 2009, the first week of Glenn Beck's newly minted Fox News show, he had Amity Shlaes on as a guest to discuss her book. Shlaes would appear on Beck's program multiple times in the ensuing months and years. Yet in June 2008, even before Beck joined Fox News, he had featured Shlaes' book on his CNN Headline News program. Thus, Beck must be credited as being one of the first major conservative hosts to recognize Shlaes' work. This early promotion of Shlaes reflects a more general quality of Beck's programming style. The format innovations Beck brought to Fox News were characterized by a stronger emphasis on popular education, conservative scholarship, and – resembling the stylistic qualities of radio (which is his career base) – a more free-flowing and less rushed format structure that was more conducive to longwinded historical and intellectual conversations.

While Beck's show was unconventional in more ways than I can outline here, his program on Fox was immediately successful and lifted, almost single-handedly, the ratings of Fox News' daytime programming bloc to unprecedented levels.[12] This was partly due to Beck's astute recognition that conservative talk media audiences are as attracted to educational-historical content as they are to inside the beltway politics and horse-race style political coverage. Confirming Beck's programming instincts, according to a YouGov's Brandindex survey conducted in 2010 that compared which top five brands Republicans and Democrats most identify with, Republicans cited Fox News as number one. Their second choice: the History Channel.[13]

Yet because Beck's program was so new and unconventional in relation to Fox News' most established programs, it would be problematic to use Beck's show as a representative example of how Fox uses expert

---

[12] Pew Research Center (March 15, 2010). *The State of the News Media: An Annual Report on American Journalism 2010*. As the report states, "Glenn Beck's average of 2.32 million viewers in 2009 – up 96% from the previous year in that slot – was high especially given his 5 p.m. time slot. Beck's program popularity was a key reason for Fox's ratings surge in daytime over all."

[13] Ives (2010).

knowledge to support its conservative ideological interpretations. The *Glenn Beck* show was quite different from that of *The O'Reilly Factor*, Fox's flagship program. Host Bill O'Reilly started his career at the tabloid television show *Inside Edition*; accordingly, his style is far more compatible with the rapid, sound-bite-driven pace of television news. Moreover, O'Reilly's program remained true to the "cable magazine" format by including segments that have clear, recognizable boundaries (e.g. traditional newscasts, *Crossfire*-like partisan debates, documentaries, interviews, roundtable discussions, light-hearted pop culture segments).[14] This is not to say that O'Reilly did not significantly engage the issue of the Depression, promote books, or turn to conservative intellectuals in framing the economic crisis. O'Reilly's show simply did not offer the in-depth documentaries and elaborate historical discussions that Beck's program used.

During the recession, *The O'Reilly Factor* displayed the same general use of expert knowledge and the same sophisticated balance of populist and technocratic voices that we see on *Glenn Beck* and *Hannity*. However, more than Beck or Hannity, O'Reilly *personally* attempted to embody the populist-intellectual tactic by claiming to be *both* a "blue-collar guy" (October 6, 2010) and a "historian" (September 9, 2009). In the years following the recession, O'Reilly would supersede Beck as the Right's number one popular historian. In 2011, he published a history book entitled *Killing Lincoln*. This bestseller would be followed by five more suspense thriller–styled history books with "killing" in the title.[15]

---

[14] I take the term "cable magazine" from Chris Peters. In "No-Spin Zones: The Rise of the American Cable News Magazine and Bill O'Reilly" (2010), Peters defines a cable magazine as something which "suggests an affinity with news magazines such as *60 Minutes* which have been around for decades; quasi-investigative journalism, typically an hour in length, that consider events in greater detail than the network newscasts. These shows also have a semblance of Sunday-Morning talk shows, like *Meet the Press*, with prominent political interviewees and roundtable discussions. A hint of the traditional newscast is found in these broadcasts with reports that are virtually indiscernible from stories that would be filed on the CBS Evening News. Political debate shows like *Crossfire* lend their embrace of conflict and volume. There is an occasional flavor of tabloid news magazines such as *A Current Affair*; salacious stories of sex, celebrity, and crime. A more accurate description might be 'cable political talk show news magazine' but this noun-train is an awkward construction. As such, I have conceptualized them quite literally as the print news magazine adapted by the cable networks; short briefs, longer social stories, interviews, and opinion pieces brought together in a consistent format" (846–847, 1n).

[15] *Killing Kennedy* (2012), *Killing Jesus* (2013), *Killing Patton* (2014), *Killing Reagan* (2015), and *Killing England* (2017).

Each of these books would sell millions of copies, making Bill O'Reilly one of the most prolific history authors of the 2010s.

Witnessing O'Reilly's publishing success, in January 2015, Fox News partnered with Warm Springs Productions, a Historical Channel–affiliated production company, and launched a ten-week series of historical Sunday specials about the American frontier entitled *Legend & Lies: Into the West*. As the executive producer, O'Reilly is heavily featured in this series – not as a populist or a political pundit, but as an "expert." In the second season (2016), which focuses on "Founding Fathers," other Fox hosts appear in the series as historical experts such as *Fox & Friend's* Brian Kilmeade, a man who started his career as a sports broadcaster calling mixed martial arts events (MMA) but, since joining Fox, has authored popular books on George Washington and Thomas Jefferson. This trend of the conservative pundit turned part-time historian is seen in conservative talk radio as well; Glenn Beck, Mark Levin, and Rush Limbaugh have all written popular books on Revolutionary era history. Yet, as I detail later in this chapter, issues arise when conservative pundits attempt to play both ends of the populist-intellectual spectrum. Even television performers as skilled as O'Reilly encountered problems trying to juggle these contradictory identities.[16]

A top Fox News host since 1999, Sean Hannity had been well familiar with the network's broadcasting conventions and, like O'Reilly, had adhered primarily to the cable magazine format during the Great Recession years. However, Hannity was clearly influenced by Beck and the broader trend toward historical debate that had accelerated in the recession period. Like Beck, Hannity's program has aired short, historical documentaries about the Depression and devoted segments not just to the topic of the Depression but to scholarship *about* the Depression. And in an April 7, 2009 episode, Hannity did an entire segment on Shlaes' book *The Forgotten Man*. This one segment offers a particularly suitable example of how Fox News' top shows deploy conservative intellectual culture, as it represents a middle ground between Beck's stylistic eccentricity and O'Reilly's conventionalism.

---

[16] For example, in 2006, in a recurring segment where O'Reilly responds to viewer mail, one viewer criticized O'Reilly's elite educational credentials and charged him with elitism, the major critique O'Reilly has long waged against political liberals. In an attempt to recuperate his working-class credibility, O'Reilly rebutted, "It's not my Harvard degree that makes me smarter sir, it's my degree from the school of hard knocks that gives me advantage" (December 5, 2006).

My analysis begins by considering how *Hannity*'s "Forgotten Man" segment had been set up earlier in the program with a preview. At a practical level, previews keep viewers tuned in through the commercial break; but they are also useful as analytical objects, as they provide condensed versions of the full segment's rhetorical framework. They create a flow and thematic continuity across the hour-long program because they can pre-frame the content coming ahead.

In this particular preview, Hannity will tell the audience, "It is the anniversary of FDR's famous 'forgotten man' address. But liberals have forgotten who the forgotten man *really* is. [It's a] very important history lesson that we all need to remember." As Hannity says this, the viewer is shown a video window with the famous black and white footage of Roosevelt signing the Social Security Act underneath a title reading "HISTORY LESSON." Placed next to this window is a second window previewing another segment on the program lineup. It shows footage of then Democratic Congressman Barney Frank speaking at a podium. A title reads, "FRANK GETS SCHOOLED." Hannity smiles and says, "Barney Frank goes face to face with a very sharp college student on the issue of the economy – and let's just say the congressman . . . doesn't keep his cool."

The obvious contrast between the middlebrow history segment and the one featuring Frank next to it is meant to appeal to the viewer's baser desire to witness partisan combat and an emotional outburst. Their combination demonstrates how a given *Hannity* episode encompasses different cultural appeals, which serve in one moment of the show a "higher-minded" desire for enlightenment and in another moment a more juvenile pleasure in seeing a political enemy embarrassed and defeated. Placing these previews together highlights the way Fox programs bridge different taste cultures and rationalizes their connections. Gaining knowledge from an informative historical segment offers the viewer argumentative ammunition to "school" someone else in a political debate whom they may have squabbled with online or with family members.

The segment itself begins by comparing historic quotes from Franklin Roosevelt and William Graham Sumner. The first quote comes in the form of a crackling recording of Roosevelt's voice, with the audio clip replaying the most famous lines from his 1932 "Forgotten Man" radio address: "These unhappy times call for the building up of plans that rest upon the forgotten, the unorganized, but the indispensable unit of economic power, for plans like those of 1917 that build from the bottom up

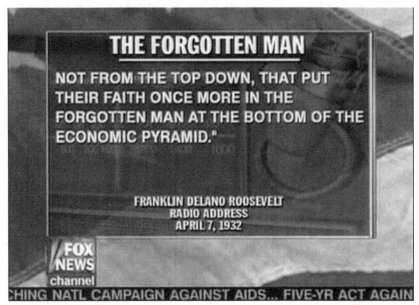

FIGURE 5.2 FDR's "Forgotten Man" address

and not from the top down, that put their faith once more in the forgotten man at the bottom of the economic pyramid." Cued with this recording, an image of an antique radio is shown on screen with an accompanying text that follows the quote (see Figure 5.2). The second quote, which I will detail shortly, is spoken by Hannity and recites Sumner's basic argument in his "Forgotten Man" essay.

By beginning the segment this way, Hannity replicates the same juxtaposition of quotes that Shlaes uses as an epigraph in the book's introduction. This pairing nicely introduces the rhetorical parameters of Shlaes' book – its key concepts and ideological positions. Additionally, these quotes are useful because they meet the needs of the fast-paced production style of television, condensing the book's two competing political definitions of the forgotten man into useable sound bites.

While summarizing a 400-page book into a seven minute segment obviously has its limitations, the television medium and news format have their advantages as well. It is especially through electronic forms of mass media that Roosevelt, and by extension the Depression, is remembered in the national consciousness. As a television program, *Hannity* can represent the book's interpretation of the Depression's history on communicative registers (e.g. audio, film) that speak to the "collective memory" of the Depression in a way that Shales' book, in its printed form, cannot.[17] The audio clip and the image of the antique radio invoke Roosevelt's "fireside chats," which were the monthly radio addresses that have been credited with endearing millions of Americans to FDR and that still symbolize his personable presidential style. Like the crackling sonic quality of the radio recording, the film clip shown of FDR's signing the Social Security Act in the preview bears the mark of its time period, with the black and white tonal palette, the scratches and grain particles, and the flickering image all being qualities that characterize old film stock. It is these characteristics that help the viewer situate the historical moment of the Great Depression and the 1930s. From an entertainment standpoint, these media artifacts, like a teaser scene in a movie, draw the viewer into the segment and serve to maintain the viewer's attention during the drier policy discussion that follows. From a political-ideological standpoint, using these artifacts and iconography enables the *Hannity* program to place the viewer's more *general,* popular understanding of the Great Depression in dialogue with Shlaes' *particular* intellectual retelling of the event.

Having primed the viewer with familiar representations of the Depression, the segment then transitions and introduces the second quote. Hannity informs the viewer that "FDR took the idea of the 'Forgotten Man' from Yale professor William Graham Sumner who wrote about the 'Forgotten Man' half a century earlier." Hannity continues and begins to paraphrase Sumner's argument:

Now Sumner described two people, A and B, who realized that a third person, X, is suffering in some way, and decide that X needs federal assistance. A and B, however, can't pay for that assistance on their own, so they need to raise taxes on C. The forgotten man is roped in to pay for the various programs that A and B deem necessary, and FDR, however, claimed that X was the forgotten man, all

---

[17] According to sociologist Michael Schudson, collective memory should not be conceptualized as an aggregate product of millions of individual memories that coalesce like raindrops into a pool. This implies it is something that develops in an organic way without systematic direction or intention. Collective memory, he emphasizes, is produced by and located in specific institutions, and is handed through a select set of symbols through "particular cultural forms and transmitted in particular cultural vehicles" (1992: 5). These symbols (iconic photos, memorable phrases, historical figures), cultural forms (speeches, TV shows, textbooks) and cultural vehicles (public education, media industries, communication technologies) are at once ways through which we encounter a shared sense of our nation's past and what gives collective memory a tactility, a way to handle and shape it for specific purposes and political interests. Also see Zelizer, 1992; Edy, 2006; Olick, 2014.

FIGURE 5.3 Visual diagram of Sumner's theory

designed, you know [here Hannity starts getting tripped up on the awkward letter scheme], to bring up these federal interventions aimed at helping X, all at the expense of C who is the *original* forgotten man. Sound familiar?

Hannity's verbal articulation of Sumner's forgotten man argument provides the basic story of government theft and taxpayer victimization that underlies Shlaes' reinterpretation of the New Deal and Fox News' coverage of the recession overall (see Chapter 4). But by itself, Sumner's letter-scheme-oriented argument comes across as overly abstract and vague.

Hannity remedies this. As Hannity explains Sumner's theory, a colorful diagram appears on the screen showing cartoon figures, money, arrows, designating letters, and the smiling faces of Democratic Senate leader Harry Reid and President Barack Obama (see Figure 5.3).

This visual diagram works to flesh out this schema by assigning social and political identities to each letter and figure. "C", the figure at the center of the visual diagram, is depicted as a forward-looking entrepreneur who stands at the origin of the money stream, as indicated by the arrows, and is thus presented as the sole wealth-generator and producer in the cast of characters. The virtue and patriotism of "C" is reinforced and signaled by the awkwardly photoshopped American flag on his shoulder. The fusing of "A" and "B" with the faces of Obama and Reid not only ties these letters to government and the system of taxation in general but also more specifically to the Democratic opposition. By situating Sumner's esoteric and century-old theory within the preexisting partisan structure of the *Hannity* program and by using this theory to interpret current policy (e.g. the Stimulus Act), Sumner's work becomes endowed with more immediate importance and is made to "sound familiar."

In his verbal explanation of Sumner, Hannity has inserted FDR's definition of the forgotten man into Sumner's schema ("FDR ... claimed that X was the forgotten man") and is thereby able to present the schema, following Shlaes' book, as a way to reinterpret the history of the New Deal. In the visual diagram, figure X receives government assistance and addresses the audience with his hands out. In this way, Hannity has reframed the leftist vision of the forgotten man as a parasitic character standing in direct contrast to the proletarian-producer image that FDR has conveyed in the quote played moments earlier. But Hannity's analysis of the FDR broadcast only discusses how New Deal rhetoric like the "forgotten man" speech had called for more progressive taxation and government programs; it conveniently omits FDR's moral critique against "economic royalists" and corporate political influence that had been at the heart of the New Deal coalition Forgotten Man narrative.

Moving on to the interview portion of the segment, Shlaes now appears on set with Hannity. Underneath the mid-shot of Shlaes is a banner indicating her professional credentials: "Amity Shlaes: Senior Fellow at the Council on Foreign Relations." Addressing her across the anchor desk, Hannity attempts to summarize Shlaes' book, saying, "You tell the story of A, the progressive of the 1920s and 1930s whose good intentions, supposedly, inspired the New Deal, and the story of C, the American who paid for it, and was not thought of." Wasting little time, Hannity then leads the discussion directly into contemporary politics. "This is where we are today ... for example, in New York City, we have nine million people, and 42,242 of those people pay fifty percent of the tax bill. Is that C?," he asks Shlaes. She smiles in affirmation, saying:

That's the C of New York, yes, and we have Cs all across the country. Maybe the person who doesn't get the mortgage break who was paying his mortgage before ... or the person who doesn't fall into one of those groups that gets favored by one of the bailouts. That's one of the concerns. You always leave someone out, that forgotten man.

When Roosevelt evoked the term in the 1930s, he was describing those who were being exploited "at the bottom of the economic pyramid." In stark contrast, Shlaes and Hannity describe those "not thought of" who are at the *top* of the tax code. The letter scheme used by Shlaes and Hannity to describe different economic actors (e.g. A, B, C) references the social theory of the previously mentioned nineteenth-century intellectual William Graham Sumner. As cited earlier in the quotes of Republican politicians and Fox pundits, Sumner had first coined the term "the forgotten man" in his 1883 essay of the same name. A fierce critic of early forms of welfare, his ardent advocacy of laissez-faire ideology often blended with his social Darwinist ideas.

While Hannity's use of the forgotten man trope closely echoes Sumner's definition, in this episode Hannity also deftly engaged the forgotten man of FDR's famous speech, since it is this historical reference that is most recognizable within American popular culture.[18] Wisely, the program did not simply offer its audience a novel intellectual argument about the Depression and then expect them to accept it by sheer expert-academic fiat. A strategy like this, returning to Eyal's model, is only doable in "closed" institutional settings like academia or in the medical field where experts have great "autonomy" and influence over dictating how consumer needs are defined. Commercial news organizations like Fox, however, being ratings-dependent, feel more pressure to tailor the intellectual content they present to meet the bases of knowledge its audience is expected to have. For these reasons, the *Hannity* segment

---

[18] After Roosevelt's pivotal "Forgotten Man" radio address in Albany, New York in 1932, the forgotten man trope not only spread in the political culture of the 1930s but was manifest in pop culture as well, appearing in the era's most iconic movies and songs. For example, the song "Remember My Forgotten Man" from Al Dubin used often in Harry Warren's *Gold Digger* series of Hollywood films was one of the most popular songs of the 1930s. This song was a direct reference to FDR's speech and played on a similar theme about unrewarded labor, as evident in the lyrics: "Remember my forgotten man, You had him cultivate the land; He walked behind the plow, The sweat fell from his brow, But look at him right now!" Interestingly, Shlaes and Fox News' reintroduction of the term in the late 2000s was not the first time a major conservative political figure or organization had attempted to use the term and reinterpret it in a conservative light. As Gary Wills documents, President Richard Nixon used the term "forgotten Americans" in his speech at the 1968 Republican convention in Miami as a sort of precursor to his more famous term "Silent Majority." Nixon took this term from the 1964 Barry Goldwater campaign where Goldwater's speechwriter Michael Bernstein would use the term "Forgotten American" (Wills, 1970. 310fn 37, 38). More recently, Donald Trump utilized the term "forgotten Americans" throughout his 2016 presidential campaign and mentioned the term ("forgotten men and women") in his January 2017 inaugural address (Trump, 2017).

featured commentary and media artifacts about Roosevelt as much as it discussed Sumner's theory in the abstract.

Yet in drawing attention to FDR, and especially to his famous Forgotten Man speech, Shlaes and Hannity stand to jeopardize their own particular free-market interpretation of the Depression's history. FDR's speech and the Depression era images that the segment included still carry the anti-corporate politics and moral critiques of the New Deal coalition. To make the term ideologically useful, Hannity's "Forgotten Man" segment, following Shlaes' book, endeavors to use Sumner's laissez-faire social theory to supplant the term's residual leftist connotations. This is done chiefly by encoding the forgotten man trope with a different class identification – that is, he is no longer among those who emerge from the bottom of tax code but is instead among those emerging from the top. The result of this redefinition of who the social protagonist of the Great Depression actually is allows Hannity to draw very different policy lessons from the historic economic downturn than those offered by the original leftist theorists.

In the final portion of the interview, we see how *Hannity* executes the populist-intellectual tactic not only through the program's format and visual-audio presentation, but also through the juxtaposition of Hannity and Shlaes' divergent communicative styles and embodied performances. When making her final historical critique, Shlaes uses abstract, dispassionate language, and attaches to the New Deal government words like "arbitrary" and "problematic." In contrast, Hannity follows Shlaes' final point by stating, "and now it [the present-day government] is bigger ... And if he [Obama] gets everything he wants, and he will – we are robbing, stealing from our kids and our grandkids, we're taking a baseball bat and smashing open their piggy banks and taking every last cent they've got, and that is morally corrupt as far as I'm concerned." Unlike Shlaes' analytical language, Hannity's rhetoric and physical gestures graphically frame his notion of government expansion as that of an aggressor "smashing our children['s] ... piggy banks." As he says this line, he mimes the swinging of a bat with his arms (see Figure 5.4).

In Hannity's rhetoric, increasing the role of government in the market doesn't simply "problematize" the workings of abstract, political and social structures like the nation and the economy; it is a palpable threat to the closest members of one's inner circle. As elaborated in Chapter 3, Hannity adopts an *invested* anchoring address that connects the issue under discussion to one's personal background and interpersonal relationships. This connection provides the moral basis and justification for

FIGURE 5.4 *Hannity*'s body language

taking Hannity's anti-Obama, anti-statist position. Shlaes' response to Hannity's dramatic, moralistic comment is telling. Instead of adding to it, she first gives a blank facial expression and says nothing; then she offers something of a grimaced smile, as if she is simultaneously put off and amused by Hannity's colorful take on redistributive tax policy (see Figure 5.5). In returning Hannity's final, impassioned point with silence, Shlaes creates a visibly awkward moment, which demonstrates her unease with addressing political issues in such moral and personal terms.

POLICING THE INTELLECTUAL CONTENT OF
A POPULIST SHOW

In the previous section, I illustrated how the *Hannity* program translated the main historical argument of Shlaes' book into popular discourse and made the book's content compatible with "good television." However, this intellectual-to-popular translation is not without its risks. Incorporating such content might threaten Hannity's performance as a culturally ordinary guy whose taste and knowledge are in line with his viewers'. For example, the algebraic language of William Graham Sumner's argument,

FIGURE 5.5 Amity Shlaes' reaction

his status as a "Yale professor," and the pedagogical role Hannity assumes ("history lesson") in explaining Sumner's theory all convey an air of cultural elitism. To maintain the populist sensibility of the show and prevent a social break between Hannity and the everyday viewer, Hannity uses various representational techniques to distance himself from intellectual culture and formal expertise.

Returning to the way Sumner's theory had been visualized in the diagram cited earlier (see Figure 5.3), we might ask why one of the most profitable news networks in history, with all the high-tech video effects and animation technologies at its disposal, would present such an important historical argument in such a seemingly shoddy and childish manner. The cartoon images of the businessmen could very well have been cut and pasted from a children's coloring book, while the tilted smiling heads of Barack Obama and Harry Reid resemble the bobble-head dolls one finds on a car dashboard or at sporting events. The rudimentary and silly nature of the visuals could be read as a conscious effort by *Hannity*'s producers to appeal to the audience by "dumbing down" their programming. Such a reading would be in line with veteran network anchor Ted Koppel's ongoing critiques against Fox News and cable news more generally (see Chapter 1). However, this reading fails to explain an important aspect of the segment: if *Hannity*'s strategy were to simply sell eyeballs and offer diluted "common denominator" entertainment, why would the program take the book of an economic historian and a mostly unknown intellectual from the nineteenth century as its focus?

Borrowing a term from Dan Rather, we can say that the visual diagram undoubtedly works to "showbiznify" Shales' historical argument. However, I argue that the purpose of layering the argument with burlesque visual representations is as much an ideological tactic intended to maintain the working-class voice and authority of the show as it is a commercially motivated accommodation to mass consumerism and infotainment. For Shlaes' intellectual work and argument to successfully operate within the populist representational strategy of the *Hannity* program, its veneer of prestige and distinction must be, to a degree, desecrated, unofficialized, and brought down to earth. In short, the tactical purpose of the diagram's flippant, humorous aesthetic allows the *Hannity* program to cover (and validate) Shlaes' intellectual work without coming across as being a particularly intellectual program.

A further indicator of how the *Hannity* program tempers the intellectual quality of Shlaes and Sumner's work becomes evident in host Sean Hannity's next distancing act. When Hannity first spelled out Sumner's theory earlier in the segment, his facial expression seemed to suggest that he recognized how tangled and abstract Sumner's letter-schemed model might sound to the viewer. In order to separate himself from Sumner's language and the pedagogical role attached to it, Hannity has to deprecate his authority and educational pretensions. Furrowing his eyebrows, but smiling, Hannity will parody the stern face of a teacher and say to the viewer, "And by the way, we'll have a test on that coming up in five minutes." A camera man is then heard laughing at Hannity's joke offscreen.

These types of distancing practices were commonly used by all three of Fox News' top hosts during the recession period. For example, in one episode of *Glenn Beck*, Beck was introducing early-twentieth-century Russian economist Nikolai Kondratiev and his wave theory of capitalism. Finding himself pontificating rather deep in the discursive weeds, the host suddenly quipped in a sarcastic aside, "It's so popular with the people I hang out with" (February 24, 2010). Before finally summarizing up the theory, Beck said, "Hang on, I need my pipe," and, impersonating a professor, put a wooden pipe in his mouth and adopted a stereotypical WASP accent that sounded very much like Thurston Howell III, the billionaire character from the 1960s' sitcom *Gilligan's Island*.

We see similar distancing practices on *The O'Reilly Factor*. In one segment, guest John Stossel was referencing conservative economist Friedrich Hayek. In the middle of their conversation O'Reilly interrupted him and said, "Hayek?" Stossel clarified, "Friedrich Hayek, the economist." Still expressing an ignorance of Hayek, O'Reilly asked again, "Hayek?" The conversation moved on to a debate about whether Stossel thought Obama was a socialist. Stossel said, "I call him an interventionist." O'Reilly responded, "Nobody knows what that means ... And nobody knows Hayek" (May 4, 2010). Considering O'Reilly's master's degree from Harvard's John F. Kennedy School of Government and his knowledge of American history, particularly of the conservative movement, it is hard to believe O'Reilly had never heard of Hayek. But feigning ignorance makes perfect sense as a way to protect the populist media persona he has developed.

We see the same kind of distancing strategies at play in *The Factor*'s recurrent "Word of the Day" segment, where O'Reilly introduced "obscure and obsolete" words like *sagacious* (September 23, 2008) and *pettifogger* (January 28, 2009).[19] Mocking their eloquent nature, he often verbalized such words slowly with his chin lifted. Or, to take a more recent example, when O'Reilly had been unashamedly promoting one of his newest history books on air as a perfect father's day present, he said, "Any of my history books, dad will enjoy, *if*..." (with O'Reilly now offering up a dramatic pause) "... he is 'a man of letters'" (January 3, 2015).

THE "INVESTED" POPULIST AND THE "DISINVESTED" EXPERT

In Chapter 2, I explained how Fox News' populist programming discourse radically simplifies the political public sphere by dividing it into two rival media systems and knowledge infrastructures, one for the elite and one for the people. The network's populist conceptualization of the political field breaks from normative, liberal theories of deliberative democracy. But it also alters the traditional epistemological standards of professional journalism and changes how evidence is evaluated in public debates. Rather than seeking to produce the truth-effects that disinterested anchoring styles once yielded in the network era, Fox's top hosts

---

[19] Billoreilly.com. Words of the Day [Online archive]. Retrieved from: www.billoreilly.com/factor-words-of-the-day.

abandon the professional tenet of neutrality and embrace what I call an *invested* disposition (drawing from Bourdieu; 1984: 34–50).

In the interview portion of the "Forgotten Man" segment, Amity Shlaes counters the impassioned, *invested* style of Hannity by exhibiting a *disinvested* disposition. This disposition symbolizes the methodological soundness of her research and her intellectual autonomy and integrity (coming back to Eyal's model). Most scholarship that engages how expert groups struggle for autonomy adopt an organizational perspective. By examining Shlaes' appearance on *Hannity*, I seek to demonstrate the representational aspects of this struggle – that is, how experts, particularly those with lower academic credibility, manufacture their image as autonomous thinkers and researchers through televised *performances* of technocratic reason.

The stark epistemological and dispositional differences between Shlaes and Hannity are most evident when the central political critique of the segment is most forcefully articulated. Hannity tells Shlaes, "There is a myth or a concept, and I think Barack Obama's trying to duplicate this, that the New Deal literally got us out of the Depression. Now, my father and mother grew up during the Depression. All right? Very tough times, and they describe them to me often, but the reality is the New Deal did not get us out of the Depression, did it?" Shlaes responds, "That's right, and the data say it, it's not hard. The Dow never came back, unemployment never got down really below ten percent, maybe one year if you're charitable ... GDP per capita not back in real terms either. All the basic numbers don't look good for that period."

By mentioning how his parents "grew up during the Depression" and then following this statement with "All right?" Hannity affirms the value of a lived-memory of the Depression and in doing so reframes the cultural criteria of what it means to "know" something about its history. Beyond citing his parent's experience, Hannity stresses his familiarity with it by telling Shlaes how his parents, "describe them [the hard times of the Depression] to me often." He elongates the word "often," raises his eyebrows, and then smirks, suggesting a relationship with his parents that is so close as to be endearingly burdensome. Hannity offers no logic for how his parents' experience of the "hard times" of the Depression follows from his suggestion that the New Deal didn't work. However, in stressing his closeness to his parents and their past, Hannity seeks to establish not necessarily the truth of his argument but his right to speak on the topic. In the face of this Great Depression expert, Hannity is able to counter Shlaes' formal expertise by grounding his knowledge on interpersonal relationships and lived experience. His authority is established through his self-presentation as the cultural bearer of his parents' legacy – which is, by extension, the legacy of the Depression generation.

In a segment about the Great Depression on *The O'Reilly Factor*, Bill O'Reilly and his guests use the same combination of invested and disinvested analytical approaches, mentioning "my dad was a teenager when the Depression happened" in one moment and then, in another moment, citing the abstract, economic historical record: "you know this history on this stuff, stimulus heavy spending does little to help us out of morass" (February 17, 2009). We see the same balancing of different epistemic cultures and modes of analysis on *The Factor* when addressing the other major event of the "Greatest Generation" legacy: World War II. In a debate about the ethics of using a nuclear bomb against Japan during the war, O'Reilly said with assurance that the US government had estimated the death toll would have been worse had the Allied forces invaded the Japanese mainland. When his guest questioned this assertion, O'Reilly countered with the family reference: "my father was on a [navy] ship on the way to Japan. So it wasn't unknowable" (May 4, 2009). In another episode, by contrast, O'Reilly aligns himself with professional historiography as he and his academic guest criticize actor Tom Hank's World War II series, claiming it is guilty of "presentism," an academic term that describes how historical events can be distorted by the historian's contemporary perspective (March 12, 2010).

Once again, more than Beck and Hannity, O'Reilly consistently attempted to the execute the populist-intellectual tactic single handedly. However, returning to the Hannity "Forgotten Man" segment, often Fox's populist hosts rely more heavily on others to play the role of expert. While Hannity emphasizes the personal and social ties he has to the historical topic of the Great Depression, Shlaes' strategy of legitimation displays the opposite tendency. Shlaes does not share a similar biographical story or draw a common thread between her background and Hannity's, as is found in the typical reaction one gets with *Hannity*'s celebrity guests and guests from the talk radio world or from other Fox shows. Instead, as a professional historian and good social scientist, she affirms the "truth" of the New Deal's failure by citing empirical evidence. Immediately after Hannity shares his anecdote about his parents, Shlaes goes on to list a set of economic statistics from the era (e.g. unemployment, the Dow, GDP), which, she insists, conclusively proves the New Deal's ineffectiveness.

Shlaes' ability to display a comfortable mastery of historical statistics aligns Hannity's more overtly partisan statements about the "myth" of the New Deal that "Obama's trying to duplicate" with an empirical notion of the past. Having the best handle of the tools and methods of social science, professional historians like Shlaes exude the notion that they have a special access to what, in a material, phenomenal sense, *really* happened in history. In contrast to the open-ended quality of collective memory and the idiosyncratic character of personal histories like the one Hannity cites, Shlaes' critique of the New Deal bears the qualities of scientific knowledge: exactitude and universal credibility. However, the truth-value of Shlaes' evidence depends on her ability to represent it as separate from her own interests and political ties. Unlike Hannity, whose personal background, political convictions and social affiliations are central to how he approaches the Depression's history and any other news topic, Shlaes stresses that the "data say it" – in other words, the historical record speaks for itself. This rhetorical tactic works to remove Shlaes from the political debate her book did so much to ignite.

This rhetorical move is especially pronounced when Hannity asks about the great success of her book. "Did you ever think it [*The Forgotten Man*] would ever be this huge?" he elatedly asks Shlaes. The structure of Hannity's question already implies a personal relationship between Shlaes and her object of analysis (i.e. the Depression) and, in turn, implies connections between her intellectual work (i.e. her book) and her own ambitions – be they monetary, prestige-based or political. Shlaes pauses for a moment before answering, indicating a discomfort with the framing of the question. When she finally responds, she says, "I never expected a downturn like this. Let's just say that." Hannity then ends the interview with a similar question: "Why do you think the book has taken off so much?" She answers, "Just because we need to take a second look at the period; and what compelled me, Sean, as... I didn't need to write it retroactively. The people in the period said it." In saying that "I didn't need to write it retroactively," Shlaes indicates the awareness that her revision of the New Deal's history, like all interpretations of history, could be seen as politically motivated and presentistic. To address this liability, she again separates herself from the book's historical conclusions. "The people in the period said it," she concludes. In other words, it's not *her* saying it!

Shlaes has deployed the same rhetoric of autonomy in interviews with other news outlets as well. For example, just weeks after the *Hannity* segment aired, a *Politico* reporter wanted to hear Shlaes' thoughts on how her book was being referenced by congressional Republicans to support their critique of the stimulus bill. "Insofar as certain policymakers are reading the book," she told the reporter, "on the authorly level, that's really gratifying ... And if certain politicians find *The Forgotten Man* useful for making arguments, that's great, but that does not mean that I endorse the individual action of the individual lawmaker... *Books have lives* [my emphasis], and stuff happens to them that you never plan" (April 21, 2009). Here, she repeats the same view of her book's being a self-referential, autonomous, intellectual product. This, of course, conceals the social relations, institutions, and political interests behind the book's production, promotion, and dissemination.

Even the most well-known experts of the Great Depression, such as Robert S. McElvaine, who vigorously refutes her book on historical grounds, acknowledges Shlaes' gifts as a writer.[20] But what Shlaes' rhetoric of intellectual *autonomy* obscures is the relations of *dependency* that exist between her research and the politically-driven institutions that have sustained it for decades. Winning the International Policy Network's Bastiat Prize in 2002 is an earlier example of how support for her work on economic history has been predicated on its conformity to the ideological needs of free-market think tanks. And the astounding publicity that *The Forgotten Man* has received from Fox News and the Republican Party during the Great Recession provides a more recent example of similar political relations of dependency.

SWITCHING ROLES: THE COMMUNICATIVE VERSATILITY OF THE FOX NEWS PUNDIT

So far, I have primarily highlighted the communicative differences between Hannity and Shlaes and how they perform divergent analytical dispositions and use opposing class-cultural bases of knowledge. However, pegging the host and guests as purely occupying the roles of "populist" and "intellectual" overlooks the communicative versatility of both Shlaes and Hannity and oversimplifies how the populist-intellectual tactic operates. Although he certainly leans more toward a populist orientation, at moments in the discussion Hannity shifts his expressive style and uses disinterested modes of analysis that convey his commitment to scientific-journalistic values of objectivity and neutrality. This ability to alter his disposition and assume a professional posture is significant because it allows his popular audience to imagine that they, like Hannity, can enjoy "double access" to high and low culture (Gripsrud, 1989).

---

[20] For a forceful, *academic* critique of Shlaes' *Forgotten Man*, see McElvaine, 2009.

In the exchange outlined in the beginning of this section, after Shlaes offers a list of economic indices to demonstrate the New Deal's supposed ineffectiveness, Hannity attempts to contribute to the statistical discourse Shlaes initiates, inserting, against her numbers, the added observation, "but mostly it [the unemployment rate] hovered at 20 percent." Hannity's citation of statistical evidence not only sought to enhance his credibility as a speaker; it also served to make social scientific discourses of experts like Shlaes appear less alien and elite. This straddling of populist and professional voices seeks to resolve the underlying tensions and contradictions between, using Bakhtinian terms, the "official" and "unofficial" culture that Shlaes and Hannity represent. But these reconciliatory gestures do not always work.

For example, in Hannity's transition from his parents' experience to *his* use of statistical discourse, subtle differences were exposed between Hannity and Shlaes. When Hannity adds to Shlaes' numbers ("but mostly it hovered at 20 percent"), Shlaes actually corrects his inflated numbers in the next line saying, "fourteen, fifteen, like that." This undermines Hannity's attempt to stand next to Shlaes as an intellectual equal. Hannity once again becomes lay, popular, and culturally subordinate. Aware of the power relations behind her corrective gesture and how it could mark her as a "know-it-all," Shlaes attempts to downplay the degree of Hannity's significant error by ending her sentence with "like that." Here we see how the populist host is not the only actor in the execution of PIT working to contain the tensions between popular and professional bases of knowledge and cultural authority.

Intellectuals and academics can be as communicatively versatile as their TV populist counterparts. In fact, most experts that appear on Fox News, and on television in general, do so because they understand and are comfortable with the communicative requirements of the television medium and/or have past experience of speaking on television and radio. Like Shlaes, these experts have often worked as journalists for major newspapers and have thus gained the skills to translate the esoteric language and presentational style of the intellectual field into the exoteric language of the journalistic field.

An intellectual's awareness of the popular aesthetic of any given cable show – from talk shows to the infotainment programs found on networks like the History Channel or Discovery – heightens the expert's apprehension of using disciplinary jargon and encourages them to popularly accent their language and self-presentation. For example, an expert on Roman weaponry on the History Channel might tell the audience that "the chariot was the stealth bomber of its day," or say that the emperor Nero was "one bad hombre." Sometimes this translation works and sometimes, if unsuccessful, an intellectual can appear even more awkward and foreign to the popular audience. However, if the translation is not attempted at all and the intellectuals choose to strictly express themselves in hyper-formalized ways, they will display a *social* disconnectedness that can mark their voices as condescending – or, worse, as irrelevant.

When successfully embodying the populist-intellectual tactic, the intellectual guests are simultaneously able to convey their expertise and educational pedigree and the notion that their intelligence and knowledge-set complements and affirms that of the ordinary viewers. After Hannity summarized Sumner's argument using the Yale professor's letter scheme to designate a taxpaying producer, a politician, and a welfare recipient, Hannity acknowledged the limits of his authority and conceded the role of teacher to Shlaes. This gesture points to her status as an expert. Hannity deferentially says, "Maybe you can make more sense of that than I just tried to describe." In return, she downplayed her distance from popular knowledge (and by extension Hannity and the audience) and stressed how the subject matter under consideration is comprehensible to commonsense thinking – the only reason it seems otherwise being due to the arcane ways in which the argument is presented. Shlaes would state, "Well, it's pretty simple. The algebra sounds complicated, but the forgotten man is the taxpayer who subsidizes a project that the government wants. Maybe it's a good project. Often, it's a not-so-good project. And that's what happened in the New Deal." Looking at Hannity's setup of PIT and Shlaes' follow-through, we see how her argument is simultaneously stamped with elite distinction and made to appear accessible to the popular audience ("it's not hard").

The populist-intellectual tactic requires that the actors involved demonstrate a communicative flexibility, one which allows them to temporarily assume contrary subjectivities so as to repair culturally contentious moments between popular and professional brands of knowledge. However, if the boundaries separating different classed subjectivities are transgressed too often and the actors do not commit to the performance of a particular class-cultural disposition and analytical posture, the representational tactic loses its main purpose: to exhibit a consensus about the history of the Depression that spans different class-cultural bases of authority. The consensus cannot be represented without the prior and continued representation of class-cultural differences between Hannity and Shlaes. The authenticity of both Hannity's populist and Shlaes's intellectual roles are threatened if either one oscillates too frequently between a professional and populist posture. Moreover, having academics and experts on Hannity and other top Fox News programs allows the populist host to cede the professional class voice. Thus by contrasting himself with the guest's intellectual performance, Hannity can further accentuate his performance as an everyday guy.

EXPERTISE MUST BE PERFORMED

Political parties entail more than the pursuit of legislative goals, electoral victories and the spoils of government power. Political parties – or at least effective ones – also operate as educational organizations. The cultural-ideological role of parties was a central focus of Antonio Gramsci's writing;[21] he particularly emphasized the way in which parties cultivate and promote what he called "organic intellectuals" – that is, knowledge producers who help develop new "common sense" notions of class and morality that, if successful, could become widely shared values that cut across multiple social sectors (Laclau & Mouffe, 2001: 67). The dominance of neoliberal ideas both in the United States and internationally exemplifies many of Gramsci's core ideas about hegemony and the importance of intellectual leadership. One of the most defining features of neoliberalism has been the movement's concerted investment in intellectual production, and in particular the production of knowledge that, sociologist Stephanie Mudge writes, "provid[es] symbolic resources to political elites in the form of explanations for the failures of Keynesian and developmental policies and a new set of recommendations for economic recovery" (2008: 708). The contemporary example of Amity Shlaes' book *The Forgotten Man* demonstrates how this long term intellectual mission is active and ongoing.

However, any political group attempting to reshape common sense in order to secure hegemonic power must, Gramsci stressed, devise ways to bridge different levels of ideology, linking theoretical ideas with popular beliefs. He writes:

---

[21] Following James P. Hawley's summary of Gramsci's work, Gramsci conceptualized the party as "an organization of culture and education, a state of a new type in gestation" (1980: 586). Also see Gramsci, 1971.

Common sense is the folklore of philosophy and always stands midway between folklore proper (folklore as it is normally understood) and philosophy, science, and economics of the scientist. Common sense creates the folklore of the future, relatively rigidified phase of popular knowledge in a given time and place.[22]

Mirroring these Gramscian insights, Fox News' interpretative strategy seemed to recognize that in order to create a new "folklore" of the Great Depression, its ideological framing of it had to communicate on different class-cultural registers of authority. With the concept of the populist-intellectual tactic, I have strived to add to and, in some ways, go beyond Gramscian frameworks. By overly focusing on macrological ideological structures and broad, epochal political shifts, hegemony theorists have underexamined the intricate but no less important role that representational tactics and embodied performative styles play within political media texts. I introduce the concept of PIT as a theoretical tool that describes the hegemonizing media techniques that facilitate the execution of broader hegemonic strategies.

Hopefully, in reading this chapter, the reader no longer sees Fox News programs as merely soapboxes for blowhards and partisan hacks. Liberal media critics underestimate the degree to which Fox News serves a popular platform for conservative intellectual culture. Granted, conservative writers, researchers and experts appear on discussion panels with country singers and sports stars, and their research is presented with extravagant or comical graphics. Yet the presence of such experts and the promotion and translation of their intellectual products are recurrent features of Fox News' top shows. Even when intellectuals and academics do not appear in the broadcasts, the academic studies and scholarly standards used for measuring the truth-value of the political claims are nevertheless invoked and regularly cited – regardless of how superficially and problematically applied. The fact that these "scholarly" sources predominantly come from conservative think tanks does not negate the fact that the producers of Fox's top programs employ and concern themselves with displaying professional, technocratic forms of credibility.

The intellectual aspects of a given Fox News program are often disregarded by Fox's critics because of their assumptions about the Fox News audience. The stereotypical conception is one of an uneducated viewer who requires overstimulation via flashy graphics and attractive blonde anchors; a viewer who is easily mystified by cultural symbols and

---

[22] Gramsci (1985), p. 421.

responsive to partisan propaganda. This conception precludes the possibility that Fox News' viewership might actually have a desire to engage (and in fact sees themselves as participating) in an intellectual culture. Fox News shows like *Hannity* provide just the model for doing this without losing their working-class cultural appeal. Simply because a mass audience may not *privilege* word-based forms of information, expert opinion, and elite cultural styles, does not mean that a majority non-college-educated audience discounts or does not want to evaluate the empirical accuracy of a given argument or piece of information.

The producers of *Hannity* and at Fox News in general seem to realize that while speakers may effectively signal their "official" competence by citing credentials and displaying professional modes of analysis, the display of expertise has less *popular* legitimacy if those same speakers are not vouched for by or do not themselves perform the roles of politically loyal, morally concerned individuals. In other words, if the characters of the expert guests are in question and if their moral stakes in the issue are not suggested by the populist host, their demonstration of elite knowledge is less powerful. Likewise, however, the populist host, being unofficial and uncertified, is even less legitimate on his/her own.

It must not be forgotten that even though the legitimacy of empirical knowledge and technocratic voices have been shaken by the rise of postmodern culture and contested by conservative critiques of educated elites, the empirical mode of argumentation is still the dominant way for making truth-claims in the US public sphere. As seen in the "Forgotten Man" segment, Hannity, the stand-in layman, seeks affirmation again and again from the expert when making points about the Depression, and this is replicated on *Glenn Beck* and *The O'Reilly Factor*. The validity of popular memory and experiential knowledge are still dependent on how much these lay epistemic resources align with expert voices. This remains true even in the most wild, partisan sectors of the American news landscape. Sure, sensationalist, conspiracy theory stories are a staple of online conservative outlets like The Drudge Report, Breitbart, and InfoWars but, like all news organizations, these outlets regularly rely on "studies," "statistics," and "experts" in order to "debunk" what they see as "liberal," "globalist" lies.

Focusing so much on the way conservative media has departed from the liberal empirical knowledge tradition, liberal critics have largely overlooked the way conservative media still pay deference to expert knowledge and rely on it to legitimate their political arguments and news interpretations. Rather than viewing Fox News' top programs as anti-intellectual, this chapter has strived to show how *analytically ambidextrous* Fox News hosts and their guest can be. As opposed to merely fact-checking Fox News, it may behoove liberal journalists to try to learn from and possibly emulate this kind of epistemological diversity and versatility. Using the example of Amity Shlaes and the success of her book at rewriting the Depression's history, this chapter also seeks to question the liberal intellectual orientation toward "closure" strategies of legitimation and aversion to the "openness," media-centric strategies of right-wing think tanks.

The inefficacy of the "closure" strategies of higher educational expertise are no more apparent than with the issue of climate change. Liberals continue to stress how the vast majority of scientists and peer-reviewed studies support the idea that humans are causing climate change, yet, a significant amount Americans continue to not believe this scientifically established fact to be true.[23] The success of the expert-activists of the right demonstrate how research and "facts" do not speak for themselves. No different than populism, expertise must be *performed*, ideally on the most mass mediated stage available.

[23] Nuccitelli (2013).

Conclusion: Trumpian Populism

Fox News' Respectable Future Clashes with Its Tabloid Past

Every tabloid, as soon as it gets into safe waters, begins to grow intellectual.
–H. L. Mencken

Substituting for the recently fired Bill O'Reilly, on April 21, 2017, the usually affable conservative comedian Greg Gutfeld opened *The O'Reilly Factor* with somber tone, "Thanks for watching this final edition of *The Factor*. This is a strange and historic day for all of us on the show." At the close of the show, Gutfeld elaborated on the historical significance of the moment: "In the twenty years since *The Factor* has been on the air Bill changed the way news is done. And his show became a sanctuary for you, our loyal viewers who are not being well-served by the mainstream media ... but," reiterating the awkwardness of doing O'Reilly's last program, "I've never been in a situation like this before. How do I turn out the lights on such a venerable and amazing show? I can't. It's not my show and it's not my place." And so ended *The O'Reilly Factor*, the show that first put Fox News on the map and kept the network in the driver's seat for the next two decades.

The beginning of Bill O'Reilly's end started on January 10, 2017, when the *New York Times* published a story by investigative reporters Emily Steel and Michael Schmidt about a former Fox News employee, Juliet Huddy, who, in 2011, accused O'Reilly of stifling her career for denying his sexual advances. Reportedly, Fox News paid a "high six figures" sum to keep Ms. Huddy quiet about the case. Steel and Schmidt's follow-up story on April 1, 2017, proved to be a backbreaker as it revealed that Fox News had paid more than $13 million to settle sexual harassment charges against O'Reilly from five separate women. This bad publicity, combined with activist pressure on companies buying ad space on *The O'Reilly Factor*, created a mass exodus of corporate brands from the show, which in turn forced Fox News to finally take O'Reilly off the air (after which it was revealed that Fox News paid an astounding $32 million in January of 2017 to settle yet another sexual harassment charge against O'Reilly[1]).

One of the interesting things about O'Reilly's firing is that the 2017 *New York Times* investigative reports were not the first time the public had learned of O'Reilly's embroilment in sexual harassment suits. The first case, involving former producer Andrea Mackris, was publicly revealed to the press in 2004.[2] Fox News and O'Reilly had no problem weathering the public scandal then. What made the 2017 reports so damning was the timing of their release. They came on the heels of the biggest scandal in Fox's history. In July of 2016, *Fox & Friends* co-host Gretchen Carlson filed sexual harassment charges against Fox News CEO Roger Ailes, charges that were corroborated by similar charges and testimonies from other Fox employees, notably Fox's primetime star host Megyn Kelly. Ailes, one of the most powerful political figures in America, was promptly terminated as Fox's chief executive and would pass away less than a year later of medical problems related to his longtime battle with hemophilia.

The great irony of Ailes and O'Reilly's removal is that of all the powerful political enemies that tried to take them down over the years, the biggest blows against them came from within Fox News; specifically, from women producers and journalists who exposed the sexist culture of the network's internal workplace environment. Decades of criticism questioning Fox's objectivity and journalistic credibility, on the other hand, was a line of attack that seldom drew blood. However, while these scandals are critical events in Fox's history, in some ways they cloud analysts from seeing how Ailes and O'Reilly's departure supported a new institutional trajectory for the network that was already underway before the scandals came to light.

In June of 2013, Fox News' parent company News Corp. officially split into two companies. The television and film sectors of the media conglomerate became one company, Twenty-First Century Fox, Inc., and the publishing division retained the original name of the company News Corp. This organizational restructuring paved the way for Murdoch's sons, Lachlan and James, to take the executive reins of Twenty-First

---

[1] Steel & Schmidt (October 21, 2017).   [2] NBCnews.com (2004).

Century Fox in 2015, thus, giving them a greater role in shaping Fox News' future. Tensions have long existed between Murdoch's sons and Fox CEO Roger Ailes. For most of Fox's history Rupert Murdoch has backed Ailes' creative leadership over his children's more progressive and professionally styled vision for Fox. However, as it became increasingly obvious that Fox's aging, conservative audience was not a sustainable base on which to build a long-term audience strategy, in late 2013 the network started to make moves to reach out to younger audiences and independents.

Enter Megyn Kelly.

On October 7, 2013, Fox News undraped its new primetime lineup, something that had not been altered in a decade. The addition of *The Kelly File*, hosted by former lawyer Megyn Kelly, was the spotlight of this announcement. This new show was given *Hannity*'s 9:00PM spot, then Fox's second ranked show, bumping it to 10:00PM. In contrast to *Hannity* – the red meat partisan program that had held that spot for years – *The Kelly File* presented itself as a straighter, less opinionated program. A *New York Times* article entitled, "The Megyn Kelly Moment" hailed the new primetime host as the woman who "will define Fox's future" (Rutenberg, 2015). And for a while this seemed to be the case. As a glowing *New York Times* profile on Kelly documented, her program was "the only cable-news program in the 9 p.m. time slot to show year-over-year growth in overall viewership and in the 25-to-54 demographic." *The Kelly File*, the article noted, closed out 2014 with the second highest rating for a cable news show (beating *Hannity*) and even surpassed O'Reilly's ratings on a few occasions.

While Kelly's news coverage and analysis generally conformed to Fox News' conservative ideological slant, liberal media critics applauded her for playing devil's advocate and challenging conservative guests, particularly on gender-related issues. One notable instance is when she challenged conservative blogger Erick Erickson's claim that "kids will most likely do best in households where they have a mom at home nurturing them while dad is out bringing home the bacon." Kelly responds, "Your science, Erick, is not supported by the American Psychological Association, the American Academy of Pediatrics, a Colombia University study, a University of North Carolina study ... Why are we supposed to take your word for it, Erick Erikson?"[3]

---

[3] Martysoffice (May 31, 2013).

Kelly's performance of a "straight" news anchor committed to the values of facticity and journalistic independence was operating smoothly in Fox News' primetime schedule up until her fateful exchange with then candidate Donald Trump in the first debate of the Republican primary. That night on August 6, 2015, Kelly did not play the part of Republican partisan. To her credit, she, like her co-moderators Bret Bair and Chris Wallace, posed truly tough questions to Trump and the other candidates on the stage. The most contentious question of the night involved gender and sexism. Kelly addressed Trump saying, "You've called women you don't like fat pigs, dogs, slobs and disgusting animals ... how will you answer the charge that you are part of the war on women?" To tremendous applause in crowd, Trump responds, "The big problem this country has is being politically correct."

After the debate, Trump – with his "blood coming out of wherever" comment on *CNN Tonight* – suggested that Kelly's toughness as a moderator was related to menstruation. This sexist comment received widespread condemnation from media pundits and politicians. However, Fox viewers voiced their support for Trump over Kelly in email responses forcing Fox's corporate leadership to question whether their new programing direction was "too cosmopolitan" for the network's hard-core audience base (Drezner, 2015). Kelly's confrontation with Trump, combined with her testimony against Ailes, put her in conflict with her Fox News mentor Bill O'Reilly, who defended Trump and Ailes in each incident.[4] Though the Murdoch family was reportedly willing to offer Kelly a $20 million-a-year contract, Kelly decided to leave Fox News for NBC in January of 2017.

In the first debate of the 2016 Republican primary, Fox News sought to spotlight its "straight" news anchors, old and new. However, the confrontation between Trump and the moderators and Kelly's subsequent departure from Fox News illustrates the contradictions that arise when a network built on a tabloid-populist ethos strives to attain journalistic prestige and establishment legitimacy. Trump's political style, more than any Republican candidate in the 2016 race, expressed Fox's *original* programming style.

Of course, Trump has a long history with the tabloid media sector in America (Grove, 2017). In his 1992 essay "The Idiot Culture" veteran Watergate reporter Carl Berstein specifically singles out a story about

---

[4] Steel & Schmidt (April 14, 2017).

Donald Trump to exemplify the broader trend toward tabloidization. On the day Nelson Mandela was released from prison, Bernstein lamented, Trump's affair with Marla Maples and divorce from Ivanka Trump was the top story. "The Best Sex I Ever Had," was the headline Murdoch's *New York Post* ran about the affair on February 16, 1990. In addition to Murdoch's *Post*, Trump has had a long and close relationship with the tabloid news baron David Pecker who owns properties like the *National Enquirer*.[5] This is to say nothing of Trump's central presence in two of most dominant forms of markedly "lowbrow" media, reality television and entertainment wrestling. For fourteen seasons, he starred in and produced one of the most successful reality television shows in network history and he was a central "character" in the fictional domain of World Wrestling Entertainment (WWE), so much so that he was inducted in the WWE Hall of Fame.

Long before declaring his presidential run on July 16, 2015, Donald Trump had an extensive relationship with Fox News as well. In 2011, Trump became a "regular guest" on *Fox & Friends*, complete with his own segment "Monday Mornings with Trump."[6] Even before he took on this formalized role, he appeared as a guest on *Hannity*, *The O'Reilly Factor*, and other top shows going as far back as the late 1990s. This exposure undoubtedly helped prime his candidacy with the conservative base. Of course, Trump's conversion from a Democrat to a Republican was critical to achieving the media platform that Fox granted him. However, the strong compatibility of Trump's *style* with Fox News' traditional corporate brand was equally crucial. Trump embodied Fox's populist-tabloid presentational style like no other Republican presidential candidate had before. And though Rupert Murdoch, Roger Ailes and other major Fox News figures expressed opposition to Trump's candidacy during the Republican primaries, once Trump entered into the general election against Democrat Hillary Clinton, Fox fell quickly in line with the Trump campaign, becoming its most ardent media supporter.[7]

While Hannity, arguably the greatest Trump advocate, continues to represent Fox News' original working-class populist brand, the bow-tie-wearing Tucker Carlson, the host Fox News selected to replace Bill O'Reilly at the 8:00PM timeslot, could not be any less blue-collar, regional

---

[5] Borchers (2016).
[6] Montopoli (2011). For a broader overview of Trump's relationship with Fox see Power, 2015.
[7] Kludt (2016).

or ethnic. In *Washington Post* article Daniel W. Drezner raises the possibility of a rival conservative network shaking Fox's control by being, ironically, more partisan, more populist and more tabloid (2015). The "alt-right" Breitbart News and Alex Jones' conspiracy-driven InfoWars pose competitive threats from the online sphere, while new conservative television ventures such as One America News Network, Newsmax TV, Blaze TV, and Sinclair Broadcasting Group have created more competition in the television arena. Yet as marketers and advertisers know all too well, brand loyalties, once established, are quite difficult to break. It remains to be seen how safe it is for Fox News to rebrand itself as a younger, hipper, more professionally styled news network. The political ascendancy of Donald Trump suggests that the Fox News audience still prefers populism over prestige.

A DEFENSE OF POPULISM

In the last decade, scholarship on populism has grown exponentially. This growth was significantly triggered by the contemporaneous rise of right-wing populist movements in northern Europe and left-wing populist movements in southern Europe and Latin America in the 1990s and 2000s. And the 2016 "Brexit" referendum in the United Kingdom and Trump's presidential victory in the United States has only heightened the concept's salience in the 2010s. As an Americanist, I have strived to reveal the nuances of how populism is deployed in the US political context and, more, how its logic guides the rules of news branding in the US media market. This book's textual analyses of Fox News programming have shown how populism can speak to class inequality in powerful, culturally resonant ways *and* can also distort or conceal its root causes. I have also critiqued the racist and sexist dimensions of populist narrative traditions and iconographies in the United States as well as the way that populism, as a performance style, creates unique pitfalls for women politicians and for politicians of color. But what I disagree with, however, is a position that some scholars have recently advanced, which is that populism, at its logical core, is *inherently* averse to the multicultural values of the Democratic Left.

This perspective explains the Democratic Party's repulsion to populist rhetorical styles as being as a product of its greater demographic diversity and inclusiveness and, conversely, explains the singularity of the conservative populist identity to the Republican Party's racial homogeneity. Jan-Werner Müller's new book *What Is Populism?* (2016) lends support to this view by arguing that populism's tendency to formulate a "people" through excluding an "elite" is antithetical to democratic pluralism. With populism, power centers must be, first and foremost, confronted not deliberated with and, indeed, the discourse's tendency to target an enemy faction contradicts the liberal democratic tenet of total civic inclusiveness. Whether or not this rhetorical trait is, *on principle*, xenophobic or hostile to multiculturalism as Müller suggests, is quite debatable.

Many anti-populist critiques from the left seem to assume that "small l" liberal democracy is a naturally more inclusive alternative to populist forms of democratic action. But, while liberal democracy may rhetorically celebrate pluralism on the surface, such politics – as populism scholar Benjamin Moffit has pointed out (2016) – can involve various *technocratic* forms of exclusion that play out through procedural and juridical processes within party and government institutions, and through the marginalization of voices and expressive styles that do not conform to the *professional* communication norms of the liberal, "bourgeois" public sphere. These so-called "rational" communication standards, as Nancy Fraser has noted, carry their own racist, sexist, and classist baggage (1990). And while populism's constant evocation of a lost, traditional past must be critically interrogated, one should not treat "traditional culture" as an automatic stand-in for political conservatism (Hall, 1998). In turn, one cannot assume discourses of modernity and secularism are *naturally* progressive either. Joan Scott, one of the pioneers of gender history, argues the opposite showing how these discourses have historically justified the subordination of women to the "femininized familial sphere meant to complement the rational masculinist realms of politics and economics" (2017: 3).[8] Her analysis also illustrates how these nominally "progressive" discourses have been used to legitimate Islamophobic ideas and policies.

In *An Army of Women* (1997), Michael Goldberg shows how the populist styled political culture of the People's Party was in many ways more hospitable for women to assert a "public," political identity than the

---

[8] In *Modernity Reimagined: An Analytic Guide* (2017), Chandra Mukerji cogently traces modernity's various discursive threads across several centuries. Mukerji's analysis captures both the complexity and contingency of modernity's social and cultural politics. However, supporting Scott's gender-based critique, Mukerji makes clear, "it was only in the late 18th century when philosophers articulated principles of modernity that men and women were reimagined as opposite in character. Men became the natural leaders of the modern world while women became their opposite: carries of outmoded and artificial traditions of social rank" (95).

"respectable," middle-class style of the established political parties during the Gilded Age. The dominant political institutions of the 1890s treated women's participation in politics as violating the sacred Victorian "ethic of domesticity" (5). The Irish-American firebrand Mary Lease embodied the solidarities between the Gilded Age "Women's movement" and Populist organizations like the Farmer's Alliance. Lease started her political career in the Women's Christian Temperance Union (WCTU) in the 1880s and then joined the Populist Party in the 1890s to become one of the most sought-after Populist Party speakers. "In an era when political speeches were mass entertainment," historian Rebecca Edwards writes, Lease, "excelled at holding an audience's attention." Lease, Edwards continues, "laced her speeches with quotations of Shakespeare and the Bible, and she learned to handle hecklers with scathing sarcasm" (2000: 60). Even while Republican Party leaders slandered her with gendered slurs like "man-wife" (Goldberg, 1997: 261), Lease's humor, tenacity, and confrontational class rhetoric endeared her to audiences and the Populist Party's rank-and-file.

Lease, like contemporary conservative women activists, saw women's political participation as a Christian duty of motherhood rather than its betrayal. But, unlike Sarah Palin's free-market–friendly populism, Lease used the rhetoric of "Momism" (Eliasoph, 1998: 183–189) to attack banks and corporations. Speaking before an audience of suffragists and WCTU members, she said, "Monopoly is taking our homes from us by an infamous system of mortgage foreclosure ... Do you wonder the women are joining the [Farmer's] Alliance? I wonder if there is a woman in all this broad land who can afford to stay out?" (Edwards, 2000: 59). Lease's example complicates the idea that populism is or has to be the exclusive purview of men.

Yet even while Goldberg applauds the Populist Party for being more gender inclusive than other mainstream political organizations of the Gilded Age, just like Republican male leaders, the male leaders of the Populist Party often failed to recognize the way gender inequalities are perpetuated *within* the private sphere of the family farm and in the leadership structure of the movement itself.

Coming back to Müller's criticism of populism, there are many historical examples of how – in order to keep factional schisms at bay and maintain a singular political identity – populists have failed to address the social differences and specific grievances between participant groups in their movement. This is a valid critique of the New Deal coalition of the 1930s, which I discussed in Chapter 4 and is – to a lesser extent – a fair critique of the recent example of Bernie Sanders' populist campaign during the 2016 Democratic primaries, as Sanders' supporter Naomi Klein has acknowledged.[9] It is vital to recognize how, in a patriarchal society where whiteness is normative, populist representational inclinations can easily lead movements to repeat the historic pattern of treating the white, male working class as the default image of the "people." As the New Deal exemplified, who is and who is not included in the *symbolic* construction of "the working class" affects *policy* outcomes that have real world economic consequences.

However, while liberal critiques of populism have raised legitimate concerns, these critiques must always be weighed next to the repeated failure of the Democratic Party and Democratic Party-aligned media to *engage* and activate working-class citizens (both white and nonwhite) with professional class news personalities and technocratic politicians. In *The Populist Explosion* (2016) John Judis argues that the 2016 "Bernie Sanders for President" movement, for all its flaws, ultimately showed that populism and multiculturalism can coexist within the same representational system. Moving beyond the US context, critics who naturalize populism's association with white supremacy must also consider the way leftist movements abroad have used populist rhetorical styles to attack racism. We see this with Spain's Podemos movement, Greece's Syriza movement and in the rhetoric and embodied indigenous–racial identities of former Latin-American populist presidents such as Hugo Chavez in Venezuela and Evo Morales in Bolivia.[10]

Political theorist Chantal Mouffe has vigorously argued that the primary mandate of the contemporary left is to "construct a people," and not merely identify and micro-advertise to existing constituencies (Mouffe et al., 2016). Whether or not one agrees with Mouffe, it is highly problematic to assume the *process* of constructing a "people" by a political movement is somehow purely vertical and does not entail vigorous contestation, negotiation, and coalition-building practices among group members. As the Jamaican-born, British cultural theorist Stuart Hall has

---

[9] In *No Is Not Enough: Resisting Trump's Shock Politics and Winning the World We Need* (2017), Naomi Klein, a full-throated Bernie Sanders supporter, maintains that one of the shortcomings of Sander's leftwing populist movement was its inability to engage and speak to people of color, namely African American and Latinx American citizens. She applauds Sanders' economic populism but stresses how it must be articulated in, drawing from Kimberlé Crenshaw's term, an "intersectional" manner that accounts for the role of race and gender play in the broader reproduction of economic inequalities.

[10] de la Torre, 2010; de la Torre & Anderson, 2013.

stressed, "The stubborn truth is that social interests are contradictory. There is no automatic correspondence between class location, political position, and ideological inclination. Majorities have to be 'made' and 'won' – not passively reflected" (1988c: 27).

Even for the most seemingly homogeneous political communities, populism, like hegemony itself, is "hard work."[11] Election cycle after election cycle, conservative activists have effectively bridged social gaps between suit and tie Wall Street Republicans and blue-collar, Reagan Democrats, between Ron Paul libertarian men and the women of the Religious Right, between conservatives in the South and Sunbelt and conservatives in the Northeast and Rustbelt. At the level of conservative intellectual culture, the Burkean emphasis on *conserv*ing traditional ways of life somehow coexists with neoliberal economic theory that, drawing from economist Joseph Schumpeter's concept of "creative-destruction," celebrates ceaseless societal revolution through capitalism (Grossberg, 2005: 132–134). There are no natural or logical connections between these intellectual threads in the same way there is no natural or logical connection between being pro-gun, pro-life, denying climate change, or supporting tax cuts for the rich. And yet, thanks to decades of ideological labor performed by conservative activists, think tanks and media organizations, any one of these conservative positions conjures, almost automatically, each and every other position in the conservative political package.

The coalescing function of rhetorically taking on "the elite" is performed by outlets across the entire conservative media establishment, from Fox News to Rush Limbaugh's talk radio show to the pages of the *Wall Street Journal* (Cappella & Jamieson, 2008: 59–74). During the late-2000s economic crisis, however, Fox News played a special role in this regard. Fox's top programs provided Tea Party activists with a consistent set of populist moral narratives that kept the movement "on message," a messaging coherency the leftist Occupy Wall Street movement of 2011 evidently lacked. Fox's initial opposition to Trump in the 2016 Republican primaries and Trump's eventual victory reveals the limits of Fox's power. With this said, one is hard-pressed to identify a media organization that exerts the same level of political pressure on the Democratic Party as Fox News does with the "Grand Old Party" (GOP) – the Republican Party. Emulating Fox's populist rhetorical style carries many risks for the

---

[11] This is a homage to Stuart Hall, who once said, "Hegemonizing is hard work." Found in Lipsitz, June, 1988.

Democratic Party and its media allies but so, too, does a continual reliance on the same professional class cultural style and confrontation-averse centrism that has repeatedly led to messaging entropy, voter/viewer apathy and ideological defeat.

LEARNING FROM FOX NEWS

In 1926, Italian intellectual Antonio Gramsci was imprisoned by the fascist Mussolini regime. While incarcerated, Gramsci somehow continued to develop his ideas about the relationship between culture and politics in his now famous "Prison Notebooks." Gramsci, a left-wing Marxist, regularly reviewed the right-wing periodicals of his day such as the *Critica Fascista*, and the ideas of prolific right-wing writers such as Giovanni Gentile and Luigi Pirandello. As Gramsci scholar Timothy Brennan writes, "Gramsci tended to *learn* [my emphasis] by absorbing the lessons of the popular conservative forces of his day ... He modeled his arguments as answers to those in the ascendant of modern thought, whatever their persuasion" (2006: 251). Gramsci cared little about exposing the Italian right's techniques of deception. Instead, he was far more interested in learning the deeper cultural currents that gave the dominant ideas of his political era their moral force and "common sense" quality. Contemporary analysts of TV news would do well to adopt Gramsci's approach in emphasizing culture over supposed instances of deceit.

I conclude this book by exploring three tendencies that have hindered left analysts from approaching Fox News from the learning posture that Gramsci modeled. In accounting for Fox News' commercial success and political power, left-leaning critics should abandon three prevailing and related analytical dead-ends. First, research on Fox News has analytically privileged the issue of ideological indoctrination at the expense of stylistic analysis. Second, analysts have often used a deception-based mode of analysis that explains the power of conservative media messaging only in terms of how it promotes "false consciousness." Lastly, there is a tendency to approach the conservative media audience as being hopelessly bigoted or anti-intellectual. This view leads the analysts to only see the reactionary elements of conservative political discourse and overlook its utopian qualities. Let us begin with the first tendency.

If there is one concept that has emerged above all others in the academic literature on Fox News and partisan media it is the concept of "selective exposure." Contemporary political science and political communication scholars have reintroduced this psychological theory from the "limited effects" tradition of mass communication research that developed in the 1950s.[12] Selective exposure describes people's cognitive tendency to select information that is congenial to their politics and, conversely, to avoid the "cognitive dissonance" such people experience when presented with ideas and facts that challenge their existing worldview.

As this research has shown, *both* conservatives and liberals are susceptible to this mental habit. As a result, both political communities exist – to varying degrees – in their own cultural–ideological silos (Pew, 2004; Iyengar & Hahn, 2009). Yet while the selective exposure research on partisan media has shed light on the social, psychological and media industrial processes that have created and continue to perpetuate the polarized state of today's news and politics, popular critics from the left and right have unfortunately taken the basic lines of argumentation of this literature, even as they overlook its nuanced conclusions.

From the left, we have examples such as Jen Senko's documentary *The Brainwashing of My Dad* (2015). This film explores the consequences that conservative talk media has on interpersonal relationships. Using the case of her own father, Senko's film dramatically illustrates the very real ways in which partisanship can tear families apart. As evident by the film's title, the documentary presents a psychologized image of the talk radio listener and Fox News viewer as someone primarily driven by irrational, fear-based impulses. But while this film provides a good historical context for the rise of conservative media, it ultimately falls back on a problematic analytical approach that has typified leftist critiques of conservative political constituencies as far back as Richard Hofstadter's "paranoid style" analysis of McCarthyism in the 1950s.[13]

The Brainwashing of My Dad suggests that the political identity of conservative audiences is primarily formed not from these audiences' own active and deliberative intellectual exploration or sense of morality, but

---

[12] Sunstein, 2001; Tsfati & Cappella 2003; Prior, 2007; Bennett & Iyengar, 2008; Cappella & Jamieson, 2008; Stroud, 2011; Arseneaux & Johnson, 2013; Levendusky, 2013.

[13] See Hofstadter, 1965. "The Pseudo-Conservative Revolt – 1954." In *The Paranoid Style in American Politics, and Other Essays.* This essay first appeared in Daniel Bell's edited volume *The New American Right* (1955). This volume was itself expanded and updated as *The Radical Right* (1963). For a thorough overview of Hofstadter's writing on conservative populism and of his main critics, see "chapter 5: Richard Hofstadter's "Paranoid Style Revisited: The Tea Party, Past is Prologue" in Robert Hortwitz's book *America's Right: Anti-establishment Conservatism from Goldwater to the Tea Party* (2013).

rather from the repetitive onslaught onto otherwise passive and compliant receivers of ideological messages via a powerful media apparatus. The hammering gradually breaks down whatever critical capacities the audience member might have possessed and thus makes them more impressionable to the propagandistic techniques of conservative political operatives. Akin to the cult member who has been sequestered from friends, family and the outside world by the cult leader, the documentary, with its leftist critique, understands the conservative audience member as having already been subsumed within a media culture that hammers home a single point of view.

Some of the major selective exposure studies, however, contradict this depiction of conservative media audiences as mentally vulnerable couch potatoes. For example, Joseph Cappella and Kathleen Jamieson's *Echo Chamber* (2008) and Matthew Levendusky's *How Partisan Media Polarize America* (2013) show that consumers of Rush Limbaugh and Fox News make up some of the most politically *active* segments of the US citizenry. Cappella and Jamieson attribute this, in part, to how the style of conservative media gives the audience a greater sense of urgency and a sense that they have the power to affect public policy (13–38). The Fox News audience's belief in its political agency was acutely on display during the Tea Party protests of 2009, a belief that was largely confirmed by the historic number of congressional seats Republicans captured in the 2010 midterms.

With their "active audience theory," Kevin Arceneaux and Martin Johnson argue that practicing "selective exposure" is itself a form of audience agency (2013). Moreover, their research demonstrates that, when compared to nonpartisan news audiences and strictly entertainment-seeking audiences, partisan media consumers tend to be the most *active* and *discerning* media interpreters among these different groups. In short, partisan media audiences tend to be less impressionable, not more, than other segments of the national television audience.

Conservatives, of course, have their own selective exposure-*like* arguments to "explain away" the thinking of political liberals. They dismiss the reasoning or veracity of leftist political arguments by depicting higher education, the supposed source of all liberal views, as a sequestered (e.g. "ivory tower"), cult-like experience. In fact, a recent 2017 Pew study actually shows that more than half of Republicans view higher education as having a negative impact on American society (Fingerhut, 2017). This view follows a rhetorical pattern that William F. Buckley, one of founders of the conservative intellectual movement, established long ago in his classic book *God and Man at Yale* (1951). The notion that American universities indoctrinate America's youth to become liberal has been the *bête noir* of Fox New programming for quite some time. One 2007 content study on *The O'Reilly Factor* listed "academics" as one of the program's most consistent "villains" (Conway et al., 2007). Continuing this legacy, *Tucker Carlson Tonight* has a recurrent segment called "Campus Craziness,"[14] where host Tucker Carlson invites college professors and student activists to the show solely in order to confront them for their "extreme" "anti-American" views and to depict them as "brainwashed."

Too often debates over partisan journalism and media bias have devolved into contests to prove that one political culture is more intellectually isolated and out of touch with reality than the other. This framing of the topic has inevitably led to a dialogical and analytical deadlock. Placing the emphasis on Fox News' political style as opposed to its political bias, as this book has done, provides a new avenue for engaging the network which, I hope, can refresh and expand the discussion on political media.

The second analytical pitfall is the deception-based interpretive approach. This mode of analysis is most pronounced in activist exposés such as Robert Greenwald's film *Outfoxed: Rupert Murdoch's War on Journalism* (2004) and David Brock and Ari Rabin-Havt's book *The Fox Effect: How Roger Ailes Turned a Network into a Propaganda Machine* (2012). These projects claim, in a nutshell, that Fox News misinforms its viewers and functions as a propaganda arm of the Republican Party. The type of textual analysis these works offer primarily consists of comparing erroneous statements made during Fox News broadcasts with the factual record. In providing a slew of empirical examples where Fox News programs engaged in manipulative and deceptive editing and framing tactics, *The Fox Effect* and *Outfoxed* provide plenty of ammunition to support the idea that Fox is a politically driven news operation.

However, only being able to show how your political opposition propagates lies falls into the trap of what German philosopher Ernst Bloch aptly termed a "half-Enlightenment." Bloch argued for a "double-coded" method of ideology critique, which this study has sought to follow by considering both the deceptive qualities of Fox's programming and the elements that ring true for audiences.[15] Indeed, this book

---

[14] *Fox News Insider* (March 3, 2017).
[15] For an overview of and strong argument for the resuscitation of Ernst Bloch's method of cultural criticism, see Kellner, 1997.

has critiqued the distorted and misleading ways in which Fox represents social inequality in America, particularly with regard to race, gender, and class. However, it also has sought to demonstrate how Fox's nostalgia for a "traditional past," coupled with its utopian free-market vision of the future, draws critical attention to what the current social system lacks. On this register, Fox News' top programs have *elucidated*, not masked, key contradictions between the "American Dream" and structural social realities. In particular, Fox News' populist imaginary has highlighted class tensions and incongruities between the lower middle class and educated professionals.

Conservative media figures like Hannity, O'Reilly, and Glenn Beck succeed in large part because they use populist rhetorical traditions to critique power and articulate a utopian–moral vision of a better future. Unfortunately, the left response thus far has offered only "thin" descriptions of these populist undercurrents, while instead conducting elaborate, in-depth examinations of Fox hosts' most reactionary and authoritarian qualities.

Consensus School intellectuals such as sociologist Daniel Bell and historian Richard Hofstadter did much to establish this reactionary-focused interpretive stance. Taking the ascendant conservative movements of the 1950s and 1960s such as McCarthyism and the "Goldwater for President" movement as their objects of study, they conceptualized the "paranoid style" of conservative populism as a rhetorical tool for inciting the white middle class's "status anxiety," or *fears* about losing their race-based and newly gained economic privileges.[16] The pathologizing nature of such terms recurs in the documentary film mentioned earlier here, *The Brain Washing of My Dad* (2015), as well as countless liberal think pieces in the wake of Donald Trump's 2016 presidential victory.

In *The Reactionary Mind* (2011), Corey Robin takes this argument further and suggests that the very DNA of conservative thought, going as far back as Edmund Burke and the politics of eighteeth-century England and France, is rooted in a reactionary impulse to protect social hierarchy in all its forms. Robin argues that conservative intellectual thinking has

---

[16] Alice O'Connor has critiqued Hofstadter's "status anxiety" thesis for reducing the appeal of conservative populist formations such as McCarthyism and the Barry Goldwater for President movement to "a bundle of impulses and resentments" (109). For another critical take on Hofstadter's "status anxiety" argument, see Kazin, 1998: 191–192. For a supportive take on Hofstadter's "status anxiety" argument, see chapter 5 of Robert Horwitz's 2013 book *America's Right: Anti-Establishment Conservatism from Goldwater to the Tea Party*.

rested on a preference for the possibility of individual supremacy over the ideal of social equality. Thus, since the development of popular democracy, the "permanent political project" of the conservative movement has been and continues to be an attempt to make "privilege palatable to the democratic masses" (100).

Robin's genealogy persuasively demonstrates how central counterrevolutionary ideas have been to the conservative intellectual tradition and, to his credit, his analysis accounts for this tradition's historical contingency and mutability. However, his general argument that the conservative philosophical system (its "reactionary mind") fundamentally hinges on a mission to make "privilege palatable" leads the analysts to a dead end, that is, if their goal is to better understand why conservative policies and ideas have achieved widespread moral legitimacy. When one believes conservative populism is essentially driven by the motivation to protect one's privilege and power – an inherently selfish, unredeeming motivation – the analyst is relieved from having to engage with its moral logic and the social-political basis of its antiestablishment crusade.

In this book, I have strived to do what the majority of writing on Fox News seldom does, which is challenge a leftist reader to see elements of their own belief system within the culture of conservative media – or, at the very least, to see conservatives as moral thinkers. Political elites must make certain concessions, whether symbolic or material, to factions of the subordinate masses in order to maintain their position of power;[17] thus, it should make sense that discourses defending forms of privilege and hierarchy would be accompanied by and entangled with egalitarian, progressive, and even subversive ideas. According to Gramsci, the key to challenging a rival hegemonic project is as much about exposing its reactionary elements as it is about identifying and taking back its popular-democratic elements. Literary theorist Kenneth Burke has said that much of politics involves "the stealing back and forth of symbols" (1984: 103). Since the postwar era, conservatives have seized a great deal of symbolic property from the leftist movements of the 1890s and 1930s and have even appropriated culturally transgressive themes from the New Left of the 1960s. This exchange of political symbols may be lopsided, in part, because conservative political communicators seem to have a broader imagination for what elements of the national popular culture are desirable, contestable and usable. In other words, they have been, in some

---

[17] Laclau (1977: 173); Gramsci (1996).

ways, better practitioners of hegemony and better examples of Gramsci's learning posture.

The anti-aristocratic, egalitarian values of political populism and tabloid journalism are deeply embedded in American popular culture. Therefore, it is unlikely that any successful discourse in media and politics can rely solely on appeals to social supremacy without making some sort of underdog identity claim. Seeking to understand how conservatives understand themselves as social underdogs does not have to mean one defers the question of how conservative populism appeals to patriarchal values and white supremacy. On the contrary, this book has illustrated how the latent, egalitarian elements of conservative populism provide cover for its reactionary currents by blunting moral critiques from the left while evading moral reflection from within. This is one of the reasons why "forgotten man" populist narratives and working-class performers like Bill O'Reilly have been so important to the conservative movement. Nothing more likely blinds someone from considering another group's oppression as when they have been given a narrative about their own oppression. But of course this point cuts in both political directions.

Postscript

Fox News and the "Alt-Right": Populism and Nationalism

The term "alt-right" gained widespread currency during the 2016 presidential election and, for a brief moment, its main leaders and affiliated media outlets were all the rage among the US commentariat. The label was supposed to signify a new, "alternative" brand of conservatism; one that was unapologetically built on white identity politics and anti-feminism and that emphasized economic nationalist positions over conservatism's traditional free-trade internationalism. Other commentators maintained that this was simply a rehashing of the Old Right's "paleo-conservative" tendencies, a subset of conservatism that was exemplified by figures such as Republican Senator Robert Taft in the 1940s and conservative columnist Pat Buchanan in the 1990s.[1] The peak of the term's public legitimacy can be dated to Steven Bannon's comments at the 2016 Republican National Convention, when he nominated his online site Breitbart News to be *the* "platform of the alt-right."[2] In August of 2016, then candidate Donald Trump would make the Breitbart CEO his chief advisor, a move that seemed to signal – in light of Bannon's public comments a month prior – that Trump wanted to officially align his campaign with the budding alt-right movement as well.

Fast-forward to 2017, conservative politicians and conservative media began running from the term like the plague. According to Angela Nagle, a leading expert of the alt-right, the events that transpired in Charlottesville, Virginia, on August 11 and 12, 2017, marked the end of the movement.[3] The "Unite the Right" protest event against the removal of

---

[1] Lyons (January 20, 2017). Also see Rosenberg (October 8, 2016).
[2] Posner (August 22, 2016).   [3] Nagle (August 15, 2017).

the Robert E. Lee statue, a confederate commander, brought the white supremacist elements of the alt-right out into the open. Seeing Klu Klux Klan and Neo-Nazi groups march alongside the more youthful, hipster-looking leaders of the alt-right such as Richard Spencer, disabused any previous idea that the alt-right's racist rhetoric was ironic or performatively transgressive. The vehicular murder of Heather Heyer at a counter-protest event by self-described Neo-Nazi James Alex Fields especially punctuated the serious, non-ironic militancy of the alt-right.

During the 2015–2016 presidential campaign, Spencer and other alt-right figures such as former Breitbart editor Milo Yiannopoulos were treated as semi-legitimate public speakers and interview subjects, but, in a post-election, post-Charlottesville context, they had become marginalized pariahs. Steven Bannon's star rose and fell almost as quickly. Trump hired Bannon as his campaign chief in August of 2016 and, just one year later, fired Bannon as the White House's "chief strategist." In January of 2018, the falling out between Trump and Bannon was so public and acrimonious that Bannon was even forced to leave Breitbart, the organization he did so much to establish. Considering the ephemerality of the alt-right movement, it is difficult, and perhaps foolish, to try and compare the style and politics of alt-right media to that of Fox News, a truly enduring conservative media institution. Nevertheless, it may be a fruitful exercise to tentatively explore the institutional and discursive ties between Fox News and Breitbart, the old guard and the new guard.

As mentioned in the Introduction, during the 2016 presidential campaign, Breitbart News momentarily stole the spotlight from Fox News. And, in this period, the online news site even adopted an oppositional posture toward Fox. But, much like other tales about "new" online media taking on "old" television media, the rivalry story about Fox News and Breitbart concealed the synergistic relationship the two organizations have had since Breitbart's founding in 2007.

Breitbart was launched by Andrew Breitbart, a conservative provocateur from California who had cutting-edge insights on how to navigate the budding online news business. In addition to working for The Drudge Report, one of most successful news aggregator sites on the political right, Breitbart helped Arianna Huffington launch what would become one of the most successful news aggregator sites on the political left, Huffington Post. Breitbart's intelligence and skill undoubtedly contributed to Breitbart News' emergence as a major media player in the 2016 election. However, what many forget is that it was Fox News that helped Breitbart achieve its first big national story. This story was based on the

2009 ACORN sting video produced by conservative activist James O'Keefe. Its sensationalist content combined with its anti-welfare politics prefigured the story's wall-to-wall coverage on Fox News. Because Fox is a "inter media agenda setting" leader (see Introduction), Breitbart's ACORN story was able to take root outside the online sector and was cited by mainstream, "legacy" media outlets from CNN to NBC to NPR (Dreier & Martin, 2010).

After Andrew Breitbart's death in 2012 due to heart failure, Steve Bannon took over Breitbart News as executive chairman. Like Andrew Breitbart, Bannon's career as a conservative media producer was catapulted by his activist work with the Tea Party movement in the Great Recession era. His stature would hit its zenith when President Donald Trump appointed him White House chief strategist in 2016, but Fox News, it could be argued, was responsible for first establishing Bannon's name in the conservative media world. Fox heavily promoted his documentary on the 2008 financial collapse *Generation Zero*, which debuted at the 2010 National Tea Party Convention and then at CPAC. Fox News pundit Jesse Watters reported how the film "blew the doors off the Tea Party convention." Moreover, Fox News' top show *Hannity* had Bannon as a guest and devoted an entire hour-long show to *Generation Zero*; "It was a massive hit," host Sean Hannity told Bannon encouragingly (February 23, 2010). In looking back at this Great Recession era documentary, one can see how its economic nationalist themes and attendant points about the evils of "crony capitalism" and the tragedy of American's lost, traditional past provided the blueprint for the slogans Trump would use in his 2016 campaign, such as "Make America Great Again" and "Drain the Swamp."

Breitbart and Bannon's history with Fox clearly influenced both Breitbart's editorial agenda and the Trump campaign's rhetoric. Trump has and continues to represent himself as a champion for the "forgotten Americans," a term that is a variation on the "forgotten man" trope Fox News hosts heavily used in their coverage of the late-2000s economic crisis and the Tea Party. And the discursive parallels continue. Breitbart and Trump's battle against "Big Journalism," "Big Hollywood," and "Big Government" repeats narrative themes that have been staples of Fox News programming for decades. Trump and Breitbart's crusade against liberal PC culture is nothing new either. Consider how Bill O'Reilly introduced *The O'Reilly Factor* (then *The O'Reilly Report*) on its maiden broadcast on October 7, 1996. "Few broadcasts take chances these days," the fresh faced O'Reilly told his audience, "and most are very *politically correct* [my emphasis]. We're going to try and be different" (Folkenflik, 2013: 56).

Donald Trump's "lowbrow," tabloid style firmly positioned him within a long line of *cultural populist* conservative politicians and media figures. However, his xenophobic, anti-immigration rhetoric, and "law and order" framing of the Black Lives Matter movement projected the reactionary politics of the alt-right, a movement and media culture that is more strongly oriented toward ethno-nationalism than populism. But what, one may ask, is the difference between populism and nationalism?

Populism and nationalism have similar rhetorical traits, hence, their frequent conflation. As mentioned in Chapter 4, populism is a "past-directed" discourse always attempting "to bring back ancient values into the contemporary world" (Taggart, 2000: 16). This parallels what historians have long recognized about nationalism, how it is also foundationally built on past-directed ideas such as "heritage" and "tradition" (Kammen, 1991). Most centrally, nationalism and populism create the solidarity of a political community in the same basic way; by accentuating a common opposition to an enemy Other. What distinguishes them however is the enemies they target.

Unlike nationalism's emphasis on *foreign* enemies, the primary threat in populist discourse – *the elite* – comes from within the body politic (Stavrakakis, 2005: 244–247) and is, thus, fixated more on social hierarchies internal to the nation. For this reason, the populist tradition has provided American politicians and news organizations – particularly tabloid ones (Ornebring & Jönsson, 2004) – with a vernacular language for describing *class tensions*. This is not to suggest such a populist–nationalist schema is without its problems.

For centuries, the populist image of the "producer" and "worker" has almost exclusively been a *white, masculine* image (Roediger, 1991; Kazin, 1998). In addition to attacking aristocrats and power elites, populist political formations have also involved scapegoating the poor and racial minorities (Berlet & Lyons, 2000; Lowndes, 2005), treating these groups as if they were *foreigners* in their own country. Historical events like the Red Scare of the 1950s particularly exemplifies how there has never been a bright line distinction between "foreign" and "domestic" enemies in the history of American politics. Moving beyond the US national context, this is especially the case in formerly colonized nations whose politics have been and still are manipulated by Western powers and/or other regional hegemons.

Returning to Fox News, the network's programming themes have historically fluctuated across a nationalist/populist spectrum. During the Great Recession, the editorial direction of Fox's top programs was more evidently weighted toward issues of wealth distribution and class. Today, Fox News' programming seems to be less focused on the cultural elitism of the media and liberals and more focused on stories about threatening Islamic terrorists and immigrant street gangs like MS-13. These contemporary topics naturally fit within one of the main political narratives of the alt-right and paleoconservatism, a story about how increased immigration and the multicultural values of the left will destroy "Western civilization" (Buchanan, 2002). Commentators from Bill Kristol, the founder of the conservative *Weekly Standard*, to Joy Reid, a liberal host on MSNBC, have argued that Fox has shifted into a white nationalist mode to better suit the political conditions of the Trump era. Both Kristol and Reid have specifically singled out Tucker Carlson as the main figure driving this trend at Fox News,[4] a charge Carlson has vigorously repudiated.[5]

Like its predecessor *The O'Reilly Factor, Tucker Carlson Tonight* places professors and university culture at the center of its vision of "the elite." However, Carlson's anti-elitist attacks focus more narrowly on campus-based identity politics and do not express a deeper class grievance against the professional class writ large. Like former Breitbart editor and rising conservative online star Ben Shapiro, Carlson is a California native whose preppie appearance, voice, and embodied affect projects the cultural sensibility of khaki-pants-wearing college Republicans. In short, Carlson's brand of whiteness lacks both the regional-ethnic and working-class edges of Bill O'Reilly and Sean Hannity's on-air personas.

There are several distinctions, however, between Carlson's Fox News show, a show designed for an older audience, and the more youthful online political culture of the alt-right. Like other Fox hosts, Carlson celebrates sincere, God-fearing "squares" who listen to country music and often presents himself, like Bill O'Reilly before him, as the protector of traditional Judeo-Christian moral norms. In contrast, the youthful denizens of right-wing websites such as 4Chan and Breitbart despise moralistic "normies" and take special pleasure in being sarcastic, nihilistic, and culturally transgressive. As Angela Nagle's book *Kill All Normies* (2017) details, the rhetoric of major alt-right figures like Richard Spencer

[4] Baragona (January 20, 2018); Harwood (January 26, 2018).
[5] Fox News Insider (January 23, 2018).

and former Breitbart editor Milo Yiannopoulos can be quite elitist. Alt-right media figures often depict themselves as avant-garde and counter-cultural, and generally view the social masses as a "blue-pilled," mindless herd, something akin to French social psychologist Gustave Le Bon's concept of "the crowd." Fox News pundits like Carlson, by contrast, still valorize the intelligence and taste of "ordinary Americans."

As explained in an earlier section, the moral class narratives of political populism have the power to conceal the authoritarian/reactionary elements of the political movement wielding them. The only underdog narrative that seems to exist within the media discourses of the alt-right is a story about a *future* (not actual) post-majoritarian Anglo-European society, where whites are marginalized. This *overt* appeal to whiteness diminishes any egalitarian or popular-democratic gesture that its leaders and media may attempt to use as an outreach-oriented legitimation strategy. Only time will tell if an alt-right-*styled* news outlet could attain the level of hegemonic influence that Fox News has achieved solely using ethno-nationalist appeals and with no attendant identity claim for the working class.

Bibliography

A *Current Affair* (January 24, 1989) [Video tape]. Los Angeles: Twentieth Century Fox. Retrieved October 9, 2014 from UCLA Film and Television Archive.

(March 7, 1989). [Video tape]. Los Angeles: Twentieth Century Fox. Retrieved October 10, 2014 from UCLA Film and Television Archive.

(April 28, 1989). [Video tape]. Los Angeles: Twentieth Century Fox. Retrieved October 10, 2014 from UCLA Film and Television Archive.

(May 31, 1989). [Video tape]. Los Angeles: Twentieth Century Fox. Retrieved October 10, 2014 from UCLA Film and Television Archive.

(July 17, 1989). [Video tape]. Los Angeles: Twentieth Century Fox. Retrieved October 9, 2014 from UCLA Film and Television Archive.

Aday, S. (2005). Chasing the Bad News: An analysis of 2005 Iraq and Afghanistan War Coverage on NBC and Fox News Channel, *Journal of Communication,* 60(1), 144–164.

Ahmed, S. (2014). *The Cultural Politics of Emotion* (2nd Edition). New York: Routledge: 54.

Ailes, R. (April 12, 2012). Lecture Presented at the School of Media & Journalism at University of North Carolina, Chapel Hill [Transcript]. Retrieved from: http://mj.unc.edu/sites/default/files/images/2012parklecture.pdf.

Alterman, E. (February 8, 1996). The GOP's Strike Force: The Rightwing Propaganda Machine dChurns Out Money, Activists and Lies. *Rolling Stone.* Retrieved from: www.rollingstone.com/politics/news/the-gops-strike-force-19960208.

(2004). *What Liberal Media?: The Truth about Bias and the News.* New York: Basic Books.

Alvarez, L. (2008). *The Power of the Zoot: Youth Culture and Resistance in World War II.* Berkeley: University of California Press.

Anderson, C. W. (2011). Deliberative, Agonistic, and Algorithmic Audiences: Journalism's Vision of Its Public in an Age of Audience Transparency. *International Journal of Communication,* 5, 533–540.

Anderson, C. W., Downie, L., & Schudson, M. (2016). *The News Media: What Everyone Needs to Know*. Oxford University Press: 162.

Arceneaux K., & Johnson, M. (2013). *Changing Minds or Changing Channels?: Partisan News in the Age of Choice*. Chicago: Chicago University Press.

Arceneaux, K., Johnson, M., Lindstädt, R., & Wielen, R. (2016). The Influence of News Media on Political Elites: Investigating Strategic Responsiveness in Congress. *American Journal of Political Science*, 60(1), 4–5, 5–29.

Arditi, B. (2005). Populism as an Internal Periphery of Democratic Politics. In F. Panizza (ed.), *Populism and the Mirror of Democracy*. London: Verso: 82–83.

Argenti, P. (2013). *Corporate Communication* (6th Edition). New York: McGraw-Hill: 2–5.

Aronowitz, S. (1992). *The Politics of Identity: Class, Culture, Social Movements*. New York: Routledge.

Arsenault, A., & Castells, M. (2008). Switching Power: Rupert Murdoch and the Global Business of Media Politics. *International Sociology*, 23(4), 488–513.

Auletta, K. (2003, May 26). Vox Fox: How Roger Ailes and Fox News Are Changing Cable News. *The New Yorker*.

Bai, M. (December 6, 2009). Cable Guise. *New York Times Magazine*, 13.

Banet-Weiser, S. (1999). *The Most Beautiful Girl in the World: Beauty Pageants and National Identity*. Berkeley: University of California Press: 82.

Baragona, J. (January 20, 2018). Joy Reid: Many Feel Tucker Carlson's Pushing a 'Blatantly White Nationalist' Point of View. *Mediaite*. Retrieved from: www.mediaite.com/tv/joy-reid-many-feel-tucker-carlsons-pushing-a-blatantly-white-nationalist-point-of-view/.

Bark, E. (July 13, 1998). Journalist Writes about What He Knows: TV News' Cutthroat World. *St. Louis Post-Dispatch*.

Barrabi, T. (June 26, 2017). ESPN Exec on Bias Allegations: "We Have No Political Agenda Whatsoever." Fox Business Network. Retrieved from: www.foxbusiness.com/features/2017/06/26/espn-exec-on-bias-allegations-have-no-political-agenda-whatsoever.html.

Bartle, J., & Bellucci, P. (2009). *Political Parties and Partisanship: Social Identity and Individual Attitudes*. New York: Routledge: 8.

Bartels, L. (2000). Partisanship and Voting Behavior. *American Journal of Political Science*, 44, 35–50.

(September 1–4, 2005). What's the Matter with What's the Matter with Kansas? Prepared for presentation at the annual meeting of American Political Science Association. Washington, DC. Retrieved from: https://my.vanderbilt.edu/larrybartels/files/2011/12/kansas_Bartles.pdf.

(2006). What's the Matter with What's the Matter with Kansas? *Quarterly Journal of Political Science*, 1(2), 201–226.

(2008). *Unequal Democracy: The Political Economy of the New Gilded Age*. Princeton: Princeton University Press: 83–93.

Bartlett, B. (May 11, 2015). *How Fox News Changed American Media and Political Dynamics*. Retrieved from: https://papers.ssrn.com/sol3/papers.cfm?abstract_id=2604679.

Battaglio, S. (January 15, 2003). How Young Fox Slyly Moved Past CNN: Flash (or fluff) Helped Channel Win News Crown. *New York Daily News*. Retrieved from: www.nydailynews.com/archives/nydn-features/young-fox-slyly-moved-cnn-flash-fluff-helped-channel-win-news-crown-article-1.660984.

(September 16, 2003). New CNN Team Seeks a Long Run. *Daily News*. Retrieved from: www.nydailynews.com/archives/nydn-features/young-fox-slyly-moved-cnn-flash-fluff-helped-channel-win-news-crown-article-1.660984.

Baum, M. (2003). *Soft News Goes to War: Public Opinion and American Foreign Policy in the New Media Age*. Princeton, NJ: Princeton University Press: 37–39.

Baum, M., & Groeling, T. (2008). New Media and the Polarization of American Political Discourse. *Political Communication*, 25, 345–365.

Baym, G. (2009). *From Cronkite to Colbert: the Evolution of Broadcast News*. Oxford: Oxford University Press: 20.

Beck, G. (January 6, 2009). *Glenn Beck*. [Transcript]. New York: Fox News Channel. Retrieved July 3, 2011, from Factiva database (Dow Jones).

(January 16, 2009). *Glenn Beck*. [Transcript]. New York: Fox News Channel. Retrieved July 3, 2011, from Factiva database (Dow Jones).

(January 26, 2009). *Glenn Beck* [Video file]. New York: Fox News Channel. Retrieved January 5, 2012, from UCLA Communication Studies Archive, University of California, Los Angeles.

(June 16, 2009). *Glenn Beck* [Video file]. New York: Fox News Channel. Retrieved March 12, 2012, from UCLA Communication Studies Archive, University of California, Los Angeles.

(February 2, 2009). *Glenn Beck* [Video file]. New York: Fox News Channel. Retrieved June 25, 2011, from UCLA Communication Studies Archive, University of California, Los Angeles.

(February 24, 2010). *Glenn Beck* [Video file]. New York: Fox News Channel. Retrieved December 2, 2011, from UCLA Communication Studies Archive, University of California, Los Angeles.

(March 13, 2009). *Glenn Beck* [Video file]. New York: Fox News Channel. Retrieved September 16, 2011, from UCLA Communication Studies Archive, University of California, Los Angeles.

(June 17, 2009). *Glenn Beck* [Transcript]. New York: Fox News Channel. Retrieved July 3, 2011, from Factiva database (Dow Jones).

(June 29, 2009). *Glenn Beck* [Video file]. New York: Fox News Channel. Retrieved September 16, 2011, from UCLA Communication Studies Archive, University of California, Los Angeles.

(August 17, 2009). *Glenn Beck* [Video file]. New York: Fox News Channel. Retrieved June 25, 2011, from UCLA Communication Studies Archive, University of California, Los Angeles.

(November 10, 2009). *Glenn Beck*. [Transcript]. New York: Fox News Channel. Retrieved July 3, 2011, from Factiva database (Dow Jones).

(June 8, 2010). *Glenn Beck* [Video file]. New York: Fox News Channel. Retrieved January 5, 2012, from UCLA Communication Studies Archive, University of California, Los Angeles.

(August 11, 2010). *Glenn Beck* [Video file]. New York: Fox News Channel. Retrieved December 2, 2011, from UCLA Communication Studies Archive, University of California, Los Angeles.

(November 4, 2010). *Glenn Beck* [Video file]. New York: Fox News Channel. Retrieved January 5, 2012, from UCLA Communication Studies Archive, University of California, Los Angeles.

Beck, U., & Giddens, A. (1994). *Reflexive Modernization: Politics, Tradition and Aesthetics in the Modern Social Order*. Stanford, CA: Stanford University Press.

Becker, R. (2006). *Gay TV and Straight America*. New Brunswick, NJ: Rutgers University Press: 95.

Bell, D. (1973). *The Coming of Post-Industrial Society*. New York: Basic Books.

Benkler, Y., Faris, R., Roberts, H., & Zuckerman, E. (March 3, 2017). Study: Breitbart-Led Right-wing Media Ecosystem Altered Broader Media Agenda. *Columbia Journalism Review*. Retrieved from: www.cjr.org/analysis/breit bart-media-trump-harvard-study.php.

Bennett, W. L. & Iyengar, S. (2008). A New Era of Minimal Effects? The Changing Foundations of Political Communication. *Journal of Communication, 58*: 707–731.

Benson, R. (2013). *Shaping Immigration News: A French-American Comparison*. Cambridge: Cambridge University Press.

Benson, R., & Neveu, E. (2005). *Bourdieu and the Journalistic Field*. Cambridge, UK: Polity Press.

Berke, R. (January 30, 1994). Political Memo: G.O.P.-TV: New Image in Appeal to Voters. *New York Times*. Retrieved from: www.nytimes.com/1994/01/30/ us/political-memo-gop-tv-new-image-in-appeal-to-voters.html.

Berlet, C., & Lyons, M. (2000). *Right-Wing Populism in America: Too Close for Comfort*. New York: Guilford Press.

Berr, J. (January 24, 2011). After Olbermann, Is Comcast Set to Overhaul MSNBC? Don't Bet on It. *Daily Finance*. Retrieved from: www.dailyfi nance.com/2011/01/24/after-olbermann-is-comcast-set-to-overhaul-msnbc-dont-bet-on/.

Berry, M., & Sobieraj, S. (2014). *The Outrage Industry: Political Opinion and the New Incivility*. New York: Oxford University Press: 66–94.

Berry, P. (April 19, 2017). Here Are 10 of Bill O'Reilly's Most Infamous Hip-Hop Moments. *XXL*. Retrieved from: www.xxlmag.com/news/2017/04/bill-oreilly-hip-hop-moments/.

Bérubé, M. (2009). *The Left at War*. New York: New York University Press.

Bettie, J. (1995). Class dismissed? Roseanne and the Changing Face of Working-class Iconography. *Social Text, 45*, 134.

(2003). *Women without Class: Girls, Race, and Identity*. Berkeley: University of California Press: 49–56.

Bird, E. (1992). *For Enquiring Minds: A Cultural Study of Supermarket Tabloids* (1st Edition). Knoxville: University of Tennessee Press: 30, 34.

Biressi, A., & Nunn, H. (2008). Introduction. In A. Biressi & H. Nunn (eds.), *The Tabloid Reader*. Berkshire, England: McGraw-Hill/Open University Press: 14.

Blumenthal, M. (May 21, 2010). Reliance on Cable News: More than We Thought? *Huffington Post.* Retrieved from: www.huffingtonpost.com/mark-blumenthal/reliance_on_cable_news_more_th_b_727639.html.

Bolce, L., De Maio, G., & Muzzio, D. (1996). Dial-in Democracy: Talk Radio and the 1994 Election. *Political Science Quarterly,* 111, 457–483.

Borchers, C. (March 28, 2016). The Very Cozy Relationship between Donald Trump and the National Enquirer. *Washington Post.* Retrieved from: www.washingtonpost.com/news/the-fix/wp/2016/03/28/the-very-cozy-relationship-between-donald-trump-and-the-national-enquirer/.

Boss, K. (June 9, 1991). Talk-Show Hosts Convene, Hear Their King of Bombast. *The Seattle Times.* Retrieved from: http://community.seattletimes.nwsource.com/archive/?date=19910609&slug=1287993.

Bourdieu, P. (1984). *Distinction: A Social Critique of the Judgment of Taste* (R. Nice, trans.), Cambridge, MA: Harvard University Press: 25, 33, 34–50, 41, 43, 44–50, 190, 381.

(1999). *On Television,* (P. Ferguson, trans.). New York: The New Press.

Braid, M. (September 14, 2004). The Naked Truth. BBC. Retrieved from: http://news.bbc.co.uk/1/hi/magazine/3651850.stm.

Brandingm3 (October 27, 2010). MSNBC: Lean Forward [Video file]. YouTube. Retrieved from: www.youtube.com/watch?v=4CQAcewckXo.

Brennan, T. (2006). *Wars of Position: the Cultural Politics of Left and Right.* New York: Columbia University Press: 251.

Briggs-Bruce, B. (1979). An Introduction to the Idea of the New Class. In B. Briggs-Bruce (ed.), *The New Class?* New Brunswick, NJ: Transaction Books.

Briggs, C., & Hallin, D. (2016). *Making Health Public: How News Coverage Is Remaking Media, Medicine, and Contemporary Life.* New York: Routledge.

Brinkley, A. (1982). *Voices of Protest: Huey Long, Father Coughlin and the Great Depression.* New York: Vintage.

Broadcasting (April 4, 1988). Cable Operators Search for Space, 106.

(March 2, 1992). *The Simpsons* Bested an Original Episode of NBC's *The Cosby Show,* 72.

Broadcasting & Cable (June 21, 1993). Top 100 Companies, pp. 36–39.

Brock, D. (2004). *The Republican Noise Machine: Right-Wing Media and How It Corrupts Democracy* (1st Edition). New York: Crown Publishers: 81–81.

Brock, D., & Rabin-Havt, A. (2012). *The Fox Effect: How Roger Ailes Turned a Network into a Propaganda Machine.* New York: Anchor Books: 58, 86–90.

Brooks, D. (September 17, 2009). No, It's Not about Race. *New York Times.* Retrieved from: www.nytimes.com/2009/09/18/opinion/18brooks.html.

Brown, R. (February 1, 1993). *Chancellor: Too Much Vox Populi.* Broadcasting, 8.

(November 15, 1993). NET Channel: C-Span with a Spin. *Broadcasting & Cable,* 34.

Bryan, W. J. (1913). *The Price of the Soul.* New York: Funk & Wagnalls Company: 362.

Buchanan, P. (2002). *The Death of the West: How Dying Populations and Immigrant Invasions Imperil Our Country and Civilization.* New York: Thomas Dunne Books.

Buckley, W. F. (1951). *God and Man at Yale: The Superstitions of "Academic Freedom."* Chicago: Regnery.

Burke, K. (1984). *Attitudes toward History.* Berkeley: University of California Press: 103.

Burke, M. J. (1995). *The Conundrum of Class: Public Discourse on the Social Order in America.* Chicago: University of Chicago Press.

Burkett, E. (1998). *Right Women: A Journey through the Heart of America.* New York: Touchstone: 15–16.

Burner, D. (1996). *Making Peace with the 1960s.* Princeton, NJ: Princeton University Press: 136.

Butler, J. (1990). *Gender Trouble: Feminism and the Subversion of Identity.* New York: Routledge.

Calabrese, A. (2005). U.S. Media and the Justification of the Iraq War. *Television & New Media,* 8(9), 153–175.

Caldwell, J. (1995). *Televisuality: Style, Crisis, and Authority in American Television.* New Brunswick, NJ: Rutgers University Press: 336–358.

Calhoun, C. J. (1982). *The Question of Class Struggle: Social Foundations of Popular Radicalism during the Industrial Revolution.* Chicago: University of Chicago Press.

Campbell, A., Converse, P., Miller, W., & Stokes, D. (1960). *The American Voter.* Chicago: University of Chicago Press.

Cannato, V. J. (February 2, 2013). Mayor Who Saved NYC. *New York Post.* Retrieved from: http://nypost.com/2013/02/02/mayor-who-saved-nyc/.

Canovan, M. (1981). *Populism* (1st Edition). New York: Harcourt Brace Jovanovich.

(1999) Trust the People! Populism and the Two Faces of Democracy. *Political Studies,* 47(1): 2–16.

Cappella, J., & Jamieson, K. (2008). *Echo Chamber: Rush Limbaugh and the Conservative Media Establishment.* Oxford: Oxford University Press: 13–38, 51, 143, 211–212, 246–247.

Carey, J. W. (1987). The Press and the Public Discourse. *The Center Magazine,* 20, (March/April), 6–15.

Carmody, J. (January 6, 1995). The TV Column. *Washington Post.*

Carroll, A. (2010). *Public's Trust in Corporate America Fading* [Web page]. Athens Banner-Herald. Retrieved from: http://onlineathens.com/stories/022110/bus_565562395.shtml#.VyyUs1KCzdk.

Carson, T. (January/February, 2005). The Murdoch Touch. *The Atlantic.* Retrieved from: www.theatlantic.com/magazine/archive/2005/01/the-murdoch-touch/303676/.

Carter, D. (1995). *The Politics of Rage: George Wallace, the Origins of New Conservatism, and the Transformation of American Politics.* New York: Simon & Schuster.

Cassino, D. (2016). *Fox News and American Politics: How One Channel Shapes American Politics and Society.* Abingdon, UK: Routledge.

Castells, M. (2009). *Communication Power,* Oxford: Oxford University Press: 91, 164.

Cavuto, N. (September 21, 2008). *Cavuto* [Transcript]. New York Fox Business Network. Retrieved July 7, 2011, from Factiva database (Dow Jones).

Ceaser, J., & Busch, A. (2005). *Red Over Blue: The 2004 Elections and American Politics.* Lanham, MD: Rowman & Littlefield.

Chafets, Z. (2013). *Roger Ailes: Off Camera.* London: Sentinel: 125, 193, 227.

Chait, J. (March 18, 2009). Wasting Away in Hooverville. *The New Republic.* Retrieved from: www.tnr.com/article/books/wasting-away-hooverville.

Chariton, J. (January 2, 2014). 2013 Ratings: MSNBC Stays in Second in Primetime, Falls to Third in Total Day. *Adweek.* Retrieved from: www.adweek.com/tvnewser/2013-ratings-msnbc-stays-in-second-in-primetime-falls-to-third-in-total-day/210039.

Chenoweth, N. (2001). *Rupert Murdoch: The Untold Story of the World's Greatest Media Wizard.* New York: Crown Business.

Chinoy, E. (1955). *Auto Workers and the American Dream.* Garden City, NY: Doubleday.

Clinton, J., & Enamorado, T. (2014). The National News Media's Effect on Congress: How Fox News Affected Elites in Congress. *The Journal of Politics, 76*(04), 928–943.

Cmiel, K. (1991). *Democratic Eloquence: The Fight Over Popular Speech in Nineteenth-Century America.* Berkeley: University of California Press.

CNN (November, 2008). *Election Center 2008.* Retrieved from: www.cnn.com/ELECTION/2008/results/polls/#USP00p1.

(October 11, 2009). Interview with White House Communications Director; Obama Wins Nobel Peace Prize [Transcript]. *Reliable Sources.* Retrieved from: http://transcripts.cnn.com/TRANSCRIPTS/0910/11/rs.01.html.

Coe, S. (March 2, 1992). Diller's New Departure; Fox's New Order. *Broadcasting,* 4–6.

Cohen, N. (March 1, 2018). Trump Losing College-Educated Whites? He Never Won Them in the First Place: New Evidence That Exit Polls Are a Very Flawed Vehicle for Doing Post-Election Analysis. *New York Times.* Retrieved from: www.nytimes.com/2018/02/27/upshot/trump-losing-college-educated-whites-he-never-won-them-in-the-first-place.html.

Cohen, P. (April 27, 2010). 'Epistemic Closure'? Those Are Fighting Words. *New York Times.* Retrieved from: www.nytimes.com/2010/04/28/books/28conserv.html.

Coller, A., & O'Connor, P. (April 21, 2009). Why GOP Is Devouring One Book. *Politico.* Retrieved from: www.politico.com/news/stories/0409/21477.html.

Collins, S. (2004). *Crazy Like a Fox: The Inside Story of How Fox News Beat CNN.* New York: Portfolio: 68, 72, 106, 140, 141, 143.

Columbia Journalism Review, (Jan/Feb, 1980,), 18(5), 22.

Conboy, M. (2002). *The Press and Popular Culture.* London: Sage Publications: 51–54.

Cook, J. (July 11, 2011). Roger Ailes' Secret Nixon-Era Blueprint for Fox News. *Gawker.* Retrieved from: http://gawker.com/5814150/roger-ailes-secret-nixon-era-blueprint-for-fox-news.

Cooper, D. (2008). *Naked Launch: Creating Fox News*. New York: 4 LLC [ebook]. Also Retrieved from: www.dancooper.tv/NakedLaunch.htm.

Conservative Political Action Conference (February 12, 1994). Conservative Opportunities through Technology [Video File]. Retrieved from: www.c-span.org/video/?54536-1%2Fconservative-opportunities-technology.

Conway, M., Maria, E., & Grieves, K. (2007). Villains, Victims and the Virtuous in Bill O'Reilly's "No-Spin Zone." *Journalism Studies*, 8(2): 197–223, 207–210.

Cosgrove, S. (1984). Zoot-Suit and Style Warfare. *History Workshop*, 18 (Autumn), 77–91.

Couldry, N. (2004). Theorizing Media as Practice. *Social Semiotics*, 14 (2): 115–132.

Cowie, J. (2010). *Stayin' Alive: the 1970s and the Last Days of the Working Class*. New York: The New Press.

Crenshaw, K. (1989). Demarginalizing the Intersection of Race and Sex: A Black Feminist Critique of Antidiscrimination Doctrine, Feminist Theory and Anti-racist Politics. *University of Chicago Legal Forum*, 140: 139–167.

Critchlow, D. (2006). *Phyllis Schlafly and Grassroots Conservatism: A Woman's Crusade*. Princeton, NJ: Princeton University Press.

Curtin, M. (1995). *Redeeming the Wasteland: Television Documentary and Cold War Politics*. New Brunswick, NJ: Rutgers University Press: 9, 217.

Curtin, M. & Shattuc, J. (2009). *The American Television Industry*. New York: Palgrave Macmillan: 157.

Cvetkovich, A. (2012). *Depression: A Public Feeling*. Durham, NC: Duke University Press.

Dávila, A. (2001). *Latinos, Inc.: The Marketing and Making of People*. Berkley, CA: University of California Press.

Davis, M. (1986). *Prisoners of the American Dream: Politics and Economy in the History of the US Working Class*, London: Verso.

Dawson, E., Brescoll, V., & Uhlmann E. (2008). Status Fragility. Paper Presented at Behavioral Decision Research in Management Conference; San Diego, CA.

DellaVigna, S., & Kaplan, E. (May 10, 2005). The Fox News Effect: Media Bias and Voting. Working paper. New York National Bureau of Economic Research.

   (2007). The Fox News Effect: Media Bias and Voting. *The Quarterly Journal of Economics*, 122(3), 1187–1234.

de la Torre, C. (2010). *Populist Seduction in Latin America*. Athens: Ohio University Press.

de la Torre, C., & Anderson, C. (2013). *Latin American Populism in the Twenty-First Century*. Washington DC: Woodrow Wilson Center Press with Johns Hopkins University Press.

Delli Carpini, M., & Williams, B. (2001). Let Us Infotain You: Politics in the New Media Environment. In W. Bennett & R. Entman (eds.), *Mediated Politics: Communication in the Future of Democracy*. Cambridge: Cambridge University Press: 160–181.

Denning, M. (1998). *The Cultural Front: The Laboring of American Culture in the Twentieth Century*. New York: Verso.

DeParle, J. (April 16, 1995). The First Primary. *New York Times*. Retrieved from: www.nytimes.com/1995/04/16/magazine/the-first-primary.html.

Dickinson, T. (May 25, 2011). How Roger Ailes Built the Fox News Fear Factory. *Rolling Stone*. Retrieved from: www.rollingstone.com/politics/news/how-roger-ailes-built-the-fox-news-fear-factory-20110525.

Dilliplane, S. (2014). Activation, Conversion or Reinforcement? The Impact of Partisan News Exposure on Vote Choice. *American Journal of Political Science*, 58(1): 79–94.

DirectorJess8. (April 2, 2009). O'Reilly Factor Promo #1 [Video file]. YouTube. Retrieved from: www.youtube.com/watch?v=Hb50B7mu1ic.

Dooley, P., & Grosswiler, P. (1997). 'Turf wars': Journalists, New Media and the Struggle for Control of Political News. *Harvard International Journal of Press/Politics*, 2 (3): 31–51.

D. Oom. (May 29, 2013). Morton Downey vs Stripper for God!! [Video file]. Retrieved from: www.youtube.com/watch?v=JM45bTgmoog.

Dreier, P., & Martin, C. R. (2010). How ACORN Was Framed: Political Controversy and Media Agenda Setting. *Perspectives on Politics*, 8(3), 761–792.

Drezner, D. (August 11, 2015). Why Donald Trump Got the Best of Fox News. *The Washington Post*. Retrieved from: www.washingtonpost.com/postevery thing/wp/2015/08/11/why-donald-trump-got-the-best-of-fox-news/.

Drotner, K. (1992). Modernity and Media Panics. In M. Skovmand & K. Schrøder (eds.), *Media Cultures Reappraising Transnational*. London: Routledge.

Duggan, L. (2003). Introduction. *Twilight of Equality?: Neoliberalism, Cultural Politics, and the Attack on Democracy*. Boston: Beacon Press.

Edwards, R. (2000). Mary Lease and the Sources of Populist Protest. In B. Campbell (ed.), *The Human Tradition in the Gilded Age and the Progressive Era*. Wilmington, Delaware: Scholarly Resources, Inc.: 59, 60.

Edy, J. (2006). *Troubled Pasts: News and the Collective Memory of Social Unrest*. Philadelphia: Temple University Press.

Ehrlich, M. (1996). The Journalism of Outrageousness: Tabloid Television News vs. Investigative News. *Journalism & Mass Communication Monographs*, (155), 1, 1–24.

Eliasoph, N. (1998). *Avoiding Politics: How Americans Produce Apathy in Everyday Life*. Cambridge: Cambridge University Press: 183–189.

Entman, R. (1993). Framing: Toward Clarification of a Fractured Paradigm. *Journal of Communication*, 43(4): 51–8.

Eyal, G. (2002). Dangerous Liaisons between Military Intelligence and Middle Eastern Studies in Israel. *Theory & Society*, 31(5), 653–693.

(2006). *The Disenchantment of the Orient: Expertise in Arab Affairs and the Israeli State*. Stanford, CA: Stanford University Press.

Farhi, P. (December 13, 2000). The Life of O'Reilly. *Washington Post*. Retrieved from: www.washingtonpost.com/ac2/wp-dyn/A62722-2000Dec12.

(May 26, 2011). MSNBC's Schultz Suspended after Using Slur to Refer to Ingraham. *Washington Post*. Retrieved from: www.washingtonpost.com/life style/style/schultz-suspended-after-using-slur-to-refer-to-ingraham/2011/05/26/AGbbozBH_story.html.

(March 19, 2012). C-SPAN Founder Lamb Steps Down after 34 Years. *Washington Post*. Retrieved from: www.washingtonpost.com/lifestyle/style/c-span-founder-lamb-steps-down-after-34-years/2012/03/19/gIQACR71NS_story .html.

Faue, E. (1991). *Community of Suffering & Struggle: Women, Men, and the Labor Movement in Minneapolis, 1915–1945*. Chapel Hill: University of North Carolina Press: 20.

Feder, J. (2006). *"Song of the South": Country Music, Race, Region, and the Politics of Culture, 1920–1974* (Doctoral dissertation). PhD, University of California, Los Angeles. Advisor: Robert Fink.

Feldman, L., Maibach, E., Roser-Renouf, C., & Leiserowitz, A. (2012). Climate on Cable: The Nature and Impact of Global Warming Coverage on Fox News, CNN, and MSNBC. *The International Journal of Press/Politics*, 17(1), 3–31.

Fingerhut, H. (July 10, 2017). Sharp Partisan Divisions in Views of National Institutions. Pew Research Center. Retrieved from: www.people-press.org/2017/07/10/sharp-partisan-divisions-in-views-of-national-institutions/.

Fiske, J. (1992). Popularity and the Politics of Information. In P. Dahlgren & C. Sparks (eds.), *Journalism and Popular Culture*: 49–50.

Fiske, S., Bergsieker, H., Russel, A., & Williams, L. (2009). Images of Black Americans. Then, "Them," and Now, "Obama!." *Du Bois Review*, Spring 6(1).

Fitzgerald, T. (November 5, 2013). Why Cable News Is so Incredibly Influential: Generates Buzz Because Its Audience Is so Engaged. *Media Life Magazine*. Retrieved from: http://medialifemagazine.com/cable-news-incredibly-influential/.

Fleisher, R., & Bond, J. (2000). *Polarized Politics: Congress and the President in a Partisan Era*. Washington, DC: CQ Press.

Folkenflik, D. (2013). *Murdoch's World: The Last of the Old Media Empires*. New York: PublicAffairs: 28–29, 56.

Foner, E. (1970). *Free Soil, Free Labor, Free Men: The Ideology of the Republican Party before the Civil War*, New York: Oxford University Press.

Forty-Eight Hours. (March 2, 1989). Hot TV [Video file]. New York: CBS Network. Retrieved June 5, 2015 from The Paley Center for Media.

Foucault, M. (1965). *Madness and Civilization*, (R. Howard, trans.). New York: Vintage Books.

(1970). *The Order of Things*, New York: Pantheon Books.

(1977). *Discipline and Punish*, (A. Sheridan, trans.). New York: Pantheon.

Fox News Channel (April 29, 2004). Bill O'Reilly's Bio [Web page]. Retrieved from: www.foxnews.com/story/2004/04/29/bill-oreilly-bio.html.

Fox News Insider (June 20, 2011). Bill O'Reilly Goes Head-to-Head with Rapper Who Called Obama a Terrorist [Video file]. YouTube. Retrieved from: www.youtube.com/watch?v=HmM9_Y5uiW4.

(March 3, 2017). Campus Craziness. Retrieved from: http://insider.foxnews .com/tag/campus-craziness.

(January 23, 2018). "Our Views Are Not Extreme": Tucker Fires Back at Joy Reid for 'White Nationalist' Criticism. Retrieved from: http://insider.fox news.com/2018/01/23/tucker-carlson-fires-back-joy-reid-calling-him-white-nationalist.

Frank, T. (1997). *The Conquest of Cool: Business Culture, Counterculture, and the Rise of Hip Consumerism.* Chicago: University of Chicago Press.

(2004). *What's the Matter with Kansas? How Conservatives Won the Heart of America* (1st Edition). New York: Metropolitan Books: 113, 196–199.

(2005). Class Is Dismissed [Web Blog Post], p. 3. Retrieved from: www.tcfrank .com/media/TCFRANK_Class_Dismissed_2005.pdf.

(2012). *Pity the Billionaire: The Hard Times Swindle and the Unlikely Comeback of the Right* (1st Edition). New York: Metropolitan Books/Henry Holt: 135.

(2016). *Listen, Liberal: Or, What Ever Happened to the Party of the People?* New York: Metropolitan Books.

Franken, A. (2003). *Lies and the Lying Liars Who Tell Them: A Fair and Balanced Look at the Right,* New York: Penguin.

Fraser, N. (1990). Rethinking the Public Sphere: A Contribution to the Critique of Actually Existing Democracy. *Social Text,* 25/26, 56–80.

Fraser, S. (1989). The "Labor Question." In S. Fraser & G. Gerstle (eds.), *The Rise and the Fall of the New Deal Order, 1930–1980.* Princeton, NJ: Princeton University Press: 56, 57, 70–71.

Fraser, S., & Gerstle, G. (1989). Introduction. In S. Fraser & G. Gerstle (eds.), *The Rise and Fall of the New Deal Order, 1930–1980.* Princeton, NJ: Princeton University Press: xiv, 296.

Freidson, E. (1986) *Professional Powers: A Study of the Institutionalization of Formal Knowledge.* Chicago: University of Chicago Press.

Fried, L. (November 25, 1994). GOP to Invade TV. *Greensboro News & Record.*

Galbraith, J. (2007). *The New Industrial State* (First Princeton Edition). Princeton, NJ: Princeton University Press: 350.

Gallup (2016). Media Use and Evaluation: Historical Trends. Retrieved from: www.gallup.com/poll/1663/media-use-evaluation.aspx.

Gamson, J. (1998). *Freaks Talk Back: Tabloid Talk Shows and Sexual Nonconformity.* Chicago: University of Chicago Press: 30.

Gans, H. (1999). *Popular Culture and High Culture: An Analysis and Evaluation of Taste* (Revised Edition). New York: Basic Books.

Geertz, C. (1973). *The Interpretation of Cultures: Selected Essays.* New York: Basic Books.

Gerstner, D. (2006). *Manly Arts: Masculinity and Nation in Early American Cinema.* Durham, NC: Duke University Press.

Gigot, P. (October 11, 2008). *Journal Editorial Report* [Transcript]. New York: Fox News Channel. Retrieved July 3, 2011, from Factiva database (Dow Jones).

Gilliam, F., & Iyengar, S. (2000). Prime Suspects: The Influence of Local Television News on the Viewing Public. *American Journal of Political Science,* 44(3), 566.

Gilroy, P., Grossberg, L., & McRobbie, A. (2000). *Without Guarantees: In Honour of Stuart Hall.* London: Verso: 321.

Glynn, K. (2000). *Tabloid Culture: Trash Taste, Popular Power, and the Transformation of American Television.* Durham, NC: Duke University Press: 28.

Goetz, T. (September/October, 1994). I'm Not a Reporter: But I Play One on GOP-TV. *Columbia Journalism Review*, 13–14.

(July–August 1995). Cable: Who's Connected? *Columbia Journalism Review*, 34(2), 17–18.

Goffman, E. (1959). *The Presentation of Self in Everyday Life*. Garden City, NY: Doubleday.

Goldberg, M. L. (1997). *An Army Women: Gender and Politics in the Gilded Age Kansas*. Baltimore: The John Hopkins University Press: 5, 261.

Gomery, D. (July–August 1996). *American Journalism Review*, 18(6), 52.

Goodman, W. (October 10, 1996). Fox's 24-hour News Is Oddly Familiar. *New York Times*.

Goodwyn, L. (1978). *The Populist Moment: A Short History of the Agrarian Revolt in America*. New York: Oxford University Press.

GOP-TV (February 13, 1994). C-Span Interview with RNC Chair Haley Barbour [Video file]. C-Span.org. Retrieved from: www.c-span.org/video/?54527-1/gop-tv.

Gottfried, J., Barthel, M., Shearer, E., & Mitchell, A. (February 4, 2016). The 2016 Presidential Campaign: A News Event That's Hard to Miss. Pew Research Center. Retrieved from: www.journalism.org/2016/02/04/the-2016-presidential-campaign-a-news-event-thats-hard-to-miss/.

Gottlieb, M. (March 24, 1993). Cuomo Called by Murdoch on the *Post*. *New York Times*. Retrieved from: www.nytimes.com/1993/03/24/nyregion/cuomo-called-by-murdoch-on-the-post.html.

Gould, S. (March/April 1975). Coors Brews the News, *Columbia Journalism Review*.

Gouldner, A. (1979). *The Future of the Intellectuals and the Rise of the New Class*. London: Macmillan: 47.

Gramsci, A. (1971). *Selections from the Prison Notebooks*, (Q. Hoare, & G. Nowell-Smith, trans.). New York: International Publishers.

(1985) *Selections from Cultural Writings*. D. Forgacs & G. Nowell-Smith, (eds.), (W. Boelhower, trans.). Cambridge, MA: Harvard University Press.

(1996). *Prison Notebooks* (Vol. 2), (J. A. Buttigieg, trans.). New York: Columbia University Press.

Grann, D. (October 27, 1997). Robespierre of the Right. *The New Republic*. Retrieved from: https://newrepublic.com/article/61338/robespierre-the-right.

Green, D., Palmquist, B., & Schickler, E. (2002). *Partisan Hearts and Minds: Political Parties and the Social Identities of Voters*. New Haven, CT: Yale University Press.

Green, D., & Schickler, E. (2009). A Spirited Defense of Party Identification against Its Critics. In J. Bartle & P. Bellucci, (eds.), *Political Parties and Partisanship: Social Identity and Individual Attitudes*, New York: Routledge: 180–199.

Greenwald, R. (Director) (2004). *Outfoxed: Rupert Murdoch's War on Journalism* [Motion picture]. United States: Carolina Productions.

Grim, R. (May 2, 2017). With Trump in the White House, MSNBC Is Resisting The Resistance. *Huffington Post*. Retrieved from: www.huffingtonpost.com/entry/andy-lack-msnbc-donald-trump_us_5907422de4b0bb2d086fb7a8.

Grindstaff, L. (2002). *The Money Shot: Trash, Class, and the Making of TV Talk Shows*. Chicago: University of Chicago Press: 50.

Gripsrud, J. (1989). "High Culture" Revisited, *Cultural Studies*, 3(2), 194–207.

Groeling, T. (2008). Who's the Fairest of them All? An Empirical Test for Partisan Bias on ABC, CBS, NBC, and Fox News. *Presidential Studies Quarterly*, 38 (4), 631–657.

Groseclose, T., & Milyo, J. (2005). A Measure of Media Bias. *The Quarterly Journal of Economics*, 120(4), 1191–1237.

Grossberg, L. (1992). *We Got to Get Out of This Place: Popular Conservatism and Postmodern Culture*. New York: Routledge.

(2005). *Caught in the Crossfire: Kids, Politics, and America's Future*. Boulder, CO: Paradigm Publishers: 132–134.

Grove, L. (2017, Fall). Best Press He's Ever Had. *Columbia Journalism Review*. Retrieved from: www.cjr.org/special_report/trump-tabloids-daily-news-new-york-post-press.php.

Grynbaum, M. (February 17, 2017). Trump Calls the News Media the "Enemy of the American People." *New York Times*. Retrieved from: www.nytimes.com/2017/02/17/business/trump-calls-the-news-media-the-enemy-of-the-people.html.

Guttfield, G. (April 21, 2016). *The O'Reilly Factor* [Video file]. YouTube. Retrieved from: www.youtube.com/watch?v=ao5kRO4_lAY.

Hagey, K., & Martin, J. (September 27, 2010). Fox Primary: Complicated, Contractual. *Politico*. Retrieved from: www.politico.com/story/2010/09/fox-primary-complicated-contractual-042745.

Haidt, J. (2012). *The Righteous Mind: Why Good People Are Divided by Politics and Religion*. New York: Pantheon Books.

Hall, S. (1975). Introduction. In A. Smith, (ed.), *Paper Voices: the Popular Press and Social Change, 1935–1965*. London: Chatto & Windus.

(1988a). *The Hard Road to Renewal: Thatcherism and the Crisis of the Left*. New York: Verso: 4, 48.

(1988b). Toad in the Garden: Thatcherism among the Theorists. In Cary Nelson and Lawrence Grossberg (eds.), *Marxism and the Interpretation of Culture*. Urbana: University of Illinois Press: 44.

(1988c). Thatcher's Lessons. *Marxism Today*, 27.

(1998). Notes on Deconstructing "the Popular." In J. Storey (ed.), *Cultural Theory and Popular Culture: a Reader* (2nd Edition). London: Prentice Hall.

Hall, S., Critcher, C., Jefferson, T., Clarke, J., & Roberts, B. (1981). The Social Production of News. In S. Cohen and J. Young, (eds.), *The Manufacture of News: Deviance, Social Problems and the Mass Media*. London: Constable/Sage: 342–345.

Hallin, D. (1990). Whatever Happened to the News. *Media & Values*, 50, 2–4.

(1994). *We Keep America on Top of the World*. New York: Routledge.

(2000). Commercialism and Professionalism in the American News Media. In J. Curran and M. Gurevitch (eds.), *Mass Media and Society* (Third Edition). London: Oxford University Press: 1, 234.

(2006). The Passing of the "High Modernism" of American Journalism Revisited. *Political Communication Report*, 16(1), 1.

Hallin, D. C., & Mancini, P. (2004). *Comparing Media Systems: Three Models of Media and Politics.* Cambridge, England: Cambridge University Press: 210–211.

Hannity, S. (January 19, 2009). *Hannity* [Transcript]. New York: Fox News Channel. Retrieved July 3, 2011, from Factiva database (Dow Jones).

  (January 22, 2009). *Hannity* [Transcript]. New York: Fox News Channel. Retrieved July 3, 2011, from Factiva database (Dow Jones).

  (January 26, 2009). *Hannity* [Transcript]. New York: Fox News Channel. Retrieved July 7, 2011, from Factiva database (Dow Jones).

  (January 29, 2009). *Hannity* [Transcript]. New York: Fox News Channel. Retrieved July 8, 2011, from Factiva database (Dow Jones).

  (February 18, 2009). *Hannity* [Transcript]. New York: Fox News Channel. Retrieved July 3, 2011, from Factiva database (Dow Jones).

  (February 20, 2009). *Hannity* [Transcript]. New York: Fox News Channel. Retrieved July 3, 2011, from Factiva database (Dow Jones).

  (February 24, 2009). *Hannity* [Transcript]. New York: Fox News Channel. Retrieved July 3, 2011, from Factiva database (Dow Jones).

  (March 24, 2009). *Hannity* [Transcript]. New York: Fox News Channel. Retrieved November 10, 2011, from Factiva database (Dow Jones).

  (April 7, 2009). *Hannity* [Transcript]. New York: Fox News Channel. Retrieved July 3, 2011, from Factiva database (Dow Jones).

  (April 10, 2010). *Hannity* [Transcript]. New York: Fox News Channel. Retrieved July 3, 2011, from Factiva database (Dow Jones).

  (April 21, 2009). *Hannity* [Transcript]. New York: Fox News Channel. Retrieved July 3, 2011, from Factiva database (Dow Jones).

  (May 19, 2009). *Hannity* [Transcript]. New York: Fox News Channel. Retrieved July 3, 2011, from Factiva database (Dow Jones).

  (July 6, 2009). *Hannity* [Video]. New York: Fox News Channel. Retrieved September 27, 2011, from UCLA Communication Studies Archive, University of California, Los Angeles.

  (November 10, 2009). *Hannity* [Transcript]. New York: Fox News Channel. Retrieved July 3, 2011, from Factiva database (Dow Jones).

  (December 9, 2009). *Hannity* [Transcript]. New York: Fox News Channel. Retrieved November 10, 2011, from Factiva database (Dow Jones).

  (April 10, 2010). *Hannity* [Transcript]. New York: Fox News Channel. Retrieved July 3, 2011, from Factiva database (Dow Jones).

  (April 13, 2010). *Hannity* [Transcript]. New York: Fox News Channel. Retrieved July 3, 2011, from Factiva database (Dow Jones).

  (April 14, 2010). *Hannity* [Transcript]. New York: Fox News Channel. Retrieved July 3, 2011, from Factiva database (Dow Jones).

  (April 21, 2010). *Hannity* [Transcript]. New York: Fox News Channel. Retrieved July 3, 2011, from Factiva database (Dow Jones).

  (June 6, 2010). *Hannity* [Video]. New York: Fox News Channel. Retrieved December 2, 2011, from UCLA Communication Studies Archive, University of California, Los Angeles.

  (December 14, 2010). *Hannity* [Transcript]. New York: Fox News Channel. Retrieved July 3, 2011, from Factiva database (Dow Jones).

Hannity, S., & Colmes, A. (April 11, 2008). Hannity [Transcript]. New York: Fox News Channel. Retrieved July 3, 2011, from Factiva database (Dow Jones).

(September 16, 2008). *Hannity & Colmes* [Transcript]. New York: Fox News Channel. Retrieved July 3, 2011, from Factiva database (Dow Jones).

(November 17, 2008). *Hannity & Colmes* [Transcript]. New York Fox News Channel. Retrieved November 10, 2011, from Factiva database (Dow Jones).

Hariman, R. (1995). *Political Style: The Artistry of Power*. Chicago: University of Chicago Press: 10.

Harris, P. (February 2, 2011). Glenn Beck and the echoes of Charles Coughlin. *The Guardian*. Retrieved from: www.theguardian.com/commentisfree/cifamerica/2011/feb/02/far-right-glenn-beck.

Hart, P. (2002). *The Oh Really? Factor: Unspinning Fox News Channel's Bill O'Reilly*. New York: Seven Stories Press: 17, 88.

Harvey, D. (2005). *A Brief History of Neoliberalism*. Oxford, England: Oxford University Press.

Harwood, J. (January 26, 2018). Bill Kristol Hits Fox News, Tucker Carlson for "Dumbing Down" Coverage, Pushing "Ethno-nationalism." *CNBC.com*. Retrieved from: www.cnbc.com/2018/01/24/bill-kristol-takes-on-fox-news-tucker-carlson.html.

Hauser, G. (1998). Vernacular Dialogue and the Rhetoricality of Public Opinion. *Communication Monographs*, 65(2): 83–107.

Hawley, J. (1980). Antonio Gramsci's Marxism: Class, State, and Work. *Social Problems*, 27(5), 586.

Hemmer, N. (2016). *Messengers of the Right: Conservative Media and the Transformation of American Politics*. Philadelphia: University of Pennsylvania Press: 14.

Hendershot, H. (2011). *What's Fair on the Air?: Cold War Right-Wing Broadcasting and the Public Interest*. Chicago: University of Chicago: 13, 16.

Hendrickson, C., & Galston, W. A. (November 30, 2016). The Educational Rift in the 2016 Election. Brookings Institution. Retrieved from: www.brookings.edu/blog/fixgov/2016/11/18/educational-rift-in-2016-election/.

Hetherington, M. J. (2010). Resurgent Mass Partisanship: The Role of Elite Polarization. In R. G. Niemi, H. F. Weisberg, & D. C. Kimball (eds.), *Controversies in Voting Behavior*. Washington, DC: CQ Press.

Hilburn, R. (April 4, 1989). Morton Downey Jr. – The Mouth Goes on the Record. *Los Angeles Times*. Retrieved from: http://articles.latimes.com/1989-04-04/entertainment/ca-1068_1_morton-downey.

Hilmes, M. (1997). *Radio Voices: American Broadcasting, 1922–1952*. Minneapolis: University of Minnesota Press: 16.

Himmelstein, J. (1990). *To the Right: The Transformation of American Conservatism*. Berkeley: University of California Press.

Hmielowski, J., Beam, M., & Hutchens, M. (2015). Structural Changes in Media and Attitude Polarization: Examining the Contributions of TV News before and after the Telecommunications Act of 1996. *International Journal of Public Opinion Research*, 28(2), 153–172.

Hofstadter, R. (1965).The Pseudo-Conservative Revolt – 1954. In *The Paranoid Style in American Politics, and Other Essays*. New York: Knopf.

(2008). Pseudo-conservatism Revisited – 1965. In *The Paranoid Style in American politics*. New York: Vintage Books.

Hogeland, W. (September/October 2010). Real Americans. *Boston Review*. Retrieved from: http://bostonreview.net/BR35.5/hogeland.php.

Holcomb, J. (April 29, 2015). Cable News: Fact Sheet. In *State of the News Media 2015*. Pew Research Center. Retrieved from: www.journalism.org/2015/04/29/state-of-the-news-media-2015/.

Holcomb, J., Mitchell, A., & Rosenstiel, T. (2012). Section: Cable: CNN Ends Its Ratings Slides Slide, Fox Falls Again. In *The State of the News Media 2012: An Annual Report on American Journalism*. Pew Research Center. Retrieved from: http://stateofthemedia.org/2012/cable-cnn-ends-its-ratings-slide-fox-falls-again/.

Hollander, B. (Spring 2008). Tuning Out or Tuning Elsewhere? Partisanship, Polarization and Media Migration, from 1998 to 2006. *Journal of Mass Communication Quarterly*. 85(1), 32.

Holt, J. (2011). *Empires of Entertainment: Media industries and the Politics of Deregulation, 1980–1996*. New Brunswick, NJ: Rutgers University Press: 118.

Hoover Institution (February 26, 2010). Interview with Roger Ailes, President of Fox News Channel [Video File]. YouTube. Retrieved from: www.youtube.com/watch?v=lHYa9IupxRs.

Hopkins, D., & Ladd, J. (2012). *The Reinforcing Effects of Fox News*. Working paper Georgetown University. Retrieved from: http://people.iq.harvard.edu/~dhopkins/FoxPersuasion021212.pdf.

Horton, D., & Wohl, R. (1956). Mass Communication and Para-social Interaction: Observations on Intimacy at a Distance. *Psychiatry*, 19, 215–229.

Horwitz, R. (2013). *America's Right: Anti-Establishment Conservatism from Goldwater to the Tea Party*. Cambridge, England: Polity Press.

Huang, P. J., Jacoby, S., Strickland, M., & Rebecca, K. K. (November 8, 2016). Election 2016: Exit Polls. *New York Times*. Retrieved from: www.nytimes.com/interactive/2016/11/08/us/politics/election-exit-polls.html.

Hubbs, N. (2014). *Rednecks, Queers, and Country Music*. Berkley: University of California Press: 12–18.

Huertas, A., & Kriegsman, R. (2014). *Science of Spin? Assessing the Accuracy of Cable News Coverage of Climate Science*. New York: Union of Concerned Scientists. Retrieved from: www.ucsusa.org/assets/documents/global_warming/Science-or-Spin-report.pdf.

Huffington Post (February 7, 2012). Cable News Main Source For 2012 Presidential Campaign Viewers. *Huffingtonpost*. Retrieved from: www.huffingtonpost.com/2012/02/07/cable-news-2012-presidential-campaign-coverage_n_1260716.html.

Huston, J. (1998). *Securing the Fruits of Labor: The American Concept of Wealth Distribution, 1765–1900*, Baton Rouge: Louisiana State University Press.

Huyssen, A. (1986). *After the Great Divide: Modernism, Mass culture, Postmodernism*. Bloomington: Indiana University Press.

Inglehart R. F., & Norris, P. (2016). Trump, Brexit, and the Rise of Populism: Economic Have-Nots and Cultural Backlash, HKS Faculty Research Working Paper Series. Retrieved from: https://research.hks.harvard.edu/pub lications/workingpapers/Index.aspx.

Inside Edition (January 24, 1989). [Video tape]. Los Angeles: King World Productions. Retrieved October 9, 2014 from UCLA Film and Television Archive.

Isenberg, N. (2016). *White Trash: The 400-year old Untold History of Class in America*. New York: Viking.

Iskandar, A. (2005). The Great American Bubble: Fox News Channel, the "Mirage" of Objectivity, and the Isolation of American Public Opinion.' In L. Artz & Y. Kamlipour (eds.), *Bring 'Em On: Media and Politics in the Iraq War*. Lanham, MD: Rowman and Littlefield: 155–174.

Ives, N. (October 25, 2010). Consumers' Hearts Bleed Red – and Blue: Top U.S. Brands Favored Much Higher Among One Political Party or the Other, Survey Finds. *Advertising Age*. Retrieved from: http://adage.com/article/news/top-u-s-brands-favored-democrats-republicans/146663/.

Iyengar, S., & Hahn, K. (2009). Red Media, Blue Media: Evidence of Ideological Selectivity in Media Use. *Journal of Communication*, 59(1), 19–39.

Iyengar, S., Sood, G., & Lelkes, Y. (2012). Affect, Not Ideology: A Social Identity Perspective on Polarization. *Public Opinion Quarterly*, 76 (3), 406, 407, 427.

Jackman, M., & Jackman, V. (1985). *Class Awareness in the United States*. Berkeley: University of California Press.

Jacobs, R., & Townsley, E. (2011). *The Space of Opinion: Media Intellectuals and the Public Sphere*. Oxford, NY: Oxford University Press.

Jacoby, S. (2008). *The Age of American Unreason*. New York: Pantheon Books.

Jaramillo, D. (2009). *Ugly War, Pretty Package: How CNN and Fox News Made the Invasion of the Iraq High Concept*, Bloomington: Indiana University Press: 21–40, 30, 36–38.

Jenkins, H. (2006). *Convergence Culture: Where Old and New Media Collide*. New York: New York University Press: 61.

Jennocuse (September 8, 2011). Chuck Todd Commercial [Video file]. YouTube. Retrieved from: www.youtube.com/watch?v=pRuqgWbbN-s.

Johnston, R. (2008). Modeling Campaign Dynamics on the Web in the 2008 National Annenberg Election Study. *Journal of Elections, Public Opinion and Parties*, 18(4), 401–412.

Johnson, S. (August 15, 1996). Some Media Chafe Under Choreography of "News." *Chicago Tribune*. Retrieved from: http://articles.chicagotribune.com/1996-08-15/news/9608150224_1_convention-coverage-goptv-repub lican-convention.

Johnson, V. (2008). *Heartland TV: Prime Time Television and the Struggle for U.S. Identity*. New York: New York University Press: 150–151.

Jones, G. (1983). Rethinking Chartism. In *Languages of Class: Studies in English Working Class History, 1832–1902*. Cambridge, NY: Cambridge University Press.

Jones, J. (2012). Fox News and the Performance of Ideology. *Cinema Journal*, 51(4), 180.

Judis, J. (June 17, 2007). Back to the Future. *The American Prospect*. Retrieved May 20, 2017, from http://prospect.org/article/back-future.

(May 19, 2010). Tea Minus Zero: The Tea Party Menace Will Not Go Quietly. *The New Republic*. Retrieved from: www.tnr.com/article/politics/tea-minus-zero.

(2016). *The Populist Explosion: How the Great Recession Transformed American and European Politics*. New York: Columbia Global Reports.

Jutel, O. (2013) "American Populism and the New Political Economy of the Media Field," *Political Economy of Communication*, 1(1), 26–42.

(2015) The Liberal Field of Journalism and the Political – *The New York Times*, Fox News and the Tea Party. *Journalism: Theory, Practice and Criticism*, 17(8), 1131–1132.

Kammen, M. (1991). *Mystic Chords of Memory: The Transformation of Tradition in American Culture*. New York: Vintage Books.

Kamp, D. (February 1999). The Tabloid Decade. *Vanity Fair*.

Kaplan, R. (2002). *Politics and the American Press: The Rise of Objectivity, 1865–1920*, Cambridge, England: Cambridge University Press.

Katz, S. (1976). Thomas Jefferson and the Right to Property in Revolutionary America. *Journal of Law and Economics*, 19(3), 467–488.

Kazin, M. (1998). *The Populist Persuasion: An American History* (Revised Edition). Ithaca: Cornell University Press, 4, 13, 119, 191–192, 232.

Kearns, B. (1999). *Tabloid Baby*. Nashville, TN: Celebrity Books: 20, 21.

Keeble, R. (2009). *Ethics for Journalists* (2nd Edition). New York: Routledge: 160, 205–206.

Keister, L. A., & Southgate, D. E. (2012). *Inequality: A Contemporary Approach to Race, Class, and Gender*. Cambridge,NY: Cambridge University Press.

Kelley, R. (1996). *Race Rebels: Culture, Politics, and the Black Working Class*. New York: Simon and Schuster Adult Publishing Group.

Kellner, D. (1997). Ernst Bloch, Utopia and Ideology Critique: *Illuminations: The Critical Theory Project*. Retrieved from: https://pages.gseis.ucla.edu/faculty/kellner/Illumina%20Folder/kell1.htm.

Kelly, M., Hemmer, B., & Hill, E. D. (November 13, 2008). *America's News Headquarters* [Transcript]. New York: Fox News Channel. Retrieved July 9, 2011, from Factiva database (Dow Jones).

(December 1, 2008). *America's News Headquarters* [Transcript]. New York: Fox News Channel. Retrieved July 9, 2011, from Factiva database (Dow Jones).

Kimmel, D. (2004). *The Fourth Network: How Fox Broke the Rules and Reinvented Television*. Chicago: Ivan R. Dee.

King, M. L. (2010). Where Are We? In V. Harding, (ed.), *Where Do We Go From Here: Chaos or Community?* Boston: Beacon Press: 7.

Kissel, R. (December 13, 2013). Fox News Remains Ratings Champ as 2013 Comes to Close. *Variety*. Retrieved from: http://variety.com/2013/tv/news/fox-news-remains-ratings-dynamo-as-2013-comes-to-close-1200964903/.

Kitman, M. (2007). *The Man Who Would Not Shut Up: The Rise of Bill O'Reilly*. New York: St. Martin's: 78, 135, 137, 138.

Kitty, A., & Greenwald, R. (2005). *Outfoxed: Rupert Murdoch's War on Journalism*. New York: Disinformation: 49.

Klein, N. (2017). *No Is Not Enough: Resisting Trump's Shock Politics and Winning the World We Need*. Chicago: Haymarket Books.

Kludt, T. (April 16, 2016). How Rupert Murdoch Warmed up to Donald Trump's Candidacy. CNNmoney.com. Retrieved from: http://money.cnn.com/2016/04/15/media/rupert-murdoch-donald-trump/index.html.

Knorr-Cretina, K. (1999). *Epistemic Cultures: How the Sciences Make Knowledge*. Cambridge, MA: Harvard University Press.

Kogan, R. (August 17, 2015). Morton Downey Jr. Paved the Way for the Angry Talk Show Host of Today. *Chicago Tribune*. Retrieved from: www.chicagotribune.com/entertainment/tv/ct-morton-downey-jr-documentary-20150817-story.html.

Koger, G. (2010). *Filibustering: A Political History of Obstruction in the House and Senate*. Chicago: University of Chicago Press.

Kolbert, E. (November 27, 1993). TV Chanel Plans Conservative Talk, All Day, All Night. *New York Times*.

Koppel, T. (November 14, 2010). The Case against News We Can Choose. *Washington Post*. Retrieved from: www.washingtonpost.com/wpdyn/content/article/2010/11/12/AR2010111206508.html.

(September 20, 2012). War of Words: Partisan Ranting Is "Marketing of Fear" [Video file]. MSNBC.com. Retrieved from: www.nbcnews.com/video/rock-center/49113264#49113264.

Kramer, S., & Miller, D. (Directors). (2013). *Évocateur: The Morton Downey Jr. Movie* [DVD]. Magnolia Pictures.

Krasnow, E., Longley, L., & Terry, H. (1982). *Politics of Broadcast Regulation* (3rd Edition). New York: St. Martin's Press: 71–72.

Kull, S., Ramsay, C., & Lewis, E. (2003). Misperceptions, the Media, and the Iraq War. *Political Science Quarterly*, 118(4), 569–98.

Kuntz, T. (January 8, 1995). Word for Word/National Empowerment Television: You Want Your Newt TV? Whether You Do or You Don't, It's Here. *New York Times*. Retrieved from: www.nytimes.com/1995/01/08/weekinreview/word-for-word-national-empowerment-television-you-want-your-newt-tv-whether-you.html

Kurtz, H. (January 22, 1988). The N.Y. Post's Hard Decline. *Washington Post*. Retrieved from: www.washingtonpost.com/archive/lifestyle/1988/01/22/the-ny-posts-hard-decline/a461ba70-6646-4099-9caf-98848df13012/.

(February 10, 1994). With a News Look, Partisan TV Networks Downlink Conservatism. *The Washington Post*. Retrieved from: www.washingtonpost.com/archive/politics/1994/02/10/with-a-news-look-partisan-tv-networks-downlink-conservatism/8a9642ca-3b60-42c8-8668-7e99301e86ba/.

(November 12, 1994). Crossing the Line in California? *Washington Post*. Retrieved from: www.washingtonpost.com/archive/lifestyle/1994/11/12/crossing-the-line-in-california/e02c9d8b-79d9-44be-beb4-b6a6fcd8fbea/.

(1997). *Hot Air: All Talk, All the Time*, New York: Basic Books.

(March 26, 1999). Crazy Like a Fox: Question His News Judgment, Perhaps, but Never Underestimate Roger Ailes. *Washington Post*. Retrieved from: www .washingtonpost.com/archive/lifestyle/1999/03/26/crazy-like-a-fox-question-his-news-judgment-perhaps-but-never-underestimate-roger-ailes/a959339f-acaf-4823-8238-27da13eb77be/.

La Chapelle, P. (2007). *Proud to Be an Okie: Cultural Politics, Country Music, and Migration to Southern California*. Berkeley: University of California Press.

Laclau, E., & C. Mouffe. (2001). *Hegemony & Socialist Strategy: Towards a Radical Democratic Politics* (2nd Edition.). London: Verso: 67.

Laclau, E. (1977). *Politics and Ideology in Marxist Theory*. London: Verso: 173.

(2005a). *On Populist Reason*. New York: Verso.

(2005b). Populism: What's in a Name? In F. Panizza (ed.), *Populism and the Mirror of Democracy*. London: Verso.

(2007). *Emancipation(s)*. London: Verso.

Lafayette, J. (September 9, 1996). "Fairness" Will Set Fox News Apart. *Electronic Media*.

Lakoff, G. (1996). *Moral Politics: How Liberals and Conservatives Think*. Chicago: Chicago University Press.

(2004). *Don't Think of an Elephant!: Know Your Values and Frame the Debate: The Essential Guide for Progressives*. White River Junction: Chelsea Green Publishing Company.

(2008). *The Political Mind: Why You Can't Understand 21st-Century American Politics with an 18th-Century Brain*. New York: Viking.

La Monica, P. (2009). *Inside Rupert's Brain*. New York: Portfolio: 83–84.

Lamont, M. (1992). *Money, Morals, and Manners: The Culture of the French and American Upper-middle Class*. Chicago: University of Chicago Press.

(2000). *The Dignity of Working Men: Morality and the Boundaries of Race, Class, and Immigration*. Cambridge, MA: Harvard University Press: 9, 104, 108–109.

Langer, J. (1998). *Tabloid Television: Popular Journalism and the "Other News."* New York: Routledge.

Lawler, S. (2005). Disgusted Subjects: The Making of Middle-Class Identities. *Sociological Review*, 53(3), 429–46.

Layman, G., Carsey, T., & Horowitz, J. (2006). Party Polarization in the American Electorate. *Annual Review of Political Science*, 46, 768–803.

Ledbetter, J. (1997). *Made Possible By...: The Death of Public Broadcasting in the United States*. New York: Verso.

Lee, A. (2002). *The Bizarre Careers of John R. Brinkley*. Lexington: University Press of Kentucky.

Lee, J. (November 29, 1993). Conservative TV: "C-Span with an Attitude." *USA Today*.

Leuchtenburg, W. (2009). *In the Shadow of FDR: From Harry Truman to Barack Obama* (4th Edition). Ithaca, NY: Cornell University Press: 299–312, 304, 306.

Levendusky, M. (2013). *How Partisan Media Polarize America*. Chicago: University of Chicago Press: 12, 13, 24–49.

Levere, J. (January 30, 2002). The Fox News Channel Tops CNN's Audience, and Casts Its Eyes toward Its Advertising Rates. *New York Times.* Retrieved from: www.nytimes.com/2002/01/30/business/media-business-advertising-fox-channel-tops-cnn-s-audience-casts-its-eyes-toward.html.

Levin, G. (September 9–15, 1996). Fox News Sets Slate. *Variety.*

Lewis, M. (November 8, 1996). 41: Politics. *This American Life.* National Public Radio [transcript]. Retrieved from: www.thisamericanlife.org/radio-archives/episode/41/transcript.

Lieberman, D. (September 23, 1996). Ailes Tackles Toughest Assignment Cable Channel Battles Budget, Clock, Rivals. *USA Today.*

Lippman, J. (January 24, 1990). NATPE 1990: Trash, Crash Genres of Past, *Variety,* 159.

Lippmann, W. (1922). *Public Opinion.* New York: Harcourt, Brace and Co.

Lipsitz, G. (1988 June). The Struggle for Hegemony. *The Journal of American History,* 75(1), 146.

(2001). *American Studies in a Moment of Danger.* Minneapolis: University of Minnesota Press: 47–50.

Litherland, B. (2014). Breaking *Kayfabe* Is Easy, Cheap and Never Entertaining: Twitter Rivalries in Professional Wrestling. *Celebrity Studies,* 5 (4).

Lorber, J. (1994). *Chapter One: "Night to His Day": The Social Construction of Gender.* Paradoxes of Gender. New Haven, Connecticut: Yale University Press.

Lott, E. (1993). *Love & Theft: Blackface Minstrelsy and the American Working Class.* New York: Oxford University Press.

(2007). Class. In B. Burgett & G. Hendler (eds.), *Keywords for American Cultural Studies.* New York: New York University Press.

Lowndes, J. (2005). From Founding Violence to Political Hegemony: The Conservative Populism of George Wallace. In F. Panizza, (ed.), *Populism and the Mirror of Democracy.* New York: Verso: 171.

Luhby, T., & Agiesta, J. (November 9, 2016). Exit Polls: Clinton Fails to Energize African Americans, Latinos and the Young. CNN.com. Retrieved from: www.cnn.com/ 2016/ 11/ 08/ politics/ first-exit-polls-2016/.

Lyons, M. (January 20, 2017). Ctrl-Alt-Delete: The Origins and Ideology of the Alternative Right. *Political Research Associates.* Retrieved February 05, 2018, from: www.politicalresearch.org/2017/01/20/ctrl-alt-delete-report-on-the-alternative-right/.

Mahler, J. (May 21, 2005). What Rupert Wrought. *New York Magazine.* Retrieved from: http://nymag.com/nymetro/news/people/features/11673/.

(2006). *Ladies and Gentlemen, The Bronx Is Burning: 1977, Baseball, Politics, and the Battle for the Soul of a City.* New York: Picador: 34.

Mahoney, W. (March 2, 1992). Diller Tight-Lipped on Plans after Fox. *Advertising Age,* 63 (9).

Malone, B. (2002). *Country Music U.S.A* (2nd Edition). Austin: University of Texas Press, 2002: 75.

Mannies, J. (November 3, 1993). Conservatives Rushing to Be New Limbaugh. *St. Louis Post Dispatch.*

Marcus, R. (July 26, 1996). Amway Says It Was Unnamed Donor to Help Broadcast GOP Convention. *Washington Post*. Retrieved from: www.washington post.com/archive/politics/1996/07/26/amway-says-it-was-unnamed-donor-to-help-broadcast-gop-convention/fdefcb71-221a-4b55-94f0-ecc6336eb263/.

Martin G., & Yurukoglu, A. (2017). Bias in Cable News: Persuasion and Polarization. *American Economic Review*, 107(9), 2587. Retrieved from: https://pubs.aeaweb.org/doi/pdfplus/10.1257/aer.20160812.

Martysoffice (May 31, 2013). Megyn Kelly Attacks Erickson and Dobbs On Sexism: 'Who Died and Made You Scientist-in-Chief?! [Video File]. YouTube. Retrieved from: www.youtube.com/watch?v=d6vecZLWupM.

McCarty, N., Poole, K., & Rosenthal, H. (2001). The Hunt for Discipline in Congress. *The American Political Science Review*, 95, 673–687.

McChesney, R. (1999). *Rich Media, Poor Democracy: Communication Politics in Dubious Times*. New York: New Press.

(2003). Foreword: The Golden Age of Irony. In: P. Hart, (ed.), *The Oh Really? Factor: Unspinning Fox News Channel's Bill O'Reilly*. New York: Seven Stories Press.

McClellan, S. (1992, June 1). Fox Fills in the Blanks. *Broadcasting*, pp. 18–19

McClennen, S., & Maisel, R. (2014) *Is Satire Saving Our Nation: Mockery and American Politics*. New York: Palgrave Macmillan

McCombs, M. (2005). A Look at Agenda-setting: Past, Present and Future. *Journalism Studies*, 6(4), 549–550.

McDermott, T. (2010). Dumb like a Fox. *Columbia Journalism Review*, 48(6), 8.

McElvaine, R. (2009). *The Introduction to the Twenty-fifth Anniversary Edition. In the Great Depression: America, 1929–1941* (Reprint Edition). New York: Times Books.

McGerr, M. (1986). *The Decline of Popular Politics: The American North, 1865–1928*. Oxford, NY: Oxford University Press: 58.

McGirr, L. (2001). *Suburban Warriors: The Origins of the New American Right*. Princeton, NJ: Princeton University Press.

McGuigan, J. (1992). *Cultural Populism*. London: Routledge.

McIlwain, C. D. (2007). Perceptions of Leadership and the Challenge of Obama's Blackness. *Journal of Black Studies*, 38(1), 64–74.

McKnight, D. (2013). *Murdoch's Politics: How One Man's Thirst for Wealth and Power Shapes Our World*. London: Pluto: 13, 27–29, 70, 71, 74, 75.

McMurria, J. (2017). *Republic on the Wire: Cable Television, Pluralism and the Politics of New Technologies, 1948–1984*. New Brunswick, NJ: Rutgers University Press.

McNair, B. (1998). *The Sociology of Journalism*. London: Arnold Publishers.

McRobbie, A. (1994). *Postmodernism & Popular Culture*. New York: Routledge.

Meacham, J. (January 30, 1995). Surfing on Newt's Network. *Newsweek*.

Media Matters for America (July 2004). O'Reilly: "Fox Does Tilt Right"; Said GOP "Very Uneasy with Fox" – Even after Cheney, Ralph Reed Touted Fox. Retrieved from: http://mediamatters.org/research/200407210007.

Mediaite (August 10, 2012). Thursday Ratings: Ed Schultz Beats CNN and Rest of MSNBC in Total Viewers. Retrieved from: www.mediaite.com/tv/thursday-ratings-ed-schultz-beats-cnn-and-rest-of-msnbc-in-total-viewers/.

Medvetz, T. (2012). *Think Tanks in America*. Chicago: University of Chicago Press: 102–105, 109, 137–140.

Meek, R.L. (1976). *Studies in the Labor Theory of Value* (2nd Edition). New York: Monthly Review Press.

Meroney, J. (1997). The Fox News Gamble. *American Enterprise*, 8(5), 41.

MightyFalcon2011 (January 26, 2014). Inside Edition 8/3/1993 [Video file]. YouTube. Retrieved from: www.youtube.com/watch?v=4FGGHN2Godo.

Milano, B. (August 31, 2017). Benkler Report Focuses on Partisanship, Propaganda and Disinformation in the 2016 U.S. presidential election. Harvard Law Today. Retrieved from: https://today.law.harvard.edu/benkler-report-focuses-partisanship-propaganda-disinformation-2016-u-s-presidential-election/.

Mitchell, A., Gottfried, J., Barthel, M., & Shearer, E. (July 7, 2016). Pathways to News. Pew Research Center. Retrieved from: www.journalism.org/2016/07/07/pathways-to-news/.

Mittell, J. (2010). *Television and American Culture*. New York: Oxford University Press.

(October 19, 2016). Donald Trump Doesn't Need to Broaden His Appeal. The Rise of Cable TV Explains Why. Vox. Retrieved from: www.vox.com/culture/2016/10/19/13304908/trump-television-narrowcasting.

Moffit, B. (2016). *Global Rise of Populism: Performance, Political Style and Representation*. Redwood City, CA: Stanford University Press.

Moffitt, B., & Ostiguy, P. (October 20, 2016). Of Course Donald Trump Goes Low. That's the Populists' Winning Style. Retrieved from: www.washingtonpost.com/news/monkey-cage/wp/2016/10/20/of-course-donald-trump-goes-low-thats-the-populists-winning-style/.

Moffitt, B., & Tormey, S. (2014). *Rethinking Populism: Politics, Mediatisation and Political Style*. Political Studies, 62, 385–386, 338.

Mone, L., & Hertog, R. (2004). *Turning Intellect into Influence*. New York: Reed Press.

Montgomery, D. (1981). *Beyond Equality: Labor and the Radical Republicans, 1862–1872: With a Bibliographical Afterword*. Urbana: University of Illinois Press.

Montopoli, B. (April 1, 2011). Donald Trump Gets Regular Fox News Spot. *CBSnews.com*. Retrieved from: www.cbsnews.com/news/donald-trump-gets-regular-fox-news-spot/.

Morahan, L. (July 7, 2008). Conservative Icon Weyrich Warns "Moral Minority" Still Dwindling. Retrieved from: www.cnsnews.com/news/article/conservative-icon-weyrich-warns-moral-minority-still-dwindling.

Moreton, B. (2010). *To Serve God and Wal-Mart: The Making of Christian Free Enterprise*. Cambridge, MA: Harvard University Press

Morris, J. S. (2005). The Fox News Factor. *The Harvard International Journal of Press/Politics*, 10(3), 56–79.

Mouffe, C., Errejon, I., & Jones, O. (2016). *Podemos: In the Name of the People*, (S. Canos, trans.). London: Lawrence & Wishart.

Mudde, C. (2007) *Populist Radical Right Parties in Europe*. Cambridge, England: Cambridge University Press.

Mudde, C. & Kaltwasser, C. (2011). "Voices of the Peoples: Populism in Europe and Latin America Compared," Kellogg Institute Working Paper. Notre Dame, IN: Kellogg Institute.

Mudge, S. (2008). What Is Neo-liberalism? *Socio-Economic Review*, 6: 703–31.

(2011). What's Left of Leftism?: Neoliberal Politics in Western Party Systems, 1945–2004. *Social Science History*, 35(3), 346.

Mukerji, C. (2007). Cultural Genealogy: Method for a Historical Sociology of Culture or Cultural Sociology of History, *Cultural Sociology*, 1(1), 49–71.

(2009). *Impossible Engineering: Technology and Territoriality on the Canal du Midi*, Princeton, NJ: Princeton University Press.

(2017) *Modernity Reimagined: An Analytic Guide*. New York: Routledge: 95.

Mundy, A. (January 1, 1996). A Division Divided. *MediaWeek*, 6(1): 16.

Nadler, A. (2016). *Making the News Popular: Mobilizing U.S. News Audiences*. Champagne, IL: University of Illinois Press.

Nagle, A. (August 15, 2017). Goodbye, Pepe: The End of the Alt-right. *The Baffler*. Retrieved from: https://thebaffler.com/latest/goodbye-pepe.

(2017).*Kill All Normies: Online Culture Wars from 4chan to Tumblr to Trump and the Alt-Right*. Winchester, UK: Zero Books.

Nash, G. (1998). *The Conservative Intellectual Movement in America, since 1945*. Wilmington: Intercollegiate Studies Institute: 335.

National Empowerment Television (September 1994). [Business proposal]. Proposal NET National Empowerment Television Changing the Picture, Truth Tobacco Industry Documents (Box 21230), University of California, San Francisco Library. Retrieved from: www.industrydocumentslibrary.ucsf.edu/tobacco/docs/#id=xnpko101.

(December 13, 1994). *The Progress Report*. C-Span [Video file]. Retrieved from: www.c-span.org/video/?62168-1/national-empowerment-television.

(April 5, 1995). [Broadcast]. *Freedom's Challenge* NTSC 525/60 950405. Truth Tobacco Industry Documents (Collection: Philip Morris Records), University of California, San Francisco Library. Retrieved from: www.indus trydocumentslibrary.ucsf.edu/tobacco/docs/#id=xjwc0072.

NBC News (October 10, 2010). MSNBC Rachel Maddow [Video file]. YouTube. Retrieved from: www.youtube.com/watch?v=kE23NuY5T44.

NBCnews.com (October 21, 2004). O'Reilly Lawyer Explains the Extortion Suit Against Andrea Mackris. Retrieved from: www.nbcnews.com/id/6298207/ns/msnbc-the_abrams_report/t/oreillys-lawyer-explains-extortion-suit-against-andrea-mackris/#.WWpKE1KZOCR.

(June 10, 2009). "The Ed Show" for Tuesday, June 9 [Transcript]. Retrieved from: www.nbcnews.com/id/31205888/ns/msnbc-the_ed_show/t/ed-show-tuesday-june/#.WWZEHVKZPox.

New York Times (June 16, 2009). Obama Interview with John Harwood [Transcript]. Retrieved from: www.nytimes.com/2009/06/16/us/politics/16harwood.text.html.

Nichols, B. (1991). *Representing Reality*. Bloomington: Indiana University Press: 3–4.

Nietzsche, F. (1956). *Birth of Tragedy and the Genealogy of Morals*, (G. Francis, trans.). Garden City, NY: Doubleday.

Noble, D. (1985). *The End of American History: Democracy, Capitalism, and the Metaphor of Two Worlds in Anglo-American Historical Writing, 1880–1980*. Minneapolis: University of Minnesota Press.

Norrell, R. J. (1990). After Thirty Years of "New" Labour History, There Is Still No Socialism in Reagan Country. *The Historical Journal*, 33(1), 227–238.

Norton, M. (2011). A Structural Hermeneutics of *The O'Reilly Factor*. *Theory and Society*, 40, 317, 325, 327.

Nuccitelli, D. (May 16, 2013). Survey Finds 97% Climate Science Papers Agree Warming Is Man-made. *The Guardian*. Retrieved from: www.theguardian .com/environment/climate-consensus-97-per-cent/2013/may/16/climate-change-scienceofclimatechange.

nytimers (February 25, 2009). Weekender 345 010609 60 [Video file]. YouTube. Retrieved from: www.youtube.com/watch?v=gInOA9LmdiE.

O'Connor, A. (2007). *Social Science for What?: Philanthropy and the Social Question in a World Turned Rightside Up*. New York: Russell Sage Foundation: 73–75, 109.

OECD. (2016). *Education at a Glance 2016: OECD Indicators*, OECD Publishing, Paris. Retrieved from: http://dx.doi.org/10.1787/eag-2016-en.

Olick, J. (2014). Reflections on the Undeveloped Relations between Journalism and Memory Studies. In B. Zelizer & K. Tenenboim-Weinblatt (eds.), *Journalism and Memory*. Basingstoke, England: Palgrave Macmillan.

O'Reilly, B. (March 12, 2002). *The O'Reilly Factor: The Good, the Bad, and the Completely Ridiculous in American Life*. New York: Three Rivers Press.

(December 5, 2006). *The O'Reilly Factor* [Transcript]. New York: Fox New Channel. Retrieved November 10, 2011, from Factiva database (Dow Jones).

(August 16, 2008). *The O'Reilly Factor* [Transcript]. New York: Fox New Channel. Retrieved July 3, 2011, from Factiva database (Dow Jones).

(September 1, 2008). *The O'Reilly Factor* [Transcript]. New York: Fox New Channel. Retrieved July 3, 2011, from Factiva database (Dow Jones).

(September 16, 2008). *The O'Reilly Factor* [Transcript]. New York: Fox New Channel. Retrieved November 10, 2011, from Factiva database (Dow Jones).

(December 1, 2008). *The O'Reilly Factor* [Transcript]. New York: Fox New Channel. Retrieved October 6, 2011, from Factiva database (Dow Jones).

(January 5, 2009). *The O'Reilly Factor* [Transcript]. New York: Fox New Channel. Retrieved July 3, 2011, from Factiva database (Dow Jones).

(January 7, 2009). *The O'Reilly Factor* [Transcript]. New York: Fox New Channel. Retrieved July 3, 2011, from Factiva database (Dow Jones).

(January 29, 2009). *The O'Reilly Factor* [Transcript]. New York: Fox New Channel. Retrieved July 3, 2011, from Factiva database (Dow Jones).

(February 17, 2009). *The O'Reilly Factor* [Transcript]. New York: Fox New Channel. Retrieved July 3, 2011, from Factiva database (Dow Jones).

(March 5, 2009). *The O'Reilly Factor* [Transcript]. New York: Fox New Channel. Retrieved July 3, 2011, from Factiva database (Dow Jones).

(March 10, 2009). *The O'Reilly Factor* [Transcript]. New York: Fox New Channel.Retrieved July 3, 2011, from Factiva database (Dow Jones).

(March 12, 2009). *The O'Reilly Factor* [Transcript]. New York: Fox New Channel. Retrieved July 3, 2011, from Factiva database (Dow Jones).

(April 15, 2009). *The O'Reilly Factor* [Transcript]. New York: Fox News Channel. Retrieved July 3, 2011, from Factiva database (Dow Jones).

(May 4, 2009). *The O'Reilly Factor* [Transcript]. New York: Fox News Channel. Retrieved July 3, 2011, from Factiva database (Dow Jones).

(July 30, 2009). *The O'Reilly Factor* [Transcript]. New York: Fox News Channel. Retrieved July 3, 2011, from Factiva database (Dow Jones).

(August 13, 2009). *The O'Reilly Factor* [Transcript]. New York: Fox New Channel. Retrieved November 10, 2011, from Factiva database (Dow Jones).

(September 9, 2009). *The O'Reilly Factor* [Transcript]. New York: Fox News Channel. Retrieved July 3, 2011, from Factiva database (Dow Jones).

(October 7, 2009). *The O'Reilly Factor* [Transcript]. New York: Fox News Channel. Retrieved July 3, 2011, from Factiva database (Dow Jones).

(November 20, 2009). *The O'Reilly Factor* [Transcript]. New York: Fox New Channel. Retrieved July 3, 2011, from Factiva database (Dow Jones).

(November 23, 2009). *The O'Reilly Factor* [Transcript]. New York: Fox New Channel. Retrieved July 3, 2011, from Factiva database (Dow Jones).

(January 22, 2010). *The O'Reilly Factor* [Transcript]. New York: Fox New Channel. Retrieved July 2, 2011, from Factiva database (Dow Jones).

(February 15, 2010). *The O'Reilly Factor* [Transcript]. New York: Fox New Channel. Retrieved July 2, 2011, from Factiva database (Dow Jones).

(March 12, 2010). *The O'Reilly Factor* [Transcript]. New York: Fox New Channel. Retrieved July 1, 2011, from Factiva database (Dow Jones).

(March 22, 2010). *The O'Reilly Factor* [Video file]. New York: Fox News Channel. Retrieved June 23, 2011, from UCLA Communication Studies Archive, University of California, Los Angeles.

(March 24, 2010). *The O'Reilly Factor* [Video file]. New York: Fox New Channel. Retrieved November 26, 2011, from UCLA Communication Studies Archive, University of California, Los Angeles.

(May 4, 2010). *The O'Reilly Factor* [Transcript]. New York: Fox New Channel. Retrieved July 1, 2011, from Factiva database (Dow Jones).

(September 22, 2010). *The O'Reilly Factor* [Transcript]. New York: Fox New Channel. Retrieved June 28 1, 2011, from Factiva database (Dow Jones).

(October 6, 2010). *The O'Reilly Factor* [Transcript]. New York: Fox News Channel. Retrieved July 3, 2011, from Factiva database (Dow Jones).

(November 8, 2010). *The O'Reilly Factor* [Transcript]. New York: Fox New Channel. Retrieved November 10, 2011, from Factiva database (Dow Jones).

(November 15, 2010). *The O'Reilly Factor* [Transcript]. New York: Fox New Channel. Retrieved November 10, 2011, from Factiva database (Dow Jones).

(January 3, 2015). *The O'Reilly Factor.* [Broadcast]. New York: Fox News Channel.

(Producer) (2015). *Legend & Lies: Into the West [Broadcast].* New York: Fox News Channel.

(2016) *Legend & Lies: The Patriots* [Broadcast]. New York: Fox News Channel.

O'Reilly B., & Dugard, M. (2011). *Killing Lincoln: The Shocking Assassination That Changed America Forever,* New York: Henry Holt & Co.

(2012). *Killing Kennedy: The End of Camelot.* New York: Henry Holt & Co.

(2013). *Killing Jesus: A History.* New York: Henry Holt & Co.

(2014). *Killing Patton: The Strange Death of World War II's Most Audacious General.* New York: Henry Holt & Co.

(2015). *Killing Reagan: A Violent Assault That Changed a Presidency.* New York, New York: Henry Holt & Co.

(2017). *Killing England: The Brutal Struggle for American Independence.* New York: Henry Holt & Co.

Örnebring, H., & Jönsson, A. M. (2004). Tabloid Journalism and the Public Sphere: A Historical Perspective on Tabloid Journalism. *Journalism Studies,* 5(3), 288.

Ostrow, J. (October 8, 1996). Fox News Channel so Busy it Might Make You Dizzy. *The Denver Post.*

Otterson, J. (March 28, 2017). Cable News Ratings: Fox News Breaks Records, MSNBC Posts Significant Growth. *Variety.* Retrieved from: http://variety.com/2017/tv/news/cable-news-ratings-fox-news-msnbc-1202017940/.

Ouellette, L. (1999). Inventing the Cosmo Girl: Class Identity and Girl-style American Dreams. *Media, Culture & Society,* 21(3): 377.

(2002). *Viewers Like You? How Public TV Failed the People.* New York: Columbia University Press: 58, 181.

(May 24, 2017). #Notokay: Trump as an Affective State. Verbal Presentation at the Populism, Post-Truth Politics and Participatory Culture: Interventions in the Intersection of Popular and Political Communication Preconference at the International Communication Conference in San Diego.

Owens, L. (October 7, 2011). Forty-year Low in America's View of Wall Street. *CNN.com.* Retrieved from: www.cnn.com/2011/10/07/opinion/owens-wall-street-disapproval/.

Ozzi, D. (January 23, 2015). A Brief History of Bill O'Reilly Knowing Dick about Hip-Hop. *Vice.* Retrieved from: https://noisey.vice.com/en_us/article/rb88qa/a-brief-history-of-bill-oreilly-knowing-dick-about-hip-hop.

Palmer, B. (1980). *"Man Over Money": The Southern Populist Critique of American Capitalism.* Chapel Hill: University of North Carolina Press.

Palmer, G. (1957). Attitudes toward Work in an Industrial Community. *American Journal of Sociology,* 63, 17–26.

Panizza, F. (2000). Neopopulism and Its Limits in Collor's Brazil. *Bulletin of Latin American Research,* 19(2), 177–192.

(2005). Introduction. In F. Panizza (ed.), *Populism and the Mirror of Democracy.* London: Verso, 2005: 6.

Parker, A., & Costa, R. (April 23, 2017). "Everyone Tunes in": Inside Trump's Obsession with Cable TV. *Washington Post.* Retrieved from: www.washingtonpost.com/politics/everyone-tunes-in-inside-trumps-obsession-with-cable-tv/2017/04/23/3c52bd6c-25e3-11e7-a1b3-faff0034e2de_story.html.

Parson, P. (2008). *Blue Skies: A History of Cable Television.* Philadelphia: Temple University Press.

Patterson, T. E. (2000). *Doing Well and Doing Good: How Soft News and Critical Journalism Are Shrinking the News Audience and Weakening Democracy: And What News Outlets Can Do about It.* Joan Shorenstein Center on the Press, Politics and Public Policy, John F. Kennedy School of Government, Harvard University.

Peck, R. (2014a) You Say Rich, I Say Job Creator: How Fox News Framed the Great Recession through the Moral Discourse of Producerism. *Media, Culture & Society*, 36, (4), 526–35.

(November 5, 2014b). Is Fox News the Smartest Journalism Ever?: Tabloid Television Is Great at Manipulating America's Long History of Elitism and Class Conflict. *Zócalo Public Square*. Retrieved from: www.zocalopublicsquare.org/2014/11/05/is-fox-news-the-smartest-journalism-ever/ideas/nexus/.

(July 2017). Usurping the Usable Past: How Fox News Remembered the Great Depression during the Great Recession. *Journalism*, 18, (6), 680–699.

Pecknold, D. (2007). *The Selling Sound: The Rise of the Country Music Industry*. Durham, NC: Duke University Press: 219.

Pelizzon, V. P. & West, N. M. (2010). *Tabloid, Inc.: Crimes, Newspapers, Narratives*. Columbus: Ohio State University Press.

Perlstein, R. (2001). *Before the Storm: Barry Goldwater and the Unmaking of the American Consensus*. New York: Hill and Wang.

(2008) *Nixonland: The Rise of a President and the Fracturing of America*. New York: Scribner.

(2014). *The Invisible Bridge: The Fall of Nixon and the Rise of Reagan*. New York: Simon & Schuster Paperbacks.

Perren, A. (2004). *Deregulation, Integration and a New Era of Media Conglomerates: The Case of Fox, 1985–1995* (Doctoral dissertation). PhD, University of Texas at Austin. Advisor: Thomas Schatz.

Peters, C. (2010) No-Spin Zones: The Rise of the American Cable News Magazine and Bill O'Reilly. *Journalism Studies*, 11(6), 842, 845, 846–847, 853, 1n.

Peterson, R. (1997). *Creating Country Music: Fabricating Authenticity*. Chicago: University of Chicago Press.

Petrocik, J., Benoit, W., & Hansen, G. (2003). Issue Ownership and Presidential Campaigning, 1952–2000. *Political Science Quarterly*, 118(4), 599–626.

Pew Research Center (2004). *News Audiences Increasingly Politicized*. Pew Research Center. Retrieved from: www.people-press.org/2004/06/08/news-audiences-increasingly-politicized/.

(August 5, 2005). GOP Makes Gains among the Working Class, While Democrats Hold on to the Union Vote. Retrieved from: www.people-press.org/2005/08/02/gop-makes-gains-among-the-working-class-while-democrats-hold-on-to-the-union-vote/.

(January 6, 2007). Pew Research Center. Section: Public Attitude. In *The State of the News Media 2007*. Retrieved from: www.stateofthemedia.org/2007/cable-tv-intro/public-attitude/.

(April 15, 2007). Public Knowledge of Current Affairs Little Changed by News and Information Revolutions. Pew Research Center. Retrieved from: www.people-press.org/2007/04/15/public-knowledge-of-current-affairs-little-changed-by-news-and-information-revolutions/.

(2007). *The State of the News Media 2007: An Annual Report on American Journalism*. Retrieved from: www.stateofthemedia.org/2007/.

(April 9, 2008). Inside the Middle Class: Bad Times Hit the Good Life. Retrieved from: www.pewsocialtrends.org/2008/04/09/inside-the-middle-class-bad-times-hit-the-good-life/.

(October 29, 2008). The Color of News: How Different Media Have Covered the General Election. Retrieved from: www.journalism.org/node/13436.

(October 5, 2009). Covering the Great Recession: How the Media Have Depicted the Economic Crisis During Obama's Presidency. Retrieved from: www.journalism.org/analysis_report/covering_great_recession.

(October 30, 2009). Partisanship and Cable News Audiences. Retrieved from: www.pewresearch.org/2009/10/30/partisanship-and-cable-news-audiences/.

(March 15, 2010). *The State of the News Media: An Annual Report on American Journalism 2010*. Retrieved from: http://assets.pewresearch.org .s3.amazonaws.com/files/journalism/State-of-the-News-Media-Report-2010-FINAL.pdf

(September 12, 2010). Section 4: Who Is Listening, Watching, Reading: And Why. In *Americans Spending More Time Following the News*. Retrieved from: www.people-press.org/2010/09/12/americans-spending-more-time-following-the-news/.

(March 13, 2011). Cable: Audience vs. Economics. In *The State of the News Media 2011*. Retrieved from: www.stateofthemedia.org/2011/cable-essay/data-page-2/.

(September 27, 2012). Section 4: Demographics and Political Views of News Audiences. In *In Changing News Landscape, Even Television Is Vulnerable*. Retrieved from: www.people-press.org/2012/09/27/section-4-demographics-and-political-views-of-news-audiences/.

(June 16, 2016). *State of the News Media 2016*, p. 24. Retrieved from: http://assets.pewresearch.org/wpcontent/uploads/sites/13/2016/06/30143308/state-of-the-news-media-report-2016-final.pdf.

Phillips-Fein, K. (2009). *Invisible Hands: The Making of the Conservative Movement from the New Deal to Reagan*, New York: W. W. Norton & Company: 163–169.

Pierce, C. (August 22, 2002). Fox Populi: What Do the Barking Heads of Fox News Channel and Other Murdoch Media Have That CNN, Rather and Donahue Don't? A True Virtuous, Tabloid Soul. *Salon.com*. Retrieved from: www.salon.com/2002/08/22/fox_19/.

Plummer, S. (September 10, 2011). Koppel Speaks on Media Changing Priorities, Political Atmosphere: Ted Koppel Kicks Off the Tulsa Town Hall Lecture Series. *Tulsa World*. Retrieved from: www.tulsaworld.com/news/local/koppel-speaks-on-media-changing-priorities-political-atmosphere/article_82daec2f-ba1a-504a-b710-5f35241a0eod.html.

Politico (July 21, 2011). Cenk Uygur, MSNBC Differ on Why He Left: On Media. Retrieved from: www.politico.com/blogs/onmedia/0711/Cenk_Uygur_MSNBC_differ_on_why_he_left.htm.

Pollack, N. (1966). *The Populist Response to Industrial America: Midwestern Populist Thought*. New York: Norton.

Posner, S. (August 22, 2016). How Donald Trump's Campaign Chief Created an Online Haven for White Nationalists. *Mother Jones.com*. Retrieved from: www.motherjones.com/politics/2016/08/stephen-bannon-donald-trump-alt-right-breitbart-news/.

Power, L. (July 22, 2015). Donald Trump and Fox & Friends' Symbiotic Relationship. Media Matters. Retrieved from: www.mediamatters.org/blog/2015/07/22/donald-trump-and-fox-amp-friends-symbiotic-rela/204533.

Prior, M. (2007). *Post-Broadcast Democracy: How Media Choice Increases Inequality in Political Involvement and Polarizes Elections*. Cambridge, NY: Cambridge University Press: 94.

(2013). Media and Political Polarization. *Annual Review of Political Science*, 16, 101–127.

Qian, Z. (1997). Breaking the Racial Barriers: Variations in Interracial Marriage between 1980 and 1990. *Demography*, 34(2), 263–276.

Quick, B., Andrew, R. S., & Kernen, J. (February 19, 2009). *Squawk Box* [Transcript]. New York: CNBC. Retrieved October 11, 2011, from Factiva database (Dow Jones).

RealClearPolitics (February 6, 2009). Sen. Mitch McConnell, Speech on Senate Floor. Retrieved from: www.realclearpolitics.com/articles/2009/02/leader_mcconnell_wont_work.html.

Reed, B. (October 31, 2009). Glenn Beck Peddles Populism for Rich Guys. *Alternet*. Retrieved from: www.alternet.org/news/143624 glenn_beck_peddles_populism_for_rich_guys/?page=entire.

Rich, A. (2001). The Politics of Expertise in Congress and the News Media. *Social Science Quarterly*, 82(3): 586.

(2004). *Think Tanks, Public Policy, and the Politics of Expertise*. Cambridge, England: Cambridge University Press.

Ries, A., & Trout, J. (1981). *Positioning: The Battle for your Mind*. New York: Warner Books.

(1986). *Marketing Warfare*. New York: McGraw-Hill.

Robin, C. (2011). *The Reactionary Mind: Conservatism from Edmund Burke to Sarah Palin*. New York: Oxford University Press: 100.

Robinson, R., & Kelly, J. (1979). Class as Conceived by Marx and Dahrendorf: Effects on Income Inequality and Politics in the United States and Great Britain. *American Sociological Review*, 44(1), 38–58.

Robles-Anderson, E., & Svensson, P. (2016). One Damn Slide After Another: PowerPoint at Every Occasion for Speech. *Computational Culture*, 5.

Rocky Mountain News (August 25, 1974). Interview with Joseph Coors.

Rodriguez, A. (1999). *Making Latino News: Race, Class, Language*. London: Sage.

Roediger, D. (1991). *The Wages of Whiteness: Race and the Making of the American Working Class*. New York: Verso.

Roosevelt, F. (March 4, 1933). Inaugural Address. The American President Project. Retrieved from: www.presidency.ucsb.edu/ws/?pid=14473.

(June 27, 1936). Acceptance Speech for the Renomination for the Presidency. The American Presidency Project. Retrieved from: www.presidency.ucsb.edu/ws/index.php?pid=15314.

(October 31, 1936). Address at Madison Square Garden, New York City. The American President Project. Retrieved from: www.presidency.ucsb.edu/ws/?pid=15219.

Rosenberg, P. (October 8, 2016). From the "Old right" to the Alt-right: How the Conservative ideology of FDR's Day Fueled the Rise of Trump. *Salon.com*. Retrieved from: www.salon.com/2016/10/08/from-the-old-right-to-the-alt-right-how-the-conservative-ideology-of-fdrs-day-fueled-the-rise-of-trump/.

Rothman, N. (May 23, 2013). What's Wrong with MSNBC's Chris Hayes? *Mediaite*. Retrieved from: www.mediaite.com/tv/whats-wrong-with-msnbcs-chris-hayes/.

Roush, M. (October 8, 1996). Fox News Channel: Not Crafty Enough. *USA Today*.

Rubin, J. (1992). *The Making of Middlebrow Culture*. Chapel Hill: University of Northern Carolina Press.

Rust, M. (May 22, 1995). TV Cameras Turn Right. *Insight On the News*.

Rutenberg, J. (September 17, 2000). The Right Strategy for Fox; Conservative Cable Channel Gains in Ratings War. *New York Times*. Retrieved from: www.nytimes.com/2000/09/18/business/the-right-strategy-for-fox-conservative-cable-channel-gains-in-ratings-war.html.

(January 15, 2003,). War or No, News on Cable Already Provides the Drama. *New York Times*. Retrieved from: www.nytimes.com/2003/01/15/business/media/15TUBE.html.

(February 24, 2003). Inside CNN, a Struggle to Be Less "Tabloid." *New York Times*. Retrieved from: www.nytimes.com/2003/02/24/business/inside-cnn-a-struggle-to-be-less-tabloid.html.

(April 16, 2003). A Nation at War: The News Media: Cable's War Coverage Suggests a New "Fox Effect" on Television Journalism. *New York Times*. Retrieved from: www.nytimes.com/2003/04/16/us/nation-war-media-cable-s-war-coverage-suggests-new-fox-effect-television.html.

(January 21, 2015). The Megyn Kelly Moment. *New York Times*. Retrieved from: www.nytimes.com/2015/01/25/magazine/the-megyn-kelly-moment.html.

Sareen, A. (March 13, 2013). Ed Schultz Leaving MSNBC Weeknights, Moving to Weekends. *Huffington Post*. Retrieved from: www.huffingtonpost.com/2013/03/13/ed-schultz-time-slot-leaving-weeknight_n_2871383.html.

Saurette, P., & Gunster, S. (2011). Ears Wide Shut: Epistemological Populism, Argutainment and Canadian Conservative Talk Radio. *Canadian Journal of Political Science*, 44 (1), 195–218.

Sawr, M., & Hindess, B. (2004). *Us and Them: Anti-Elitism in Australia*. Perth, WA: Curtin University of Technology.

Saxton, A. (1990). *The Rise and Fall of the White Republic: Class Politics and Mass Culture in Nineteenth-century America*. New York: Verso.

Sayer, A. (2005). *The Moral Significance of Class*. Cambridge, England: Cambridge University Press.

Schechter, D. (2003). *Embedded: Weapons of Mass Deception: How the Media Failed to Cover the War on Iraq*. Amherst, New York: Prometheus Books.

Scheuer, J. (2001). *The Sound Bite Society: How Television Helps the Right and Hurts the Left*, London: Routledge.

Schiller, D. (1996). *Theorizing Communication: A History*. Oxford, England: Oxford University Press: 4–20.

Schlesinger, A. (2002). *The Age of Roosevelt: The Crisis of the Old Order, 1919–1933* (Vol. 1). New York: Houghton Mifflin Company.

Schoestz, D. (March 23, 2010). David Frum on GOP: Now We Work for Fox. *ABC News*. Retrieved from: http://abcnews.go.com/blogs/headlines/2010/03/david-frum-on-gop-now-we-work-for-fox/.

Schudson, M. (1978). *Discovering the News: A Social History of American Newspapers*. New York: Basic Books: 109, 112, 118, 127–129.

(1992). *Watergate in American Memory: How We Remember, Forget, and Reconstruct the Past*. New York: Basic Books: 5, 53.

(2003). *The Sociology of News*. New York: W.W. Norton & Co.: 112.

Schuessle, A. (2000). *A Logic of Expressive Choice*. Princeton, NJ: Princeton University Press.

Schwartz, C. R., & Mare, R. D. (2005). Trends in Educational Assortative Marriage from 1940 to 2003. *Demography*, 42(4), 621–646.

Scott, J. (2017). *Sex and Secularism*. Princeton, NJ: Princeton University Press: 3.

Seelye, K. (December 12, 1994). Republicans Get a Pep Talk from Rush Limbaugh. *New York Times*. Retrieved from: www.nytimes.com/1994/12/12/us/republicans-get-a-pep-talk-from-rush-limbaugh.html.

Sella, M. (June 24, 2001). The Red-State Network. *New York Times*. Retrieved from: www.nytimes.com/2001/06/24/magazine/the-red-state-network.html.

Senko, J. (Director). (2015). The Brain Washing of My Dad *[Film]*. New York: Jsenko Productions.

Seplow, S. (October 31, 1995). GOP-TV Plugs in Party Line Republicans Are Pushing Their Message Via Cable. *The Philadelphia Inquirer*.

Shapiro, I. (1991). Resources, Capacities, and Ownership. *Political Theory*, 19 (1), 47.

Shaw, D. (2006). *The Race to 270*. Chicago: University of Chicago Press.

Shawcross, W. (1997). *Murdoch: The Making of a Media Empire* (Reprint Edition). New York: Simon & Schuster: 160.

Shea, D. (March 30, 2010). Fox News' 2009 Ratings Records: Network Sees Best Year Ever. *Huffington Post*. Retrieved from: www.huffingtonpost.com/2009/12/29/fox-news-2009-ratings-rec_n_406325.html.

(July 26, 2010). Fox News Audience Just 1.38% Black. *Huffington Post*. Retrieved from: www.huffingtonpost.com/2010/07/26/fox-news-audience-just-13_n_659800.html.

(October 1, 2010). Rick Sanchez: Jon Stewart A "Bigot," Jews Run CNN & All Media. Retrieved from: www.huffingtonpost.com/2010/10/01/rick-sanchez-jon-stewart-_n_746764.html.

Sherman, G. (October 3, 2010). Chasing Fox: The Loud, Cartoonish Blood Sport That's Engorged MSNBC, Exhausted CNN: And Is Making Our Body Politic Delirious. *New York Magazine*. Retrieved from: http://nymag.com/news/media/68717/.

(2014). *The Loudest Voice in the Room: How the Brilliant, Bombastic Roger Ailes Built Fox News: And Divided a Country*, New York: Random House: xv, 70, 72, 72–74, 101–107, 106–107, 151, 185, 187, 192, 241, 242–243, 277, 291.

Shlaes, A. (1999). *The Greedy Hand: How Taxes Drive Americans Crazy and What to Do About It*. New York: Random House.

(2007) *The Forgotten Man: A New History of the Great Depression*. New York: HarperCollins.

(2013). *Coolidge*. New York: HarperCollins.

Silver, N. (May 3, 2016). The Mythology of Trump's "Working Class" Support. *FiveThirtyEight*. Retrieved from: https://fivethirtyeight.com/features/the-mythology-of-trumps-working-class-support/.

(November 22, 2016). Education, Not Income, Predicted Who Would Vote for Trump. *FiveThirtyEight*. Retrieved from: http://fivethirtyeight.com/features/education-not-income-predicted-who-would-vote-for-trump/.

Skeggs, B. (2004). *Class, Self, Culture*. New York: Routledge.

Skocpol, T., & Williamson, V. (2012). *The Tea Party and the Remaking of Republican Conservatism*. NY: Oxford University Press: 8, 135.

Smith, S. (April 26, 2016). A Wider Ideological Gap between More and Less Educated Adults. Pew Research Center. Retrieved from: www.people-press.org/2016/04/26/a-wider-ideological-gap-between-more-and-less-educated-adults/.

Sombart, W. (1976). *Why is There No Socialism in the United States?* (P. Hocking & C. T. Husbands, trans.). London: Macmillan.

Soundbitten. (December 20, 2002). Show and Prove: Bill O'Reilly's Hip-Hop problem. Retrieved from: www.soundbitten.com/oreilly.html.

Sparks, C. (2000). Introduction: Panic Over Tabloids News. In C. Sparks & J. Tulloch (eds.), *Tabloid Tales: Global Debates Over Media Standards*. Lanham, MD: Rowman & Littlefield: 1.

Spruill, M. (2008). Gender and America's Right Turn. In B. J. Schulman & J. E. Zelizer (eds.), *Rightward Bound: Making America Conservative in the 1970s*. Cambridge, MA: Harvard University Press.

Stacey, J. (1990). *Brave New Families: Stories of Domestic Upheaval in Late-Twentieth-Century America*. New York: Basic Books.

Stavrakakis, Y. (2005). Religion and Populism in Contemporary Greece. In F. Panizza (ed.), *Populism and the Mirror of Democracy*. London: Verso.

Steel, E., & Schmidt, M. (January 10, 2017). Fox News Settled Sexual Harassment Allegations Against Bill O'Reilly, Documents Show. *New York Times*. Retrieved from: www.nytimes.com/2017/01/10/business/media/bill-oreilly-sexual-harassment-fox-news-juliet-huddy.html.

(April 1, 2017). Bill O'Reilly Thrives at Fox News, Even as Harassment Settlements Add Up. *New York Times*. Retrieved from: www.nytimes.com/2017/04/01/business/media/bill-oreilly-sexual-harassment-fox-news.html.

(April 14, 2017). O'Reilly's Behavior Said to Have Helped Drive Megyn Kelly Out at Fox. *New York Times*. Retrieved from: www.nytimes.com/2017/04/14/business/media/oreilly-behavior-megyn-kelly-fox.html.

(October 21, 2017). Bill O'Reilly Settled New Harassment Claim, Then Fox Renewed His Contract. *New York Times*. Retrieved from: www.nytimes.com/2017/10/21/business/media/bill-oreilly-sexual-harassment.html.

Steel, R. (1980). *Walter Lippmann and the American Century*. Boston: Little, Brown: 180–185.

Stein, J. (April 19, 2017). The Democratic Party's Messaging Rift, in One Short Video [Video file]. *Vox*. Retrieved from: www.vox.com/policy-and-politics/2017/4/19/15359498/democratic-party-sanders-perez.

Steinberg, B. (October 23, 2017). CNN Fights "Fake News" Claims with New "Facts First" Campaign. *Variety*. Retrieved from: http://variety.com/2017/tv/news/cnn-advertising-fake-news-facts-first-1202596220/.

Stelter, B. (May 2, 2008). Fox and Democrats Become Strange Bedfellows. *New York Times*. Retrieved from: www.nytimes.com/2008/05/02/technology/02iht-fox.1.12516015.html.

(July 20, 2011). Sharpton Close to Being MSNBC Anchor. *New York Times*. Retrieved from: www.nytimes.com/2011/07/21/business/media/sharpton-close-to-being-msnbc-anchor.html.

Stewart, J. (October 4, 2010). Hurty Sanchez. *The Daily Show with Jon Stewart* [Video file]. Retrieved from: www.cc.com/video-clips/k0bl4z/the-daily-show-with-jon-stewart-hurty-sanchez.

Stonecash, J. M., Brewer, M. D., & Mariani, M. D. (2003). *Diverging Parties: Social Change, Realignment, and Party Polarization*. Boulder, CO: Westview.

Strömbäck, J. (2016). Mediatization. *The International Encyclopedia of Political Communication*, 1–9.

Stroud, N. (2011). *Niche News: The Politics of News Choice*, New York: Oxford University Press.

Strupp, J. (September 22, 2004). Murdoch Says Fox Would Have Been "Crucified" For CBS Mistake. *Editor & Publisher*. Retrieved from: www.editorandpublisher.com/PrintArticle/Murdoch-Says-Fox-Would-Have-Been-Crucified-for-CBS-Mistake.

Sumner, W. G. (2007). *Forgotten Man and Other Essays*. Old Chelsea Station: Cosimo Inc.

Sunstein, C. (2001). *Republic.com*. Princeton, NJ: Princeton University Press.

Swint, K. (2008). *Dark Genius: The Influential Career of Legendary Political Operative and Fox News Founder Roger Ailes*. New York: Union Square Press: 3, 10, 67–69, 114, 138, 166.

Taggart, P. (2000). *Populism*. Buckingham, England: Open University Press: 16.

Tantaros, A. (2016). *Tied up in Knots: How Getting What We Wanted Made Women Miserable*. New York: Broadside Books: 231.

Taub, A. (April 12, 2017). Why Americans Vote "against Their Interest": Partisanship. *New York Times*. Retrieved from: www.nytimes.com/2017/04/12/upshot/why-americans-vote-against-their-interest-partisanship.html.

Tavernise, S. (February 2012) Education Gap Grows between Rich and Poor, Studies Say. *New York Times*. Retrieved from: www.nytimes.com/2012/02/10/education/education-gap-grows-between-rich-and-poor-studies-show.html?pagewanted=all.

Taylor, C. (July 19, 1996). Fall TV: Fox Will Jump into the "Very Competitive" All-News Arena. *Seattle Times*.

Teixeira, R. A., & Rogers, J. (2001). *America's Forgotten Majority: Why the White Working Class Still Matters*. New York: Basic Books.

The Indianapolis Star (November 20, 1994). Conservative Cable Network Planned.

Thompson, E. P. (1963). *The Making of the English Working Class*. London: Gollancz.

TIME Magazine Cover (2008, November 24). The New New Deal. *Time*. Retrieved from: http://content.time.com/time/covers/0,16641,20081124,00 .html.

Tomasky, M. (November 3, 2010).Turnout: Explains A Lot. *The Guardian*. Retrieved from: www.guardian.co.uk/commentisfree/michaeltomasky/2010/ nov/03/us-midterm-elections-2010-turnout-says-a-lot.

Trump, D. (January 20, 2017). The Inaugural Address. White House Press Office. Retrieved from: www.whitehouse.gov/inaugural-address.

Tsfati, Y., & Cappella, J. (2003). Do People Watch What They Do Not Trust? Exploring the Association between News Media Skepticism and Exposure. *Communication Research*, 30(5), 504–529.

Turner, C. (2004). *Planet Simpson: How a Cartoon Masterpiece Documented an Era and Defined a Generation*. Cambridge, MA: Da Capo Press: 225–226.

Turow, J. (1997). *Breaking Up America: Advertisers and the New Media World*, Chicago: University of Chicago Press.

Tyson, A., & Maniam, S. (November 9, 2016). Behind Trump's Victory: Divisions by Race, Gender, Education. Pew Research Center. Retrieved from: www.pewresearch.org/fact-tank/2016/11/09/behind-trumps-victory-divisions-by-race-gender-education/.

United States Census Bureau (September 2009). Media Household Income for States: 2007 and 2008. American Community Surveys. Retrieved from: www.census.gov/prod/2009pubs/acsbr08-2.pdf.

(May 19, 2016). Newsroom Archive. Retrieved from: www.census.gov/news room/releases/archives/education/cb12-33.html.

USAhistorywriter (March 11, 2014). Bill O'Reilly vs. Russell Simmons Over Hip Hop & Beyoncé. [Video file]. YouTube. Retrieved from: www.youtube.com/ watch?v=8BDzN2NA6GM.

Vaillant, D. (2004). Bare-Knuckled Broadcasting: Enlisting Manly Respectability and Racial Paternalism in the Battle against Chain Stores, Chain Stations, and the Federal Radio Commission on Louisiana's KWKH, 1924–33. *Radio Journal: International Studies in Broadcast & Audio Media*, 1(3), 193–211.

VampiressOnDaProwlq (February 20, 2011). Ed Schultz: WI Labor Protests: Limbaugh Calls Workers Freeloaders [Video file]. YouTube. Retrieved from: www.youtube.com/watch?v=Tjx_9WC_yko.

Van Horn R., & Mirowski, P. (2009). The Rise of the Chicago School of Economics and the Birth of Neoliberalism. In P. Mirowski & D. Plehwe D. (eds.), *The Road from Mont Pèlerin: The Making of the Neoliberal Thought Collective*. Cambridge, MA: Harvard University Press: 139–178.

Vanneman, R., & Cannon, L. W. (1987). *The American Perception of Class*. Philadelphia: Temple University Press: 83–87.

Variety (December 28, 1989). Twentieth-century Fox TV Thrilled with "Current Affair" Success: Granddaddy of Sleaze Racks up Ratings; Only in 11 Markets 1 Year Ago, Now in 129.

Viguerie, R., & Franke, D. (2004). *America's Right Turn: How Conservatives Used New and Alternative Media to Take Power,* Chicago: Bonus Books, Inc.: 214–215.

Viles, P. (1993). Dan Rather Blasts TV News. *Broadcasting and Cable,* 12.

Voloshinov, V. (1973). *Marxism and the Philosophy of Language.* New York: Seminar Press: 23.

Vyse, G. (May 1, 2017). MSNBC Is Getting Whiter and More Conservative: Even though Their Liberal Hosts Have Soaring Ratings under Trump. *The New Republic.* Retrieved from: https://newrepublic.com/minutes/142434/msnbc-getting-whiter-conservativeeven-though-liberal-hosts-soaring-ratings-trump.

Wallsten, P., & Yadron, D. (November 3, 2010). Democratic Coalition Crumbles, Exit Polls Say. *Wall Street Journal.* Retrieved from: www.wsj.com/articles/SB10001424052748703778304575590860891293580.

Walters, R. (2007). Barack Obama and the Politics of Blackness. *Journal of Black Studies,* 38(1), 7–29.

Weigel, D. (February 3, 2009). The GOP's Anti-Stimulus Manifesto. *The Washington Independent.* Retrieved from: http://washingtonindependent.com/28819/amity-shlaes.

(May 27, 2016). Why the Young Turks, and Their Viewers, Love Bernie Sanders. *Washington Post.* Retrieved from: www.washingtonpost.com/politics/why-the-young-turks-and-their-viewers-love-bernie-sanders/2016/05/27/bd15e02e-2386-11e6-aa84 42391ba52c91_story.html.

Weinger, M. (March 13, 2013). Limbaugh, Hannity Lead Talkers' Top 100. *Politico.* Retrieved from: www.politico.com/blogs/media/2013/03/limbaugh-hannity-lead-talkers-top-100-159206.

Wdshelt (July 7, 2012). Inside Edition Reports on Reginald Denny Rescue [Video file]. YouTube. Retrieved from: www.youtube.com/watch?v=AFQlx9R-hz8.

White, H. (1980). The Value of Narrativity in the Representation of Reality. *Critical Inquiry,* 7(1), 5–27.

(1987). *The Content of the Form: Narrative Discourse and Historical Representation.* Baltimore: Johns Hopkins University Press.

White, K. C. (2018). *The Branding of Right-Wing Activism: The News Media and the Tea Party.* Oxford: Oxford University Press.

Wilentz, S. (Fall 1984). Against American Exceptionalism: Class Consciousness and the American Labor Movement, 1790–1920. *International Labor and Working-class History,* 26, 1–24.

(1986). *Chants Democratic: New York City & the Rise of the American Working Class, 1788–1850.* New York: Oxford University Press.

(2002). *America's Lost Egalitarian Tradition. Daedalus,* 131(1), 77.

Williams, A. (February–March 1995). Citizen Weyrich: NET's Conservative Media Empire, *Afterimage,* 22(7–8).

Williams, J. (2017). *White Working Class: Overcoming Class Cluelessness in America.* Boston: Harvard Business Review Press.

Williams, R. (1978). *Marxism & Literature.* New York: Oxford University Press: 108.

(1985). *Keywords: A Vocabulary of Culture and Society.* Oxford: Oxford University Press: 64, 112–115.

(1991). Base and Superstructure in Marxist Cultural Theory. In C. Mukerji & M. Schudson (eds.), *Rethinking Popular Culture: Contemporary Perspectives in Cultural Studies*, Berkeley: University of California Press.

Williamson Jr., C. (June 9, 1978). Country & Western Marxism: To the Nashville Station. *National Review*, 30(23), 711–717.

Willman, C. (2005). *Rednecks and Bluenecks: The Politics of Country Music.* London: The New Press: 4–5.

Wills, G. (1970). *Nixon Agonistes: The Crisis of the Self-Made Man.* Boston: Houghton Mifflin: 310, 311.

Wilstein, M. (December 15, 2014). Only 1% of Fox News Viewers Are Black. *Mediaite.* Retrieved from: www.mediaite.com/tv/only-1-of-fox-news-viewers-are-black/.

Winfield, B. (1994). *FDR and the News Media.* New York: Columbia University Press: 128.

Wolcott, J. (August 2001). Fox Populi? *Vanity Fair.* Retrieved from: www.vanity fair.com/culture/features/2001/08/wolcott-200108.

Wolff, M. (2008). *The Man Who Owns the News: Inside the Secret World of Rupert Murdoch.* New York, Broadway Books: 71–72, 205, 210, 282.

Wormald, B. (2005). Differences among Cable Channels (Iraq War Reportage). Pew Research Center. Retrieved from: www.journalism.org/2005/03/15/dif ferences-among-cable-channels-iraq-war-reportage/.

Wright, E.O. (1985). *Classes.* London: Verso: 19–63.

Wuthnow, R. (1988). *The Restructuring of American Religion.* Princeton, NJ: Princeton University Press: 155–156, 163.

Yazakchattiest (December 4, 2011). Meow: Anderson Cooper vs. Ed Schultz— CATFIGHT! [Video file].

YouTube Retrieved from: www.youtube.com/watch?v=zy6FnILnCrY.

Zelizer, B. (1992). *Covering the Body: The Kennedy Assassination, the Media, and the Shaping of Collective Memory.* Chicago: University of Chicago Press.

(June 1995). Reading the Past against the Grain: The Shape of Memory Studies. *Critical Studies in Mass Communication*, 214–239. 227.

Zieber, K. (January 12, 2012). Right-wing Media Lash Out at Michelle Obama for Addressing "Angry Black Woman" Stereotype. *Media Matters.* Retrieved from: www.mediamatters.org/research/2012/01/12/right-wing-media-lash-out-at-michelle-obama-for/186063.

Zizzo, D. (October 11, 1993). Conservatives Broadcasting Own Message. *The Oklahoman.* Retrieved from: http://newsok.com/article/2444674.

Zook, K (1999). *Color by Fox: The Fox Network and the Revolution in Black Television.* New York: Oxford University Press.

Zoonen, L. V. (2005). *Entertaining the Citizen: When Politics and Popular Culture Converge.* Lanham, MD: Rowman & Littlefield.

(2006). The Personal, the Political, and the Popular: A Woman's Guide to Celebrity Politics. *European Journal of Cultural Studies*, 9 (3), 298.

Index

academics, 124, 129, 132, 235. *See also* higher education and New Class

ACORN, 3n11, 240–241

advertising: of CNN, 47–48, 54, 152; of *Daily Show*, 101, 101n19; of failed conservative networks, 20–22, 24, 31–32; of Fox News, 11–14, 23–25, 48 (*see* "Fair & Balanced" ad campaign); of MSNBC, 11, 13, 88–89; of the *New York Times*, 12–13, 62; rates for cable news, 46n11, 54

aesthetics: Ailes' emphasis on, 35–36; austere look of network era journalism, 17–18, 66–67; differences between CNN and Fox News, 54, 116, 141–142; similarities between, 140; modern politics is driven by, 16–17; prioritized in tabloid media, 43–44, 55

affect: "affective economics," 46; "affective polarization," 48–49; theories of, 91–92

Affordable Care Act (ACA), 6, 93–94, 186n1

agenda setting, 3n10, 3–4, 241

African Americans: Black Entertainment Television (BET), 86–87; exclusion from populist working-class imaginary, 113–114, 162n8, 162–163, 173–182, 242; percentage of Fox's audience versus MSNBC's and CNN's, 111, 111n35, 134n10

Ailes, Roger: on authenticity, 50–51; criticism of liberal media, 23, 151; on journalism, 35–36; mocking MSNBC, 50;

on moral rhetoric, 184; on performance and personality, 95; pre-Fox News career, 17, 35–36, 51, 131; relationship with Rush Limbaugh, 22, 22n42; sexual harassment scandals, 8–9, 117, 119n47, 223; views on the wealthy, 165; on visual aesthetics, 35–36

alt-right, 8, 239–244

anti-cultural elitism. *See* cultural populism

anti-intellectualism, 129–130, 151, 185, 187, 220–221

anti-statism, anti-government, 5, 161, 169, 241. *See also* free-market ideology and neoliberalism

audience: cable news demographics, 133–136, 133–136nn10–19; fandom, 46n11; fragmentation in the post-network era, 45–46; polarization of, 42, 47–49, 58, 82–83

aspirational style, 18, 62–65, 102; populist *vs.*, 12n26, 12–14, 27, 42, 62, 151

"authoritarian populism," 68, 81

Baym, Geoffrey, 67, 86–87, 101–102, 140, 148

Beck, Glenn, *Glenn Beck* (TV show): programming innovations on Fox News, 155, 198; role with the 9/12 Project and the Tea Party, 7, 155; suspicion of experts and credentials, 146; working-class self-presentation, 102–103, 116

Bernstein, Carl, 56, 225–226

bias. *See* media bias

Bourdieu, Pierre: on body image, 118; "cultural capital," 124, 126; "disinvested disposition," 64–65, 101, 192–193, 212–213; "invested disposition," 102, 148n33, 148–150, 207, 212–213; "ethical disposition," 107, 148–149; "principle of conformity" vs. "principle of distinction," 125–126

Breitbart News, 8, 10, 151, 220, 227, 239–243

Brock, David, 18n30, 21, 93, 165n9, 235. *See also* Media Matters

Bryan, William Jennings, 61, 127–128

Buckley, William F., Jr., 27, 30, 130–131, 234

Buchanan, Pat, 131, 239, 243

Bush, George H., 32, 72

Bush, George W., 1, 4, 7, 110, 122, 133, 136n22

business class, 20, 123, 126, 154, 156–158, 168–170

cable news: audience demographics (*see* audience); audience size, 3, 3n9, 53; criticism of 55, 55n25, 58–59, 107, 209–210; network news *vs.*, 17–18, 45–48, 46n11, 66–67, 86–87; political influence of, 2, 2nn4–7, 3nn10–11, 2–4, 234; and polarization, 47–49, 58–59, 82–83. *See also* opinion journalism

cable and satellite technologies, 24n45, 33–34, 42, 44–46, 82

Carlson, Tucker, 114, 226, 235, 243–244

Cavuto, Neil, 5–6, 149–150, 153–154, 179

celebrities: conservative celebrities, 124, 144–146; Fox's animosity toward, 91, 124, 143–145, 241; prevalence in modern news, 140–141. *See also* soft news

civil rights movement, 86, 132, 163

class: conservative redefinition of, 126–133; cultural theories of, 124–126, 139; and education, 137–138; and income, 136, 136n19, 136nn21–22, 137–138, 158, 172n11, 183; moral-populist understandings of, 138–139, 158–159, 182–184; and status, 138; US vs. French perceptions of, 125–126. *See also* business class, New Class, professional class, small business owners and working class

climate change denial, 221

Clinton, Bill, 3, 57, 80–81

Clinton, Hillary, 111, 115–116, 119, 134n10, 226

Clinton-Lewinsky scandal, 3, 80–81

CNN: audience demographics (*see* audience); coverage of Tea Party, 5; competition with and counter-programming to Fox News, 23–24, 47, 48, 54; hails audience as a "fact-based community," 152; Murdoch's criticism as being "too liberal," 23; journalistic philosophy vs. Fox News,' 95; and Ted Turner, 23–24, 28, 95; and Time Warner, 28, 29n55

Colbert, Stephen, *Colbert Report, The* (TV show), 100–102, 107, 142, 152

Comedy-based news, 99–102

conservatism, conservatives; criticism of liberal media bias, 14–15; 21–23, 132; Fox as main news source for, 9, 9n20; MSNBC's recruitment of, 109, 109n33; political philosophy, 231, 237; as reactionary, 233n13, 233–234; 236–237. *See also* anti-statism, free-market ideology and neoliberalism

conservative media: "first generation" vs. "second generation," 25–26, 36–37; Fox News as pioneer of, 9, 21, 26; Limbaugh and talk radio's role in establishing, 22n42, 22–23; pillars of, 5, 231. *See also* failed conservative networks

conservative movement: alt-right, 8, 227, 239–244; internal tensions within, 131, 231; paleoconservatism, 239, 243; and the Powell Memo, 190; pro-business class agenda, 5, 153–154, 156–158, 164–171; "Republican Revolution", 47, 117; and the Tea Party, 5–8, 176, 231; think tanks and the intellectual establishment, 19, 19n33, 130–131, 164–165, 186n1, 190; and women activists, 117, 117n46

Cooper, Anderson, 106–107, 140–141

Coughlin, Father Charles, 65nn34–35, 65–66, 128, 128n5, 130

country music, 50, 66, 109–110, 115, 125, 125n4, 132, 132n9, 140, 140n29, 144–146

Cronkite, Walter, 58, 67, 86

cultural populism, anti-cultural elitism: crux of Fox programming, 4–5, 37, 50, 62, 133; definitions of, 126, 127; expressed as epistemic differences, 146–151; expressed as taste differences, 140–146; history of, 127–133; as a news style, 12–14, 42–44, 68–69, 77–80; social logic of, 125–126. *See also* the "Silent Majority" and New Class

culture war, 4, 178

Current Affair, A (TV show), 35–36, 44, 50, 55–56, 73–81, 199n14

Daily Show, The (TV show), 93, 99–102, 105, 105n21, 141, 185. *See also* Stewart, Jon

Democracy, democratic theory, 43, 64, 89, 99n17, 101, 211, 228, 237

Democratic Party, Democrats; aversion to populism, 108–111, 111n34, 227–228, 231–232; embrace of the civil rights and the feminist movement, 163–164; demographic constituencies, 134nn10–11, 134n17; and the labor movement, 160–162; losing "tabloid soul," 109–110; and the "politics of difference," 88–89

deregulation, 57, 57n29

Echo Chamber (book), by Kathleen Jamieson and Joseph Cappella, 58, 234

education: and class, 137–138; conservative suspicion of, 124, 146–147, 235; level of Fox News' audience, 134n11, 134n17, 134–136, 135n18. *See also* academics and higher education

elections, U.S.: of 1896, 61; of 1968, 131, 162, 206n18; of 1972, 131; of 1994, 22, 47, 191n6; of 2008, 1, 90, 114–115, 171, 181; of 2010, 1, 234; of 2016, 8–9, 119, 131, 134, 134n10, 134n17, 206n18, 225, 230, 239–240

entertainment. *See* soft news and tabloidization

epistemology: empirical vs. lay knowledge, 25n47, 25–26, 185–188, 187n2, 201–203, 211–214, 216–221; "epistemic closure" and "post-fact" politics, 152; "epistemic culture," 147–148, 152, 185, 213; epistemological strategies of Fox hosts, 25–26, 147–151, 211–214

experts, expertise; "activist-experts" vs. university experts, 191n6, 191–193; conservative antipathy toward, 129–133, 146–147, 190; experts and the professional class, 147n31; "journalist-intellectuals," 194; populist opposition to, 127–128

failed conservative networks, 20–26, 33–34, 37, 80, 82; Conservative Television Network (CTN), 22, 29n54; GOP-TV, 21, 29, 32–33, 35; National Empowerment Television (NET), 20, 22, 25n46, 28, 29n52, 31n58, 31n60, 33n67; Republican Exchange Satellite Network (RESN), 21, 29n54, 32n61; Television News, Inc. (TVN), 24, 24n45

Fairness Doctrine, 66

"Fair & Balanced" ad campaign, 14, 23–25, 48

fake news, 25, 152

false consciousness, 122–123, 232

family values, 71, 81, 117, 164

feminism, feminist movement, 163–164; conservative opposition to, 117n46, 117–118, 239. *See also* gender

Forgotten Man: archetype of economic hardship, 155–156, 206n18; conservative reimagination of, 196, 204–206, 241

Forgotten Man, The (book), by Amity Shlaes, 186, 188, 193–197, 195n8, 200, 214–215, 215n20, 218

Fox Broadcasting Company, 32, 44, 71–72, 72n43, 74

Fox News Channel: appeals to working-class taste, 5, 12, 51–52, 54, 102–103, 118–119, 140–146, 209–210, 219–220; attacking liberal media bias, 14–15, 21, 24n45, 54, 122; audience demographics, (*see* audience); audience's political activeness, 6–7, 234; as a brand community, 47–48; conservative bias, 3, 3n11, 18, 18nn30–32; competition with and counter-programming strategy to CNN, 23–24, 47–48, 54; and MSNBC, 2–3, 11–12, 47–50, 52, 54, 85–86, 88–89; free-market ideological orientation, 5, 20, 153, (chap. 4) (chap. 5) 236; "Fox News Effect" and debates over impact, 3, 3nn10–11, 83, 83nn55–58; financial success of, 3, 3n8,

28, 46n11; influence over Republican
Party, 5–8, 231; key creative figures (*see*
Rupert Murdoch, Roger Ailes, or Bill
O'Reilly); liberal perception as racists and
xenophobic, 233, 243; mocked by *Daily
Show* and *Colbert Report*, 100, 142, 185;
narrative skill, 93; overcoming
distribution obstacles, 29n55, 70;
partisan marketing strategy and style, 6,
9, 42, 44, 47–49; perception as
Republican propaganda, 7, 21, 219–220,
235; performance and personality-driven,
95–96; platform for conservative
intellectuals and think tanks, 70, 186n1,
186–188, 196n11, 196–197; precursors
to (*see* the *Sun*, the *New York Post*, and
A Current Affair, failed conservative
networks); presentational innovations,
35; politicizing cultural tastes, 42, 44;
populist conceptualization of public
sphere, 85–99; racializing stimulus
debate, 173–182; ratings dominance, 3, 5,
9, 9n20, 23–24; regional appeals (*see*
regional identity); sexual harassment
scandals, 8, 117, 119n47, 222–223; and
the tabloid style (*see under* tabloid
journalism); Tea Party movement
advocacy, 5–8, 135n18, 155, 175–176,
197, 231, 234; tensions with the Obama
administration, 6–7; transforming US
journalism, 9, 9n21; and Trump, 8–10,
225–227, 239–241
Frank, Thomas, 122–123, 133, 136,
136–137n22, 197. *See also What's the
Matter with Kansas?* (book)
free-market ideology, 19, 51, 57, 130,
164–165, 165n9, 179, 190, 195n8, 229;
and Fox News, 5, 20, 153, (chap. 4)
(chap. 5) 236. *See also* anti-statism and
neoliberalism
Friedman, Milton, 130, 164, 190

gender, 115–118, 228n8, 228–229;
masculine biases of populist
communication styles, 65, 115–120, 164,
230, 230n9. *See also* patriarchy and
women
generational differences, 177–182
Gingrich, Newt, 30–32, 31n58, 32n61,
35–36, 195n8
Giuliani, Rudy, 70, 196

Great Depression, 2, 39, 160, 178–179,
(chap. 5)
Greatest Generation, 178–179, 213
Great Recession, late 2000s economic
downturn, 1–2, 4–5, 20, 121, 138,
(chap. 4) (chap. 5) 241, 243
Gramsci, Antonio, 218–219, 223–233,
237–238. *See also* hegemony

Hall, Stuart, 2, 19, 68, 81, 121, 123, 187,
187n2, 189, 228, 230–231
Hallin, Daniel, 64, 67–68, 93, 189n3
Hannity, Sean, *Hannity* (TV show): anti-
welfare rhetoric, 175–178; career in talk
radio, 50, 75; and country music, 66, 103,
141–143; regional appeal (*see* regional
identity); and Trump, 226; working-
class self-presentation, 26, 103, 142,
147–148
hegemony theory, 18–19, 218–219,
237–238
high-modern journalism, 67, 78, 101, 148,
152
higher education, 126, 128–129, 129nn6–7,
131, 172, 172n11, 192, 221, 234–235
Hofstadter, Richard. *See* "paranoid style"
Hume, Brit, 80, 80n51, 112, 136

immigrants, immigration, 122, 242–243
Inside Edition (TV show), 22n42, 35–36,
50, 52, 56, 75–80
intellectuals: activist-experts, 191–193;
conservative intellectual movement, 70,
70n40, 130–131, 193–194, 234–237;
Fox's opposition to, 4–5, 25–26, 146–147;
Fox as a platform for, (chap. 5). *See also*
experts, think tanks, academics and
higher education
Internet, 2, 8, 9, 227, 240, 243
"intersectionality," 122, 230n9
Iraq War, 3, 3n11, 4, 142
Islamophobia, 122, 228, 243

Jackson, Andrew, 60, 159, 162, 171
Jefferson, Thomas, 159, 162, 171, 181, 200
"job creators," 154, 165–173

Kazin, Michael, *The Populist Persuasion*
(book), 19, 112n36, 126, 128–130, 138,
158–159, 162, 236n16
Kelly, Megyn, 8, 135n18, 223–225

Keynesian economics, 7, 129, 161, 178, 191, 218
knowledge. *See also* epistemology
Koppel, Ted, 55, 58–59, 67, 75–76, 85, 209

Labor Theory of Value, 159–162, 167
labor unions, labor movement, 106–108, 132–133, 160–162, 162n8
Laclau, Ernesto: 43, 86–91, 138–139, 218, 237n17
Lakoff, George, 183
Lamont, Michèle, 124–126, 138n25, 172n11, 183
Latinx Americans, 86–87, 230n9
liberalism, liberals: aversion to cultural populism; 61, 89, 108–110, 146–147, 184, 221; and economic populism, 123–125, 160–163; and higher education, 127, 129, 131, 191–192; and multiculturalism, 89, 227–228, 230, 243; professional/"hip" taste culture; 12–14, 36, 49–50, 54, 101–102, 115, 115n45, 143, 191. *See also* Progressive movement and Democractic Party
Limbaugh, Rush, *The Rush Limbaugh Show* (radio show), 5, 22, 22n42, 22–23, 36, 36n76, 106–107, 117, 146, 147, 200, 231, 234
Lippmann, Walter, 64, 67
Loudest Voice in the Room (book). *See* Sherman, Gabriel

Maddow, Rachel, *The Rachel Maddow Show* (TV show), 11–13, 106, 140–141
marketing/markets: and affective economics, 46–47; narrowcasting, 44–47; "positioning" strategies, 48; "flyover" vs. "slumpy," 52–53. *See also* "Fair & Balanced"
McCarthy, Joseph, 4, 129–132, 233, 236
media bias: conservative criticism of, 14–15, 20–26, 48–51, 94, 121–122, 151; liberal criticism of, 7, 18, 18n30, 21, 54, 233–234
Media Matters, 18n30, 93
"media metacommentary," 15, 77–78
middlebrow. *See* aspirational style
morality, moral discourses: and narrative, 93–95; and populism, 138–139, 182, 237; power of, 158–159, 182–184
MSNBC: audience demographics (*see* audience); competition with and counter-

programming to Fox News, 2–3, 11–14, 47–50, 85–86, 88–89, 141; emulating Fox's partisan style and opinion news format, 9, 11–12; hails audience as "fact-based community," 12, 185
multichannel era. *See* post-network era
multiculturalism, 89, 227–228, 230, 243
Murdoch, Rupert: blamed for tabloidizing American culture, 56, 71–75; business acumen, 28, 71, 194, 194n7; criticism of liberal media, 23, 51; feud with Ted Turner, 23, 28; on journalism, 36n76, 40–42, 68–69, 73; political influence of, 68–70, 193; pre-Fox News career, 27–28, 41–42, 55–56, 68–74, 79–81, 193–194, 194n7
Murrow, Edward, 66

narrative, narrativity, 93–94
narrowcasting. *See* niche marketing
National Empowerment Television (NET). *See under* failed conservative networks
National Review, The, 131
nationalism: and Fox News, 4, 243; similarities and differences with populism, 177–178, 242; white nationalism, 239–240, 243–244
neoliberalism, neoliberals, 123n2, 190, 218
network era, 17–18, 46, 86, 146, 148, 211. *See also* high-modern journalism
New Class, 130n8, 130–133, 147n31
News Corporation: anti-elitist marketing strategies, 41–42, 51, 71–72, 109; Australian and British roots, 40, 44, 73; conglomerate structure, 28, 57, 193; distribution battle with Time Warner, 29n55, 70; innovating reality programming and tabloid television, 71, 73–75; launching Fox Broadcasting Company; 71; and the tabloid tradition, 40–42, 68–75
New Deal: Fox's criticism of, 181–182, (chap. 5); gender and race-based exclusions, 162n8, 162–163; and producer populism, 160–162. *See also* Franklin Roosevelt and revisionism
New York Post, 41–42, 44, 69, 70, 70n39, 73, 75, 81, 89, 226
New York Times: advertising of (*see* advertising); as elitist foil for

conservatives, 70, 89–90, 94; role in creating objectivity regime, 61–62
niche marketing, 42, 45–48, 71, 82n54, 86
9/11, 4. *See also* terrorism
Nixon, Richard: 81, 131–133, 162, 172, 190–191, 206n18

Obama, Barack: challenges as first black president, 111–114; Franklin Roosevelt comparisons, 1, 197, 212; and Fox News, 6–7; painted as elitist, 90, 90n7, 100, 168–170; professional class political style, 112, 119–120; reaching out to hip-hop community, 114; Tea Party opposition to, 6–7, 176
objectivity, 14, 24–25, 64–67, 148–149, 152, 215. *See also* high-modern journalism
opinion journalism, 9, 9n21, 57–58, 199n14. *See also* media metacommentary
O'Reilly, Bill, *The O'Reilly Factor* (TV show): assuming the voice of the "people"/working-class, 52, 75–76, 85–87, 86n2, 89, 98, 99–100, 141; pioneer of opinion journalism, 22n42, 52, 58; popular history author, 199–200; pre-Fox News career, 75–80; regional identity of, (*see* regional identity); sexual harassment suits, 222–223; on taxes and wealth distribution, 169, 173–174

Palin, Sarah, 53, 91, 119, 119n47, 131, 147, 168–170, 229
"paranoid style," 233, 233n13, 236
partisanship, partisan media: theoretical approaches to, 14–17, 44, 48–49, 58–61, 232–235. *See also* polarization
patriarchy, 115–116, 119–120, 230. *See also* gender
performance: Ailes' emphasis on, 95; centrality to populist communication strategies, 16, 26, 88, 219; performance theory, 96–97; relationship to narrative, 95–96
Pierce, Charles, 40, 42, 104, 109
Phillips, Kevin, 131
polarization, 27, 42, 47–49, 58, 82–83, 233. *See also* partisanship, partisan media
political correctness, 69n38, 225, 241–242
postmodernism, postmodern journalism, 87, 101–102, 152–153, 220

popular culture, pop culture: blending with news, 101, 140–146
Popular Front, 110, 162n8
"popular intellect," 147, 151, 185
populism: aesthetic vs. organizational, 32–34; as antithetical to liberal, pluralist democracy, 88–89, 227–228; compared to tabloid journalism, 43–44; defenses of, 228–232; economic populism (distributional) vs. identitarian, 123–124; epistemological aspects of (*see* "popular intellect"); expressed as a taste politics, 37, (*see* popular culture); genealogies of, 127–133, 158–165; and mediatization, 16, 88, 88n4; and nationalism, 177–178, 242–243; and masculinity (*see under* gender); as a performative style (*see under* performance); and producer ethic (*see* producerism); race and gender biases of, 111–120, 162–164, 229–230; regional elements (*see* regional identity); Republican capture of, 130–132, 162–163; and social class (*see under* class); technocratic style *vs.*, (*see* technocracy); theories of, 32–33, 43, 79, 88–89, 99n17, 126, 227–228
Populist Party, 127, 160, 229
Post-fact/truth politics and news, 26, 152–153. *See also* epistemology
post-network era, 42, 46n11, 46–47, 194
producerism/producer ethic: anti-corporate producerism, 159–162; "entrepreneurial producerism," 155–158, 165–173; history of, 158–165; theoretical tenets of, 158–159. *See also* "job creators" and the Forgotten Man
professionalism, 13–14, 61, 67
professional class, 13, 50, 66, 101–102, 111, 116, 120, 125, 147n31, 230, 232, 243. *See also* New Class
Progressive movement, 61, 64, 127, 130, 171, 191
propaganda: Fox accused of being, 21, 91, 235

race: cable news demographics (*see* audience); challenges for politicians of color (*see* Obama, Barack); and popular culture, 114–115; and scapegoating, 157–158, 162, 180–181, 242; and traditional values, 178. *See also* welfare and whiteness

radio: political talk radio, 15, 22, 50, 54, 66, 75, 106, 147n32; populist broadcasters of the 1930s, 65–66, 97, 128, 130
Rather, Dan, 32, 59, 67, 210
ratings: and cable news, 2, 2n4, 5n14, 9, 29–30n55, 46n11, 53, 53n23, 106n25, 198n12; and network news, 57, 57n29, 66–67; network vs. cable, 3, 3n9
Reagan, Ronald, 19, 32, 57, 70, 163, 190–191
reality programming, 44, 71, 119
red-state/blue-state rhetoric, 53
regional identity, 50, 51–53, 115n45, 148, 243
religion, religious: gender ideology, 117–119; and populism, 127–128; secularism *vs.*, 64n32, 64. *See also* culture war and family values
Republican Party: Ailes' consultancy work for, 7, 17, 131; and cultural populism, 129–133; demographic constituencies, 134, 134nn10–12, 134n17; Fox's influence over, 6–8; realignment in Nixon era, 131–133, 162–164; "Republican Revolution" of 1996, 47, 117; "Republican tsunami" of 2010, 1, 1n2; and the Tea Party, 5–7; and think tanks, 19–20, 190–191; and Trump, 8, 226, 239
revisionism, 177–178, 179, 181–182, 188, 201–208, 213–214. *See also* "selective tradition"
Roosevelt, Franklin Delano, 1, 66, 110–111, 113, 155, 160–161, 178–179, 197, 201–203, 206n18, 206–207

Satire. *See* comedy-based news
Schlafly, Phyllis, 117
Schultz, Ed, *The Ed Show* (TV Show), 105–109
"selective exposure," 58–59, 232–234
"selective tradition," 20, 237
sexual harassment, 8–9, 117, 119n47, 222–223
Sherman, Gabriel, *Loudest Voice in the Room* (book), 12, 18, 21n38, 24, 24n45, 29n55, 35, 36, 46n11, 49, 51n19, 80n51, 135n18
Shlaes, Amity, 186–189, 192–198, 200, 202–210, 212–218, 221
"Silent Majority," 132–133, 162–164, 206n18

small business owners, 102, 155–156, 168, 170–173
socialism, 107, 123, 129, 170–171, 173–174, 191, 211
soft news, 42n5, 42–43, 57–58, 68–69, 79–81, 140–141. *See also* "tabloidization"
Stewart, Jon, 93, 100–101, 105, 107
Stimulus Act, 7, 175–178, 194, 205
style, stylistic analysis, 11–18, 88
Sun, The (British newspaper), 41, 41nn3–4, 68–69, 79
Swint, Kerwin, *Dark Genius* (book), 17, 23–24, 35, 45

"tabloidization," 27, 27n49, 55–58, 225–226
tabloid journalism: the aspirational style *vs.*, 12n46, 12–14, 27, 42, 62; definition of, 42n5, 42–44; liberal aversion to, 54, 109; and Fox News, 10, 27, 34–37, 44, 56, 65, 81; history of, 55–62, 65; laments about, 31–33, 54–62, 73–75, 107, 226; and Murdoch, 40–42, 68–75; and populism, 33, 43–44, 60, 79; and social class, 41–42, 44, 59–62, 109, 139–140; and Trump, 17, 119, 225–226; US vs. UK, 41–44, 68–69. *See also* celebrities and soft news
talk radio; role establishing conservative media market, 22, 22n42; ties to cable news, 15, 50, 56, 75, 106, 147n32, 198, 231. *See also* radio and Rush Limbaugh
"taste culture," 13, 126, 146, 148n33
taxes, 153, 156, 158, 165–167, 171, 173–174, 195, 203–208, 231
Tea Party movement: and Fox News, 3, 3n11, 5–8, 135n18, 155, 175–176, 197, 231, 243
technocracy, technocratic styles, 110, 116, 130–131, 162, 188, 199, 219–220, 228
Television News Inc. (TVN). *See under* failed conservative networks
terrorism, terrorists, 4, 153, 243
telecommunication policy, 57, 57n29, 66
think tanks: growth of conservative think tanks, 164–165, 190, 192; theoretical approaches to, 191–193; think tanks and Fox News, 185–188, 186n1
Time Warner, 28, 29n55, 57, 70

traditional values, 26, 51, 81, 117, 170, 177–178, 184, 243
trickle-down economics, 158. *See also* free-market ideology and neoliberalism
Trump, Donald: and the alt-right, 8, 239–240; attacks on the media, 25, 151; and Fox News, 8–10, 224–227, 241–243; populist style of, 16–17, 110, 113, 119–120, 206n18, 241–243; voting base of, 134, 134n10, 134n17, 136n22
Twentieth Century Fox, 71
Twenty-First Century Fox, 10, 68, 69n38, 223–224

Wallace, George, 129–133, 163
What's the Matter with Kansas? (book), by Thomas Frank, 122–123, 136–137n21
wealth inequality, wealth distribution, 4, 19–20, 103, 122–124, 127, 136–138, (chap. 4) (chap. 5) 243. *See also* taxes
welfare: racial framing of, 157–158, 162–163, 174–182, 206, 240–241
Weyrich, Paul, 25n46, 28, 29n52, 33, 35, 36–37, 190

white nationalism. *See under* nationalism
white supremacy, white supremacists, 130, 238, 240–242
whiteness, 51, 122, 162, 230, 242–244
Williams, Raymond, 19–20, 128, 166
Wolff, Michael, 40n2, 41, 68, 81
women: and conservative activism, 117, 117n46; exclusion from populist working-class imaginary, 162n8, 162–164; feminine brands of populism, 116–120, 228–229. *See also* feminism
working class: anti-corporate sentiment, 160n4, 160–161; anti-elitist attitudes, 125–126; debates over definition, 133–140; epistemology (*see* "popular intellect"); and "false consciousness," 122–123; Fox's claim to represent, 11, 40, 52, 85–87, 89, 98–99, 136; and masculinity (*see under* gender); populist moral reasoning of, 126, 138–139, 159–160, 184; racial segmentation of (*see* race); small business ownership aspirations, 172, 172n11

xenophobia, 122, 228, 242

Other Books in the Series (*continued from page ii*)

Richard Gunther and Anthony Mughan, eds., *Democracy and the Media: A Comparative Perspective*

Daniel C. Hallin and Paolo Mancini, *Comparing Media Systems: Three Models of Media and Politics*

Daniel C. Hallin and Paolo Mancini, eds., *Comparing Media Systems Beyond the Western World*

Roderick P. Hart, *Civic Hope: How Ordinary Citizens Keep Democracy Alive*

Robert B. Horwitz, *Communication and Democratic Reform in South Africa*

Philip N. Howard, *New Media Campaigns and the Managed Citizen*

Ruud Koopmans and Paul Statham, eds., *The Making of a European Public Sphere: Media Discourse and Political Contention*

L. Sandy Maisel, Darrell M. West, and Brett M. Clifton, *Evaluating Campaign Quality: Can the Electoral Process Be Improved?*

Douglas M. McLeod and Dhavan V. Shah, *News Frames and National Security*

Pippa Norris, *Digital Divide: Civic Engagement, Information Poverty, and the Internet Worldwide*

Pippa Norris, *A Virtuous Circle: Political Communications in Postindustrial Society*

Victor Pickard, *How America Lost the Battle for Media Democracy: Corporate Libertarianism and the Future of Media Reform*

Sue Robinson, *Networked News, Racial Divides: How Power & Privilege Shape Public Discourse in Progressive Communities*

Margaret Scammell, *Consumer Democracy: The Marketing of Politics*

Adam F. Simon, *The Winning Message: Candidate Behavior, Campaign Discourse*

Daniela Stockmann, *Media Commercialization and Authoritarian Rule in China*

Bruce A. Williams and Michael X. Delli Carpini, *After Broadcast News: Media Regimes, Democracy, and the New Information Environment*

Gadi Wolfsfeld, *Media and the Path to Peace*